Engineering Elixir Applications

Navigate Each Stage of Software Delivery with Confidence

Ellie Fairholm
Josep Giralt D'Lacoste

The Pragmatic Bookshelf

Dallas, Texas

See our complete catalog of hands-on, practical,
and Pragmatic content for software developers:
https://pragprog.com

Sales, volume licensing, and support:
support@pragprog.com

Derivative works, AI training and testing,
international translations, and other rights:
rights@pragprog.com

The team that produced this book includes:

Publisher: Dave Thomas
COO: Janet Furlow
Executive Editor: Susannah Davidson
Series Editor: Sophie DeBenedetto
Development Editor: Nicole Taché
Copy Editor: Corina Lebegioara
Indexing: Potomac Indexing, LLC

Copyright © 2024 The Pragmatic Programmers, LLC.

All rights reserved. No part of this publication may be reproduced by any means, nor may any derivative works be made from this publication, nor may this content be used to train or test an artificial intelligence system, without the prior consent of the publisher.

When we are aware that a term used in this book is claimed as a trademark, the designation is printed with an initial capital letter or in all capitals.

The Pragmatic Starter Kit, The Pragmatic Programmer, Pragmatic Programming, Pragmatic Bookshelf, PragProg, and the linking *g* device are trademarks of The Pragmatic Programmers, LLC.

Every precaution was taken in the preparation of this book. However, the publisher assumes no responsibility for errors or omissions or for damages that may result from the use of information (including program listings) contained herein.

ISBN-13: 979-8-88865-067-7
Book version: P1.0—December 2024

*To each other. For always being
the other's rock.*

Contents

Foreword xi

Acknowledgments xiii

Going Back to the Root of the DevOps Paradigm xv

1. **Introduction to the Journey** 1
   Introducing the BEAMOps Paradigm 2
   The Book's Tech Stack 5
   Set Up Your Environment 7

2. **Use Terraform to Create GitHub Issues and Milestones** . . 13
   Get to Know Terraform 14
   Create Your First Resource Using the GitHub Provider 17
   Examine the Terraform State 26
   Terraform Variables 31
   Resource Dependencies 43
   What Have You Learned? 47

3. **Build and Dockerize a Phoenix LiveView Application** . . 49
   Releases and the mix release Command 50
   Docker Fundamentals 56
   Build Your First Docker Image 61
   Run Your First Docker Container 63
   Write Multistage Dockerfiles 67
   What Have You Learned? 77

4. Set Up Integration Pipelines with GitHub Actions . . . 79
Mandatory CI Steps for a CI Pipeline   80
Build a Docker Image and Push to the GitHub Registry   103
Amend Your GitHub Workflow Triggers   115
What Have You Learned?   117

5. The Dev Environment and Docker Compose 119
Rebuild Your Phoenix Application with Ecto   119
Run Your Multiservice Application Manually   122
Get to Know Docker Compose   128
Create Your First Docker Compose File   134
Get to Know Docker Swarm   149
What Have You Learned?   155

6. The Production Environment and Packer 157
Create Your AWS Production Environment Manually   158
Import an Existing Infrastructure Resource with Terraform   166
Get to Know Packer   190
Build Your First Amazon Machine Image (AMI)   194
Putting Packer and Terraform Together   200
What Have You Learned?   207

7. Continuous Deployment and Repository Secrets . . . 209
Handle Sensitive Data with Docker Secrets   210
Encrypt Secret Data with SOPS   222
Deploy Manually to Understand Requirements   227
Turn Deploy Commands into a Convenience Script   232
Enable Continuous Deployment   236
What Have You Learned?   249

8. Revise Your AWS Stack to Create a Multinode Swarm . . 251
Create and Distribute Multiple EC2 Instances   252
Create a Multinode Swarm   255
Automate the Initial Deployment of Your Application   277
What Have You Learned?   284

9. Distributed Erlang 285
Get to Know Distributed Erlang 286
Manually Implement a Local Distributed Erlang Cluster 288
Automate the Creation of a Distributed Erlang Cluster in a Remote
Docker Swarm 300
What Have You Learned? 308

10. Autoscaling and Optimizing Your Deployment Strategy . . 311
Autoscale Your Phoenix LiveView Application 312
Add a Load Balancer to Your Auto Scaling Group 337
Minimize Downtime with Automatic Rollbacks 343
Clean Up Dangling Docker Resources 347
What Have You Learned? 350

11. Instrument Your Application with Logs and Metrics . . . 353
Design Your Instrumentation Architecture 354
Collect Your Application Logs 357
Configure Default Monitoring Metrics 369
What Have You Learned? 384

12. Create a Custom PromEx Metric and Grafana Alert . . . 387
Implement Your Own PromEx Metric and Grafana Dashboard 388
Add Alerts to Your Metrics Configuration 405
Deploy the BEAMOps Kanban Image to AWS in Production 411
What Have You Learned? 413
Wrapping Up the Journey 414

Index 417

Foreword

Around ten years ago, I began the journey of learning a new programming language called Elixir and its web framework, Phoenix. As a pragmatic developer, I learned them by building something more complex than a typical to-do list. I decided to create a Trello clone using Elixir, Phoenix, and React. I took some time off during the holidays to read and code. Instantly, I fell in love with Elixir and Phoenix, and I knew right then that I had found my favorite tech stack, one that I wouldn't trade for any other.

The evolution of the Elixir ecosystem over the years has been fascinating. It has provided us with tools to develop everything from real-time web applications to APIs, large data processing systems, embedded systems, machine learning, and AI. Libraries such as Plug, Phoenix LiveView, Ecto, Broadway, GenStage, LibCluster, Oban, and Nx are just some of the fantastic tools available for us to build any solution you can imagine using a single technology.

Focusing my professional career on Elixir has allowed me to work in different types of companies and projects, enabling me to solve various problems. My role has always been more of a full-stack engineer, helping where I was needed. Although I feel comfortable working both on the front- and backend, I've always struggled a bit when doing operational tasks such as CI/CD pipelines, deployments, and whatnot. At some companies I've worked for, there were dedicated DevOps teams on which I could rely for these tasks, making my life a lot easier. However, I've also worked for smaller companies that couldn't afford to hire a dedicated team for these operations, so we had to get the job done. Nowadays, we can use PaaS tools to deploy our projects with a single command from a terminal. Still, I've always felt like I was cheating while using them due to the magical abstraction layer they offer.

Working with Elixir has also allowed me to meet and work with incredible and brilliant people. I've always loved being part of small teams—sharing knowledge, learning from others, and building up the team and the relationships based on teamwork, collaboration, and respect for each other. One of the outstanding people I've met along the way is Pep, who is not only brilliant but also the teammate you want by your side while fighting in the trenches. Therefore, when he told me he was writing a book with Ellie about developing, testing, deploying, and debugging Elixir applications, I couldn't be more excited and thankful.

If you, like myself, encounter challenges balancing development and operations, this book is a remarkable breakthrough. It unveils a novel approach to work, engaging you comprehensively in every phase of the software development lifecycle while empowering you both as a proficient engineer and a collaborative team player. Embrace the enlightening journey into a new way of thinking and working, where innovation and collaboration reign supreme, paving the way for enhanced productivity and success in your endeavors. Welcome to the BEAMOps paradigm.

Ricardo García Vega
Elixir Engineer

Acknowledgments

We'd like to thank everyone at PragProg who has helped us get our ideas out there.

Special thanks go to Manuel Rubio for introducing us to PragProg and to Sophie DeBenedetto for helping us shape our proposal. The biggest thanks go to Nicole Taché, our editor, for all of her support, for her eagle-eye, and for making us sound our best.

A huge thank you to Ricardo García Vega, whose expertise and generosity in helping us write the application for this book cannot be overstated. We're both better Elixir developers because of you.

Thank you, also, to our technical reviewers: Emma Turner, Francisco De Lucas Consuegra, Mohamed Boudra, Alvaro Vilanova, Zi Makki, Alex de Sousa, Deniz Demirel, Jordan Mackie, Andrea Franz, and Stefan Turalski. Thank you for helping us refine our ideas and improve our explanations.

Lastly, we want to thank each other. Writing a book with your partner could have been stressful, but we've learned a lot from one another and this experience has brought us closer together. Here's to working on many more projects together in the future.

Going Back to the Root of the DevOps Paradigm

As engineers or developers, working in our development environments is comfortable. Developing new features comes easily, but transitioning those features from our local machines to a production environment often seems like a mystical process that "just happens." This is due, in large part, to the separation of "dev" and "ops" people within software teams.

The "DevOps" concept was born out of the need for engineers to be able to tackle anything, whether on the dev or ops side. But nowadays, the vast majority of "DevOps" teams are really "ops" teams that aren't really aware of what's going on in the application layer, or "dev" side. We want to help change that. We want to take engineering teams back to the root of what "DevOps" is. We want to empower you to be a multidisciplinary programmer who understands not only how to develop software but also how to deploy it. Being able to do both is a superpower in today's tech industry. It gives you confidence in what you're deploying and a more comprehensive understanding of how new features behave in a real-world environment.

To that end, this book introduces a new paradigm, BEAMOps, a specific type of DevOps that focuses on developing BEAM applications. Core BEAMOps principles include environment integrity, scalability, and infrastructure as code. By pairing these principles with the fault-tolerant nature of the BEAM, you'll deliver reliable and robust software applications.

In this book, we'll guide you through each of the BEAMOps principles and explain how you can apply them to each step of software project delivery, from start to finish. You'll learn how to manage a project, package an application, create integration pipelines, provision infrastructure, build base machine images for remote servers, automate deployments, distribute an application as part of an Erlang cluster, orchestrate an application, autoscale an application, and finally, instrument an application.

That's enough about the book for now. Let's talk about YOU.

Is This Book for You?

This book is written for advanced beginners or intermediate programmers who are familiar with Elixir and basic shell usage but feel stuck when it comes to deploying and scaling their applications. The complexity of the Elixir code is minimal; rather, the focus is on how to package and ship an application to production in a reliable and iterative manner. As a result, managers of software teams with little coding experience can also benefit from the general themes that we explore.

The techniques discussed in this book are suitable for mid-size or personal projects as they'll give you a basis for understanding all the steps involved in shipping an application. The efficient programming practices in this book will set you up with transferable skills that can be applied to many different technologies.

We've written this book for people who like to "jump over the fence" and get stuck in an issue rather than "throw it over the fence." We want to empower you to learn something new and not be scared of the unknown. After all, magic often happens when you're outside of your comfort zone.

What's in This Book?

Reading this book will feel like we're taking a journey together. Each chapter tackles a specific part of the software delivery process and builds on content from the previous chapters. For this reason, we recommend that you read it sequentially.

Chapter 1: Introduction to the Journey, on page 1

This chapter will formally introduce you to the BEAMOps paradigm and its core principles. You'll learn how the different stages of software delivery relate to the BEAMOps principles. You'll also set up your development environment and install all of the tools you'll need to complete your journey.

Chapter 2: Use Terraform to Create GitHub Issues and Milestones, on page 13

Terraform is an infrastructure-as-code tool that lets you safely provision and manage infrastructure. This chapter will discuss the project management stage of delivering a software product. It will ease you into Terraform by demonstrating how you can use it to create familiar GitHub resources: repositories and issues. You'll create issues and milestones for each of the different stages of software delivery covered in this book. And in each of the subsequent chapters, you'll close at least one of the issues/milestones that you created.

Chapter 3: Build and Dockerize a Phoenix LiveView Application, on page 49

Docker is a platform designed to help you build and run containerized applications so that they can be shared and run in a consistent manner. It is essential for creating integrity between environments. This chapter will guide you through creating a production-ready build for a Phoenix Live View application. You'll create a basic Phoenix application and then take a crash course in creating OTP releases and containerizing your application using Docker.

Chapter 4: Set Up Integration Pipelines with GitHub Actions, on page 79

Integration pipelines are an important part of the software delivery process—they help you ensure that your code works as you expect it to. In this chapter, you'll write your own continuous integration (CI) pipeline using GitHub Actions and including the mandatory steps for an ideal CI for an Elixir application.

Chapter 5: The Dev Environment and Docker Compose, on page 119

You want to ensure environment integrity for both simple and more complex applications. In this chapter, you'll create an application suite that is made up of more than one service. To do this, you'll add a database to the application that you created in Chapter 3. You'll also learn about Docker Compose, Docker Swarm, and the Docker CLI commands needed to run your application locally. This will allow you to create an environment template for a multi-service application.

Chapter 6: The Production Environment and Packer, on page 157

This chapter will cover the provisioning of remote environments. You'll be introduced to Packer, a tool that allows you to automate the creation of the base machine images for virtual machines. You'll combine Terraform and Packer to create/provision a production environment in AWS and then deploy your basic application to a single-node swarm in production.

Chapter 7: Continuous Deployment and Repository Secrets, on page 209

Continuous deployment (CD) is an essential part of the software delivery process. It ensures environment integrity by making sure that your application is always deployed to production in the same way. In this chapter, you'll create a CD pipeline with GitHub Actions that automates the deployment of your application once code is merged into the main branch of your repository. You'll also learn how to hide any sensitive data in your code using SOPS and make them available to your application with Docker secrets.

Chapter 8: Revise Your AWS Stack to Create a Multinode Swarm, on page 251

Distributing your infrastructure is important, as it makes the software you deliver more fault-tolerant. In this chapter, you'll adapt your production Terraform configuration to create a multinode swarm, rather than a single-node one. To do this, you'll learn about AWS services such as the SSM Parameter Store and IAM roles/policies. You'll make your application highly available by distributing the different nodes in your Docker Swarm in different AWS availability zones (or data centers).

Chapter 9: Distributed Erlang, on page 285

Connecting multiple replicas of Elixir applications into a distributed cluster is a great way to harness the power of the BEAM. In this chapter, you'll learn how to join different Erlang nodes to form a cluster and the benefits of doing so. You'll deploy an application, lovingly written by our friend Ricardo García Vega, that uses Phoenix's Pub/Sub module to pass data between the multiple nodes in your Erlang cluster.

Chapter 10: Autoscaling and Optimizing Your Deployment Strategy, on page 311

In this chapter, we'll discuss how to make your production environment more reliable by configuring your application to automatically scale based on the CPU usage of your remote servers. You'll optimize your production environment by adding an AWS Auto Scaling group and Load Balancer to your infrastructure. You'll learn how to ensure zero-downtime deployments by automatically rolling back your application upon failed deployments. You'll also understand how to improve the health of your production resources by cleaning up any unused artifacts any time you deploy.

Chapter 11: Instrument Your Application with Logs and Metrics, on page 353

Instrumentation is the last important step in the software delivery cycle, as it allows you to monitor your applications after they have left your machine and are deployed to production. You'll use Grafana, Promtail, and Loki to log your application and Prometheus and PromEx to collect the basic metrics produced by the main Elixir libraries in your Phoenix application.

Chapter 12: Create a Custom PromEx Metric and Grafana Alert, on page 387

This chapter builds on the basic instrumentation that you implemented in Chapter 11 and discusses how you can implement your own custom metric for your Phoenix application. We'll also explore how to set up alerts for your application so that you're notified when unexpected issues arise in any of your environments.

Any time we introduce a new technology in a chapter, we always take care to break it down for you. If getting too detailed is outside of the scope of this book, we'll always point you to other resources where you can find more information.

At the end of every chapter, you'll see a section titled "The Extra Mile." These sections include further exercises for you if you're eager to apply what you've learned to novel scenarios. The essential content that you need to know is covered in the chapter, but these sections contain fun exercises that will give your brain a workout. The exercises aren't guided, but we'll point you to the answers to the related questions.

Online Resources

The full source code for this book, along with all images, can be found at the Pragmatic Programmers site for this book.[1] There, you'll also find a link to the book's errata page listing any updates and corrections made to the book, as well as a way for you to report any errata you may find.

That's enough chit-chat. Let's begin our journey!

---

1. https://pragprog.com/titles/beamops/engineering-elixir-applications/

CHAPTER 1

Introduction to the Journey

Welcome to *Engineering Elixir Applications*!

In this book, we'll go on a step-by-step journey through each stage of the software delivery process. We'll start at the very beginning with project management, before moving into the shipping and maintenance of a production application. Along the way, we'll look at containerization, continuous integration, continuous delivery, provisioning virtual machines, application distribution, autoscaling, and instrumentation. When you've finished reading this book, you'll have a production environment that looks like this:

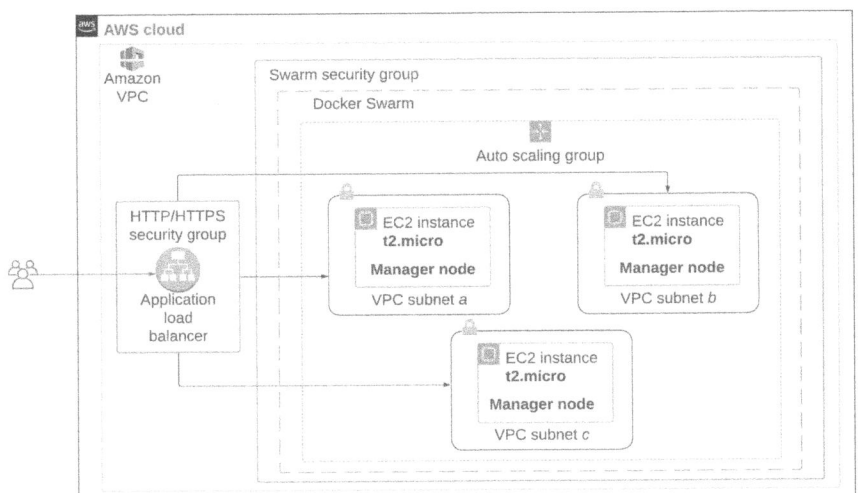

You'll have a multinode Docker Swarm that's distributed across multiple availability zones (data centers) in AWS and that autoscales according to the average CPU usage of the servers hosting your application. Yes, this book covers a lot of material—you could probably write a whole book on each of its chapters! Discussing each stage of software delivery, while comprehensive, means we've made a trade-off. We can't take a deep dive into every little detail. Our goal is to give you a solid foundation of how software applications should be delivered when pushing out features beyond your localhost.

We've written this book to help engineers jump over the fence, from the developer world to the operations world. We think knowledge should be shared rather than kept under lock and key. They do say that "sharing is caring." In this book, we'll be talking about software delivery in the context of the BEAMOps paradigm—a new approach to software writing that's an extension of the DevOps paradigm but with a particular focus on BEAM applications. Let's take a deeper look at what BEAMOps actually means and how you can become a BEAMOps developer.

Introducing the BEAMOps Paradigm

Throughout this book, we'll be talking about something called "BEAMOps." As we said, this is an extension of the well-known DevOps paradigm, but with a focus on the development of BEAM applications. We love the BEAM ecosystem because of its fault-tolerant nature. The concurrency, distribution, and message-passing capabilities of the BEAM make the technologies within its ecosystem ideal for creating reliable and scalable applications. The BEAMOps paradigm recognizes these advantages and sets forth a related set of seven principles:

- Project Management
- Ownership
- Infrastructure-as-Code (IaC)
- Environment Integrity
- Scalability
- Kaizen Principle
- Continuous Deployment

The intention of the BEAMOps paradigm is to create a well-rounded working environment that encourages cooperation and empathy. Let's walk through each principle.

Project Management

You may be surprised to read "project management" as a BEAMOps principle. Isn't managing a project the responsibility of a project manager or product owner? Our answer is yes and no. BEAMOps, at its core, is about sharing responsibilities. You'll see in Chapter 2 that we recommend using a technology that developers are familiar with for project planning, as it helps bridge the gap between project planning and execution. We don't want to imply that project managers aren't important or that developers can (or should) do their job for them. Instead, we want to empower engineers to be part of the project management process so that they can feel more involved with their projects and experience a sense of shared ownership.

Ownership

Speaking of ownership, this is another key BEAMOps value. When we say "ownership," we mean avoiding the "throw it over the fence" culture, where people are inclined to disregard tasks that don't fall squarely in their domain. Let's take project management as an example. Throwing it over the fence could look like a "frontend" developer not writing/updating a Dockerfile because they think "that's not my job." Owning tasks is important to promote not only team efficiency but also a collaborative environment. To make a software product—and the team delivering it—the best that it can be, it's important that team members don't pigeonhole themselves, but rather develop confidence in all areas of software delivery. Being a multidisciplinary engineer who is able to touch any part of the development stack for an application will boost your career options and make working in a team easier and more enjoyable. You've already made the first step to becoming multidisciplinary by just picking up this book!

Infrastructure-as-Code (IaC)

The third BEAMOps principle is infrastructure-as-code (IaC). Defining your infrastructure in code is a must when delivering a software product because it allows you to specify all of the different components and express how they're related. IaC removes the tedium of manual infrastructure creation, allowing you to easily and automatically spin up new environments that use the exact same resources as your other ones. IaC is especially helpful when new members join your team. IaC is a core theme of this book, and you'll see it in various chapters, most notably in Chapter 2 when you'll be introduced to Terraform. We'll also discuss IaC in Chapters 6, 8, and 10, where you'll build on the basic knowledge you gain in Chapter 2 and create your production resources.

Environment Integrity

Closely related to IaC is environment integrity—another key aspect of the BEAMOps paradigm. Environment integrity is achieved when each of your project's different environments use the same resources, whether that be the same versions of tools and packages or the same infrastructure resources. By using the same resources, your software will behave predictably across different stages and environments and it will be easier to develop new features and debug existing ones. Reusing existing IaC files to create your project's infrastructure is a great way to ensure environment integrity because it helps maintain consistency across various environments.

As well as IaC, containerization is another way to ensure environment integrity. Containerization, as you'll see in Chapters 3 and 5, is the practice of packaging an application and its dependencies together in a standardized unit, or container, that can be run in any environment. Containerizing your environment is paramount to reducing the "it works on my machine" problem.

Scalability

For your application to be reliable, it must be able to scale according to its load. When your goal is to provide a continuous service with minimal downtime, scaling is essential. In Chapter 10, we'll look at how you can implement autoscaling so that your application's production resources can grow and shrink depending on how much capacity your application needs to run.

Kaizen Principle

The sixth BEAMOps principle is the Kaizen principle. Kaizen is a Japanese term for "continuous improvement," and the Kaizen principle is the idea that small, continuous changes can lead to significant improvements. Joe Armstrong, one of the co-creators of Erlang, said something important that relates to this concept:

> Make it work, then make it beautiful. Then if you really, really have to, make it fast. 90 percent of the time, if you make it beautiful, it will already be fast. So really, just make it beautiful!

These are words that we live by. Operating as perfectionists much of the time, we engineers often find it difficult to know where to start with a problem. That is why the Kaizen principle is so important. Start out by making something work. Then, bit by bit, make improvements until you have something beautiful. Trying to make something "perfect" in one go is just not possible. You'll get lost and overwhelmed with the workload, so start small and gradually build from there. We'll discuss this more in Chapter 4.

Continuous Deployment

The last cornerstone of the BEAMOps paradigm is continuous deployment. Continuously deploying your work goes hand in hand with the Kaizen principle, allowing you to quickly and easily ship small, incremental changes. Continuously deploying an application also shortens the feedback loop and time to market of new features. It helps you take responsibility for the features you're developing and gives you a sense of ownership of those features once they leave your machine and become part of your continuous deployment pipeline.

BEAMOps is about using the BEAM as a basis for software applications and empowering engineers to actively participate in all stages of software delivery so that their application, their work, is the best it can be. After you finish reading this book, you'll be a BEAMOps developer. You'll be able to demonstrate all of the BEAMOps principles in your daily work, which will help you become a better engineer, take a step forward in your career, and enjoy tackling new challenges.

The Book's Tech Stack

We're going to use a lot of technologies in this journey. As we mentioned, because of the vast number of topics we'll cover in this book, you won't become an expert in any of the technologies by the end, but you'll have a good working understanding of what they are and how to use them. Along the way, we'll point you to some other books and materials if you wish to deepen your knowledge. The technologies you'll be using in your journey are:

- Elixir
- Terraform
- Docker, Docker Compose, and Docker Swarm
- GitHub Actions and ghcr.io
- AWS and EC2
- Packer
- SOPS
- Grafana

We're not married to any of these technologies. We've chosen them because we feel they best facilitate a key goal of this book—to help Elixir engineers jump over the fence into the operations world. Some people out there may prefer other technologies, such as Kubernetes over Docker Swarm or GCP over AWS. But we chose these technologies for two main reasons:

- Popularity: Each of the technologies in the list is widely used in the industry and has a large community of users. This means that you can find a lot of resources and support online if you run into any issues.

- Ease of use: We believe that you, the reader, are going to be most comfortable with these technologies because they're relatively easy to get the hang of and will provide you with the transferrable skills you need to jump over that fence.

In this book, you'll use Docker to build, store, and orchestrate your application. Docker has had a profound impact on the software industry by simplifying the process of building, shipping, and running applications. It has empowered developers to focus on writing code without worrying about the underlying infrastructure, leading to faster development cycles, improved reliability, and increased agility. Docker is great because it is agnostic to the technology of your application or environment and is important for environment integrity and consistency.

In terms of orchestration, Docker can be run in swarm mode which allows you to manage a cluster of Docker hosts, deploy services across them, and scale those services as needed. But there are other tools that you can use to achieve orchestration, such as Kubernetes. While Kubernetes is more widely used in the operations world today, due to its powerful capabilities, it's less straightforward to learn. Kubernetes is also strictly an orchestration tool, which means it doesn't have the capability to build self-contained image packages—you'd have to use an external tool, such as Docker, to do this. In this book, we use Docker for both building and orchestrating so that you can fully understand the concept of orchestration without having to switch contexts and learn a new technology. If you ever want to use Kubernetes to orchestrate an application, you can reuse the Dockerfiles you'll create in this book.

Where we can, we've tried to decouple the infrastructure logic from AWS. For example, rather than using AWS's native CI pipelines tool, AWS CodePipelines, we've chosen to use GitHub Actions. This is because GitHub is a tool familiar to almost all developers and GitHub Actions have multiple open source actions that you can use. After you finish this book, for example, should you choose to use an Azure stack, or any other option, in the future rather than AWS, you won't have a steep learning curve if you want to know how to create CI pipelines. For this same reason, we've chosen that the production environment you'll create will be a Docker Swarm built on EC2 instances that are provisioned with Packer. There are AWS-specific technologies that you could use to create your production environment, such as AWS's ECS service,[1] but using Docker and Packer—which again are two open source platforms—means that you can reuse a lot of your knowledge in this book should you be working on a future project that's not AWS-based. For us, it's the programming concepts that these technologies give you, such as containerization, environment integrity, and OS provisioning, that are important rather than the technologies themselves.

---

1. https://docs.aws.amazon.com/AmazonECS/latest/APIReference/Welcome.html

Security Disclaimer

This journey is about introducing you, a developer, to the operations world using the BEAMOps paradigm. To easily guide you through these concepts, we've simplified some aspects of security.

When dealing with security, it's hard to draw a boundary between sharing knowledge and exposing vulnerabilities. We've tried to walk the line, but we are aware that some of the practices described in this book might not be enough to protect your systems when they're in production. For example, in Chapter 11 we've completely disabled the authentication of the Grafana UI (don't worry if you don't know what Grafana is right now—you'll learn all about it later). We've disabled this authentication for educational purposes, simply to assist your understanding of what Grafana is. We encourage you to seek additional resources and/or professional advice when dealing with system security.

Now that you know the stack you'll use throughout the book, it's time to prepare your environment and install all the tools you need.

Set Up Your Environment

We've decided to use a tool called asdf to manage the versions of the different packages that you'll use. We chose asdf because it's a popular version manager that we believe will keep things simple. As you'll see in Chapter 4, when you create a continuous integration pipeline, using asdf and defining your packages in a .tool-versions file can help ensure environment integrity for your application.

Preparing your environment will consist of five steps:

1. Installing asdf (if you haven't done so already)
2. Installing all of the plugins (bar Docker) and their versions that you'll use throughout the book
3. Installing Docker Desktop—a Docker GUI that installs everything you need to be able to use Docker
4. Creating an AWS account
5. Configuring the GitHub CLI that you installed in step 2

If you already have asdf installed in your environment, skip step 1 and move straight on to step 2.

Install asdf

To install asdf, follow steps 1, 2, and 3 of the "Getting Started"[2] section of the official asdf documentation. This will walk you through installing the dependencies required for asdf as well as asdf itself, given your specific setup.

Great! Now that you've installed asdf, it's time to install the various plugins and their versions that you'll use throughout the book.

Install the Plugins and Their Versions Used Throughout the Book

As we mentioned in the previous section, this book uses a fair number of technologies. To define the plugins and versions that your application will need, you'll create two files: a bash script to install the asdf plugins and another script to define the versions for these plugins.

An asdf plugin is a module that provides the necessary functionality to manage the installing, configuring, and switching between different versions of a certain package. A version, as it sounds, is the version of that tool/plugin that you want to use—for example, version 1.16.0 of Elixir.

You'll create the plugin and version files as part of your application so that all developers contributing to your project can use the same package versions and run your application in the same way. This is your first step in practicing one of the BEAMOps principles: environment integrity.

To create the bash script that installs the plugins, you first need to create the directory you'll use throughout this book to house your application. To do this, create a new folder at a path of your choice called kanban. Then create a scripts folder inside that, which has an asdf_plugins.sh file with the following code:

```bash
#!/usr/bin/env bash
# in scripts/asdf_plugins.sh
# install necessary plugins
plugins=(
  "github-cli"
  "packer"
  "terraform"
  "awscli"
  "elixir"
  "erlang"
  "postgres"
  "jq"
  "age"
  "sops"
)
```

---

2. https://asdf-vm.com/guide/getting-started.html#getting-started

```
for plugin in "${plugins[@]}"; do
    asdf plugin-add "$plugin" || true
    # the "|| true" ignore errors if a certain plugin already exists
done
echo "Installation complete."
echo "Please restart your terminal or source your profile file."
```

As you can see, this script installs the Elixir, Erlang, Terraform, Packer, Postgres, jq, GitHub CLI, and AWS CLI asdf plugins. cd into the scripts directory inside the project folder that you just created, make this script executable by running chmod +x scripts/asdf_plugins.sh and then run the script to install these plugins. Remember that these plugins aren't the tools themselves, just the asdf helper modules for those tools. Note that the script will not error if any of these plugins already exist in your environment.

Terrific. You've installed the plugins. But asdf is only useful if you install the tools themselves and manage their versions. To do this, you'll create a .tool-versions file, which will define the packages that you wish to install and the versions that you wish to use. You'll use this file later in the book when you create your CI pipeline, making sure that your application is run using the same versions of the same technologies. Create your .tool-versions file in the root of your kanban folder and then copy in this code snippet:

```
github-cli 2.42.1
terraform 1.7.1
awscli 2.15.15
elixir 1.16.0-otp-26
erlang 26.2.1
postgres 15.2
packer 1.9.0
age 1.1.1
jq 1.7
sops 3.8.1
```

The .tool-versions file must be in the root so that the packages defined in that file are available at all paths within your kanban folder. Now that you've created your .tool-versions file, cd back to the root of your project folder and run asdf install to install the specific versions of the tools that you need. Your terminal should look like this:

```
$ cd ../
$ asdf install
...
```

Nice! You've installed the tools and versions that you need. If you want to check the versions of the tools that you installed, you can run the following commands in your terminal:

```
$ gh --version
$ packer --version
$ terraform --version
$ aws --version
$ elixir --version
$ erl -eval 'erlang:display(erlang:system_info(otp_release)), halt().' \
  -noshell
$ psql --version
```

Make sure that the versions match the ones in the .tool-versions file. Now, on to step 3: installing Docker Desktop.

Install Docker Desktop

Docker Desktop is a graphical user interface (GUI) that allows you to set up and run a complete Docker development environment. It includes the Docker daemon (dockerd), the Docker client (docker), Docker Compose, Docker Content Trust, Kubernetes, and Credential Helper. Don't worry if that all sounds overwhelming right now; we'll dig deeper into these components in Chapter 3. For now, all you need to know is that the easiest way to install Docker on your computer is to install Docker Desktop.

To install Docker Desktop, navigate to the Docker Desktop[3] page of the official Docker documentation and follow the installation instructions for the specific OS that you're using.

Alternatively, if you're a Mac user and use Homebrew, you can install Docker Desktop with one simple command. Docker Desktop is an application and not just a brew package, so you'll need to install it with cask. You can install it by running the following command in your terminal:

```
$ brew install --cask docker
```

Once the installation is complete, start Docker Desktop by manually opening the application. When you do this, you'll need to accept the license. Select the default settings, continue without signing in, and skip the survey. Once you're done, you can check that Docker is running properly by executing the following command in your terminal:

```
$ docker ps
CONTAINER ID   IMAGE     COMMAND   CREATED   STATUS   PORTS   NAMES
```

That's it. You've installed Docker.

---

3. https://docs.docker.com/desktop/

> **Run Docker to Run Commands**
>
>  When running Docker commands, you always need to have the Docker application running in the background. If not, the Docker daemon won't be running and you won't be able to run docker commands.

On to step 4: creating an AWS account.

Create Your AWS Account

Once you start creating your remote production environment, you'll need to have an AWS account. If you don't already have one, you can create one by following the instructions in the Amazon documentation.[4]

You shouldn't incur any costs while implementing the infrastructure in this book. The type of instances that you'll launch is part of the free tier that AWS offers for one year for new accounts. However, depending on how long your resources remain active, some small charges could apply. To be safe, you should always destroy your AWS resources at the end of each chapter. Don't worry if you forget; we'll always remind you.

And now, for the last step in setting up your environment: configuring the GitHub CLI.

Configure the GitHub CLI

To configure the GitHub CLI, run the gh auth login command to authenticate it with your GitHub account. Then, if you use ssh as the protocol to clone and push to repositories, update the gh CLI's preferred protocol accordingly:

```
$ gh auth login
...
$ gh config set git_protocol ssh --host github.com
```

And that's it! You've installed and configured all of the tools that you'll need throughout this book, and you're ready to start your journey to becoming a BEAMOps developer! We hope that you enjoy the adventure we're about to have together.

---

4. https://portal.aws.amazon.com/billing/signup#/start/email

Our first step: getting to know Terraform and using it to set up the project management tools (milestones) that you'll complete throughout the book.

Don't worry about creating a repository for this book and committing any of the code we've done in this chapter so far. You'll do this using Terraform in the next chapter.

Grab a coffee or tea, turn the page, and we'll get started!

CHAPTER 2

Use Terraform to Create GitHub Issues and Milestones

In the previous chapter, you were introduced to the BEAMOps paradigm and the importance of owning each step of the software delivery process. The foundational step of that delivery process is project management. Traditionally, this step doesn't fall under the scope of a developer, but we're here to change that. In this chapter, you'll learn to own the project management stage of an application.

You might be surprised or confused to see GitHub and Terraform in the title of this chapter. You may know Terraform as a declarative language used to define and manage infrastructure resources. And you may know GitHub as a version control and code-hosting platform. So, what do these two technologies have to do with project management?

Well, Terraform has a GitHub provider that allows you to manage GitHub repositories and project-planning resources like issues and milestones. This is important because becoming a superpowered BEAMOps developer is about ownership, lifting blockers, and, above all, reducing delivery times. We know how much time is lost in gathering requirements and the miscommunication caused by the number of times a message jumps from one person to another. To ensure there is as much alignment across the team as possible, we propose using a tool that has a Terraform provider, such as GitHub, to manage a project. This allows for more collaboration and less distance between product and development teams. Another benefit to using Terraform is that any configuration files you create can be reused in the future to easily spin up new projects. This makes the planning or organization phase of a project less painful and time-consuming. So, in this book, in addition to storing your codebase in GitHub, you'll also use GitHub to manage your project and deliver and test your application. This approach is particularly useful for small teams, short-term projects with well-known deliverables, or consultants who need to quickly spin up new projects.

In this chapter, you'll use Terraform to create your GitHub repository and your project's milestones, issues, and labels. You'll also use Terraform resource blocks, variables, and provider configurations to create GitHub infrastructure resources. On top of that, you'll learn the CLI commands used to operate Terraform configuration files and modules. We'll cover the basic commands used to manage a Terraform development workflow, as well as the commands used to check the infrastructure state and enter/use a Terraform interactive console.

Let's start by going over the Terraform fundamentals.

Get to Know Terraform

Terraform is an infrastructure-as-code (IaC) tool developed by Hashicorp. It lets you declare cloud, on-premise, or high-level resources via the declarative language HCL. Thanks to its human-friendly syntax, HCL can be used to create easy-to-read Terraform configuration files that allow you to version, reuse, and share infrastructure as code. Defining your project and business resources in an IaC tool such as Terraform helps reduce knowledge silos and encourages teams to embrace common, shared knowledge. Using a tool like Terraform also reduces human error by automating the creation, modification, and destruction of infrastructure resources. This provides consistent and reproducible results.

A modern infrastructure contains many interconnected pieces. For example, it may have an EC2 instance, a load balancer, or even a GitHub repository. Terraform offers a single unified workflow that integrates all of these pieces, and its use of implicit or explicit dependencies tells us the order in which these resources must be created, updated, or destroyed.

While we're going to use Terraform in this book, it's important to note that there are other IaC tools. One example is Pulumi. If you're interested in the key differences between Terraform and Pulumi, please visit their docs.[1]

Before jumping into an HCL 101, you first need to understand the Terraform Core and the Terraform state.

---

1. https://www.pulumi.com/docs/intro/vs/terraform#differences

The Terraform Core

The Terraform Core is the entry point to Terraform. It's Terraform's underlying execution engine, which is responsible for parsing and understanding configurations based on the Terraform configuration files that you create. It manages resource dependencies, creates execution plans, and interacts with various providers to make changes to infrastructure resources and the Terraform state that reflects them.

Don't worry if this seems like too much to take in right now; you'll be more confident in your understanding by the end of this chapter. Now let's look at the Terraform state.

The Terraform State

The Terraform state maps real-world resources to the resources defined in your configuration files. Writing or editing a configuration file alone doesn't update the state. To actually make changes and create/destroy/update resources, you need to run the command terraform apply. When you do this, the Terraform Core compares your current Terraform state with your Terraform configuration file. It then creates any resources defined in your configuration file that are not in the state and similarly destroys any resources that are in the state but not defined in your configuration file. The state also saves metadata about resource dependencies.

By default, Terraform stores its state locally in a file named terraform.tfstate. When working with Terraform in a team, using a local file makes working with Terraform complicated because each user will have their own local version of the state. When using Terraform in a project with multiple contributors you must store your Terraform state in a remote environment, such as AWS. Each person must make sure they always have the latest state data before running any Terraform commands, and they must not run any Terraform commands at the same time as someone else. In this book, we will only focus on a local Terraform state. You can find information about a remote state in the official Terraform docs.[2]

For now, this is all that you need to know about the Terraform state. As we progress through the book, we'll expand on this definition.

Now that you understand two crucial Terraform concepts, let's look at HCL, the language Terraform uses.

---

2. https://developer.hashicorp.com/terraform/language/state/remote

HCL 101: The Language That Terraform Uses

Terraform configurations are written in .tf files using HCL. HCL stands for Hashicorp Configuration Language. It's a language that's used across many tools that Hashicorp offers, such as Terraform and Packer, and you'll use it throughout this book.

Terraform uses HCL to define resources, create dependencies, and define what data will be fetched. HCL's two main syntax constructs are blocks and arguments. Here is a visual representation of a block:

```
<BLOCK TYPE> "<BLOCK INSTANCE>" "<BLOCK LABEL>" {
  # Block body
  <IDENTIFIER> = <EXPRESSION> # Argument
}
```

Now, let's use a GitHub resource definition to dissect each of the different components in an HCL block. The GitHub repository resource is defined like so:

```
resource "github_repository" "main" {
  name        = "kanban"
  description = "Taking the BEAM to production pragmatically."
  visibility  = "private"
}
```

In the previous example, you can see that the <BLOCK TYPE> we have used is resource. In HCL, there are seven main block types that you can have: a terraform block to define general configurations, a resource, a variable, a module, a data source, an output, or a locals value. You'll see an example of each one as you go through the book.

For the <BLOCK INSTANCE> we have used github_repository. This identifies which provider resource we wish to instantiate. We'll elaborate on how to use these providers in the next section,

The <BLOCK LABEL> we've used is main. A block label is the identifier that the Terraform state will use to refer to this particular resource. As a result, it must always be a unique value.

In the block body, you can see what are examples of arguments. An argument is a combination of an identifier and its assigned value. Let's take visibility = "private" as an example. This line as a whole is an argument. The visibility variable is an example of an <IDENTIFIER>. An identifier is the name of an argument. The private value is an <EXPRESSION>. Expressions are the values that are assigned to identifiers. An expression can be a raw value like a string, as in the example provided, or a more complex code block such as a for loop or a built-in Terraform function.

Defined in the same way as arguments, with an identifier and an expression, HCL also uses meta-arguments. Meta-arguments are a special type of argument that modifies the behavior of other arguments. They can be used to define default values, loop through a set or map, and set certain constraints or certain dependencies between arguments and/or resources. They are used to provide additional context, configuration, and information beyond what can be expressed by simple arguments alone. You'll see an example of a meta-argument later in this chapter.

As we mentioned and as the <BLOCK INSTANCE> shows, the HCL block we just looked at is an example of the GitHub repository resource. This resource is exposed by the Terraform GitHub provider. We'll now discuss what a Terraform provider is.

Terraform Providers

Terraform interacts with the external world (APIs) via plugins called providers. There are four types of providers:

- Cloud (such as AWS, GCP, Azure)
- On premise (such as openstack, VMware)
- Platform as a service (such as Heroku, k8s, lambdas)
- Software as a service (such as Datadog, fastly, GitHub)

A provider exposes a set of resources and/or data sources that Terraform can manage. A resource block declares one or more infrastructure objects, whether that be compute resources like EC2 or virtual networks like AWS Virtual Private Cloud—anything that a cloud provider, a platform as a service, or a software as a service exposes via an API. In this chapter, the resources you'll create are a GitHub repository as well as GitHub milestones, labels, and issues. Let's now look at how to use the GitHub provider.

Create Your First Resource Using the GitHub Provider

To declare or use any resources, the first step is always to tell the Terraform Core which providers' resources you wish to use by creating a required_providers block (if you don't already have one defined in your Terraform configuration file) and adding that provider as an argument.

Any time you want to use a provider, you need to check its docs in the Terraform registry.[3] Each provider has a Use Provider button that, when pressed, shows a pop-up with the instructions you need to include in your Terraform

---

3. https://registry.terraform.io/browse/providers

configuration file. These instructions will be similar across providers and will define three things for each provider: its name, its source in the Terraform registry, and the version to be used by the core.

At the time of this writing, the basic GitHub provider configuration looks like this:

```
terraform {
  required_providers {
    github = {
      source  = "integrations/github"
      version = "5.41.0"
    }
  }
}

provider "github" {
  owner = "YOUR_GITHUB_USERNAME"
}
```

To use this GitHub provider, you'll need to create a Terraform configuration file and paste the preceding code snippet into it. Your configuration file will be called main.tf. cd into your kanban folder you created in the previous chapter, and, once inside, create this main.tf file in a new folder called modules/integrations/github/project_management, where the project_management folder is inside the github folder and so on. Now paste the previous code block into your newly created main.tf file, replacing the owner argument value with your GitHub username. As you can see, the code example starts with a terraform block. This block uses nested block types to tell the Terraform Core what configuration to use. One of the nested block types you can specify is required_providers. This tells the Terraform Core which providers you'll use in your project. Any time you add any new providers to your Terraform configuration, to be able to use any of these providers' resources, you need to run the command terraform init. This command initializes Terraform. cd into your modules/integrations/github/project_management folder and run this command, we will then talk about what is happening behind the scenes:

```
$ cd modules/integrations/github/project_management
$ terraform init
Initializing the backend...

Initializing provider plugins...
- Finding integrations/github versions matching "5.41.0"...
- Installing integrations/github v5.41.0...
- Installed integrations/github v5.41.0 (signed by a HashiCorp...

Partner and community providers are signed by their developers.
If you'd like to know more about provider signing, you can read about it
here: https://www.terraform.io/docs/cli/plugins/signing.html
```

```
Terraform has created a lock file .terraform.lock.hcl to record the
provider selections it made above. Include this file in your version
control repository so that Terraform can guarantee to make the same
selections by default when you run "terraform init" in the future.

Terraform has been successfully initialized!

You may now begin working with Terraform. Try running "terraform plan"
to see any changes that are required for your infrastructure. All
Terraform commands should now work.

If you ever set or change modules or backend configuration for Terraform,
rerun this command to reinitialize your working directory. If you forget,
other commands will detect it and remind you to do so if necessary.
```

When you execute terraform init, the Terraform binary looks for any files with the .tf extension in the folder where it was executed and performs four actions:

- Backend initialization
- Installation of child modules and provider plugins
- Generation (if not present) of a .terraform folder where all plugins and child modules are installed after being downloaded
- Generation of a .terraform.lock.hcl

Think of the .terraform.lock.hcl as a typical dependency lock, similar to a mix.lock or rebar.lock. In this instance, however, it lists the providers from your main.tf Terraform configuration file.

As the .terraform.lock.hcl file is a dot file, use the command tree -a . to see the lock and the folder where all providers are downloaded:

```
$ tree -a .
.
├── .terraform
│   └── providers
│       └── registry.terraform.io
│           └── integrations
│               └── github
│                   └── 5.41.0
│                       └── darwin_amd64
│                           ├── CHANGELOG.md
│                           ├── LICENSE
│                           ├── README.md
│                           └── terraform-provider-github_v5.41.0
├── .terraform.lock.hcl
└── main.tf
```

> **Copy and Paste for Version Control**
>
>  Bear in mind that the versions might change when you look at the registry provider docs. To be sure that you'll have the same output, copy and paste the examples in this book.

This is great! You now have a Terraform setup that includes the GitHub provider and you're ready to create your first resource with Terraform. Our first aim will be to create a repository called "kanban." This is the repository you'll use throughout this book. To simplify things, we'll use a monolithic approach, so you'll only need to create one repository. Once the repository is created, you'll create the milestones, labels, and issues. The next section will look specifically at creating the GitHub repository.

Create Your First Resource: A GitHub Repository

So far, you know that a provider adds a set of resources. In the previous section, you configured the GitHub provider, and you're now ready to use the set of resources that it exposes. You're going to add a GitHub repository resource to your Terraform configuration file.

To find the name of a particular resource, you should always go to the Terraform registry, search for the provider you want, and look at the documentation for that resource. In this case, to create the GitHub repository, go to the provider's docs page[4] and search for github repository. You'll find the GitHub repository resource management docs. The resource you need is called github_repository.[5] The convention that Terraform uses for naming block instances of providers is PROVIDER_RESOURCE-NAME. All resource docs pages have the following structure:

- The resource name
- A small description
- A few usage examples
- The arguments that the resource allows
- The attributes that it exports
- Information on how to import an existing remote resource into your Terraform state (we'll look at this in Chapter 6)

Normally, for most of the resources, the example code snippet will provide enough detail for you to add the resource to your configuration. We would always recommend, however, that you skim the arguments reference. This way, you'll get to know all the capabilities of that particular resource. It's

---

4. https://registry.terraform.io/providers/integrations/github/latest/docs
5. https://registry.terraform.io/providers/integrations/github/latest/docs/resources/repository

important to familiarize yourself with the registry as you'll visit this whenever you want to add a resource to your configuration file or edit its arguments.

That is enough chit-chat. Let's add the github_repository resource to your config file. Open up your main.tf file and add in your resource definition under your terraform block, like this:

```
# in modules/integrations/github/project_management/main.tf
resource "github_repository" "kanban" {
  name                   = "kanban"
  description            = "Taking the BEAM to production pragmatically."
  visibility             = "private"
  has_issues             = true
  auto_init              = true
  gitignore_template     = "Terraform"
  delete_branch_on_merge = true
}
```

Most of the arguments in this resource block—such as the name, the description, or the visibility—are self-explanatory. There are two identifiers, though, that require a special mention:

- When auto_init is set to true, the repository won't be created empty. Instead, it'll have an initial commit with an empty README.md and, if the gitignore_template has been specified, a .gitignore.

- If you look at the gitignore_template argument, you'll see that it has been set to be Terraform. This will create your repository with the initial .gitignore file for Terraform projects. As you progress through the book, you'll add other ignored files.

Now that you have the repository defined in your main.tf file, you can create your resource by applying the Terraform configuration. We'll look at how to do this in the next section, where we discuss the Terraform provisioning cycle and run two new commands in the terminal.

Apply a Planned Configuration Following the Provisioning Cycle

As a general rule, you should always follow the Terraform provisioning cycle—the Terraform development cycle in which you edit your configuration file, execute the *plan* command to visualize the changes that'll be made depending on your *state*, and then execute the *apply* command to make those changes. Each time you wish to apply more changes, you edit your configuration file and restart the cycle. The graph on page 22 shows a visualization of this process.

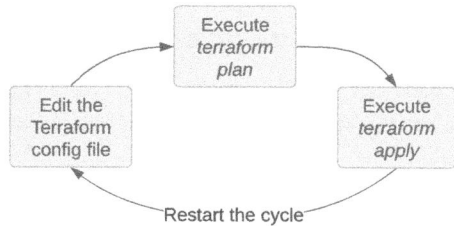

In the previous section, you completed the first step in the cycle, editing your Terraform configuration by adding your first resource to your main.tf file. Now it's time to plan. To do so, run the command terraform plan like so:

```
$ terraform plan
```

```
Terraform used the selected providers to generate the following
execution plan.
Resource actions are indicated with the following symbols:
 + create

Terraform will perform the following actions:

  # github_repository.kanban will be created
  + resource "github_repository" "kanban" {
      + allow_auto_merge            = false
      + allow_merge_commit          = true
      + allow_rebase_merge          = true
      + allow_squash_merge          = true
      + archived                    = false
      + auto_init                   = true
      + default_branch              = (known after apply)
      + delete_branch_on_merge      = true
      + description                 = "Taking the BEAM to production pragmatically."
      + etag                        = (known after apply)
      + full_name                   = (known after apply)
      + git_clone_url               = (known after apply)
      + gitignore_template          = "Terraform"
      + has_issues                  = true
      + html_url                    = (known after apply)
      + http_clone_url              = (known after apply)
      + id                          = (known after apply)
      + merge_commit_message        = "PR_TITLE"
      + merge_commit_title          = "MERGE_MESSAGE"
      + name                        = "kanban"
      + node_id                     = (known after apply)
      + private                     = (known after apply)
      + repo_id                     = (known after apply)
      + squash_merge_commit_message = "COMMIT_MESSAGES"
      + squash_merge_commit_title   = "COMMIT_OR_PR_TITLE"
      + ssh_clone_url               = (known after apply)
```

```
        + svn_url                       = (known after apply)
        + visibility                    = "private"
    }
Plan: 1 to add, 0 to change, 0 to destroy.
```

```
Note: You didn't use the -out option to save this plan, so Terraform
can't guarantee it will take exactly these actions if you run
`terraform apply` now.
```

In the example output that the Terraform Core gives when running terraform plan, you can see the GitHub repository that would be created if you were to apply your configuration. The arguments declared within the github_repository block in your main.tf file are all there. There are also some other arguments whose values will be (known after apply). This is because some attributes, such as repo_id, are generated after terraform apply is run and the provider API creates the resource. You'll also see that there is a warning at the end of the output saying that you didn't use the -out option to save your plan. The -out flag allows you to save your planned execution to a file. Doing this makes sharing Terraform configurations between team members for review a lot easier. It also guarantees that the plan generated precisely matches what will be applied later, eliminating any discrepancies that could arise from alterations in remote resources and ensuring that only changes that have been reviewed and approved are applied to the infrastructure. This could be helpful, for example, if you're applying Terraform configurations in a CI/CD pipeline. As you're just working on the application in this book by yourself, there's no need to save the plan–seeing it in the terminal is just fine.

Now that you've seen the plan, let's move to the next step in the provisioning cycle and try to run terraform apply. When you do this, you'll see another plan of the resource that will be created, and you'll be prompted to confirm you want to apply the plan. Write "yes" and press Enter. When you do this, you'll see the following error:

```
Error: POST https://api.github.com/user/repos: 401 Requires
authentication

  with github_repository.kanban,
  on main.tf line 10, in resource "github_repository" "kanban":
  10: resource "github_repository" "kanban" {
```

Why is this happening? So far, you've added a Terraform block in your configuration file where you've specified the GitHub provider and you've also declared a github_repository resource. You've told the Terraform Core *what* you want to manage (a GitHub repository) and from *whom* (the GitHub provider), but you haven't specified how the provider will authenticate itself when performing requests to the GitHub API. We'll discuss how to do this in the next section.

> **Running terraform apply**
>
>  You may have noticed when you ran the terraform apply command, the Terraform Core gave you a plan and asked you to confirm it. Recall earlier we said when running the terraform plan command, you can use the -out option to save the plan to an external file that can be used when running terraform apply. If you don't pass a plan file to the terraform apply command, the Terraform Core will automatically create a new execution plan for you and ask you to confirm it. Throughout the rest of the book, rather than running terraform plan before each terraform apply command, we'll only run terraform apply and look at the automatic plan created by the Terraform Core. We'll do this to speed up your development workflow.

Revisit the Provider Configuration: Authentication for the GitHub API

As the error in the previous section noted, the terraform apply command failed because you never authenticated yourself with the provider's API. As we mentioned previously, whenever you need information about a Terraform resource or a provider configuration, you should look at the Terraform registry. In this case, for the documentation on GitHub authentication, you can visit the Terraform registry GitHub provider documentation.[6] There you'll see that to authenticate yourself, you have two options:

- Declare a token argument in the provider block
- Set the GITHUB_TOKEN environment variable

To speed up your development cycle, we recommend setting the environment variable. If you set the argument instead, you'll be prompted to introduce the token every time you apply your plan. Alternatively, you could create an .auto.tfvars file that includes this variable, and each time a plan/apply/destroy is executed, the variable will be autoloaded and fed to the Terraform Core. We'll look at this later in this chapter. You could also hard-code the token string in the provider section of the Terraform configuration. This is not a good idea, however, because this file will be under version control and thus your GitHub token will be exposed. For now, we'll set the environment variable.

---

6. https://registry.terraform.io/providers/integrations/github/latest/docs#oauth--personal-access-token

Even if you already have a GitHub token, follow these instructions and create a classic personal access GitHub token[7] with the following scopes: repo, write:packages, delete_repo, project, and admin:org.

Then set your GITHUB_TOKEN and rerun the terraform apply command. To set the token, you can either prepend it to the terraform apply command or autoload it in your shell profile. In the following example, we've loaded it in our shell profile:

```
$ GITHUB_TOKEN=****
$ terraform apply
...
Do you want to perform these actions?
  Terraform will perform the actions described above.
  Only 'yes' will be accepted to approve.

  Enter a value: yes

github_repository.kanban: Creating...
github_repository.kanban: Creation complete after 7s [id=kanban]

Apply complete! Resources: 1 added, 0 changed, 0 destroyed.
```

Nice! You've just created your first resource using the Terraform GitHub provider. Before moving into the state revision, let's refactor a little bit.

Local Values

To avoid code repetition with values that don't change within the context of the Terraform configuration file, we suggest using local values. A locals block allows you to declare a local value that will be available in all the contexts of the Terraform file—for more information see the docs.[8] In this case, you'll use local values to avoid repeating your GitHub repository_name and github_owner. These are values that you'll need to reuse in the other resources that you'll create.

To declare a local value, you must create a locals block in your Terraform configuration file. So, in your main.tf file, create a locals block under your terraform block with your repository_name and github_owner variables as we've done here:

```
# in modules/integrations/github/project_management/main.tf
locals {
  repository_name = "kanban"
  github_owner    = "YOUR_GITHUB_USERNAME"
}
```

---

7. https://docs.github.com/en/enterprise-server@3.4/authentication/keeping-your-account-and-data-secure/creating-a-personal-access-token
8. https://developer.hashicorp.com/terraform/language/values/locals

Once you've declared your local values, you can refer to them in any other HCL block by using the variable local. You can access a specific property as you would in a map using dot notation. For example, to access the repository_name variable you defined in your locals block, you'd write local.repository_name. Replace the name value in your github_repository resource block in your main.tf file with the new repository_name local variable that you created. Your github_repository resource block should now look like this:

```
# in modules/integrations/github/project_management/main.tf
resource "github_repository" "kanban" {
  name = local.repository_name
}
```

Now, do the same with the github_owner. Normally, the GitHub provider automatically determines the owner from the GITHUB_TOKEN when authenticating with the API, but if you were to have multiple projects, things could get messy. So, it's better to be explicit and specify the owner in your Terraform configuration file, as we've done here:

```
# in modules/integrations/github/project_management/main.tf
provider "github" {
  owner = local.github_owner
}
```

It's important to keep in mind that any time you refactor anything, you must reapply the Terraform configuration to update your Terraform state. You can achieve this by simply executing another terraform apply. Do this now. In the next section, we'll look at the different commands you can use to examine the Terraform state.

Examine the Terraform State

As you're writing and editing Terraform files, it's a good idea to check the Terraform state. Doing so is an easy way to know which of your resources have been created and helps you spot if you've forgotten to apply any of your changes. A useful command is terraform state list. This command lists all the resources that are currently in your state. If you run it, the Terraform console gives the following output:

```
$ terraform state list
github_repository.kanban
```

As you can see, you currently have one resource created called github_repository.kanban. This is because in your main.tf file, you declared a github_repository resource block with the block label kanban. The Terraform state, when listing resources, will always list them in the BLOCK_INSTANCE.BLOCK_LABEL pattern—this definition is known as the resource address.

Another useful command that will show you the attributes for a specific resource is terraform state show. This command expects a resource address as an argument. For example, to see the attributes for the kanban github_repository resource, write terraform state show followed by the resource address we discovered in the earlier example:

```
$ terraform state show github_repository.kanban
# github_repository.kanban:
resource "github_repository" "kanban" {
    allow_auto_merge        = false
    allow_merge_commit      = true
    ...
```

As you can see, the terraform state show command gives a lot of information about the resource. This is useful, but sometimes you want to interact with the resource state to understand how you can link it with other resources or simply play with the terraform built-in functions. This is where the Terraform console comes in handy.

Play with the Terraform Console

Our favorite command is terraform console. As the name suggests, this command opens up an interactive Terraform console that allows you to play with the different modules within the Terraform state, as well as use Terraform built-in functions and for loops. Using this command and interacting with the console to test your code will speed up your development cycle and help you become a superpowered engineer. The upcoming terminal output gives you an example interaction with the Terraform console. Review it and then we'll discuss the commands and their outputs.

```
$ terraform console
> github_repository.kanban.name
"kanban"
> title(github_repository.kanban.name)
"Kanban"
> [for k,_v in github_repository.kanban : k]
[
  "allow_auto_merge",
  "allow_merge_commit",
  "allow_rebase_merge",
  ...
]
```

In this example, to open up the interactive Terraform console, we wrote terraform console and then pressed Enter. We then interacted with the console in three different ways:

1. We accessed the name key of the github_repository resource using its resource address: github_repository.kanban.name.

2. We passed the return value of the first command to the Terraform built-in title function: title(github_repository.kanban.name). All this function does is capitalize the received string. It's important to note that when running a function like this, you're not altering the state. The Terraform console is just showing you what the result would be if you were to use this function on the provided resource address.

3. We used the github_repository.kanban resource address to loop through the resource and return a list of the resource's keys: [for k,_v in github_repository.kanban : k].

Now that you know how to check the Terraform state and play with the Terraform console, you're ready to add some deliverables to your project. In the next section, you'll get your hands dirty with project management and create some milestones and issues.

Create Your Second Resource: GitHub Milestones

As a pragmatic engineer, you should aim to own every stage of the delivery process and, yes, this also includes project management. This is normally a tedious task that involves many people and requires many meetings. Often, communication issues and misunderstandings make this tedious task even more painful. By taking ownership of project management, you can reduce the pain points and even make it fun by turning an organizational task into a development one. As an engineer doing project management, you also have the plus of being able to go back and track tasks via version control.

Recall that in this book you're going to build and deploy a Phoenix LiveView application using GitHub Actions. You'll deliver the application into a Docker Swarm provisioned in AWS using Terraform and then add some metrics. If you think about this in terms of project management, you can think about the following milestones:

- Infrastructure
- Continuous Integration/Continuous Deployment
- Instrumentation
- Documentation
- Uncategorized

To create the milestones, you will use a new GitHub resource. Previously, we mentioned that Terraform providers are defined using the pattern PROVIDER_RESOURCE. This is the case for a top-level resource such as a repository, but a milestone isn't a top-level resource. Rather, it's a child of the top-level github_repository resource. When referring to children of a top-level resource, the pattern becomes PROVIDER_RESOURCE_NESTED-RESOURCE, so the milestone resource block instance is called github_repository_milestone. While knowing this naming pattern means that you can guess the names of resources, as we said, we always recommend referring back to the Terraform registry to check the resource arguments reference in the docs. For example, if you search for the milestone resource,[9] you'll see that you must specify the owner, repository, and title arguments and can optionally define a due_date and description.

Let's start creating the first milestone by adding the milestone resource with the <BLOCK_LABEL> epics to your main.tf file under your github_repository resource:

```
# in modules/integrations/github/project_management/main.tf

resource "github_repository_milestone" "epics" {
  owner       = local.github_owner
  repository  = local.repository_name
  title       = "Infrastructure"
  description = <<EOT
This milestone includes all the deliverables related to building the
application (e.g Dockerfile, provisioning AWS, the local environment
and the base AMI with Packer).
EOT
  due_date    = "2023-06-24"
}
```

When creating a due date for a milestone, it's always important to give yourself a buffer. When calculating the due date in the recent example, we took into account that this milestone includes the Dockerfile, the dev environment, the base AMI (Amazon Machine Image), and the AWS infrastructure. (Don't worry if you don't know what an AMI is for now—we'll discuss it in detail in Chapter 6). We estimated that this work would take around four weeks. However, we gave ourselves an extra week to account for any issues. Doing this alleviates stress and allows you time to improve your codebase and not hand over a rushed piece of work. An easy way to calculate due dates is to use the Elixir interactive shell and the built-in Date add function. The following snippet is how we calculated the date in five-weeks time:

```
iex(1)> Date.utc_today() |> Date.add(7*5) |> Date.to_string()
"2024-06-24"
```

---

9. https://registry.terraform.io/providers/integrations/github/latest/docs/resources/repository_milestone

Now that you've declared your milestone resource, run terraform apply to see what Terraform Core plans to create, type in "yes," and reapply the configuration to create the milestone resource like so:

```
$ terraform apply
Terraform used the selected providers to generate the following
execution plan.
Resource actions are indicated with the following symbols:
  + create

Terraform will perform the following actions:

  # github_repository_milestone.epics will be created
  + resource "github_repository_milestone" "epics" {
      + description = <<-EOT
            This milestone includes all the deliverables related to
            building the application (e.g Dockerfile), provisioning AWS,
            the local environment and the base AMI with Packer.
        EOT
      + due_date   = "2024-06-24"
      + id         = (known after apply)
      + number     = (known after apply)
      + owner      = "beamops"
      + repository = "kanban"
      + state      = "open"
      + title      = "Infrastructure"
    }

Plan: 1 to add, 0 to change, 0 to destroy.

Do you want to perform these actions?
  Terraform will perform the actions described above.
  Only 'yes' will be accepted to approve.

  Enter a value: yes

github_repository_milestone.epics: Creating...
github_repository_milestone.epics: Creation complete after 2s
[id=beamops/kanban/1]

Apply complete! Resources: 1 added, 0 changed, 0 destroyed.
```

Good work, you have your first infrastructure resource, a GitHub milestone! Now you just need to create four more. To do so, you could just replicate the github_repository_milestone resource four times, but as you're a pragmatic programmer, you should always aim to keep your codebase clean and tidy. Instead of replicating the resource declaration four times, in the next section, you'll parametrize the milestone resource.

Terraform Variables

As we mentioned in the earlier section on HCL 101, the variable <BLOCK TYPE> is one of the seven main Terraform constructs. Variable blocks are used to parametrize resources. They are a great way to keep your Terraform configuration DRY and clean when you want to create more than one instance of a resource. When you define a variable block, you only define the type and the description of the variable. The values of the variable will be input when applying the configuration. You may be asking yourself about the difference between a variable and a local block. They are both used to parametrize values, but a local block's values are hard-coded in your configuration file, and a variable block's values are defined independently, allowing you to set the values dynamically without having to change the configuration file.

A variable is defined using the block type variable followed by the variable name. To create the milestones variable, open up your main.tf file, declare the variable block above your github_repository_milestone resource, and give it the name milestones as we've done in the subsequent example:

```
# in modules/integrations/github/project_management/main.tf
variable "milestones" {
  type = map(object({
    title       = string
    due_date    = string
    description = string
  }))
  description = "Milestones, consider them the biggest deliverable unit."
}
```

This tells the Terraform Core to expect a milestones variable that is a map of objects containing title, due_date, and description properties. We only included these three attributes in the map as these are the attributes that will change for each milestone, and the GitHub repository name and owner will always stay the same.

At the moment, you've just created the structure of the milestone variable, but you haven't actually assigned any values to the variables themselves. If you were to try to apply these changes now, the Terraform Core would prompt you to manually input the milestones variable value, as it's not possible to define a variable block without instantiating the variable. It's always important to add the description property to any variable block that you create, as the Terraform Core will use this description, along with the variable name, written in the form var.VARIABLE_NAME, in its prompt to help you input the value. You can see the Terraform Core prompt here, as well as the response that you'd have to manually write:

```
$ terraform apply
var.milestones
  Milestones, consider them biggest deliverable unit.

  Enter a value: {"infrastructure" = { title = "Infrastructure",
  description = " This milestone includes all the deliverables related to
  building the application (e.g Dockerfile), provisioning AWS, the local
  environment and the base AMI with Packer.", due_date = "2024-06-24" }}
github_repository_milestone.epics: Refreshing state...
github_repository.kanban: Refreshing state...
No changes. Your infrastructure matches the configuration.

Terraform has compared your real infrastructure against your
configuration and found no differences, so no changes are needed.

Apply complete! Resources: 0 added, 0 changed, 0 destroyed.
```

As you can see, the configuration worked. However, having to input the variable manually wasn't convenient and means that any variables you create won't be under version control. Additionally, the Terraform Core told us that there were 0 additions, changes, or deletions. This is because, although you've created a milestones variable, we haven't linked the variable to any resource. In the next section, we'll look at how you can use variables in resource definitions by creating an autoloading variables file.

Autoload Variable Values and for_each

When using variable resources, a clean way to instantiate your variables is to define them in a .tfvars file. This file is read by the Terraform Core when terraform apply is run and any variables defined in that file will be automatically injected into the Terraform Core. This means that you won't need to manually write in the variables as you did in the previous section. So create an .auto.tfvars file and then copy and paste in the following milestone:

```
# in modules/integrations/github/project_management/.auto.tfvars

milestones = {
  "infrastructure" = {
    title       = "Infrastructure"
    due_date    = "2024-06-24"

    description = <<EOT
This milestone includes all the deliverables related to building the
application (e.g Dockerfile), provisioning AWS, the local environment
and the base AMI with Packer.
EOT
```

Now, let's apply the changes. In the upcoming example CLI output, you'll see that you won't be asked to introduce any variables because Terraform will read your .auto.tfvars file and see that you've now created one instance of the milestones variable:

```
$ terraform apply
github_repository_milestone.epics: Refreshing state...
github_repository.kanban: Refreshing state...

No changes. Your infrastructure matches the configuration.

Terraform has compared your real infrastructure against your
configuration and found no differences, so no changes are needed.

Apply complete! Resources: 0 added, 0 changed, 0 destroyed.
```

Perfect! The configuration worked. Just like in the previous section, the Terraform Core said there were 0 additions, changes, or deletions. This is because you haven't used the milestones variable to create any Terraform resources yet. You'll achieve this by refactoring the github_repository_milestone resource you created earlier to iterate over the milestones map variable and create a resource per object. To do this, you'll use the for_each meta-argument in your resource definition.

The for_each meta-argument tells the Terraform Core that you'd like to iterate over a map or a set and each iteratee will be an item of that map or set. You saw in the Terraform Core prompt in the previous section that the Terraform state refers to variables in the following pattern: var.VARIABLE_NAME. So, to tell the Core that the github_repository_milestone resource should iterate over your milestones variable, you can set the for_each identifier value to var.milestones. You can then access each of the variable's properties in the rest of the resource block by using the pattern each.value.PROPERTY_NAME. For example, on each iteration, to refer to the title property of the milestone, you'd write each.value.title. In your main.tf file, alter the epics milestone to make it refer to your milestones variable as we've done here:

```
# in modules/integrations/github/project_management/main.tf

resource "github_repository_milestone" "epics" {
  for_each    = var.milestones
  owner       = local.github_owner
  repository  = local.repository_name
  title       = each.value.title
  description = replace(each.value.description, "\n", " ")
  due_date    = each.value.due_date
}
```

> **Tidying Up Descriptions with replace**
>
>  We've used heredoc in the .auto.tfvars file to make the description content more readable and fit in the book's column limit. But to make the description nice and clean in GitHub, we've used the replace[10] built-in Terraform function to replace the newlines produced by the heredoc with spaces.

Now, apply these new changes and see what happens. You'll be asked to confirm that you wish to apply these changes. Write "yes" and press Enter:

```
$ terraform apply
github_repository_milestone.epics: Refreshing state...
github_repository.kanban: Refreshing state...

Terraform used the selected providers to generate the following
execution plan.
Resource actions are indicated with the following symbols:
  + create
  - destroy

Terraform will perform the following actions:

  # github_repository_milestone.epics will be destroyed
  # (because resource uses count or for_each)
  - resource "github_repository_milestone" "epics" {
      - description = <<-EOT
            This milestone includes all the deliverables related to
            building the application (e.g Dockerfile), provisioning AWS,
            the local environment and the base AMI with Packer.
        EOT -> null
      - due_date   = "2024-06-24" -> null
      - id         = "beamops/kanban/1" -> null
      - number     = 1 -> null
      - owner      = "beamops" -> null
      - repository = "kanban" -> null
      - state      = "open" -> null
      - title      = "Infrastructure" -> null
    }

  # github_repository_milestone.epics["infrastructure"] will be created
  + resource "github_repository_milestone" "epics" {
      + description = <<-EOT
            This milestone includes all the deliverables related to
            building the application (e.g Dockerfile), provisioning AWS,
            the local environment and the base AMI with Packer.
        EOT
      + due_date   = "2024-06-24"
      + id         = (known after apply)
      + number     = (known after apply)
```

---

10. https://developer.hashicorp.com/terraform/language/functions/replace

```
      + owner      = "beamops"
      + repository = "kanban"
      + state      = "open"
      + title      = "Infrastructure"
    }
Plan: 1 to add, 0 to change, 1 to destroy.

Do you want to perform these actions?
  Terraform will perform the actions described above.
  Only 'yes' will be accepted to approve.

  Enter a value: yes

github_repository_milestone.epics: Destroying... [id=beamops/kanban/1]
github_repository_milestone.epics["infrastructure"]: Creating...
github_repository_milestone.epics: Destruction complete after 0s
github_repository_milestone.epics["infrastructure"]: Creation complete after 2s [id=beamops/kanban/2]
Apply complete! Resources: 1 added, 0 changed, 1 destroyed.
```

As you can see, Terraform has destroyed one resource and created a new one instead of just updating the existing one. This happens because when you used the for_each meta-argument, you told the Terraform Core that your epics github_repository_milestone resource will no longer be a single resource with the name github_repository_milestone.epics, but a list of resources, where each instance has its own name within the state. If you look at the last few lines of the previous terminal execution, you can see that the infrastructure milestone's name in the Terraform state has changed from github_repository_milestone.epics to github_repository_milestone.epics["infrastructure"]. When this happened, Terraform interpreted that the first resource had been destroyed and the second one needed to be created.

Now that you've made use of your milestones variable, the only thing left to do is to add the rest of the milestones to your .auto.tfvars file. Copy in the remaining milestones listed in the upcoming code snippet so that your .auto.tfvars file looks like this:

```
# in modules/integrations/github/project_management/.auto.tfvars

milestones = {
  "infrastructure" = {
    title       = "Infrastructure"
    due_date    = "2024-06-24"
    description = <<EOT
This milestone includes all the deliverables related to building the
application (e.g Dockerfile), provisioning AWS, the local environment
and the base AMI with Packer.
EOT
  },
```

```
  "ci-cd" = {
    title       = "Continuous Deployment / Continuous Integration"
    due_date    = "2024-06-24"
    description = <<EOT
This milestone will include all deliverables that have to do with GitHub
workflows that will perform the basic checks for an Elixir application.
It will also build the Docker image and pull the latest images in
production.
EOT
  },
  "instrumentation" = {
    title       = "Instrumentation"
    due_date    = "2024-07-01"
    description = <<EOT
This milestone will include all deliverables that have to do with the
addition of basic instrumentation and BEAM specific metrics for your
application. Any task(s) related to instrumentation (independently of
which part of the stack they relate to) will be included in this
milestone.
EOT
  },
  "documentation" = {
    title       = "Documentation"
    due_date    = ""
    description = <<EOT
This milestone includes documentation for Terraform, Elixir, Packer and
others and will converge with CI when needed.
EOT
  },
  "uncategorized" = {
    title       = "Uncategorized"
    due_date    = ""
    description = <<EOT
A milestone to add all issues that do not fit in any of the other
milestones. This is an easy way to track those uncategorized tasks.
EOT
  }
}
```

Now, reapply the changes and you'll have all of the milestones in place. The milestones section in the Issues tab of the GitHub UI should now look something like the screenshot on page 37.

So, you've just parametrized your GitHub milestones and kept the Terraform configuration file clean by defining your variables in a separate file. Now that you have all of the milestones, let's move on to creating the GitHub labels and issues.

> **Documentation: Critical but Out of Scope Here**
>
>  Writing documentation is an important part of the software delivery process. It helps reduce knowledge silos of the code and makes team collaboration easier. But this book isn't about writing documentation, and even though you'll create the milestone, you won't create any documentation issues.

Create Your Third Resource: GitHub Labels

Before creating GitHub issues, you're going to create some labels using the github_issue_label resource.[11] For now, one label per milestone will suffice. When naming the labels, you'll follow a similar pattern to the one Elixir-lang follows in the Elixir repository and prepend the word "Kind" to each label, for example, Kind:Infrastructure. You'll create the labels using the same workflow that you used in the previous section when creating the milestones: you'll define the labels by using a labels variable. Each label will have a name and a color. To start, create the variable block in your main.tf file under your github_repository_milestone resource like so:

---

11. https://registry.terraform.io/providers/integrations/github/latest/docs/resources/issue_label

```
# in modules/integrations/github/project_management/main.tf
variable "labels" {
  type = map(object({
    name  = string
    color = string
  }))
  description = "The labels to tag the issues."
}
```

Now that you know what the labels variable looks like, instantiate the labels in your automatically loaded .auto.tfvars file by adding the following snippet to the end of your .auto.tfvars file, right under your previously defined milestones:

```
# in modules/integrations/github/project_management/.auto.tfvars
labels = {
  "kind-infrastructure" = {
    name  = "Kind:Infrastructure"
    color = "B60205"
  },
  "kind-ci-cd" = {
    name  = "Kind:CI-CD"
    color = "FBCA04"
  },
  "kind-instrumentation" = {
    name  = "Kind:Instrumentation"
    color = "0E8A16"
  },
  "kind-documentation" = {
    name  = "Kind:Documentation"
    color = "5319E7"
  },
  "kind-uncategorized" = {
    name  = "Kind:Uncategorized"
    color = "D93F0B"
  },
  "tech-docker" = {
    name  = "Tech:Docker"
    color = "1D76DB"
  },
  "dockerfile" = {
    name  = "Dockerfile"
    color = "3895AD"
  },
  "tech-elixir" = {
    name  = "Tech:Elixir"
    color = "D9B1FC"
  },
```

```
  "tech-gha" = {
    name  = "Tech:GHA"
    color = "66FE68"
  },
  "tech-docker-compose" = {
    name  = "Tech:Docker-Compose"
    color = "006B75"
  },
  "tech-packer" = {
    name  = "Tech:Packer"
    color = "1D76DB"
  },
  "tech-terraform" = {
    name  = "Tech:Terraform"
    color = "5319A1"
  },
  "tech-sops" = {
    name  = "Tech:SOPS"
    color = "F9D0C4"
  },
  "env-aws" = {
    name  = "Env:AWS"
    color = "D3A968"
  },
  "env-local" = {
    name  = "Env:Local"
    color = "0075ca"
  }
}
```

Finally, add the GitHub issue resource to your main.tf file under your labels variable and link it to the labels variable using the for_each meta-argument:

```
# in modules/integrations/github/project_management/main.tf
resource "github_issue_label" "issues_labels" {
  for_each   = var.labels
  repository = local.repository_name
  name       = each.value.name
  color      = each.value.color
}
```

Note that we've provided you with the resource name in the earlier example, but remember what we said earlier: each time you add a new Terraform resource, it's important to look at the registry to familiarize yourself with the correct resource name and its arguments.

Now, run terraform apply to create the list of labels. The labels section in the Issues tab of your GitHub UI should now look something like the screenshot on page 40.

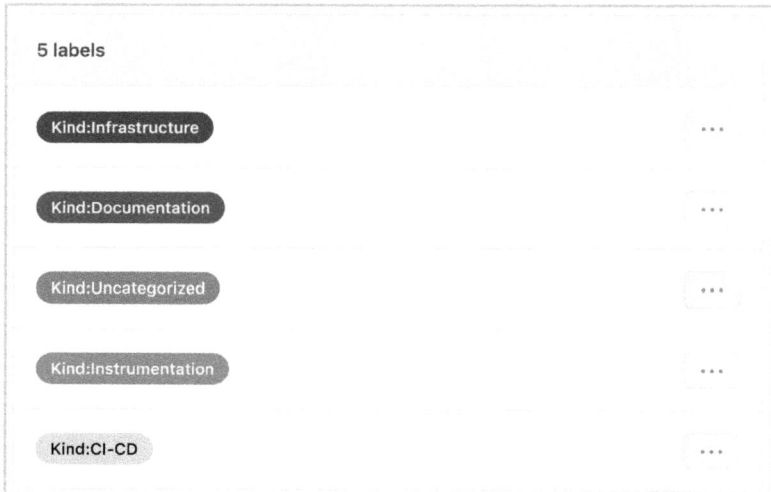

And that's how it's done! You've created your new GitHub labels in three easy steps.

Creating resources is easy, but so far, you've been doing so sequentially. As we mentioned earlier in this chapter, a big advantage to using Terraform to create project management resources is that you'll be able to spin up new projects really easily. For this to be the case, you need to make sure your files are reusable and that Terraform can apply your configuration on a single run when there are no resources in place. To ensure that you're able to do this, you need to fall in love with the CREATE–DESTROY–IMPROVE–REPEAT motto. We'll look at what this means in the next section.

Create–Destroy–Improve–Repeat

The CREATE–DESTROY–IMPROVE–REPEAT motto will become second nature to you. It's the cycle you'll use when creating software configuration files to make sure they are idempotent and will always create the same resources when applied from scratch. So far, you've been in the CREATE phase of the CREATE–DESTROY–IMPROVE–REPEAT cycle. You've created three resources in order: your repository, your milestones, and then your labels. But you don't know whether Terraform can handle creating your resources all at once. To make sure it can, you must move to the DESTROY phase and then recreate your resources. Yes, you're about to destroy what you just put a lot of effort into creating. To become a superpowered BEAMOps developer, you must not be scared of destroying resources and starting again. Restarting a project helps you think of new and better ways of achieving your goals. Destroying infrastructure is an easy way to overcome fear and gain confidence!

So let's get on with it and run the aptly named Terraform destroy command: terraform destroy. When you do so, you'll encounter a few errors. We've pasted an example execution. Run the command, type "yes" when asked if you really want to destroy all resources, and then we'll go through the errors that appear:

```
$ terraform destroy
...
Plan: 0 to add, 0 to change, 21 to destroy.

Do you really want to destroy all resources?
  Terraform will destroy all your managed infrastructure, as shown above.
  There is no undo. Only 'yes' will be accepted to confirm.

  Enter a value: yes
github_issue_label.issues_labels["documentation"]: Destroying...
github_repository_milestone.epics["documentation"]: Destroying...
github_issue_label.issues_labels["ci-cd"]: Destroying...
github_repository_milestone.epics["instrumentation"]: Destroying...
github_repository_milestone.epics["uncategorised"]: Destroying...
github_issue_label.issues_labels["instrumentation"]: Destroying...
github_issue_label.issues_labels["uncategorised"]: Destroying...
github_repository_milestone.epics["infrastructure"]: Destroying...
github_repository_milestone.epics["ci-cd"]: Destroying...
github_repository.kanban: Destroying...
github_issue_label.issues_labels["documentation"]: Destruction complete after 0s
github_issue_label.issues_labels["kind-infrastructure"]: Destroying...
github_repository_milestone.epics["ci-cd"]: Destruction complete after 1s
github_repository_milestone.epics["documentation"]: Destruction complete after 3s
github_issue_label.issues_labels["ci-cd"]: Destruction complete after 4s
github_issue_label.issues_labels["uncategorised"]: Destruction complete after 6s
github_repository.kanban: Destruction complete after 14s

│ Error: DELETE https://api.github.co.../labels/LABEL: 404 Not Found []
```

The label in your case might be different, or you might have more than one error due to the operation concurrency.

You can see that the GitHub API returned an error. It says that the label Kind:Infrastructure wasn't found when trying to perform a DELETE operation. This is because Terraform always tries to parallelize resource management operations. In this instance, your Terraform state has multiple label resources, multiple milestone resources, and a repository resource, but it doesn't know that one resource depends on another. Although for us it's obvious that you cannot have a milestone or label in a GitHub repository without the repository existing, Terraform doesn't know this.

When there are dependencies between resources, you must tell Terraform of these relationships. You might be surprised if you look at the previous example because Terraform was able to successfully delete the majority of the milestones and labels that we created, apart from the infrastructure label, even though you never told the core about the relationship between those resources and the repository. This is because, if you look at the line before the error, you'll see that the deletion of the repository resource completed just before the kind-infrastructure label was destroyed. This means that unlike all the other labels and milestones that were deleted, at the time when Terraform sent the request to the GitHub API to delete the kind-infrastructure label for your repository, the GitHub API couldn't perform the action as the repository in question no longer existed.

Dependencies aren't only important when deleting resources, they are also crucial when creating them. As we mentioned, you've been creating resources sequentially, but if you try to create all of your resources at once, you'll run into similar Not Found errors. Run the apply command in your terminal and examine the core's output. Your errors may slightly differ depending on the order in which Terraform sent off your resource requests, but they should look similar to the response we received here:

```
...
 Error: POST https://api.github.com/repos/OWNER/REPO/milestones: 404
         Not Found []

   with github_repository_milestone.epics["documentation"],
   on main.tf line 28, in resource "github_repository_milestone"
   "epics":
   28: resource "github_repository_milestone" "epics" {
...
 Error: POST https://api.github.com/repos/OWNER/REPO/milestones:: 404
         Not Found []

   with github_issue_label.issues_labels["ci-cd"],
   on main.tf line 47, in resource "github_issue_label"
   "issues_labels":
   47: resource "github_issue_label" "issues_labels" {
```

As you can see, there are more 404 Not Found errors. This is because Terraform is trying to create a milestone and an issue for a repository that doesn't yet exist. To solve these errors, you must understand how resource dependencies work in Terraform. In the next section, we'll examine the different ways in which you can tell the Terraform Core that one resource depends on another.

Resource Dependencies

Infrastructure resources are often reliant on each other and can only exist if a separate resource exists first. This is what is called a *resource dependency*. There are two ways that you can tell Terraform that one resource depends on another: implicit or explicit dependencies. Implicit, or hidden, dependencies are created by referencing one resource's exported attribute as an argument when declaring another. Terraform itself will then automatically handle the link between resources. You'll see an example of this later in the chapter.

The second method is more explicit and uses the depends_on meta-argument. As the name would suggest, adding the depends_on meta-argument to a resource tells the Terraform Core that this resource is reliant on another and either needs to be created after or deleted before the dependent resource. So, let's now execute the IMPROVE part of the CREATE–DESTROY–IMPROVE–REPEAT cycle and add the depends_on meta-argument to both your milestone and label resources in your main.tf file:

```
# in modules/integrations/github/project_management/main.tf
resource "github_repository_milestone" "epics" {
  depends_on = [github_repository.kanban]
}
resource "github_issue_label" "issues_labels" {
  depends_on = [github_repository.kanban]
}
```

In the example, the depends_on argument uses a resource address rather than the local.github_repository value that you created earlier. This is because the depends on meta-argument expects a resource address as its value to be able to link specific resources. If you were to have used the local value, the Terraform Core wouldn't be able to create the dependency.

Now that you've added this meta-argument, you can rerun terraform destroy and there will be no dependency errors as Terraform now knows in which order the resources should be created and deleted. Similarly, you can then recreate all of your resources by running another terraform apply. Go ahead and run both of these commands.

Great! You've just ensured that your Terraform configuration is working, is reusable, and is idempotent. This CREATE–DESTROY–IMPROVE–REPEAT cycle is the way to go. Get used to it, pragmatic engineer!

Now let's move on to creating the last resource: GitHub issues. We'll do so by looking at a slightly different way of using Terraform variables.

Create Your Fourth Resource: GitHub Issues

Earlier in this chapter, you used a map to define your variable block for the milestones and labels as a way to keep your Terraform configuration lean and clean. However, a Terraform variable doesn't need to be a map, so let's look at another way in which you can use variables to parametrize a Terraform resource. Rather than using a map to create the issues, you're going to use a list. Each item in the list will have a title, a body, a list of labels, and a parent milestone. As you did when defining your milestones and issues variables, you must first create your variable block. Open up your main.tf file and define your new issues variable under your github_issue_label resource as we've done here:

```
# in modules/integrations/github/project_management/main.tf
variable "issues" {
  type = list(object({
    title     = string
    body      = string
    labels    = list(string)
    milestone = string
  }))
}
```

As you can see in the previous example, the issues variable is a list of objects. Each issue has a title, a body, a list of labels, and a milestone. This milestone will be used in the resource definition to assign each issue to a specific milestone. We've chosen to use a list rather than a map so that you can keep your .auto.tfvars file tidy. In the next section, we'll discuss how to link your list variable to your issue resource.

The Count Meta-Argument for GitHub Issues

As you saw previously when using a map or set variable, you have to use the for_each meta-argument in your resource definition to iterate over our map in a key-value fashion, but when dealing with a list, you must use the count meta-argument.

The count argument takes a number as its value. This number should be equal to the length of the variable you wish to iterate over, which in this case is the issues list. You can obtain the length of the list using the built-in Terraform length[12] function. This count argument exports an index attribute that can be accessed in the rest of that resource block to refer to the object at that index of the issue list.

---

12. https://developer.hashicorp.com/terraform/language/functions/length

Now, create a GitHub issue resource in your main.tf file using the github_issue resource.[13] You'll use the count meta-argument and add the properties of the issues variable to your resource using count.index. You'll also link your issue to a certain milestone and add a label. We've given you our example code. Copy the following snippet to your issues variable and then we'll go over the complicated bits:

```
# in modules/integrations/github/project_management/main.tf
resource "github_issue" "tasks" {
  count      = length(var.issues)
  repository = github_repository.kanban.name
  title      = var.issues[count.index].title
  body       = var.issues[count.index].body
  milestone_number = github_repository_milestone.epics[
    var.issues[count.index].milestone
  ].number
  labels = [for l in var.issues[count.index].labels :
    github_issue_label.issues_labels[l].name
  ]
}
```

As you can see, we've set the count argument value to be the length of the issues variable. We've also learned from our resource dependency errors, and we've made each issue dependent on our repository. Instead of explicitly defining the resource dependency using the 'depends_on' meta-argument like last time, we've chosen to create the resource dependency implicitly and use the exported name argument. In the case of the title and body arguments, we've set these as the title and body keys of the object at that index of the issues list using count.index.

The milestone_number and labels arguments may seem a bit more complicated, but we promise they aren't. Let's break them both down.

The milestone_number argument to link each issue to a specific milestone in the Terraform state:

1. We accessed the var.issues[count.index].milestone to get the milestone related to that issue. An example of this value would be infrastructure.

2. We used the value of the accessed key in step 1 to access github_repository _milestone.epic[*].number. number is an attribute exported by the github _repository_milestone resource that refers to the number that was allocated to the milestone resource when it was created in the Terraform state. By using this argument, we've linked the issue to a certain milestone.

---

13. https://registry.terraform.io/providers/integrations/github/latest/docs/resources/issue

The labels argument links each issue to certain labels in the Terraform state:

1. A for expression iterates over var.issues[count.index].labels, which is the list of labels declared on the object at that index of the issues list. This gives us access to each label with the variable l.

2. We used this l variable as a key to access github_issue_label.issues_labels[l].name. name is an attribute exported by the resource github_issue_label.issues_labels in the Terraform state. If we follow our infrastructure example, the name would be Kind:Infrastructure, and the resulting label that would be linked from our code snippets would be kind-infrastructure.

Now that you've defined the issues variable and the issue resource, it's time to add the issues to your .auto.tfvars file. Add the following issues to the end of your .auto.tfvars file:

```
# in modules/integrations/github/project_management/.auto.tfvars
issues = [
  {
    title    = "Implement the Dockerfile's builder stage"
    body     = <<EOT
The builder stage packages all the tools and compile-time dependencies
for your application. It has to build the mix release that will be
copied in the running stage.
EOT
    labels    = ["kind-infrastructure", "dockerfile"]
    milestone = "infrastructure"
  },
  {
    title    = "Implement the Dockerfile's runner stage"
    body     = <<EOT
This stage copies the release built in the builder stage and uses it as
the entrypoint of your Docker image with the minimum system requirement
to run it.
EOT
    labels    = ["kind-infrastructure", "dockerfile"]
    milestone = "infrastructure"
  },
  {
    title    = "Elixir integration pipelines"
    body     = <<EOT
Implement a CI pipeline that includes all of the necessary steps when
delivering an Elixir application: code compilation, dependency caching,
testing, code formatting, an unused dependency check.
EOT
    labels    = ["kind-ci-cd", "tech-elixir"]
    milestone = "ci-cd"
  }
]
```

The previous example doesn't include all of the issues required to deliver this project. You can find the complete list in the .auto.tfvars file inside the 07_issues folder of the source code for this chapter on the Pragmatic Programmers website.

Now that you have everything prepared, repeat the Terraform development cycle. Destroy the whole infrastructure and recreate it. Remember, CREATE–DESTROY–IMPROVE–REPEAT. Once you've done that and you're sure your configuration is idempotent, commit your code to your newly created kanban repository. To do so, cd out of your modules/integrations/github/project_management back to the root of your project and initialize a GitHub repository. Then add the remote URL to your kanban repository and pull the README.md and .gitignore files you created earlier. Finally add, commit, and push your main.tf and .terraform .lock.hcl files. You can also include the asdf_plugins.sh and .tool-versions files that you created in the previous chapter. And that's it! You have finished setting up your project. Let's sum up what you've learned so far.

What Have You Learned?

In this chapter, you used Terraform to create project management resources in GitHub. You created a single file main.tf that contains your Terraform resources and provider. You also did some tidying of your code by using both local values and variables. Finally, you learned the differences between implicit and explicit resource dependencies.

You should feel confident using Terraform configuration files, the Terraform state, and a Terraform console. You can now quickly spin up new project management resources for future projects. We encourage you to take ownership of the planning part of a project. Project management is for everyone. Collaboration in this stage makes everyone on the team more productive and committed to the project. Now that you have an infrastructure as code template, you can spend more time writing requirements and great descriptions that will help you and your team get back to the fun stuff.

As you continue reading this book, you'll close each of the issues that you have created in this chapter. So, with the project management for your application set up, in the next chapter, you'll start the first milestone: Infrastructure. There, you'll learn how to package your Phoenix LiveView application with Docker. Doing this will allow you to run your application under the same conditions on any machine and ensure environment integrity.

> **The Extra Mile**
>
> If you wish to deepen your knowledge of the themes we've covered in this chapter and refine your BEAMOps developer superpowers, we've created a few tasks for you to do:
>
> 1. Refactor the resource blocks we've covered to get rid of the `depends_on` meta-argument and use implicit dependencies everywhere instead.
>
> 2. Refactor your `main.tf` file and split it into two different files: `main.tf` and `variables.tf`. Doing this will make your configuration easier to read. It won't affect the result of running `terraform apply` because Terraform, by default, merges all .tf files in a directory together when applying a configuration.
>
> 3. Explore the `outputs <BLOCK TYPE>` and add a few to your module, for example the milestones.

CHAPTER 3

Build and Dockerize a Phoenix LiveView Application

In the previous chapter, we stressed that becoming a superpowered BEAMOps developer is about ownership. In this chapter, you'll build on this concept by learning how to own the building stage of an Elixir application.

As we discussed in Chapter 1, a core BEAMOps principle is environment integrity—understanding that integrity across environments, and your stack in general, is a key factor to your project's success. In this book, we'll focus on two environments: development and production. Becoming a superpowered BEAMOps developer means you're able to abstract the building and running processes and avoid the classic "but it works on my machine" problem. This abstraction is key because it allows you to isolate and manage dependencies, ensuring your application is run in a consistent and reproducible way.

This chapter will cover two major concepts related to the building stage: OTP releases built with mix and Docker.

After reading this chapter, you'll understand what an OTP release is, why you should always deploy using OTP releases, and how to build and debug them in your host. You'll be able to generate a release using the phx.gen.release generator and the mix release command. You'll also be able to interpret a Dockerfile and its different stages, and you'll learn the CLI commands used to build Docker images and run Docker containers. By the end of this chapter, you'll be able to close two of the GitHub issues that you created in the previous chapter.

Let's get to it! Your first task will be to build your application using OTP releases.

Releases and the mix release Command

If you've used Elixir on a daily basis, either at work or at home, you might've encountered something called a *release*. But what is a release and what are its benefits? A release is a single unit that allows you to precompile and package your code and the runtime. Releases are used to create an executable binary of your application that can be deployed. A release contains the following:

- compiled BEAM bytecode files
- configuration files for variables used by your application
- other scripts related to the management of your application (start/stop/misc)
- BEAM VM configuration parameters

In the next section, we'll discuss the importance of OTP releases and how they'll improve your application's performance.

Why You Should Always Use OTP Releases

There are several advantages to using OTP releases when distributing your Elixir projects, but the most beneficial ones are *code preloading, configuration and customization*, and the fact that releases are *self-contained*. Let's go through each advantage one by one.

As a language, Elixir compiles into Erlang, which is run by the Erlang Virtual Machine (the BEAM). By default, when releases aren't used, the BEAM runs in interactive mode. This means that every time your Elixir program executes a function from a module that hasn't been used yet, it has to first load the function and then execute it. This extra loading step increases the execution time of your application. After running the application for a while, the execution time will eventually improve because the more the application is used, the more modules are loaded. But as a superpowered BEAMOps developer, you should never aim for your first requests to have an unusually long response time. OTP releases solve this issue. When releases are used, the BEAM runs in embedded mode rather than interactive mode. This means that once you boot your application, all of your modules will be preloaded and the execution time won't be affected.

Another benefit of OTP releases is that they allow you to have total control over how the BEAM deployment is configured and customized. We're not only talking about your application-specific configuration like a database host, but also about arguments that will be sent to the Erlang Virtual Machine when the release is booted. Being able to configure the BEAM is important for your journey as it will enable you to define all the parameters required to start the release as a node that's part of a distributed Erlang cluster. This is an important aspect of OTP releases that we'll delve into in Chapter 8.

Finally, using OTP releases produces a minimal package that contains everything needed to run your application. The package includes not only your precompiled source code but also the Erlang runtime system (ERTS). This is hugely beneficial because once you've built the release, the OS in which the release is run doesn't require Elixir or Erlang to be installed—meaning, your production artifact is really lightweight. This is important! A lightweight artifact means you'll be able to build really lean Docker images. We'll delve into Docker images and why lean Docker images are advantageous later in the chapter. For the time being, let's learn how to build a release.

Generate Your First Release

In this book, you'll work on and deploy a Phoenix LiveView application. To generate your release build files for this application, you'll use Elixir's mix build tool. You'll also use mix and Phoenix to create extra configuration and/or helper files. In this chapter, we'll focus on the helper scripts provided by the Phoenix release generator. You'll learn about the release configuration files offered by mix in Chapter 7.

To be able to build your release, you need to have version 1.7.0 of Phoenix installed in your system. You can install it using the command mix archive.install --force hex phx_new 1.7.0. The --force option means that you won't have to confirm the install. We have pasted the subsequent terminal output for reference:

```
$ mix archive.install --force hex phx_new 1.7.0
Resolving Hex dependencies...
Resolution completed in 0.012s
New:
  phx_new 1.7.0
* Getting phx_new (Hex package)
All dependencies are up to date
Compiling 11 files (.ex)
Generated phx_new app
Generated archive "phx_new-1.7.0.ez" with MIX_ENV=prod
* creating /Users/YOUR_USERNAME/.mix/archives/phx_new-1.7.0
```

Once you have Phoenix installed, cd into your kanban folder that you created in Chapter 1. This is where you'll create a new Phoenix project. To create this new project, you'll run the command mix phx.new. When you run this command, add the option --no-ecto so that Phoenix doesn't add any database support files to your project, given that you won't use them in this chapter. mix phx.new expects a path as an argument. To create the project inside your kanban folder, pass the ./ path.

When you run mix phx.new ./ --no-ecto, you'll be asked four questions. First, if you'd like to continue as the PATH_TO_YOUR_FOLDER already exists. Type "Y" and press Enter. Second, if you want to overwrite the README.md file you created in the previous chapter. Type "Y" and press Enter. Third, if you want to overwrite the .gitignore file you created in the previous chapter. As your current .gitignore file contains Terraform files, you do *not* want to do this. Type "N" and press Enter. But once the project has been created, you'll need to add common Elixir files that should be ignored to your .gitignore. You can find the list in the gitignore repository on GitHub[1] (the list is exactly the same as the files that would have been put in your .gitignore if you were to have overwritten your .gitignore file). Finally, you'll be asked if you want to fetch and install the dependencies for the project using mix deps.get. Type "Y" and press Enter. Run the mix phx.new ./ --no-ecto command and then update your .gitignore file with the commonly ignored Elixir files. See the following terminal interaction for an example of what to expect when running mix phx.new ./ --no-ecto:

```
$ mix phx.new ./ --no-ecto
The directory PATH_TO_YOUR_FOLDER already exists.
Are you sure you want to continue? [Yn] Y
...
README.md already exists, overwrite? [Yn] Y
...
.gitignore already exists, overwrite? [Yn] N
...
Fetch and install dependencies? [Yn] Y
* running mix deps.get
...
```

Now that you've installed Phoenix, created your project, and updated your .gitignore file, you're ready to take your first step in creating an Elixir release: generating release helper files using the Phoenix release generator with mix.

The command to generate the release helper files is mix phx.gen.release. When you run this command, if you haven't done so previously, you'll be asked if you want to install a local copy of rebar3, the tool used to compile Erlang dependencies. Type "Y" and press Enter. Run the command and then we'll discuss what that generator does:

---

1. https://github.com/github/gitignore/blob/main/Elixir.gitignore

```
$ mix phx.gen.release
Could not find "rebar3", which is needed to build dependency :telemetry
I can install a local copy which is just used by Mix
Shall I install rebar3?
(if running non-interactively, use "mix local.rebar --force") [Yn] Y
...
* creating rel/overlays/bin/server
* creating rel/overlays/bin/server.bat

Your application is ready to be deployed in a release!

See https://hexdocs.pm/mix/Mix.Tasks.Release.html for more information ...

Here are some useful release commands you can run in any release environment:

    # To build a release
    mix release

    # To start your system with the Phoenix server running
    _build/dev/rel/kanban/bin/server

Once the release is running you can connect to it remotely:

    _build/dev/rel/kanban/bin/kanban remote

To list all commands:

    _build/dev/rel/kanban/bin/kanban
```

As you can see, this command creates a rel/overlays folder. This folder includes custom files or configurations that will be overlaid, or included, in the release bundle during the build process. In particular, this folder includes a bin/server bash script that will serve your application. The creation of this rel folder gives you a helper script to run a release, but it doesn't create the release itself. To build the release, as the previous terminal output tells you, you'd need to run mix release. As well as building the release files, the mix release command copies over the rel/overlays directory created by mix phx.gen.release. This means that the server script, and any other configurations added to that folder, will be included in your release. Before running mix release, however, you need to compile the assets of your application, such as JavaScript and style sheets.

> **We'll Revisit --no-ecto Later**
>
> If you were to have created the Phoenix application without the --no-ecto flag, the rel folder would also include a bash script to migrate your database. Don't worry about this for now. We'll look at this in Chapter 5.

To build and compile the assets, run mix assets.deploy. This command generates and digests the minified assets for production, saving them in a file with a name that includes an md5 hash, which will change if any of the assets change. If you want to know more, you can check the Phoenix.Digester[2] module.

Finally, to build the release and copy over the Phoenix server script, run mix release. This command, by default, always uses dev as its MIX_ENV environment variable. However, as you'll deploy this release to production in later chapters, when you run the mix release command, set the MIX_ENV environment variable to prod, as we've done here:

```
$ mix assets.deploy
...
$ MIX_ENV=prod mix release
...
* assembling kanban-0.1.0 on MIX_ENV=prod
* using config/runtime.exs to configure the release at runtime
...
Release created at _build/prod/rel/kanban

    # To start your system
    _build/prod/rel/kanban/bin/kanban start
```

Great! You have the built release. To start it, follow the insrtructions given in the terminal output, and run _build/prod/rel/kanban/bin/kanban start.

```
$ _build/prod/rel/kanban/bin/kanban start
ERROR! Config provider Config.Reader failed with:
{"init terminating in do_boot",{#{'__except ....
** (RuntimeError) environment variable SECRET_KEY_BASE is missing.
You can generate one by calling: mix phx.gen.secret
...
```

Uh oh, an error! As you can see, the release isn't starting because you're missing the SECRET_KEY_BASE variable. This is a required key in all Phoenix applications when run in production mode. Here's the part of the runtime.exs file that specifies this:

```
# in kanban/config/runtime.exs
...
if config_env() == :prod do
...
  secret_key_base =
    System.get_env("SECRET_KEY_BASE") ||
      raise """
      environment variable SECRET_KEY_BASE is missing.
      You can generate one by calling: mix phx.gen.secret
      """
...
```

---

2. https://github.com/phoenixframework/phoenix/blob/v1.7.2/lib/phoenix/digester.ex

To fix this error, prepend the _build/prod/rel/kanban/bin/kanban start command with the SECRET_KEY_BASE environment variable. To create a secret key on the fly, use the mix phx.gen.secret command given to you in the previous error prompt and set the environment variable like this:

```
SECRET_KEY_BASE=$(mix phx.gen.secret) \
_build/prod/rel/kanban/bin/kanban start
```

Run the previous command, and we'll observe the output:

```
$ SECRET_KEY_BASE=$(mix phx.gen.secret) \
  _build/prod/rel/kanban/bin/kanban start
....
[info] Configuration :server was not enabled ... http/https services
won't start
```

There is an info log that says that HTTP/HTTPS services won't start because you haven't enabled the :server option in the Endpoint configuration. This happens because when starting an Elixir release that includes a Phoenix application, you need to be explicit about starting the HTTP/HTTPS server. To solve this, you could prepend the PHX_SERVER=true to your current _build/prod/rel/kanban/bin/kanban start script like this:

```
PHX_SERVER=true SECRET_KEY_BASE=$(mix phx.gen.secret) \
_build/prod/rel/kanban/bin/kanban start
```

When the PHX_SERVER environment variable is set to true, the server: true option is automatically set for you. The next code snippet from the config/runtime.exs file specifies this:

```
# in kanban/config/runtime.exs
...
if System.get_env("PHX_SERVER") do
  config :kanban, KanbanWeb.Endpoint, server: true
end
...
```

But rather than setting the environment variable yourself and then running the start script, a cleaner way to do this is to use the _build/prod/rel/kanban/bin/server script. This is the bin/server script that was created by the Phoenix release generator in your rel/overlays folder and then copied over into your release files when you ran mix release. It automatically sets the PHX_SERVER value to true for you. Open that file to see this. Using the _build/prod/rel/kanban/bin/server script is a better option as it saves you from adding an extra environment variable. Run this script, still specifying the SECRET_KEY_BASE variable as we've done and you'll be able to see your running application at http://localhost:4000, as we show on the next page.

```
$ SECRET_KEY_BASE=$(mix phx.gen.secret) _build/prod/rel/kanban/bin/server
18:38:06.109 [info] Running KanbanWeb.Endpoint with cowboy 2.10.0...
18:38:06.109 [info] Access KanbanWeb.Endpoint at https://example.com
```

You did it! You created a release and started it! You now have a light and performant way to run your Phoenix application.

As you can see, building an OTP release can be done in a few simple steps, all of which we've gone through from start to finish. As a superpowered BEAMOps developer, we always recommend following a step-by-step process like this and stripping a workflow down to its most basic requirements. First, determine what you're going to build and how, and then try to install all the requirements following a manual approach. Doing this may take a while at first, but it will help you understand how you can later automate the process, just as you'll do with Docker later in this chapter. Looking at what we've covered in this section, to build an OTP release for an Elixir Phoenix project, we can affirm that you have to follow these steps:

1. Install Elixir and Erlang.
2. Install hex and rebar.
3. Get the project dependencies using mix deps.get.
4. Compile the assets with mix assets.deploy.
5. Build the release with mix release with the MIX_ENV variable set to prod.
6. Run the release by setting the SECRET_KEY_BASE environment variable and executing the _build/prod/rel/kanban/bin/server script (which automatically sets the :server: true option for you).

Now that you know the steps required to build a Phoenix application using OTP releases, you need to ensure that you wrap them under a building technology that ensures that these steps will always be performed under the same conditions. This means that it doesn't matter where you build or run your application—the outcome will always be the same. This is where Docker comes in. Phoenix allows you to automatically create a Dockerfile for your application by passing the --docker option when running mix phx.gen.release. Being able to do this is extremely helpful, but we won't use this option in this chapter. Instead, we will go through creating that Dockerfile that the Phoenix generator would create step by step—replicating each of the six steps we mentioned—so that you can truly understand what's going on. With that said, the next section will introduce the what and why of Docker.

Docker Fundamentals

Docker is a really useful tool when it comes to abstracting the building and running processes of an application. It allows you to list a set of instructions in a file called a Dockerfile which, when read, forms a set of commands that are the basis of a runnable container. Docker is popular because it's fast and lightweight. To understand Docker, you need to know what it is replacing: virtualization. We'll look at this in the next section.

Virtualization and Virtual Machines

When using computer resources from a cloud provider, like an AWS EC2 instance or a Heroku node, these resources are presented to us with a beautiful UI and different names, but at the end of the day, they need to be in a physical server that resides in a data center. A data center has a lot of computers with RAM, CPU, storage, and networking resources. Before virtual machines came about, managing multiple applications on a single physical server was feasible but not very efficient. Even if the server had ample resources to support multiple small applications, it was common practice to dedicate a single server to each application. This was to make sure that each application had the necessary computing power, memory, and/or storage and was isolated in its own environment so it could be easily managed and not be affected by crashes to other applications.

The development of virtualization and the introduction of hypervisors revolutionized data center resource utilization by easing the creation of multiple isolated virtual machines (VMs) on a single physical server.

A hypervisor, such as VMWare ESXI, allows you to divide a server into multiple virtual machines. Each virtual machine has its own operating system and its own set of resources. This is an improvement on only using one server per application—it's a better use of resources and is much cheaper. But it isn't perfect because, as we mentioned, each virtual machine has its own OS, so if there are 10 virtual machines in the same computer, there would be 10 copies of the same OS running. This isn't efficient; it's a waste of storage. It also makes the booting process slower because you need to boot the OS for each application. This is what Docker is here to solve. Docker virtualizes software and not hardware. It uses Linux kernel features such as namespaces to virtualize the OS and cgroups to virtualize the computing resources. Using Docker means that you can run multiple virtual machines, which Docker refers to as containers, in the same computer in a more efficient way. Each container has its own set of resources but will share the same OS as all the other containers. This means that Docker is much quicker and cheaper, which is why it's so popular. In the next section, we'll go through a side-by-side comparison of virtual machines and Docker containers.

Virtual Machines vs. Docker Containers

We've said that Docker is a more efficient way to use compute resources when compared to virtual machines. But what are the specific reasons why Docker is better than a standard VM? The following table compares the key differences between the two:

VMs	Docker Containers
Heavyweight	Lightweight
Limited performance	Native performance
Each VM runs in its own OS	All containers share the host OS
Requires memory for programming and the OS	Only requires memory for programming
Hardware-level virtualization	OS virtualization
Startup time in minutes	Startup time in milliseconds
Fully isolated, more secure	Process-level isolation, less secure

You can see that the only concern that you have when using Docker is security, which we'll address later in the chapter. But overall, Docker is a better option than virtual machines in terms of performance, speed, and efficiency. The most significant benefit to Docker is that it avoids the "but it works on my machine" problem. This is because it ensures that an application is built and run consistently on each machine each time. This is why we've chosen to use Docker in this book and why we'll target a Docker Swarm in production in the coming chapters. We use Docker so that we can ensure total environment integrity. Now that you know why Docker exists, let's look at the most important concepts and terminology related to Docker.

General Docker Architecture

Docker follows a *client-server* architecture. The client, or CLI, communicates with the server, or *daemon*, using a REST API. The machine in which Docker runs is called a Docker host. Both the client and the server can run in the same host and communicate over a UNIX socket, but they can also run in different hosts as you'll see later in the book.

The Docker daemon, also known as dockerd, runs in the host and listens for the API requests sent by the Docker CLI. It performs CRUD operations on Docker objects like images, containers, networks, volumes, and so on. We'll go into detail on a few of those objects shortly.

The Docker CLI is the program we use to interact with the Docker daemon. The main three commands that you'll use are docker build, docker run, and docker pull/push. The docker build command is used to build images based on a set of instructions defined in a Dockerfile, the docker run command is used to run containers using prebuilt images, and the docker pull/push command is used to pull or push Docker local or remote images from a registry.

The following image shows a visualization of the Docker architecture:

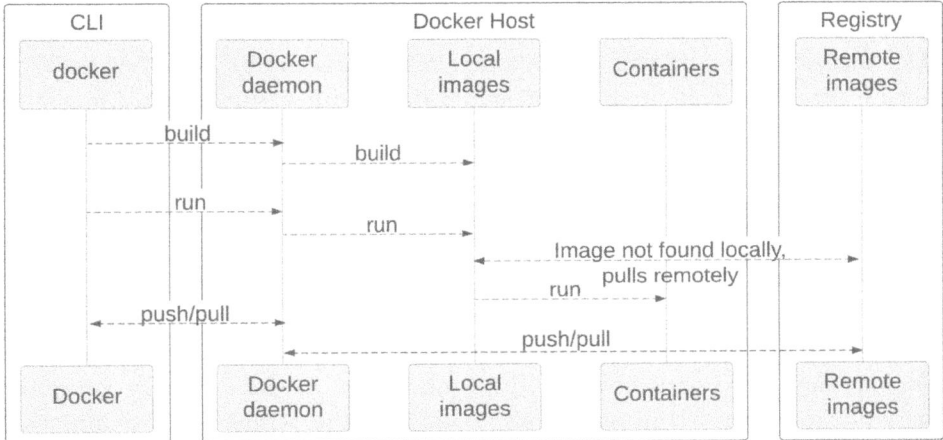

Docker Registries

A Docker registry is a place where Docker images are stored. Docker Hub is the main public registry, but there are also private registries like AWS ECR or the GitHub container registry. It's also possible to run your own registry and deploy it on your own server. Deploying your own registry isn't something that we'll touch on in this book, but if you wish to know more, take a look at their docs.[3]

Docker Objects

When using Docker, you create a set of objects. We've already mentioned one type of object a few times in this section: an image. There are many different types of objects, but the most commonly used are images and containers.

Docker Images

A Docker image is a lightweight, standalone package that includes everything needed to run a piece of software such as the code, the runtime, libraries, environment variables, and config files. These components are defined in a Dockerfile, a set of instruction statements that are used to run a Docker

---

3. https://docs.docker.com/registry/deploying/

container. You can create images from scratch, or you can build upon existing images from a registry by adding customizations. When you use an existing image as a base and add your own layers to it, this process is known as creating a derived image. For instance, you could start with the official Elixir image, add your application files to it, and perform necessary build steps, such as installing dependencies and compiling the code.

When building images, it's important to understand that each instruction in a Dockerfile creates a layer in the image. Each layer is then cached and will only be rebuilt if that instruction generates a different output. This layer caching is important to remember because it will allow you to build images faster and more efficiently.

Docker Containers

A container is a runnable instance of an image. You can create, start, stop, move, or delete a container using the Docker CLI. A container is relatively well isolated and, by default, cannot be accessed from other containers or its host machine. You can, however, pass an option to the docker run command that will expose your container to the host machine, which is something that we'll look at in detail toward the end of the chapter. Once a container is run, if no long-living process is started at the end of the Dockerfile, the container won't exist after the Dockerfile has finished executing. We'll see this in practice in a few pages when you run your first container.

It's important to note when running a container, any changes to the filesystem will be lost when the container is removed. This is because a container is based on a built image, and this built image is agnostic to any containers being run from it. For example, let's say that your container starts an nginx server that receives a request that stores something in a file. When the container is removed, this file will be gone. This is why Docker is so great. Having stateless containers helps ensure environment integrity because every recreation of the container will have the same conditions, which are defined in the image and will be shared across all environments.

Right, that's enough background! Now that you know the basic concepts of Docker, let's look at how you can build Docker images using a Dockerfile.

The Dockerfile

As we mentioned earlier, a Dockerfile defines a Docker image. The file is made up of a list of statements. Each statement has the following format:

```
INSTRUCTION argument(s)
```

Instructions are written in uppercase to distinguish them from arguments. There are many different instructions that you can use, but we'll focus on the most commonly used ones in this chapter: FROM, RUN, COPY, WORKDIR, ENV, ENTRYPOINT, and CMD.

Docker reads Dockerfile statements in order of appearance. A Dockerfile can be composed of a single stage or multiple stages. Each stage starts with a FROM instruction, whose argument specifies the parent image that the subsequent commands in that stage will use as their context when executed.

When Docker executes a FROM instruction, it will first try to find the image locally and if it isn't there, it will try to pull it from the Docker public registry. You can configure additional registries in a Docker config file, but Docker Hub is the default.

Now, let's create a Dockerfile and see the FROM command in action.

Build Your First Docker Image

To build your Dockerfile, create a file named Dockerfile in the root of the Phoenix project you created earlier in this chapter.

As we mentioned, the FROM instruction initializes a new stage of your Dockerfile and so a valid Dockerfile must start with a FROM statement. Remember, the first step in building and running a release of a Phoenix application is to have Erlang and Elixir installed. So, let's start by creating a basic Dockerfile that includes both Erlang and Elixir. To do so, paste the next FROM command into your Dockerfile, and then we'll discuss what it does:

```
# in Dockerfile
FROM hexpm/elixir:1.16.0-erlang-26.2.1-debian-bullseye-20231009-slim
```

As you can see, the argument for this FROM instruction is hexpm/elixir:1.16.0-erlang-26.2.1-debian-bullseye-20231009-slim. This image comes from a fantastic project called *Bob the builder*. We would always recommend this project when creating Dockerfiles for Erlang- and/or Elixir-based projects because its images are fast and compact.

Base Images from Bob the Builder for Elixir Applications

Bob the builder[4] is a project that was created by the hexpm team to help the community build images for Elixir applications with Docker. Bob is a genserver that periodically checks the latest versions of Elixir and Erlang and

---

4. https://github.com/hexpm/bob

then builds images with these versions targeting different Linux distributions. These are the supported distributions and their versions:

- Alpine
- Debian-Bullseye
- Debian-Buster
- Debian-Stretch
- Ubuntu-Bionic
- Ubuntu-Focal
- Ubuntu-Jammy
- Ubuntu-Trusty
- Ubuntu-Xenial

The images created by this project are great because they are more lean than the images maintained by the Erlang Ecosystem Foundation (EEF). Lean images consume fewer resources and take less time to build and run, so they are faster and cheaper to use. All *Bob the builder* image names start with hexpm/elixir. Now that you've written a basic Dockerfile that uses Erlang and Elixir, let's build your first image.

Each time you edit a Dockerfile, to apply the changes you've made, you need to build the image. You can do this by executing the command docker build. This command requires a Dockerfile and a *context*. A build's context is the set of files located in the PATH or URL you specify. These files are sent to the Docker daemon when the image is built so that the build process can refer to them. The most common way to pass a context is to use the . context which sends all of the files in the local directory to the Docker daemon. By default, the docker build command will look for a Dockerfile at the root of the build context. If you specify . as the context, Docker will read the file called Dockerfile. Alternatively, you can pass the --file option to specify a certain Dockerfile. We also recommend that you use the --tag option to tag each image you build so that you can easily distinguish one image from another and refer to that specific image when running containers. So, to build the image, run the docker build command with a tag of your choice. In the following example, we have used the tag kanban:latest and have chosen to use . as the context:

```
$ docker build --tag kanban:latest .
[+] Building 31.3s (5/5) FINISHED
 => [internal] load build definition from Dockerfile        ...  0.0s
 => => transferring dockerfile: 153B                        ...  0.0s
 => [internal] load .dockerignore                           ...  0.0s
 => => transferring context: 2B                             ...  0.0s
 => [internal] load metadata for docker.io/hexpm/elixir:1.16.0 ...  3.8s
 => [1/1] FROM docker.io/hexpm/elixir:1.16.0-erlang-26.2.1-deb ...  7.4s
```

```
 => => resolve docker.io/hexpm/elixir:1.16.0-erlang-26.2.1-deb ...  0.0s
 => => sha256:f8716e4a7fd1ee7a0da8219e3af7ffba01b3c231855d3008 ...  0.0s
 ...
 => => extracting sha256:934ce60d1040c5d4922bae5879321a3987774 ...  0.4s
 ...
 => exporting to image                                         ...  0.0s
 => => exporting layers                                        ...  0.0s
 => => writing image sha256:cb96730a598afed7a368af02438c3aad8c ...  0.0s
 => => naming to docker.io/library/kanban:latest               ...  0.0s
```

Congratulations! You've just built your first Docker image that uses version 1.16.0 or Elixir and version 26.2.1 of Erlang! Now, the next step is to create a Docker container so that you can use the versions of Erlang and Elixir that you specified.

Run Your First Docker Container

As we mentioned earlier, a Docker container is the runnable instance of a Docker image. Using the Dockerfile that you just created, create a container that has both version 25.2 of Erlang and version 1.16.0 of Elixir installed. To run a Docker container, you must execute the docker run command followed by the image name. In the previous section, we named the image kanban:latest, so to run that image you must execute the command docker run kanban:latest. Remember, if there are no long-running processes in a Docker image, once the container is run, it will die immediately. For this reason and to check that the versions of Erlang and Elixir used in the container are the ones you specified in the Dockerfile, append elixir --version to the command. Run the command docker run kanban:latest elixir --version, and then we'll look at the terminal output:

```
$ docker run kanban:latest elixir --version
Erlang/OTP 25 [erts-13.1.4] [source] [64-bit] [smp:5:5] [ds:5:5:10] ...

Elixir 1.16.0 (compiled with Erlang/OTP 25)
```

Nice! You've just run your first Docker container. As you can see, the versions of both Erlang and Elixir correspond with what was written in the Dockerfile. You've completed step one of creating an OTP Elixir release using Docker by creating a basic Docker image that already has Erlang and Elixir installed and then using that image to run a container. Next, you're going to parametrize this Dockerfile to build images dynamically and make them easier to edit.

Build Dynamically

Your current Dockerfile creates an image that uses a specific version of both Elixir and Erlang. This is great, but changing the version of Elixir and/or Erlang isn't ideal—you'd need to change the hard-coded versions in the FROM statement in the Dockerfile and then build the image again. Instead of using hard-coded variables, you can use an argument—or ARG statement—to create a reusable variable.

Previously, we said that a Dockerfile always starts with a FROM instruction. This is normally true, and the only thing that can precede a FROM statement is an ARG statement. This is useful, especially in this case, as it means that you can parameterize the FROM statement. Not only are you going to parameterize the Elixir and Erlang versions but also the OS. Replace the current content of your Dockerfile with the following code snippet:

```
# in Dockerfile
ARG EX_VSN=1.16.0
ARG OTP_VSN=26.2.1
ARG DEB_VSN=bullseye-20231009-slim
ARG BUILDER_IMG="hexpm/elixir:${EX_VSN}-erlang-${OTP_VSN}-debian-${DEB_VSN}"
FROM ${BUILDER_IMG}
```

As you can see, we've created four different ARG statements. From the ARG statements in the previous example, you can see the following:

1. Arguments are assigned with an =.
2. Argument key values are usually written in uppercase.
3. Arguments can be interpolated inside other arguments.
4. Arguments can be interpolated in other statements (in this case, the FROM statement).

Now that you've updated your Dockerfile, you must rerun docker build --tag kanban :latest . to apply these changes. Similarly, you must rerun docker run kanban:latest elixir --version to create a new container with these parametrized values and see the effect on the Erlang and Elixir versions. When you do this, you'll see that the parametrization worked and the versions of Elixir and Erlang have remained the same.

ARG statements can be overridden in the CLI by passing the --build-arg option. For example, you could override the Elixir version defined by the EX_VSN variable in your Dockerfile by running:

```
$ docker build --build-arg EX_VSN=1.13.2 --tag kanban:latest .
```

If you do that and then rerun the container using docker run kanban:latest elixir --version, you'll see that the container has been built with version 1.13.2 of Elixir rather than 1.16.0, which was specified in the Dockerfile.

So, now that you know how to parametrize an image, let's look at how you can run a container interactively to improve the way you write Dockerfiles and debug your Docker containers.

The Entrypoint, CMD, and Debugging Containers

When programming, we always recommend going step by step and not rushing to get the job done. To do this when using Docker, you can run your Docker containers interactively. This will enable you to practice your commands and be sure that they have the desired effect. We recommend that you follow this Docker development cycle:

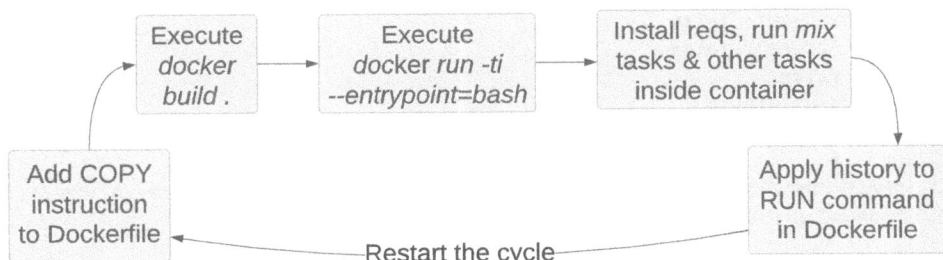

We'll elaborate more on the COPY instruction in the next section.

Running a container interactively means that when the container is run, your terminal will open the ENTRYPOINT, or CMD if no ENTRYPOINT is defined, so that you can play around with the container. To run a container interactively, you must pass the --tty and --interactive options to the docker run command. Rather than writing out those two options in full, it's much more common and less time-consuming to use their short form -ti. Let's see this command in action. In the following example, we've run the container interactively and replicated the logging of the Elixir version executed in the previous section by executing elixir --version inside the interactive container once it has started:

```
$ docker run -ti kanban:latest
root@ca695647b1e3:/# elixir --version
Erlang/OTP 24 [erts-12.3.2.9] [source] [64-bit] [smp:5:5] [ds:5:5:10] ...

Elixir 1.13.2 (compiled with Erlang/OTP 24)
root@ca695647b1e3:/#
```

As you can see, after we ran the kanban:latest image, a bash shell was loaded in the container and we were able to check the Elixir version. A bash shell was loaded because, when starting an interactive Docker container, Docker decides what executable to run by looking first for your ENTRYPOINT instruction and then, if it isn't found, your CMD instruction. The default CMD and ENTRYPOINT values for our image are bash and null. An easy way to see the configuration details of your container is to run the docker inspect command and then parse the response using jq. So, to see the data for the image we're using, exit out of your running container and run the command docker inspect kanban | jq '.[0]["Config"]'. You can see an example output here:

```
$ docker inspect kanban | jq '.[0]["Config"]'
{
  "Hostname": "",
  "Domainname": "",
  "User": "",
  "AttachStdin": false,
  "AttachStdout": false,
  "AttachStderr": false,
  "Tty": false,
  "OpenStdin": false,
  "StdinOnce": false,
  "Env": [
    "PATH=/usr/local/sbin:/usr/local/bin:/usr/sbin:/usr/bin:/sbin:/bin",
    "LANG=C.UTF-8"
  ],
  "Cmd": ["bash"],
  "Image": "",
  "Volumes": null,
  "WorkingDir": "",
  "Entrypoint": null,
  "OnBuild": null,
  "Labels": null
}
```

As you can see, the CMD value is bash and the ENTRYPOINT is null, but this isn't always the case. If you wish to specify the CMD and ENTRYPOINT values, you can either define them as instructions in your Dockerfile or use the --cmd and --entrypoint options when running docker run, which would override any definitions in your Dockerfile. To ensure that the entrypoint of an image is a bash shell, you'd add --entrypoint=bash to your docker run -ti command.

Now that you know how to run a Docker container interactively, let's replicate the rest of the Elixir release process in your Dockerfile. So far, you've been using a single-stage Dockerfile as you've only had to do one task—ensuring that Erlang and Elixir are installed. As you proceed and add more steps to a Dockerfile, it will cease being a single-stage file and will instead have multiple stages. We'll look at what this means in the next section.

Write Multistage Dockerfiles

In the early days of Docker, you could only have one FROM statement per Dockerfile. If you wanted to build and run a release of your application, you had to do the following:

1. Create a Dockerfile to build the application.
2. Run a container based on the image produced by your Dockerfile and copy the built artifact outside of that container.
3. Create a final Dockerfile, sometimes called release.Dockerfile, and copy the artifact from the previous step.

However, Docker 17.05 and later lets you create multistage Dockerfiles containing multiple FROM statements, a *stage* being a set of instructions between two FROM statements. A nice plus is that you can improve the legibility of your Dockerfile by using aliases to name different stages by adding AS <name> to the end of the FROM command. You can then refer to that particular stage throughout the rest of your Dockerfile by referring to its alias. The first stage of a Dockerfile is often the stage where your application is built. So, call that stage builder by editing the last line of your Dockerfile so that it reads like this:

```
# in Dockerfile
FROM ${BUILDER_IMG} AS builder
```

In the next section, you'll add the rest of the Elixir release steps to your Dockerfile using different stages.

The Building Stage

So far in your Dockerfile, you've told Docker that you want to use the *Bob the builder* image that has Erlang and Elixir installed. If you recall, the next step in the Elixir release process is to get all of the dependencies. To achieve this, as you did earlier, you need to install a local copy of hex and rebar. Once you have a local copy of both repos, you need to copy your mix.exs and mix.lock files into the Docker image so that you know which dependencies you need and then get those dependencies.

To achieve all of that, you'll learn four new commands: WORKDIR, RUN, ENV, and COPY. Let's go through each command one by one.

```
WORKDIR /path/to/workdir
```

The WORKDIR instruction sets the current working directory for any RUN, CMD, ENTRYPOINT, COPY, and ADD instructions that follow it in the Dockerfile.

RUN <command>

The RUN instruction executes any commands, and the resulting state of the image will be used for the next step in the Dockerfile

ENV <key>=<value>

The ENV instruction sets an environment variable using an '=' sign for assignation. That variable will then be used for all subsequent instructions in the Dockerfile. The convention is for ENV argument keys to be written in uppercase. Any quote characters in the variable value will be removed if they aren't escaped. ENV argument values can also be interpolated. It's possible to override ENV values when running the container by passing a variable of the same name to the docker run command.

COPY [--chown=<user>:<group>] [--chmod=<perms>] <src> <dest>

Finally, the COPY instruction copies files and/or folders from a <src> in your computer into a <dest> path in the filesystem of the Docker container that will be created when the Dockerfile image is built and run. In Dockerfiles used to build Linux containers, you can give certain permissions to those files by specifying the --chown and --chmod options.

We recommend that you only copy the minimum number of files needed for each stage/layer of a Dockerfile because, as we mentioned, Docker caches its layers. For example, to install the dependencies for your project you only need to copy over the mix.exs and the mix.lock files. If you were to copy over your entire source code and then get the dependencies, any time one of your source code files changes, all of your dependencies would have to be re-fetched. This would be a waste of time and resources.

Now that you know what each of those four commands do, you can put all of this into practice and edit the Dockerfile. Use the four commands to do the following:

1. Set the working directory of your Docker container to be /app.
2. Install a local copy of hex and rebar.
3. Set the MIX_ENV environment variable to prod.
4. Copy your project's dependency files.
5. Get the dependencies.

Try implementing these five steps before peeking at the next code snippet. It shows an updated version of what your Dockerfile should look like. We've added some comments to help you understand what is happening at each step:

```
# in Dockerfile
ARG EX_VSN=1.16.0
ARG OTP_VSN=26.2.1
ARG DEB_VSN=bullseye-20231009-slim

ARG BUILDER_IMG="hexpm/elixir:${EX_VSN}-erlang-${OTP_VSN}-debian-${DEB_VSN}"

FROM ${BUILDER_IMG} AS builder
# prepare build dir
WORKDIR /app
# install hex + rebar
RUN mix local.hex --force && \
    mix local.rebar --force
# set build ENV
ENV MIX_ENV="prod"
# install mix dependencies
COPY mix.exs mix.lock ./
RUN mix deps.get --only $MIX_ENV
```

Great! Your Dockerfile is ready! Now, build a new image by running docker build again:

```
$ docker build --tag kanban:latest .
[+] Building 2.3s (10/10) FINISHED
 => [internal] load build definition from Dockerfile       ...      0.0s
 => => transferring dockerfile: 42B                        ...      0.0s
 => [internal] load .dockerignore                          ...      0.0s
 => => transferring context: 2B                            ...      0.0s
 => [internal] load metadata for docker.io/hexpm/elixir:1....       0.6s
 => [1/5] FROM docker.io/hexpm/elixir:1.16.0-erlang-26.2.1...       0.0s
 => [internal] load build context                          ...      0.0s
 => => transferring context: 12.31kB                       ...      0.0s
 => [2/5] WORKDIR /app                                     ...      0.0s
 => [3/5] RUN mix local.hex --force &&     mix loca...              0.0s
 => [4/5] COPY mix.exs mix.lock ./                         ...      0.0s
 => [5/5] RUN mix deps.get --only prod                     ...      1.6s
 => exporting to image                                     ...      0.1s
 => => exporting layers                                    ...      0.1s
 => => writing image sha256:e7b80313019d4266e55a19fb7c7dde...       0.0s
 => => naming to docker.io/library/kanban:latest           ...      0.0s
                                                                    ...
Use 'docker scan' to run Snyk tests against images to find...
```

Amazing! You now have a Docker image that has Erlang and Elixir installed and has fetched all of the dependencies needed to run your project. If you run the same docker build command again, you'll see that the execution time is quicker—evidence of Docker's layer caching system. This is because the input files haven't changed, and so Docker doesn't rebuild each layer but uses the cached version of each layer instead. We've pasted the subsequent example terminal output for your reference:

```
$ docker build --tag kanban:latest .
[+] Building 0.6s (10/10) FINISHED
...
 => CACHED [2/5] WORKDIR /app                                  ...   0.0s
 => CACHED [3/5] RUN mix local.hex --force &&      mix loca ...  0.0s
 => CACHED [4/5] COPY mix.exs mix.lock ./                      ...   0.0s
 => CACHED [5/5] RUN mix deps.get --only prod                  ...   0.0s
...
```

Let's continue dockerizing the release. The next step is to compile the dependencies. To do this, you need to follow these steps:

1. Create a config folder.
2. Copy the config.exs and prod.exs files from the config folder in your application to the config folder you just created in the image.
3. Compile the dependencies using the mix deps.compile command.

You need these configuration files because normally the dependencies require configuration parameters. Have a go at doing this yourself before looking at the following resulting code snippet:

```
# in Dockerfile

RUN mkdir config

# copy compile-time config files before we compile dependencies
# to ensure any relevant config change will trigger the dependencies
# to be re-compiled.
COPY config/config.exs config/${MIX_ENV}.exs config/
RUN mix deps.compile
```

Now that you have the dependencies sorted, you can proceed to building the assets and the release. We'll look at how to do that in the next section.

Compile the Assets and Build the Release

Your current Dockerfile pulls and compiles the dependencies of your application, and now it's time to compile the assets and build the release. We will discuss these steps one by one. As we go through each step, update your Dockerfile accordingly:

1. Add the priv, the lib, and the assets folders to your Dockerfile. We advise doing so in different instructions due to the layer caching system.
2. Compile the assets.

3. Compile the release.
4. Copy the runtime.exs file
5. Copy the rel folder created by the mix phx.gen.release command that you ran earlier in this chapter.
6. Build the release using the mix release command. Unlike last time, you don't need to prepend the mix release command with the MIX_ENV environment variable, as you've already set this variable in your Dockerfile.

See the next code snippet for the steps that you should've added to the bottom of your current Dockerfile:

```
# in Dockerfile
COPY priv priv
COPY lib lib
COPY assets assets
# compile assets
RUN mix assets.deploy
# compile the release
RUN mix compile
# changes to config/runtime.exs don't require recompiling the code
COPY config/runtime.exs config/
COPY rel rel
RUN mix release
```

Great! Now update the Docker image by running docker build again:

```
$ docker build --tag kanban:latest .
[+] Building 78.6s (18/18) FINISHED
...
 => [9/16] COPY priv priv                              0.0s
 => [10/16] COPY lib lib                               0.0s
 => [11/16] COPY assets assets                         0.0s
 => [12/16] RUN mix assets.deploy                      54.3s
 => [13/16] RUN mix compile                            0.7s
 => [14/16] COPY config/runtime.exs config/            0.0s
 => [15/16] COPY rel rel                               0.0s
 => [16/16] RUN mix release                            1.2s
...
```

Perfect. Now that you have the release built, you can run the container!

The next stage in your Dockerfile will be to run the release. Rather than doing everything in one go, we recommend you run the container interactively and make sure the new steps you'll add to your Dockerfile work. It may seem like this would take more time, but it'll be much quicker as you won't have to spend hours debugging your container. So, let's run the container interactively using the docker run -ti command and then run the release manually inside the container after it starts, using the command _build/prod/rel/kanban/bin/server:

```
$ docker run -ti kanban:latest
root@00eef36219af:/app# _build/prod/rel/kanban/bin/server
ERROR! Config provider Config.Reader failed with:
{"init terminating in do_boot",{#{'__except ....
** (RuntimeError) environment variable SECRET_KEY_BASE is missing.
You can generate one by calling: mix phx.gen.secret
```

Oops! The same error as before! As you can see, you forgot to set the SECRET_KEY_BASE variable. Exit out of your interactive container. Now set the SECRET_KEY_BASE variable on the fly as you did in the first part of this chapter, by adding it to your Docker command by using the --env option, or -e for short. We've run this command in the next code snippet. Once inside the container, we've printed the environment of the bash shell so you can see that the SECRET_KEY_BASE variable has been properly set. Afterward, we have started the application by running _build/prod/rel/kanban/bin/server. Do the same and you will see that your application starts without any errors:

```
$ docker run -ti -e SECRET_KEY_BASE=$(mix phx.gen.secret) kanban:latest
root@aef49b56a801:/app# env
HOSTNAME=aef49b56a801
PWD=/app
HOME=/root
LANG=C.UTF-8
TERM=xterm
SHLVL=1
SECRET_KEY_BASE=QAPssYEIWcpPZKETIzJ9GNtVLUus+v9LKkoguahpsSt3PF4S0UquV...
PATH=/usr/local/sbin:/usr/local/bin:/usr/sbin:/usr/bin:/sbin:/bin
MIX_ENV=prod
_=/usr/bin/env
root@aef49b56a801:/app# _build/prod/rel/kanban/bin/server
13:34:35.339 [info] Running KanbanWeb.Endpoint ... :::4000 (http)
13:34:35.339 [info] Access KanbanWeb.Endpoint at https://example.com
```

Nice! You have a server running on port 4000 inside Docker!

But, if you try to go to port 4000 of your localhost in your browser, you won't be able to access the application. This is because, as we mentioned earlier, Docker containers are completely isolated from the host. This means that, by default, they cannot be accessed from the host in the outside world. As a result, you have to manually map and publish the Docker container port to a port of the host. We'll see how to do this in the next section.

Publish Docker Ports to Your Host

A Docker container can have all the same ports that a host can have, but when you run something in a Docker container on port 4000, you're not running that process on port 4000 of the host machine. For this to be the case, as we said, you have to manually map the Docker container port to a port of the host when you run the container. You can do this by adding the --publish option, or -p for short, to the docker run command. The publish option follows this format:

host-port:docker-container-port

So, to map the Docker container port 4000 to your localhost port 4000, you'd write docker run -p 4000:4000. Let's publish your Docker container so that you can access your application on port 4000 of your localhost. To do this, exit out of your running container and rerun the docker run command interactively, specifying the SECRET_KEY_BASE as you did before, but this time adding the -p option. Then, once inside the container, run the _build/prod/rel/kanban/bin/server command to start the release:

```
$ docker run -ti -e SECRET_KEY_BASE=$(mix phx.gen.secret) \
  -p 4000:4000 kanban:latest
root@4d8bda168e86:/app# _build/prod/rel/kanban/bin/server
13:34:35.339 [info] Running KanbanWeb.Endpoint ... :::4000 (http)
13:45:15.659 [info] Access KanbanWeb.Endpoint at https://example.com
```

A helpful command that you can use is docker ps. This will list all of your running Docker containers so that you can check their status. You can also add the -a option to check the status of all of your containers, running or stopped. In a separate terminal, run the docker ps command and you'll see that your kanban:latest container is up and running with the correct port mapping:

```
$ docker ps
CONTAINER ID   IMAGE   COMMAND   CREATED   STATUS   PORTS
1784fa35610c   beam... "bash"    2 sec... Up...    0.0.0.0:4000->4000/tcp
```

Now, visit https://localhost:4000 and admire your handy work.

You did it! You now know the steps needed to run your application in Docker. Let's transfer these steps to your Dockerfile by adding a new running stage.

The Running Stage

You're at the final stage! In this stage, you'll add all the steps you followed in the previous section after running the container in interactive mode to your Dockerfile.

In all the previous stages, we've been tagging all the images as kanban:latest. You can see the list of images built using the command docker images. If you run this command, you'll see that the latest image that you've built has a considerable size:

```
$ docker images
REPOSITORY      TAG          IMAGE ID         CREATED          SIZE
kanban          latest       7f68bdb73d39     32 minutes ago   263MB
```

Docker images only weigh as much as their final stage because any intermediate artifacts created in earlier stages in the Dockerfile are left behind and are not saved in the final image. The current image size is large because even though you've built the release of the application, you haven't yet created a lightweight running stage that only has the final artifact and the base OS.

Let's get to it. To implement the running stage, add a new RUNNER_IMG argument at the top of the Dockerfile that uses the DEB_VSN argument that we saw when creating the BUILDER_IMG argument. Can you see how parametrizing comes in handy? Because you've done that, it would be super easy to update the Debian version for both stages. Using just the Debian argument as your base runner image (rather than the Bob the builder image) provides the minimal requirements for running your application and makes the running stage that you'll create lean by avoiding unnecessary extra packages, such as Elixir and Erlang which your packaged release doesn't need. After you've added this new argument, the top of your Dockerfile should look like this:

```
# in Dockerfile
ARG BUILDER_IMG="hexpm/elixir:${EX_VSN}-erlang-${OTP_VSN}-debian-${DEB_VSN}"
ARG RUNNER_IMG="debian:${DEB_VSN}"

FROM ${BUILDER_IMG} AS builder
```

Next, at the bottom of your Dockerfile under the builder stage, define a new stage named runner based on the RUNNER_IMG argument you just created. This new stage must install the OS dependencies that are needed to run the release and then run that release.

While we said earlier that OTP releases are great because they don't require Erlang or Elixir to be installed (meaning you can run them in a lightweight environment), you do still need to install a few libraries, which you'll see in a moment. But these libraries are way smaller than Elixir and Erlang, so the benefit is still there.

After you install those libraries, you'll set the locale to en_US.UTF-8 and the language as en_US.en for the eventual Docker container that this composite Debian image will define. This is an important step because Elixir needs UTF-8 encoding to be able to handle text properly. The Debian image you're using doesn't have a locale set. When this happens, unless you manually specify the locale, Erlang will automatically set the locale of the Erlang VM to be Latin1.[5] If the locale isn't UTF-8, you may encounter problems with character encoding, string manipulation, and other text-related operations in your Elixir application. So you must explicitly set the locale to UTF-8 in your Dockerfile to avoid such issues.

After you've done this, you'll set the working directory to /app as you did in the builder stage. Then copy the application that was built in the builder stage that lives in the folder /app/_build/prod/rel/kanban.

Lastly, you'll run the same server release script that you've been using to start that application. (Bear in mind that the path to this script will now be a lot shorter due to you already having copied the application). We've pasted the new runner stage that you need to add to your file here:

```
# in Dockerfile
# start a new runner stage so that the final image will only contain
# the compiled release and other runtime necessities
FROM ${RUNNER_IMG} AS runner

RUN apt-get update -y \
  && apt-get install -y libstdc++6 openssl libncurses5 locales \
  && apt-get clean && rm -f /var/lib/apt/lists/*_*
# set the locale
RUN sed -i '/en_US.UTF-8/s/^# //g' /etc/locale.gen && locale-gen

ENV LANG="en_US.UTF-8"
ENV LANGUAGE="en_US:en"
ENV LC_ALL="en_US.UTF-8"

WORKDIR "/app"
RUN chown nobody /app

# set the runner ENV
ENV MIX_ENV="prod"

# only copy the final release from the build stage
COPY --from=builder \
    --chown=nobody:root /app/_build/${MIX_ENV}/rel/kanban ./

USER nobody

CMD ["/app/bin/server"]
```

---

5. https://github.com/erlang/otp/blob/922ef22d58ae5232fcb2a44776d9879e8433d71d/erts/etc/common/erlc.c#L926

As you can see, we've used the new RUNNER_IMG. We've also used an alias to name the stage runner. On top of that, we've also done these things:

- Added the RUN instruction to install the OS dependencies that we need to run the release.
- Set the locale to UTF-8.
- Added the WORKDIR instruction to set the working directory to /app, just as you did in the builder stage.
- Set the privileges of the /app folder to correspond to the nobody user. It's good practice to use the nobody user because it limits the damage that an attacker can do if they manage to gain access to the container since they will be operating under a user account with limited privileges. Additionally, running as an unprivileged user can help prevent accidental damage to the system by restricting the container's access to sensitive files and resources.
- Added the ENV instruction to set the environment to prod.
- Added the COPY instruction with the --from option to copy over the resulting artifact from the builder stage and the --chown option to assign nobody user privileges to the release binary.
- Added the USER instruction to run the container as the nobody user.
- Added the CMD instruction with the argument [/app/bin/server]. This is what will run the release when the container starts. This is the same as running _build/prod/rel/kanban/bin/server, but as you have copied the _build/prod/rel/kanban contents into /app you can just run /app/bin/server.

And that's it! You've finished writing a multistage Dockerfile that builds and runs a release of your application. Congratulations!

Exit it out of your currently running container and use the command docker build --tag kanban:latest . to rebuild our image. Then rerun the container as you did before by executing the following command:

```
$ docker run -e SECRET_KEY_BASE="$(mix phx.gen.secret)" \
      -p 4000:4000 kanban:latest
```

If you go to port 4000 of your localhost, you'll see that your application is ready to go! Now that you've achieved this, you can close the infrastructure GitHub issue that you created in the previous chapter. We'll do that in the next section.

Close Related GitHub Issues

Now that you've finished dockerizing your Phoenix application, you can close the issues related to this chapter. If you go to the Issues tab in the repository that you created in the previous chapter (shown in the following figure), you'll see that you have two issues tagged with the labels Dockerfile and Kind:Infrastructure:

- Implement the Dockerfile's builder stage
- Implement the Dockerfile's runner stage

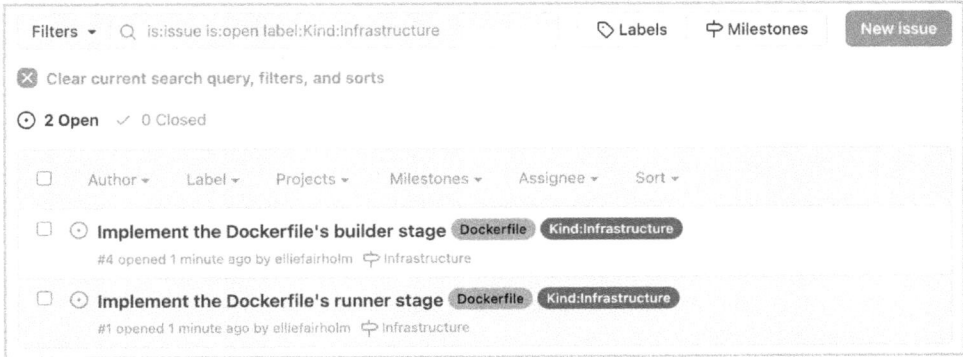

To be able to close these issues, create a new branch, commit the code you have worked on in this chapter, and submit a pull request with the multistage Dockerfile that you've implemented. Include closes #ISSUE_ID twice in your pull request description, once for each issue. Adding a closes #ISSUE_ID to a pull request is a great GitHub feature because, when that pull request is merged, the issues will close automatically.

And you're done! Mission accomplished. Let's recap what you've learned in this chapter.

What Have You Learned?

In this chapter, you built a Phoenix LiveView application using OTP releases and have dockerized it using a multistage Dockerfile. You've learned the differences between Docker and virtual machines, and you've seen why Docker is so popular for building and running applications. You know the main concepts of Dockerfiles and have executed basic Docker commands to show and build images, as well as to run containers. Lastly, you understand how to debug a Dockerfile by overriding the entrypoint and running the container interactively.

Now that you're fluent in the basics of Docker, a Dockerfile, and the core building and running commands, you can quickly containerize any Elixir application that you're working on. We encourage you to take ownership of the packaging of the application. As you'll see in future chapters, once the packaging is done, you can easily deploy the application or run it as part of a CI/CD pipeline. There will always be issues that arise at the edge of responsibility, but you'll be able to tackle them with the knowledge that you have gained in this chapter.

It's now time to take your first step in setting up a CI/CD pipeline with GitHub Actions. In the next chapter, you'll learn how to set up a CI pipeline that will give you confidence that your codebase is properly compiled, tested, and formatted. This makes your application more maintainable and minimizes bugs.

> **The Extra Mile**
>
> If you wish to deepen your knowledge of the themes we've covered in this chapter and refine your BEAMOps developer super powers, we've created a few tasks for you to do:
>
> 1. Set up your development environment using Docker. To do this, build a Docker image that specifically targets the builder stage and then run that image with a mounted volume that includes your project files.
>
> 2. Distribute your Docker image manually using the `docker save` command in one machine and then the `docker load` command in another machine. If you don't have access to two machines, you can achieve the same result by removing all of your created images after running `docker save`.

CHAPTER 4

Set Up Integration Pipelines with GitHub Actions

In Chapter 2, we explained how turning the project management of a software product into a development task improves team efficiency because it empowers the whole team and shortens the feedback loop between developers and product owners. In this chapter, you're going to learn how to further shorten this feedback loop and adopt proactive habits for testing your code by implementing a continuous integration (CI) pipeline with GitHub Actions.

A CI pipeline helps you ensure that your code works as you expect it to. It streamlines the delivery process of your application by seeking out bugs and/or issues *before* they're reported. We believe that the CI pipeline must be implemented as soon as possible when delivering a software product to ensure your code is reliable from the start.

Closely related to the CI pipeline is the concept of "continuous improvement." The Japanese term for continuous improvement is *kaizen*. By using a CI pipeline, you're following what's known as the *Kaizen principle*—the idea that small, ongoing changes can lead to significant improvements. Exercising this principle is essential in software development because it encourages better quality and more reliable code. You should always aim to ship less code, more often.

After reading this chapter, you'll understand the mandatory steps that an Elixir application must follow to safely ship to production. You'll also learn the different triggers for a GitHub Action that will run your CI pipeline, and you'll build on your understanding of Docker by pushing your Docker image to the GitHub container registry in the CI. By the end of this chapter, you'll close three of the CI/CD GitHub issues that you created in Chapter 2.

As with the previous chapter, we'll continue following our same development approach of manually implementing the necessary steps first and then automating them. Let's get started and implement the mandatory steps that each CI pipeline for an Elixir application must follow.

Mandatory CI Steps for a CI Pipeline

When implementing a CI pipeline, you must always distinguish between mandatory and nonmandatory steps. Mandatory steps are the minimum requirements that your application must meet before being shipped. Nonmandatory steps are nice-to-haves that don't affect the basic running of your application. In the case of an Elixir application, the mandatory steps are to ensure that: the code compiles, already compiled files and previously fetched dependencies are cached, the tests pass, the code is properly formatted, the code has been analyzed by Dialyzer, and that no unused dependencies exist. Let's go through each step, one by one, starting with code compilation.

Code Compilation

The first, and most important, step is to ensure your code compiles properly. As we mentioned earlier, rather than jumping straight into automation, first try to compile your code locally. To do so, use the `mix compile` command. To ensure that you compile your code from an initial, untouched state, as your CI would do, remove your _build directory from the project you created in the previous chapter and then compile your code by running `rm -rf _build && MIX_ENV=test mix compile` as we've done here:

```
$ rm -rf _build && MIX_ENV=test mix compile
==> file_system
Compiling 7 files (.ex)
...
```

You'll notice we've set the `MIX_ENV` to be test. This is the environment you'll use when running your workflow. Great. You know that your code successfully compiles. A handy way to check whether the last terminal command was successful or not is to use the bash command `echo $?`. If you run it, you'll see that your terminal prints 0, indicating a success.

Now that you know how to successfully compile your code, you can go ahead and implement your GitHub Action. However, we don't recommend doing this just yet. Instead, we advise that you also figure out a way to make your desired result fail. This is an important step in CI pipeline creation as it removes any false positives in your code. We recommend that you consistently follow this approach:

1. Make a test that fails locally.
2. Ensure that the test fails in the CI.
3. Fix the test so that it passes locally.
4. Validate that the test passes in the CI.

To make a test that fails locally, create a warning in your code by adding an unused module attribute to your lib/kanban_web.ex file. You can see how we've done so here:

```
# in lib/kanban_web.ex
defmodule KanbanWeb do
  @unused_attr ""
end
```

Now, compile your code again, but this time using the --warnings-as-errors flag as we've done here:

```
$ MIX_ENV=test mix compile --warnings-as-errors
Compiling 1 file (.ex)
warning: module attribute @unused_attr was set but never used
  lib/kanban_web.ex:2

Compilation failed due to warnings while using the --warnings-as-errors
option
```

As the name suggests, the --warnings-as-errors option turns any code warnings into errors and means that if your code has any warnings when trying to be compiled, the compilation will fail. This is a useful option in CI pipelines as it preserves the integrity of your codebase. If you don't use this flag, the daily development workflow of your application might become unhealthy. Systems deteriorate pretty quickly if you start neglecting them, and so you should always try to fix a warning as soon as it arises. To do this, you must ensure that the CI doesn't let you deliver any code that has a warning.

Now that you know how to successfully and unsuccessfully compile your codebase, let's move on to creating the GitHub Action.

Add the mix compile Step to Your CI workflow

GitHub Actions are always defined in a YAML file within the .github/workflows directory. There are eight main, first-level keys that can be used in a GitHub workflow file, which you can see in detail in their documentation.[1] We'll only be focusing on the following four keys in this chapter:

---

1. https://docs.github.com/en/actions/using-workflows/workflow-syntax-for-github-actions

- name: gives a name, or ID, which will be used to refer to your workflow. This name is displayed in the Actions tab of the repository.
- on: defines the triggers that will produce a CI job, such as pushing to a repository or opening a pull request.
- env: defines environment variables that will be available in your CI job.
- jobs: defines a list of "actions" that will be executed in the CI pipeline. Each job can have an ID, a name, a runner that specifies on which machine the job is run, environment variables, a set of steps, and a set of services.

To create your workflow, create a new .github/workflows folder at the root of your project and inside that folder a file called ci_cd.yaml and then paste the following code snippet into the file. We'll then go through each of the file components.

```yaml
# in ci_cd.yaml
name: CI/CD Elixir

on:
  push:
  workflow_dispatch:

jobs:
  ci:
    runs-on: ubuntu-latest
    name: Compile
    env:
      MIX_ENV: test
    steps:
      - uses: actions/checkout@v4

      - name: Setup Elixir
        uses: erlef/setup-beam@v1.17.3
        with:
          version-file: .tool-versions
          version-type: strict

      - name: Get dependencies
        run: mix deps.get

      - run: mix compile --warnings-as-errors
```

As you can see, we've named the workflow CI/CD Elixir. CI/CD stands for Continuous Integration/Continuous Deployment. This chapter will only focus on the CI part. You'll implement the CD part in Chapter 7. We then configured the on key of the workflow so it's triggered either by the workflow_dispatch event, which means you can manually trigger the workflow, or by the push event, meaning each time you push to your remote repository. You'll tweak these on events later, as it's not very cost-effective to trigger a workflow on each push, but we're using that event for now so that you can test the workflow. Lastly, we've used the jobs key to define an action with the ID ci and name Compile. The id is what you could use later in the workflow if you wanted to refer to that specific job, whereas the name is what will appear in the logs of the run to refer to that specific part of the workflow. The machine used to run your workflow is called a runner. We've specified that the job will run on an ubuntu-latest machine, use the MIX_ENV=test environment variable, and have the following steps:

1. Check out your project code in the runner's machine.
2. Install Elixir on the runner's machine using the .tool-versions file you created in Chapter 1.
3. Get your project's dependencies.
4. Compile your project's code.

A step is either a shell script, defined by the key run, or a predefined action, defined by the key uses. In the earlier example, we've used both keys. A predefined action is an open-source, reusable unit of code that performs a particular task, such as checking out your code or installing a programming language and making it available in your runner's path, as you can see in the first two steps of the previous code snippet. GitHub has a marketplace[2] where you can search for all different kinds of actions. When installing the project dependencies, we used the run key to execute the command mix deps.get without having to use a predefined action. This is because the previous "Setup Elixir" step installs Erlang on the runner's machine, which means that all subsequent job steps can run any mix command as normal.

You'll see that the second step sets the Elixir version by reusing the .tool-versions file that you created in Chapter 1 to define the versions of the tools your application needs. By using the same tool to set up your environment and your CI pipeline, you ensure environment integrity by making it so that your application is always being run under almost all of the same conditions.

Okay, great! You've defined your workflow. Now add and commit both your ci_cd.yaml and lib/kanban_web.ex files with a message of your choice and then push your new commit to your remote repository. Your workflow will now be running in your GitHub account. Many developers choose to see the results of their jobs in the GitHub UI. However, we recommend using the GitHub CLI as it allows you to see the workflow output directly in your terminal rather than

---

2. https://github.com/marketplace?type=actions

having to switch between your terminal and the browser. We'll look at the basic GitHub CLI commands in the next section.

> **Choosing Your Branch**
>
>  The workflow in this section only works if it's run on the main branch. This is because the workflow_dispatch trigger only works on the default branch. Pushing to main in this instance isn't an issue as you're setting up a pipeline for a project still in its development phase and you're working by yourself. If you were to be working in a team or setting up a CI pipeline for an existing project with multiple developers, you should test it by either implementing this pipeline using branches or a replica project in your personal account.

Shorten the Feedback Loop with the GitHub CLI

The GitHub CLI is a great tool that lets you interact with the GitHub API from the terminal. As a superpowered BEAMOps developer, we recommend that you integrate this tool when working with projects that host their codebase in GitHub—it will enhance your performance. If the codebase is hosted in a different service, you should try to find a similar tool.

So far, you've created a GitHub Action workflow that's triggered on push and you've pushed it to your remote repository, meaning that your workflow will either be in the process of running or will have just finished. To view the runs for a specific workflow using the GitHub CLI, you can use the command gh workflow view followed by the name of your workflow file, which in this case is ci_cd.yaml. Run this command, and we'll observe the terminal output, which should look like this:

```
$ gh workflow view ci_cd.yaml
CI/CD Elixir - ci_cd.yaml
ID: 56355710

Total runs 1
Recent runs
X  Trigger warning as errors  CI/CD Elixir  main  push  4893323052

To see more runs... try: gh run list --workflow ci_cd.yaml
To see the YAML... try: gh workflow view ci_cd.yaml --yaml
```

As you can see, this command lists all of the runs for your workflow and, as expected, the most recent run failed. If your run shows an * rather than an X next to the CI run, it means that your workflow hasn't finished running yet. Wait a few seconds and run the gh workflow view command again until you see the X. To check the logs of a particular run, use the command gh run view followed by the run ID, which in the previous example is 4893323052. As you can see in the upcoming terminal output, this command will tell you exactly which part of the workflow failed. The job with the name Compile failed at the Run mix compile --warnings-as-errors step:

```
$ gh run view 4893323052

X main CI/CD Elixir · 4893323052
Triggered via push about 6 minutes ago

JOBS
X Compile in 1m7s (ID 13261850341)
  ✓ Set up job
  ✓ Run actions/checkout@v4
  ✓ Setup Elixir v1.16.0-otp-26.2.1
  ✓ Run mix deps.get
  X Run mix compile --warnings-as-errors
  ✓ Post Run actions/checkout@v4
  ✓ Complete job

ANNOTATIONS
X Process completed with exit code 1.
Compile: .github#112

To see what failed, try: gh run view 4893323052 --log-failed
View this run on GitHub: https://github.com/.../actions/runs/4893323052
```

As the previous terminal output indicates, if you only wish to see the failed logs, you can add the --log-failed flag.

> **Quickly Navigate the GitHub UI**
>
>  The --web flag can be added to most GitHub CLI commands. It opens the command in the GitHub UI in the browser. This is a quicker way of navigating through the UI without having to click multiple times.

You did it! You replicated your failing local command in your CI, ensuring there are no false positives. Now that you have a failing job, let's fix it so the CI passes. To do so, remove the unused attribute you added earlier, commit your changes, and push again to your remote repository. Immediately after doing that, recheck the workflow runs with the command gh workflow view ci_cd.yaml, and you'll see that your job is currently running, which is indicated by the * in the following terminal output:

```
$ gh workflow view ci_cd.yaml
...
Total runs 2
Recent runs
*  Remove the unused attribute   CI/CD Elixir   main   push   4924804645
X  Trigger warning as errors     CI/CD Elixir   main   push   4893323052
...
```

Now, wait for a minute or so (feel free to make a cup of coffee) and then reexecute the same gh workflow view ci_cd.yaml command. You'll see that the run was successful, just as in this example:

```
$ gh workflow view ci_cd.yaml
...
Total runs 2
Recent runs
✓  Remove the unused attribute   CI/CD Elixir  main  push  4924804645
X  Trigger warning as errors     CI/CD Elixir  main  push  4893323052
```

Great! You have a passing job! But having to wait a minute for the run to finish isn't ideal. Whenever you see that CI jobs take a long time to execute, you should tackle the problem straight away. If you don't solve the issue as soon as it arises, then you could end up with an unhealthy CI that, instead of being a tool that bolsters your confidence, causes frustration. In the next section, we'll look at how you can speed up your CI runs by enabling a cache.

Cache the _build and deps Directories

A cache will help reduce the execution time of your CI jobs, which makes your GitHub Action workflows more cost-effective. Given this, we recommend setting up the cache in your CI as soon as possible. To be able to do this, you need to understand which folders need to be kept between runs, when to expire the cache, and how you can conditionally run certain steps depending on whether the cache has been hit or not. As always, let's first understand how to proceed locally. The two commands you're running in your workflow so far are mix deps.get and mix compile. Let's start with the mix deps.get command.

First, remove the deps directories so that you start with a clean state and then run the mix deps.get command twice, remembering to set the MIX_ENV to be test:

```
$ rm -rf deps && MIX_ENV=test mix deps.get
Resolving Hex dependencies...
...
* Getting phoenix (Hex package)
* Getting phoenix_html (Hex package)
$ MIX_ENV=test mix deps.get
Resolving Hex dependencies...
...
All dependencies are up to date
```

As you can see, the second execution is more efficient because your deps folder already existed and you didn't add or remove any dependencies. This means that mix didn't have to pull all the dependencies again. So, we can say keeping your deps folder across your CI runs would make your workflow more efficient as it would mean you wouldn't be re-fetching dependencies. To save an unnecessary execution altogether, you could go one step further and add a condition to your workflow to only run the mix deps.get command if your dependencies have changed.

Now what about the _build directory? Let's repeat the same process. Delete the _build folder and run the mix compile --warnings-as-errors command twice, changing a file in between executions. Now run the command as we've done here:

```
$ rm -rf _build && MIX_ENV=test mix compile --warnings-as-errors
10:26:21.039 [info] Compiling file system watcher for Mac...
10:26:21.563 [info] Done.
==> file_system
Compiling 7 files (.ex)
Generated file_system app
==> mime
Compiling 1 file (.ex)
...
```

Then append a new empty line to the lib/kanban.ex @moduledoc attribute file:

```
# in lib/kanban.ex
defmodule Kanban do
  @moduledoc """
  Kanban keeps the contexts that define your domain
  and business logic.

  Contexts are also responsible for managing your data, regardless
  if it comes from the database, an external API or others.
  """
end
```

Now, run the MIX_ENV=test mix compile --warnings-as-errors command again:

```
$ MIX_ENV=test mix compile --warnings-as-errors
Compiling 1 file (.ex)
```

The only file that has been compiled in the second execution was the one you changed. This should always be the case. If you're working on a project and this doesn't happen, it means you may have cross-dependencies between modules. From running the mix compile --warnings-as-errors command twice, we can say the second execution is faster because mix doesn't have to compile all the Elixir files, but rather only those that have changed since the last compilation.

In this instance, unlike with dependency fetching where we've said that you can configure your workflow so that it only runs mix deps.get when the dependencies for your application have changed, you won't add a conditional step to your workflow for your compile step. This is because you always need to run mix compile as Elixir is a compiled language and you must ensure that your code compiles properly.

Let's move this to the CI and see how you can cache both the deps and _build folders. Before you do this, undo the change you made to your lib/kanban.ex file.

Enable the Cache in the CI

You saw in the previous section that you can speed up the execution of your CI by not fetching all of your dependencies or compiling all of your code on each run. The first step in adding this to your CI is to add a cache to your workflow that keeps the _build and the deps directories across CI runs. To do this, you'll use the GitHub cache action.[3] To incorporate the cache, add the step in the following code snippet to your workflow, just after setting up the Elixir and Erlang versions and before running the mix deps.get command:

```yaml
# in ci_cd.yaml
jobs:
  ci:
    runs-on: ubuntu-latest
    name: Compile
    env:
      MIX_ENV: test
    steps:
      - name: Cache deps directory
        uses: actions/cache@v4
        id: cache-deps
        with:
          path: |
            deps
            _build
          key: ${{ runner.os }}-mix-${{ hashFiles('**/mix.lock') }}
          restore-keys: |
            ${{ runner.os }}-mix-
```

You've just added a cache to your workflow by using and customizing the predefined actions/cache@v4 action. The different attributes of the cache action do the following:

- The id key, as it would suggest, adds an ID to your cache step. The id attribute isn't required when defining a job step but in this instance is necessary as you'll use this ID later on to be able to create the conditional mix deps.get execution.

---

3. https://github.com/actions/cache

- The `path` key defines which file/directory patterns to cache and restore: the `deps` and `_build` folders.

- The `key` value defines a key for each of your cache. This key is the name that your cache will have when saved, which we've set to be a hash of the `mix.lock` file in your project. When looking for a cache to use for a run, your workflow will hash the `mix.lock` file that it checked out using the `actions/checkout@v4` action and search for a cache name with that hash. If it finds one it will use it, and if not then it won't. If the provided key doesn't match an existing cache, a new cache is automatically created once the workflow finishes running provided the job completes successfully. If the provided key *does* match an existing cache, a new cache entry is not created when the workflow finishes. This is important to remember when writing workflows because it means that if step 3 in a workflow accesses a cache, step 5 in that workflow won't be able to add files to that cache (even though it may be altering one of the files saved in the cache).

- The `restore-keys` key defines an ordered list of prefix-matched keys to use for partially restoring a stale cache. The cache action first searches for cache hits using the `key`, but if there's no hit, it searches for the `restore-keys`. Notice that the `restore-keys` value is the same as the start of the `key` value. Adding the `restore-keys` attribute to your action, means that even if your dependencies have slightly changed, *not all* of your dependencies will have to be re-fetched and *not all* of your code will have to be recompiled. This is because an older version of your `deps` and `build` folders will be restored and so your workflow will only have to fetch the new dependencies that have been added and/or compile the files that have changed. When a stale cache is used and there is a cache hit for one of the `restore-keys`, your workflow will create a new cache entry when it finishes, provided the job completes successfully.

Now, commit your changes and push them to your remote repository. Let's check the job result and pay attention to the execution time. You could do this by repeating the same process as before: listing all the runs in the workflow with `gh workflow view ci_cd.yaml` and then querying the most recent run by running `gh run view` followed by the most recent run ID. However, that's one too many executions. To make it quicker, you can use `jq` to select the most recent run ID and pass that to the `gh run view` command. Have a look at the upcoming terminal example to see how we've done this. You might have to wait a minute or so for the workflow to finish running:

```
$ gh run view $(gh run list \
                --workflow="ci_cd.yaml" \
                --limit=1 \
                --json databaseId | jq -r '.[0].databaseId')
✓ main CI/CD Elixir · 5002825177
Triggered via push about 1 minute ago
JOBS
✓ Compile in 55s (ID 13548703091)

For more information about the job, try: gh run view --job=13548703091
```

Okay! You can see that our job took 55 seconds. You may be wondering why it still took a long time even after you enabled a cache. This is because you've only just added the cache step, so this run was the first time the cache was populated. It won't be until the next run that the cache can be accessed. Let's see the cache in action by manually triggering a new workflow run. To do so, use the `gh workflow run` command followed by the name of your workflow file. After this, run the same `gh run view` command as before. Pay close attention to the execution time:

```
$ gh workflow run ci_cd.yaml
Created workflow_dispatch event for ci_cd.yaml at main
...
$ gh run view $(gh run list \
                --workflow="ci_cd.yaml" \
                --limit=1 \
                --json databaseId | jq -r '.[0].databaseId')
✓ main CI/CD Elixir · 5002851271
Triggered via workflow_dispatch about 1 minute ago
JOBS
✓ Compile in 12s (ID 13548777089)

For more information about the job, try: gh run view --job=13548777089
```

Amazing! You have a working cache step in the CI that allows you to run the application compilation in just 12 seconds by reusing the _build and deps files across CI runs. If you add --web to your previous `gh run view` command, you'll see your workflow run in the browser. Enter your workflow by clicking on the Compile box and then open the "Cache deps directory" drop-down. You'll see that your cache was used and restored using a direct match on your key attribute, as shown in the figure on page 91.

Now that you have your cache in place, you can add a conditional step to your workflow to further reduce the CI execution time.

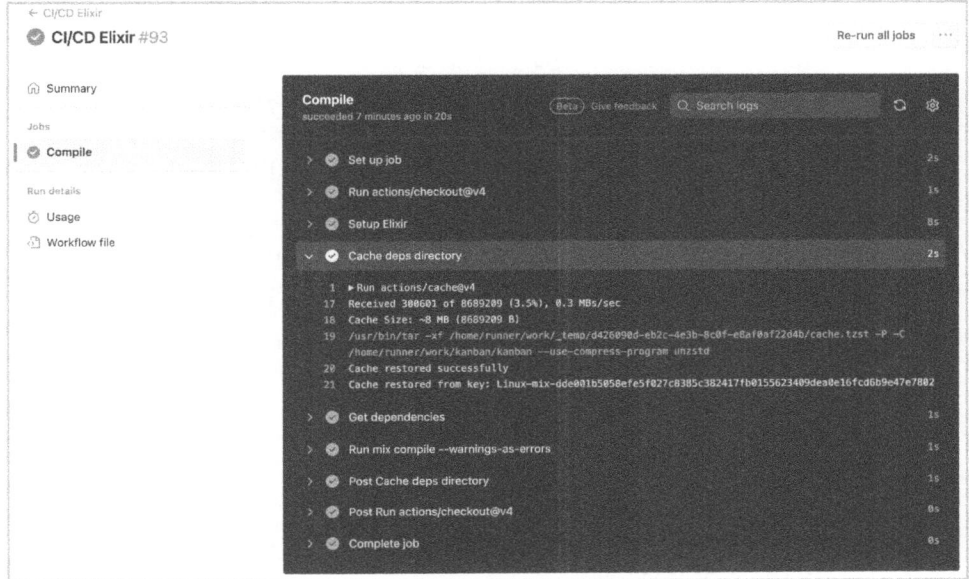

Conditional Steps

In the previous section, you configured your workflow to reuse the _build and the deps directories in consecutive CI runs if their content hasn't been changed. This is great, but you can go one step further and skip the dependency fetching step altogether if you can determine that the dependencies haven't changed.

The cache action[4] you used outputs a boolean that states whether an exact cache match was found for the key attribute. This variable can be obtained by accessing steps.STEP_ID.outputs.cache-hit, where the STEP_ID is replaced by the ID that you added to your cache step: cache-deps. This cache-hit value will only be set to true when an exact cache hit occurs for your key attribute. For a partial key match via restore-keys or a cache miss, it will be set to false. If the steps.cache-deps.outputs.cache-hit value is true, your mix.lock file hasn't changed and so your deps and _build folders can be reused. We can therefore say that if this value is *not* true, then your mix.lock file must have changed and so the dependencies must be re-fetched, meaning the mix deps.get command must be rerun.

---

4. https://docs.github.com/en/actions/using-workflows/caching-dependencies-to-speed-up-workflows#output-parameters-for-the-cache-action

> **Restoring Caches**
>
>  Just because steps.cache-deps.outputs.cache-hit is false doesn't mean that no cache will be used in your workflow. Remember that the restore-keys attribute means that your workflow can still use an old cache to speed up your workflow, but will create a new cache once it finishes running successfully.

To add this conditional to your workflow, copy the line starting with if:... in the subsequent code snippet to your Get dependencies step:

```yaml
# in ci_cd.yaml
jobs:
  ci:
    runs-on: ubuntu-latest
    name: Compile
    env:
      MIX_ENV: test
    steps:
      - name: Get dependencies
        if: steps.cache-deps.outputs.cache-hit != 'true'
        run: mix deps.get
```

Perfect! Before committing and pushing these changes, let's view a --verbose output of the 12-second run you triggered earlier to see all of the execution steps. You can do this by adding the --verbose flag to the gh run view command:

```
$ gh run view --verbose $(gh run list \
                --workflow="ci_cd.yaml" \
                --limit=1 \
                --json databaseId | jq -r '.[0].databaseId')
✓ main CI/CD Elixir · 5023905275
Triggered via workflow_dispatch about 6 minutes ago

JOBS
✓ Compile with conditional dependency fetching in 12s (ID 13607809979)
  ✓ Set up job
  ✓ Run actions/checkout@v4
  ✓ Setup Elixir v1.16.0-otp-26.2.1
  ✓ Run actions/cache@v4
  ✓ Get dependencies
  ✓ Run mix compile --warnings-as-errors
  ✓ Post Run actions/cache@v4
  ✓ Post Run actions/checkout@v4
  ✓ Complete job
```

As you can see, all the steps were run, including the Get dependencies one. Now, commit and push your most recent changes and then rerun the same --verbose log command. You'll see the Get dependencies step doesn't run this time due to the conditional you added and that, as a result, the execution time is faster than before:

```
...
JOBS
✓ Compile with conditional dependency fetching in 10s (ID 13607971397)
    ✓ Set up job
    ✓ Run actions/checkout@v4
    ✓ Setup Elixir v1.16.0-otp-26.2.1
    ✓ Run actions/cache@v4
    - Get dependencies
    ✓ Run mix compile --warnings-as-errors
    ✓ Post Run actions/cache@v4
    ✓ Post Run actions/checkout@v4
    ✓ Complete job
...
```

Great! You've further reduced the execution time of the CI by skipping the dependency fetching step. You should always keep time-saving steps like these in mind when implementing a CI step. As *The Pragmatic Programmer* states, it's extremely easy for things to become rotten if you don't take care of them.

Let's move on to the next mandatory step that a CI workflow should implement when building and testing an Elixir application: testing your application's code.

Test Your Code

We all know that tests are an important part of the development process. They give us the confidence to refactor our code and add new features. If you've been working with Elixir for a while, you're probably familiar with the many capabilities of the mix test task. If this is the first time that you're coming across the mix test command, we suggest that you take a look at the Elixir help docs by running the command mix help test. We won't go into detail on how to write efficient tests for an Elixir application, as our focus will be on adding a testing step to your CI. If you're interested in how to write tests, we recommend you check out *Testing Elixir: Effective and Robust Testing for Elixir and its Ecosystem.*[5]

Let's start from the beginning and locally run the tests that were automatically created by the Phoenix project generator in the previous chapter. We've done this here:

---

5. https://pragprog.com/titles/lmelixir/testing-elixir/

```
$ mix test
...
Finished in 0.01 seconds (0.01s async, 0.00s sync)
5 tests, 0 failures

Randomized with seed 200487
```

If you look at the previous terminal output, you'll see that the execution time is split into async and sync tests. Since Elixir is a concurrent language, it's common to have async tests that run in parallel. A handy trick to reduce your CI execution time is to use the fail-fast flag --max-failures 1, which means that as soon as one test fails, the whole test suite fails. This avoids waiting for all concurrent processes to finish. We also recommend that you add the --trace and --warnings-as-errors flags. The --trace flag will give you a more detailed output of the tests, which is useful when determining which tests may have failed in the CI. The --warnings-as-errors flag makes sure that you don't have any compilation errors in your test files. We've run the command so that you can see an example output:

```
$ mix test --max-failures 1 --trace --warnings-as-errors
...
...PageControllerTest [test/.../controllers/page_controller_test.exs]
  * test GET / (40.4ms) [L#4]

Finished in 0.07 seconds (0.03s async, 0.04s sync)
5 tests, 0 failures

Randomized with seed 132990
```

As we mentioned earlier, rather than adding an already passing test to your CI, you should add a failing one and then fix it. Let's produce a failing test by commenting the two lines of the GET / test in the test/kanban_web/controllers/page_controller_test.ex file and writing assert false like so:

```
# in test/kanban_web/controllers/page_controller_test.exs
defmodule KanbanWeb.PageControllerTest do
  use KanbanWeb.ConnCase

  test "GET /", %{conn: _conn} do
    # conn = get(conn, ~p"/")
    # assert html_response(conn, 200) =~ "Peace of mind from proto..."
    assert false
  end
end
```

Then run mix test --max-failures 1 --trace --warnings-as-errors again so that you can see that your test suite fails.

Good! Now append a test step to the end of your ci job in your ci_cd.yaml workflow that runs the command mix test --max-failures 1 --trace --warnings-as-errors and update the job name accordingly. You can see how we've done so here:

```yaml
# in ci_cd.yaml
jobs:
  ci:
    runs-on: ubuntu-latest
    name: Compile with mix test
    env:
      MIX_ENV: test
    steps:
      - name: Run tests
        run: mix test --max-failures 1 --trace --warnings-as-errors
```

Now commit your changes and push them to your remote repository to trigger the workflow. Then run the gh run view --verbose command with the jq helper and observe the logs of the latest workflow run. Once the workflow has finished running, you'll see that the job has failed because the test step you just added is, as expected, failing, like ours is here:

```
$ gh run view --verbose $(gh run list \
            --workflow="ci_cd.yaml" \
            --limit=1 \
            --json databaseId | jq -r '.[0].databaseId')
X main CI/CD Elixir · 5032493633
Triggered via push about 1 minute ago

JOBS
X Compile with mix test in 15s (ID 13629368801)
  ✓ Set up job
  ✓ Run actions/checkout@v4
  ✓ Setup Elixir v1.16.0-otp-26.2.1
  ✓ Run actions/cache@v4
  - Get dependencies
  ✓ Run mix compile --warnings-as-errors
  X Run tests
  - Post Run actions/cache@v4
  ✓ Post Run actions/checkout@v4
  ✓ Complete job
...
```

Great! Your CI is working as expected! Now restore the page_controller_test.ex by undoing your last change. Then commit and push the changes to retrigger the workflow. You'll see that when you run the same gh view run --verbose command as before, your tests pass, and they do so with a short execution time:

```
...
JOBS
✓ Compile with mix test in 16s (ID 13629467340)
...
```

Well done! You've successfully added a testing step to your CI pipeline. Now you can move on to the next mandatory step in an Elixir application: checking that the code is properly formatted.

Ensure Your Code Is Formatted

Having a step in your CI to check that your code is formatted is a must. When you're developing a new feature, it's really important to be able to focus exclusively on the diff that's produced when working on that feature. If your dev environment autoformats the code on save, you'll end up with confusing diffs that don't properly reflect the change made. This is why it's important to enforce a formatting standard in the CI, especially with a language that has a built-in formatter like Elixir. The format command for Elixir is mix format. If you add the flag --check-formatted, the command will exit with an error if the code isn't properly formatted. Let's add this format step to your pipeline.

Again, rather than starting with a passing test, create an error that will cause the mix format --check-formatted command to fail. To do this, remove a space before the assignation of the conn value in the page_controller_test.ex file, as we've done here:

```
# in test/kanban_web/controllers/page_controller_test.exs
defmodule KanbanWeb.PageControllerTest do
  use KanbanWeb.ConnCase

  test "GET /", %{conn: conn} do
  conn = get(conn, ~p"/")
    assert html_response(conn, 200) =~ "Peace of mind from proto..."
  end
end
```

Now run MIX_ENV=test mix format --check-formatted locally, and you'll see the following error that says the page_controller_test.exs file isn't formatted:

```
$ MIX_ENV=test mix format --check-formatted
** (Mix) mix format failed due to --check-formatted.
The following files are not formatted:

  * test/kanban_web/controllers/page_controller_test.exs
```

You may see other formatting errors depending on the version of Phoenix that you are using.

Fantastic! Now add a new step to your workflow that runs this same command and update your job name accordingly. Have a go yourself before looking at how we did it here:

```yaml
# in ci_cd.yaml
jobs:
  ci:
    runs-on: ubuntu-latest
    name: Compile with mix test & format
    env:
      MIX_ENV: test
    steps:
      - name: Check code is formatted
        run: mix format --check-formatted
```

Now commit your changes, push them to your remote repository, and run the run gh view --verbose command with the jq helper as you did earlier to see that the step you just added successfully fails:

```
JOBS
X Compile with mix test & format in 12s (ID 13629693622)
  ✓ Set up job
  ✓ Run actions/checkout@v4
  ✓ Setup Elixir v1.16.0-otp-26.2.1
  ✓ Run actions/cache@v4
  - Get dependencies
  ✓ Run mix compile --warnings-as-errors
  ✓ Run tests
  X Check code is formatted
  - Post Run actions/cache@v4
  ✓ Post Run actions/checkout@v4
  ✓ Complete job
```

Perfect! Now fix the error locally by adding in the space you removed before the conn assignation (as well as any other errors you may have had), run the mix format --check-code-formatted command again to make sure your code is properly formatted locally, and then commit and push your changes. If you rerun the same run gh view --verbose command, you'll see that the job passes. You now have a step in your workflow that checks that the code is properly formatted!

Nice! Now you can move on to the penultimate mandatory step in an Elixir application: analyzing your code with Dialyzer.

Static Analysis with Dialyzer

Elixir is currently a functional, dynamically typed language where the data types of variables are determined at runtime, not during compilation. This means that it's not possible to catch all errors in your code at compile time.

However, there are tools that you can use to combat this—one of them being Dialyxir.[6] Dialyxir is a wrapper around Erlang's Dialyzer[7] tool. Dialyzer is a static analysis tool that can be used to find discrepancies in your code such as type errors. Using Dialyxir in your CI pipeline will help you make sure that type-related issues are identified early and not pushed to production.

To use Dialyxir, you need to add it to your mix.exs file as a dependency. You can do this by adding the following code to your mix.exs file:

```elixir
# in mix.exs
  def project do
    [
      dialyzer: [
        plt_core_path: "priv/plts/core.plt",
        plt_file: {:no_warn, "priv/plts/project.plt"},
        plt_add_apps: [:ex_unit]
      ]
    ]
  end
  defp deps do
    [
      {:dialyxir, "~> 1.4", only: [:dev, :test], runtime: false}
    ]
  end
```

> **Use Dialyxir in Select Environments**
>
>  You may have noticed that the dependency is only being included in :dev and :test. This is because Dialyxir is a development tool that should only be used in these environments. Try to keep your production dependencies as minimal as possible in your mix.exs file whenever you can.

Great. Now that you've added the dependency, run the mix deps.get command to install it. Once it has installed properly, run it by executing mix dialyzer, as we've done here, remembering to set the MIX_ENV to test:

```
$ MIX_ENV=test mix deps.get
...
$ MIX_ENV=test mix dialyzer
...
Finding suitable PLTs
Checking PLT...
[:asn1, :castore, e_pool, :phoenix, :phoenix_ecto, :phoenix_html, ...
telemetry_metrics, ...]
```

---

6. https://github.com/jeremyjh/dialyxir
7. https://www.erlang.org/doc/man/dialyzer.html

```
Looking up modules in dialyxir_erlang-25.3.2.7_elixir-1.15.7_deps-dev.plt
Looking up modules in dialyxir_erlang-25.3.2.7_elixir-1.15.7.plt
Finding applications for dialyxir_erlang-25.3.2.7_elixir-1.15.7.plt
Finding modules for dialyxir_erlang-25.3.2.7_elixir-1.15.7.plt
...
```

When you run this command for the first time, you'll see that it takes a long time to execute. This is because Dialyzer is building the PLTs.[8] A *PLT* is a *Persistent Lookup Table*, which is a file that caches the output of Dialyzer's analysis for your project. There is one PLT for the built-in Erlang libraries, one for the built-in Elixir libraries, and another for the modules in your project. These files are used to speed up the analysis process. Once the PLTs have been built, the mix dialyzer command will execute much faster as the PLTs will already have been created.

Now that you know how Dialyxir works, let's add it to your CI pipeline. As usual, when adding your step, you'll make it fail by adding a specification that doesn't make sense, and then you'll remove that specification so the CI passes. Start by adding the following @spec line to your page_controller.ex file to make Dialyxir fail:

```elixir
# in lib/kanban_web/controllers/page_controller.ex
defmodule KanbanWeb.PageController do
  use KanbanWeb, :controller

  @spec home(Plug.Conn.t(), map()) :: []
  def home(conn, _params) do
    # The home page is often custom made,
    # so skip the default app layout.
    render(conn, :home, layout: false)
  end
end
```

You'll see that the specification we've added to the home function specifies that it should return an empty list, when in fact it returns a Plug.Conn.t(). This is a type error that will make Dialyxir fail. To see this in action, run the mix dialyzer command and you'll see the following output:

```
$ MIX_ENV=test mix dialyzer
...
Total errors: 1, Skipped: 0, Unnecessary Skips: 0
done in 0m1.31s
lib/kanban_web/controllers/page_controller.ex:4:invalid_contract
The @spec for the function doesn't match the success typing of the
function.
...
```

---

8. https://www.erlang.org/doc/apps/dialyzer/dialyzer_chapter#the-persistent-lookup-table

Great! It fails! Now add Dialyxir to your CI by adding the following new cache and new step to your ci_cd.yaml workflow, and then updating your job name accordingly:

```yaml
# in ci_cd.yaml
jobs:
  ci:
    runs-on: ubuntu-latest
    name: Compile with mix test, format & dialyzer
    env:
      MIX_ENV: test
    steps:
      - name: Cache plt files
        uses: actions/cache@v4
        env:
          EX_OTP_VERSIONS: ${{ steps.setup-beam.outputs.elixir-version }}
          KEY_BASE: plt-${{ runner.os }}-${{ env.EX_OTP_VERSIONS }}
        with:
          path: |
            priv/plts
          key: |
            ${{ env.KEY_BASE }}-${{ hashFiles('**/mix.lock') }}
          restore-keys: |
            ${{ env.KEY_BASE }}-
      - name: Dialyzer static analysis
        run: mix dialyzer --format github
```

In the previous code snippet, we've added a new cache to your workflow. This is so that you can cache the PLTs. We've created a new cache, rather than reusing your other cache because the key constraints are different. Rather than only being invalidated if the runner OS and mix.lock file change, your PLT cache will also be invalidated with the Elixir and OTP versions in your project change. You'll notice that the path we're caching is the same as the plt_file value that you added to your mix.exs file earlier.

We've also added a --format github option to the mix dialyzer command. This parameter is used to format the output of the command in a way that's easier to read in the GitHub Actions UI.

Once you've added the step to your workflow, update your .gitignore file so that it includes your PLT files like so:

```
# in .gitignore
/priv/plts/*.plt
/priv/plts/*.plt.hash
```

Then commit and push your changes to your remote repository. Your workflow will take a while to run because your PLTs are being built for the first time. Run the gh run view --verbose command with the jq helper to see that the job you just added fails:

```
JOBS
X Compile with mix test, format & dialyzer in 3m48s (ID 13629693622)
    ✓ Set up job
    ✓ Run actions/checkout@v4
    ✓ Setup Elixir v1.16.0-otp-26.2.1
    ✓ Run actions/cache@v4
    ✓ Get dependencies
    ✓ Run mix compile --warnings-as-errors
    ✓ Run tests
    ✓ Check code is formatted
    X Dialyzer static analysis
    - Post Run actions/cache@v4
    ✓ Post Run actions/checkout@v4
    ✓ Complete job
```

Perfect. You'll also notice the "Get dependencies" step wasn't skipped because your mix.lock file has changed. If you open up that step in the GitHub UI, however, you'll see a stale cache was used (thanks to your restore-keys attribute). Now fix the Dialyxir error locally by updating the specification you added to return a Plug.Conn.t() and then commit and push your changes. If you rerun the same gh run view --verbose command, you'll see the job passes. Remember, this workflow will also take a while to run. This is because your workflow failed last time and so the PLTs weren't added to your cache. The PLTs will be added to your cache on this run, so subsequent executions of your workflow will be faster.

Well done! You've successfully added Dialyxir to your CI pipeline. You can now be sure that no type errors will make it into your production code. In the next section, we'll look at the last mandatory step in an Elixir CI pipeline: cleaning up any outdated dependencies in your mix.lock file.

Clean Outdated Dependencies

Elixir's dependency manager is called mix and keeps track of the different dependencies required for your project and their versions in a mix.lock file. This file is generated when you run mix deps.get and is updated when you run mix deps.update. It won't be updated, however, when you remove a previously added dependency from the deps function in your mix.exs file, even after you rerun mix deps.get. To clean up unused dependencies, you need to manually run mix deps.clean --unlock --unused to properly remove the dependency from the mix.lock file. This is a step normally forgotten and can lead to outdated dependencies remaining in the mix.lock file of your project. This is not a huge problem, but it's a waste of resources, and every little bit counts when striving to develop a healthy project.

As usual, let's reproduce this unused dependency management locally, and then we'll move to the CI. To do this, carry out the following steps:

1. Look for the latest version of decimal in hex.pm.
2. Add this version to your mix.exs file.
3. Run the MIX_ENV=test mix deps.get command.
4. Remove the dependency from your mix.exs file.
5. Run the mix deps.unlock --check-unused command.

To search for the decimal package, use the mix hex.search command followed by the package name as we've done here:

```
$ mix hex.search decimal
Package  Description              Version  URL
decimal  Arbitrary precision...   2.1.1    https://hex.pm/packages/decimal
...
```

As you can see, the latest version of decimal is 2.1.1. Add that version of the package to the deps function of your mix.exs file by adding the following line:

```
# in mix.exs
  defp deps do
    [
      {:decimal, "~> 2.1.1"}
    ]
  end
```

Then run the MIX_ENV=test mix deps.get command to install the dependencies. Now remove the dependency you just added to your mix.exs file and run MIX_ENV=test mix deps.get again. If you observe the terminal output, you won't see any reference to decimal in the fetching process. However, if you run mix deps.unlock --check-unused, you'll see that the command returns an error because the decimal package is still there. Again, this isn't a huge problem, but if there's a way to ensure that your mix.lock file is always clean and up-to-date, why not do it? So, now that you know that the mix deps.unlock --check-unused command fails, add it to your CI workflow so that the CI fails, and then we'll look at fixing it. The following example shows how you can add that step:

```
# in ci_cd.yaml
jobs:
  ci:
    runs-on: ubuntu-latest
    name: Compile with mix test, format, dialyzer & unused deps check
```

```
env:
  MIX_ENV: test
steps:
  - name: Check unused dependencies
    run: mix deps.unlock --check-unused
```

Now trigger the workflow by committing and pushing your changes, and then view the run logs using the gh view run --verbose command with the jq helper. Your terminal output should be similar to this:

```
...
JOBS
X Compile with mix test, format, dialyzer & unused deps check in 27s ...
  ✓ Set up job
  ✓ Run actions/checkout@v4
  ✓ Setup Elixir v1.16.0-otp-26.2.1
  ✓ Run actions/cache@v4
  ✓ Get dependencies
  ✓ Run mix compile --warnings-as-errors
  ✓ Run tests
  ✓ Check code is formatted
  ✓ Dialyzer static analysis
  X Check unused dependencies
  - Post Run actions/cache@v4
  ✓ Post Run actions/checkout@v4
  ✓ Complete job
...
```

Great! It fails! You'll see that your workflow didn't take a long time to run because your PLT cache was used in your Dialyzer step. Now fix the unused dependency issue by cleaning up your mix.lock file locally. Run the mix deps.clean --unlock --unused command and then commit and push the changes that this command makes to your codebase. You'll see that, in the run that is produced, the step that was previously failing is now passing.

Fantastic! We've walked through all of the mandatory steps that will ensure that your code is of high quality. Now you can move on to automating the building of the Docker image that you created in the previous chapter. Then, you'll publish it to the GitHub Docker registry to ensure that your application can be successfully built and is available for further distribution/deployment when you enable continuous deployment.

Build a Docker Image and Push to the GitHub Registry

In the previous chapter, you learned how to generate a Docker image that builds and runs your application. However, you only did so locally. We'll now automate the building process by adding that same Dockerfile to the CI so that it's pushed to the GitHub Docker registry. This step will give you confidence that each change you make to your codebase doesn't affect its ability to be built. When working with any Docker registry, we recommend that, before adding anything to a workflow file, you follow these steps:

1. Build and tag your image locally.
2. Log in to your registry of choice.
3. Push the image to the remote registry.
4. Pull the remote image locally.
5. Test the image locally.

> **"A" Docker Registry vs. "The" Docker Registry**
>
> When you read "Docker registry," be careful not to confuse the general concept of a Docker registry with the more specific Docker registries of different Docker registry providers. *A* Docker registry, also referred to simply as a registry, is a place where Docker images can be stored. *The* Docker registry, on the other hand, refers to the official Docker registry—which is the Docker registry owned and hosted by Docker itself. There are many other different providers that host Docker registries, and the one we'll use in this chapter is the GitHub Docker registry.

Let's start by testing that the Docker image you created in the previous chapter is building locally and can successfully be deployed.

Build and Test Your Docker Image Manually

In Chapter 3 on page 62, we used the tag beamops:latest when running the docker build command, but this time around, as you'll eventually be storing the image remotely, you must prepend your tag with the GitHub Docker registry URL, following the format ghcr.io/OWNER/REPO_NAME:latest. The tag we'll use in this section is ghcr.io/beamops/kanban:latest because our GitHub username is *beamops* and our repository is called *kanban*. But when running your commands, remember to replace these values with your own username and repository name so that your tag is unique.

Build your image by running the command docker build --tag ghcr.io/OWNER/REPO _NAME:latest . as we've done here, substituting in your own GitHub details:

```
$ docker build --tag ghcr.io/beamops/kanban:latest .
...
 => exporting to image                                               0.1s
 => => exporting layers                                              0.1s
```

```
=> => writing image sha256:d5fd20f032bedf4d39720ed678599a1ee9...    0.0s
=> => naming to ghcr.io/beamops/kanban:latest                       0.0s
```

Now, use the same `docker run` command from the previous chapter to run the Docker image, injecting the same environment variable as before and mapping the ports but this time using your new tag. We've pasted the terminal interaction for you here:

```
$ docker run -e SECRET_KEY_BASE="$(mix phx.gen.secret)" \
        -p 4000:4000 ghcr.io/beamops/kanban:latest
10:50:00.139 [info] Running ... Endpoint with cowboy 2.10.0 at :::4000
10:50:00.140 [info] Access  ... Endpoint at https://example.com
```

You may see some compilation warnings in your terminal when you ran this command—don't worry about them. These errors happen because `mix phx.gen.secret` uses dev as its `MIX_ENV`. When you were figuring out which folders to cache in your CI, you deleted your _build folder and so you haven't compiled your application in dev. Because of this `mix phx.gen.secret` has to compile your project before creating the secret. These compilation warnings come from your dependencies and not your application. If you rerun the same `docker run` command again, you won't see these errors.

If you go to http://localhost:4000, you'll see your application up and running. You have a Docker image that works. Let's move on to step two: logging in to the ghcr.io GitHub Docker registry.

To do this, you'll reuse the GitHub token that you created in Chapter 2 on page 25. To log in, you must `echo` your GitHub token and then pipe it to the `docker login` command. This command takes a username, which is specified using the -u flag, and then reads your piped password using the --password-stdin flag. So, echo the GitHub token and then pipe it to the `docker login ghcr.io -u USERNAME --password-stdin` command as we've done here:

```
$ echo "$GITHUB_TOKEN" | docker login ghcr.io -u USERNAME --password-stdin
Login Succeeded
```

Once you've logged in, push the image to the GitHub registry, using the `docker push` command, which takes an image tag as its argument. To push your image, run the `docker push` command followed by the same tag you created earlier that's linked to the GitHub registry, which in our example was ghcr.io/beamops/kanban:latest. You can see the whole terminal interaction here:

```
$ docker push ghcr.io/beamops/kanban:latest
a1c234f3fc4b: Pushed
263001cf80b0: Pushed
0fc33ec1e0dd: Pushed
```

```
3ed02b6152c5: Pushed
4d92665570ce: Pushed
afd7e44a4e08: Layer already exists
latest: digest: sha256:b933422184dd5f5ce0cec4bb49... ebf13514 size: 1574
```

Now let's check that the image has been properly pushed to the registry by removing all your local images, including the one you just built, by running the command docker rmi -f $(docker images -a -q) and then executing another docker run with the same options as earlier:

```
$ docker rmi -f $(docker images -a -q)
...
$ docker run -e SECRET_KEY_BASE="$(mix phx.gen.secret)" \
            -p 4000:4000 ghcr.io/beamops/kanban
Unable to find image 'ghcr.io/beamops/kanban:latest' locally
latest: Pulling from beamops/kanban
...
Digest: sha256:b933422184dd5f5ce0cec4bb497b0a846c9bd8 ... ebf13514
Status: Downloaded newer image for ghcr.io/beamops/kanban:latest
12:11:45.119 [info] Running ... Endpoint with cowboy 2.10.0 at :::4000
12:11:45.119 [info] Access ... Endpoint at https://example.com
```

It worked! If you look at the terminal output, you can see that as Docker cannot find a local image with the tag ghcr.io/beamops/kanban, it pulled the image you just created from the Docker registry.

Now that you know the commands needed to build the Docker image and push it to the GitHub registry, you can add these new steps to your workflow file.

Add the Build and Push Steps to Your Workflow

To add the steps you completed in the previous section to your workflow, you'll create a new job using two new actions: the docker/metadata-action@v4[9] to generate the tags for the image and the docker/build-push-action@v2[10] to push the image.

As part of adding this new job to the workflow, you'll add two conditions so that the job is only run when the branch is main, the event is push, and the ci job you created earlier passes. Append the following new job, with the ID build-push to your existing ci_cd.yaml workflow, and then we'll go through it:

```
# in ci_cd.yaml

jobs:
  build-push:
    runs-on: ubuntu-latest
    needs: ci
```

---

9. https://github.com/docker/metadata-action
10. https://github.com/docker/build-push-action

```yaml
name: Build Docker image & push to ghcr.io
steps:
  - uses: actions/checkout@v4

  - name: Login to GHCR
    uses: docker/login-action@v3
    with:
      registry: ghcr.io
      username: ${{ github.repository_owner }}
      password: ${{ secrets.GH_PAT }}

  - name: Docker meta
    id: meta
    uses: docker/metadata-action@v5
    with:
      images: |
        ghcr.io/YOUR_GITHUB_USERNAME/kanban
      tags: |
        type=raw,value=latest,enable={{is_default_branch}}
        type=ref,event=pr
        type=sha,format=short

  - name: Parse versions from .tool-versions
    id: parse-asdf
    run: ./scripts/versions.sh

  - uses: docker/build-push-action@v5
    with:
      context: .
      tags: ${{ steps.meta.outputs.tags }}
      labels: ${{ steps.meta.outputs.labels }}
      push: true
      build-args: |
        ELIXIR_VERSION=${{ env.ELIXIR_VERSION }}
        OTP_VERSION=${{ env.ERLANG_VERSION }}
```

This new job, like the job created earlier, is run on an Ubuntu machine. The needs key specifies that the job should only be run after the job you created earlier, with the ID ci, passes. The first step of the job checks out your code.

The second step logs you into the GitHub Docker registry, replicating your local steps by using your repository username and your GitHub token. Your username is taken from the GitHub context, a context object that contains information about the workflow run. You'll also see this step uses a GitHub secret called GH_PAT. For you to be able to use this step, you must create a GitHub secret called GH_PAT whose value is your GitHub token. If you need help creating the secret, follow the instructions in the GitHub documentation.[11]

---

11. https://docs.github.com/en/actions/security-guides/encrypted-secrets#creating-encrypted-secrets-for-a-repository

The third step, with the ID meta, adds the appropriate tags to your image. The images key specifies the base image name tag, and the tags key adds three tags that allow you to access different image versions. The first will create a new image appended with the :latest tag whenever a pull request merges into your default branch, main. This image always contains the most up-to-date code. The second tag will create a new image when a pull request is created/updated. It will look something like :pr-12. The last tag, type=sha, creates a new image tag with the short version of a commit sha appended to the base image name for each new commit merged into main, or for each batch of commits if you're merging a pull request, taking the last commit sha. This means you're able to run, deploy, or debug a particular image from a particular commit in your version-controlled code.

The fourth step, with the name Parse versions from .tool-versions, uses a versions.sh bash script to read the Elixir and Erlang versions from your .tool-versions file and add them to the environment of the runner your action uses. To make this step work, you must create a script called versions.sh inside the scripts folder in the root of your application. We've pasted the script in the following code snippet. Create the scripts/versions.sh file and copy in the upcoming code:

```bash
#!/usr/bin/env bash

# in scripts/versions.sh

set -x

# read the version information from the ./tool-versions file
version_output=$(cat ./.tool-versions)

# extract the Elixir version
ELIXIR_VERSION=$(echo "$version_output" |
                | grep 'elixir' |
                | cut -d' ' -f2 |
                | cut -d'-' -f1)

# extract Erlang version
ERLANG_VERSION=$(echo "$version_output" | grep 'erlang' | cut -d' ' -f2)

# add the variables to the `GITHUB_ENV` (env used by the action's runner)
{
  echo "ELIXIR_VERSION=${ELIXIR_VERSION}";
  echo "ERLANG_VERSION=${ERLANG_VERSION}";
} >> "$GITHUB_ENV"
```

Remember to make this script executable by running chmod +x. This script uses cat to read the contents of your .tool-versions file and then grep to extract the Elixir and Erlang versions into two different variables. The last line adds these two variables to the GITHUB_ENV, which is the environment your runner uses to run your action. Can you see why defining the versions of the tools needed for your project in a file you'll use for both your development environment and the building of your application is so beneficial? It ensures your application is built using the same versions of Elixir and Erlang as you use in development. This will help with environment integrity and the reduction of bugs.

Lastly, the final step of your build-push job builds and pushes your image to the GitHub registry, using . as the context and reusing the tags you created in the previous meta step. It also uses the Erlang and Elixir versions extracted from your .tool-versions file as build arguments for the Dockerfile. This is what allows you to connect all the dots and ensure environment integrity.

Now that you've added this new job, commit your changes, push them to your remote repository, and check that your workflow builds and pushes your image to the registry by running the same gh run view --verbose command as before:

```
$ gh run view --verbose $(gh run list \
            --workflow="ci_cd.yaml" \
            --limit=1 \
            --json databaseId | jq -r '.[0].databaseId')
...
JOBS
✓ Compile with mix test, format, dialyzer & unused deps check in 27s ...
  ...
✓ Build Docker image & push to ghcr.io in 1m34s (ID 13724220553)
    ✓ Set up job
    ✓ Run actions/checkout@v4
    ✓ Login to GHCR
    ✓ Run docker/build-push-action@v2
    ✓ Post Run docker/build-push-action@v2
    ✓ Post Login to GHCR
    ✓ Post Run actions/checkout@v4
    ✓ Complete job
    ...
```

Great! You've automated the building and pushing of your Docker image so that you know that each code submission to your main branch doesn't affect the building of your application. You might already be thinking like a super-powered BEAMOps developer and may have noticed the job is taking 1 minute and 34 seconds to run, which is a long time. Just like earlier, you can shorten this time by using a cache. We'll look at how you can cache your Docker builds in the next section.

Cache Docker Builds

In the previous chapter, we explained Docker's caching system, whereby if layers of a Docker image don't change, they aren't rebuilt on every build but are instead reused and read from Docker's internal cache. In order to cache your Docker build in the CI, you need to add the cache-from and the cache-to keys to the docker/build-push-action step that you created earlier. The cache-from option will reuse any already built layers from the remote registry on subsequent Docker builds. The cache-to option will update the image appended with the :cache tag in the remote registry with any new layers. To use these options of the docker/build-push-action, you'll need to prepend that step with the docker/setup-buildx-action@v3 to set up a buildx builder. A buildx builder extends the basic docker build capabilities, allowing you to use a cache or build and manage multi-architecture images. It's a dependency of the docker/build-push-action when you want to implement a cache. We won't delve into the details of a buildx builder in this book, but we recommend you read their docs[12] because it's a useful tool that provides faster and optimized image builds.

Add the two options that we've mentioned to your existing docker/build-push-action@v2 step, as we've done here, remembering to replace your image name accordingly:

```yaml
# in ci_cd.yaml
jobs:
  build-push:
    runs-on: ubuntu-latest
    needs: ci
    name: Build Docker image & push to ghcr.io
    steps:
      - uses: docker/setup-buildx-action@v3
      - uses: docker/build-push-action@v5
        with:
          context: .
          cache-from: type=registry,ref=ghcr.io/beamops/kanban:cache
          cache-to: type=registry,ref=ghcr.io/beamops/kanban:cache,mode=max
          tags: ${{ steps.meta.outputs.tags }}
          labels: ${{ steps.meta.outputs.labels }}
          push: true
          build-args: |
            ELIXIR_VERSION=${{ env.ELIXIR_VERSION }}
            OTP_VERSION=${{ env.ERLANG_VERSION }}
```

Great! Now commit your changes and push them to your remote repository. When inspecting the most recent run using the gh view run command with the jq helper, remember that the first time the workflow runs, it will take longer because it's the first time the ghcr.io/beamops/kanban:cache image is populated. To see the cache in action, after your run has finished, manually trigger the

---

12. https://docs.docker.com/engine/reference/commandline/buildx/

workflow with the gh workflow run command followed by the name of your workflow file and then inspect the most recent run. You can see our example terminal interaction here:

```
$ gh workflow run ci_cd.yaml
...
$ gh run view --verbose $(gh run list \
            --workflow="ci_cd.yaml" \
            --limit=1 \
            --json databaseId | jq -r '.[0].databaseId')
✓ main CI/CD Elixir · 5081683211
Triggered via workflow_dispatch about 2 minutes ago
JOBS
✓ Compile with mix test, format, dialyzer & unused deps check in 26s ...
    ...
✓ Build Docker image & push to ghcr.io in 24s (ID 13761099732)
    ...
```

You now have a GitHub workflow that validates the integrity of your codebase and builds and pushes your Docker image to the Docker registry! However, depending on the architecture of the processor that your laptop/computer uses, you may not be able to locally run the image that your CI pipeline builds. That's not very environment-integrity-like, is it? We'll explain why this happens in the next section and look at how you can combat it.

Build Multi-Arch Docker Images

At the moment, your CI pipeline uses the default architecture of the docker/build-push-action@v5—an AMD architecture—to build your Docker image. This is a common type of architecture used across many different types of computers and will be the same architecture that your eventual production environment will use. But what happens if your local computer doesn't use an AMD architecture? And what even is the difference between AMD and other architectures?

A common example of computers that don't use an AMD architecture are those built with Apple Silicon chips. These computers use an ARM architecture. The difference between AMD and ARM architectures lies in their binary compatibility. Software compiled for AMD architectures won't run natively on ARM-architectured computers because the underlying CPU instructions that the software is trying to execute either don't exist or behave differently. This means that Docker images built in your CI pipeline which uses an AMD architecture won't run on an ARM system.

If you have an Apple Silicon laptop, for example, you won't be able to locally run the image built using your CI. This is obviously a problem and breaks environment integrity. It means that if you're working with a team of developers who each have different laptops, not all of them will be able to locally debug the remote images.

To check whether you can run the Docker image created by your CI pipeline locally, execute the `docker pull` command as we've done in the next example to pull your CI pipeline's Docker image into your local Docker registry. If you receive an error similar to the following, this means that your computer doesn't use an AMD architecture and you cannot run the remote image:

```
$ docker pull ghcr.io/beamops/kanban:latest
latest: Pulling from beamops/kanban
docker: no matching manifest for linux/arm64/v8 in the manifest list entries.
```

To make sure that everyone in a team can run the Docker images created by your CI regardless of the architecture their computer uses, you need to follow these steps:

1. Install QEMU[13] in your action's runner.

2. Specify the different types of architecture (platforms) that your Docker image should be available for when it's being built.

3. Add an environment variable to your Dockerfile to fix a known bug between QEMU and Erlang.

> **ARM-Specific Step**
>
>  Step 3 in the previous list is only necessary if you're wanting to make your Docker image available for ARM architectures. It's not a required step for making your application available for *all* architecture types.

Let's go through the steps one by one, starting with installing QEMU.

QEMU is an open-source machine emulator that lets you virtualize any system under any architecture. It's the tool that will allow your Docker build action to construct a Docker image that's suitable for multiple architectures. To install QEMU in your runner, you can use the `setup-qemu-action`.[14] Copy the following step so that it sits between your `docker/setup-buildx-action@v3` and `docker/build-push-action@v5` steps like so:

---

13. https://www.qemu.org/
14. https://github.com/docker/setup-qemu-action

```
# in ci_cd.yaml
jobs:
  build-push:
    runs-on: ubuntu-latest
    needs: ci
    name: Build Docker image & push to ghcr.io
    steps:
      - uses: docker/setup-buildx-action@v3

      - name: Set up QEMU
        uses: docker/setup-qemu-action@v3

      - uses: docker/build-push-action@v5
        with:
          context: .
          cache-from: type=registry,ref=ghcr.io/beamops/kanban:cache
          cache-to: type=registry,ref=ghcr.io/beamops/kanban:cache,mode=max
          tags: ${{ steps.meta.outputs.tags }}
```

Perfect. The runner running your action has QEMU installed. Now, for step two: specifying the different architecture types that your Docker image should support. To do this, add the platforms key to the docker/build-push-action@v5 step of your workflow. The platforms key expects a comma-separated list of platform names as a value. To make your Docker image available to be run on both AMD and ARM architectures, you should set the platforms value to be linux/amd64,linux/arm64, as we've done here:

```
- uses: docker/build-push-action@v5
  with:
    context: .
    cache-from: type=registry,ref=ghcr.io/beamops/kanban:cache
    cache-to: type=registry,ref=ghcr.io/beamops/kanban:cache,mode=max
    tags: ${{ steps.meta.outputs.tags }}
    platforms: linux/amd64,linux/arm64
    labels: ${{ steps.meta.outputs.labels }}
    push: true
```

> **A Note About AMD and ARM**
>
>  We've only suggested making your Docker image available for AMD and ARM architectures as those are the most commonly used ones. But you can set other architectures for the platforms key, which you can find in the Docker documentation.[15]

Now, for the last step in making your Docker image available for multiple platforms: adding an environment variable to your Dockerfile so that it can fix a known QEMU-Erlang bug.

---

15. https://docs.docker.com/reference/cli/docker/buildx/build/#platform

The bug between QEMU and Erlang is that the BEAM runs out of memory when trying to install the dependencies for your application due to just-in-time (JIT) compiler optimizations with versions 25+ of OTP. If you're curious for more information, check the QEMU issue on the GitLab site.[16] A workaround to this bug is adding one simple environment variable to the builder stage of your Dockerfile.

The Dockerfile that you created in the previous chapter is a replica of the one that the Phoenix release generator would have provided for you. You implemented the file manually so that you could understand each of the steps. As you'll see in the next chapter, we suggest that you always use the Phoenix release generator to generate your Dockerfile so that you'll have the most up-to-date Docker instructions. Editing a file generated by the Phoenix release generator and adding your own configurations, such as this QEMU environment variable, isn't ideal as it will mean that you'll have to maintain this change anytime you want to upgrade your Dockerfile to the latest version. However, in this case, there is no other way that you can use QEMU and build Docker images for both AMD and ARM architectures. Software is all about trade-offs, and this small trade-off of adding an environment variable will give you the big reward of environment integrity.

The environment variable that you need to add to your Dockerfile to disable this JIT behavior is as follows:

```
# in Dockerfile
FROM ${BUILDER_IMG} AS builder
ENV ERL_FLAGS="+JPperf true"
```

Now that you've made these three changes, commit and push them to GitHub. Fantastic! You've now automated the building of the Docker images in your CI so that each image can be run on both AMD and ARM architectures. This means that everyone in your team will be able to run any of the images created by your pipeline locally on their machine and debug them if necessary. You'll notice that your workflow run will take a long time, just under 10 minutes. This is because you're having to build your image to suit more than one architecture and you're therefore having to re-populate your Docker cache with your changes. Your workflow will be a lot faster on subsequent runs.

---

16. https://gitlab.com/qemu-project/qemu/-/issues/1034

> **ARM-Parallel Step**
>
>
> If you keep the ARM architecture in your platforms key, you'll notice that your workflow will take a long time to run whenever you push code to your repository. If this is a problem for you and you don't need to build your Docker image for ARM architectures, you can remove the linux/arm64 platform. In real-world production environments, we recommend that you build the ARM image in parallel in a separate job. This way deploying your application won't be blocked by having to build both Docker images.

If you were one of the unlucky ones who couldn't pull the remote image earlier, then rerun the docker pull command as before, and you'll see that you can run it without issues (provided that your computer has one of the architectures you supplied in the platforms key of the docker/build-push-action@v5).

Great! It's now time to tweak the triggers for your workflow to control when it runs.

Amend Your GitHub Workflow Triggers

Your current ci_cd.yaml workflow is configured to be triggered on every push to your remote repository. This is okay for initial development purposes but is not optimal in the long term as it will increase your GitHub Actions bill. There are many workflow triggers that you can use.[17] In the real world, you should only run the workflow when a push is made to the default branch (typically main) or when a pull request is opened and pushes are made to the branch of that pull request. To do this, you need to update the on section that you defined at the top of your workflow file so that your existing push option includes a branch restriction. You then need to create another on trigger using the pull_request option, again with a branch restriction. Leave the workflow_dispatch option as it is so you can still manually trigger your workflow. You can see the changes you have to make in this code snippet:

```yaml
# in ci_cd.yaml
on:
  push:
    branches: [main]
  pull_request:
    branches: [main]
  workflow_dispatch:
```

---

17. https://docs.github.com/en/actions/reference/events-that-trigger-workflows

Before committing this change, create a new branch with a name of your choice. Then commit your changes to this new branch and push your commit to your remote repository. If you run gh workflow view --web ci_cd.yaml just after pushing the code, you'll see that, because you changed the on configuration and committed your code to a non-default branch, the workflow hasn't been triggered.

Now create a pull request from your new branch into your main branch using the GitHub CLI. The command to do so is gh pr create. Select the default options for the instructions that appear by pressing Enter and then select "Continue in browser" as we've done here:

```
$ gh pr create
? Where should we push the 'feature-branch' branch? [Use arrows...]
> BeamOps/kanban
...

Creating pull request for feature-branch into main in BeamOps/kanban

? Title (Adds filters to triggers in the ON section)
? Body <Received>
? What's next?   [Use arrows to move, type to filter]
  Submit
  Submit as draft
> Continue in browser
```

Once in the browser, add the issue IDs for the "Elixir integration pipelines" and "Push Docker image to GitHub registry automatically" issues that you created in Chapter 2 to your pull request so that when the pull request is merged, these two ci-cd issues are completed. Once you've created the pull request, you'll see that both of your CI jobs are being run. But the only tags that are being created for your Docker image are the PR and commit sha ones.

Now merge your pull request into the main branch of your repository and then open the Actions tab in the GitHub UI. To do so, you can run the gh workflow view --web ci_cd.yaml command. You'll see that both of your CI jobs have been triggered again, as shown in the following figure. This time, because your CI is being run in main, the :latest Docker image tag will be created.

ci_cd.yaml
on: push

✅ Compile with mix test, for... 33s   ●   ● ✅ Build Docker image & pus... 30s

You've just finished implementing your CI pipeline! Mission accomplished. This gives you a good foundation from which you can build and expand your

CI pipeline. But this isn't set in stone. You should add other tools that you or your team think might be useful and would make your daily workflow easier. These steps could check the test coverage, validate the security of the image that you just pushed to the registry, or whatever else you want. Let's recap what you've learned in this chapter.

What Have You Learned?

In this chapter, you built a CI pipeline for an Elixir-based application using GitHub Actions. You learned the mandatory workflows that you should include and the different ways in which you can trigger a workflow. You considered how you can speed up your development by using the GitHub CLI. Lastly, you added the Docker image that you created in the previous chapter to the CI to ensure that your application properly builds.

Now that you have a comprehensive CI pipeline in place, you can be confident that each pull request that's merged into your main branch is properly compiled, tested, correctly formatted, built, and stored in a registry. This pipeline can be reused in the future to ensure that all of your Elixir projects follow the same standard. You now have a dependable basis from which you can employ the Kaizen principle—continuously improving your codebase with small, ongoing changes.

Now that you know all code that's merged into your main is of the same standard, it's time to homogenize your dev environment using a Docker Compose file. This will allow you to run a multiservice application in the same conditions on any machine and ensure environment integrity. We'll cover this in the next chapter.

> **The Extra Mile**
>
> If you wish to deepen your knowledge of the themes we've covered in this chapter and refine your BEAMOps developer super powers, we've created a few tasks for you to do:
>
> 1. Create an alias in your mix.exs file so that you can run all of your CI steps locally. You could even add a pre-commit hook that runs that alias. This could help you speed up your development process.
>
> 2. Make the cache of your _build and deps folders be dependent on the Elixir and Erlang versions defined in your .tool-versions file.
>
> 3. Add a step to your CI pipeline that checks the test coverage of your project using excoveralls.[a]
>
> ---
> a. https://github.com/parroty/excoveralls

CHAPTER 5

The Dev Environment and Docker Compose

So far, you've planned your project and abstracted the building process of a Phoenix application into a local Docker image. You've added a building step to a CI pipeline that creates an image and stores it in the GitHub Docker registry using GitHub Actions. This is a good start but, right now, your application doesn't depend on any other services and runs independently. This isn't an accurate reflection of a real-world project. More often, applications are made up of one or more services such as web applications, backend APIs, and/or databases.

In this chapter, you'll create an environment-agnostic template for a multiservice application. This will allow you to ensure environment integrity for more complex and realistic projects. To achieve this, you'll add a PostgreSQL (Postgres) database to your application to make it dependent on another service. You'll also use Docker Compose and Docker Swarm to run and orchestrate an application that includes more than one service. By the end of this chapter, you'll be able to easily replicate a multiservice development environment that runs in the same way each time. You'll also be able to close one of the infrastructure GitHub issues that you created in Chapter 2.

Let's jump in and show you how to manually run your database and project at the same time.

Rebuild Your Phoenix Application with Ecto

In Chapter 3, when you created your Phoenix project, you used the --no-ecto flag because we wanted the focus of that chapter to be Docker, not the configuration of a Postgres database. However, in this chapter, we want to show you how to create a reproducible development environment for an application with multiple services. Because of this, you'll need to overwrite your current Phoenix application. Don't worry, the application you'll create will be the exact same application as the one you created in Chapter 3, but with Ecto and the configuration files for a database.

To create this new application, run the same mix phx.new command as you did in Chapter 3, but this time without the --no-ecto flag. You'll see in the upcoming example we've added the --install flag to automatically install the dependencies after the project is created. Like last time, you'll be asked if you want to continue given that the PATH_TO_YOUR_FOLDER already exists. Type "Y" and press Enter. You'll then be asked if you want to override certain files. Type "Y" and press Enter to all them except for the .gitignore. You don't want to override your .gitignore file as it already contains both Elixir and Terraform files that should be ignored. You can see an example terminal interaction here:

```
$ mix phx.new ./ --install
The directory PATH_TO_YOUR_FOLDER already exists.
Are you sure you want to continue? [Yn] Y
* creating config/config.exs
config/config.exs already exists, overwrite? [Yn] Y
* creating config/dev.exs
config/dev.exs already exists, overwrite? [Yn] Y
...
* creating .gitignore
.gitignore already exists, overwrite? [Yn] N
* creating test/support/conn_case.ex
test/support/conn_case.ex already exists, overwrite? [Yn] Y
...
```

You may notice that the installation of this new project overrides your mix.exs file so that new database aliases and dependencies can be created. This means that you'll need to re-add the Dialyxir configurations that you added to your mix.exs file in your old project. You'll find these configurations on page 98.

Now that you've created your new project, you must create both the release files and the Dockerfile. We'll look at a quick and easy way to do these two tasks simultaneously in the next section.

Create a Dockerfile with the Phoenix Release Generator

In this section, you'll update your release helper files so that they include the Ecto configurations. In Chapter 3, you created a Dockerfile for your application that's the same as the Dockerfile that would be created by the Phoenix release generator. But we suggest that you re-create your Dockerfile by passing the --docker flag to the Phoenix release generator. Your current Dockerfile would work perfectly, but using the one created by the Phoenix release generator ensures that you have the most up-to-date Dockerfile possible that includes the most recent Elixir and OTP versions. So, create the release files and a new Dockerfile by running the mix phx.gen.release --docker command as we've done in the following code snippet. When asked if you want to overwrite your existing Dockerfile, type "Y" and press Enter:

```
$ mix phx.gen.release --docker
* creating rel/overlays/bin/server
* creating rel/overlays/bin/server.bat
* creating rel/overlays/bin/migrate
* creating rel/overlays/bin/migrate.bat
...
* creating Dockerfile
Dockerfile already exists, overwrite? [Yn] Y
...
```

As you can see in the previous code snippet, the release configuration folder, rel/overlays/bin, includes a greater number of files than the project you created in Chapter 3. This is because you didn't use the --no-ecto flag. In this folder, you'll now find a new migrate script that runs database migrations, as well as the same server script as before that runs your application. As we'll discuss later in the chapter, these migrations must be run before your application boots to make sure that any new features that require database modifications will work once your application starts.

Before you can use your Dockerfile, you need to add the ERL_FLAGS="+JPperf true" environment variable back in so that your CI can build multi-architecture Docker images. As we said in the previous chapter, having to maintain this environment variable in your Dockerfile each time you want to upgrade it to the latest version provided by the Phoenix release generator isn't ideal. However, it's a small price to pay for ensuring environment integrity by making your CI pipeline able to build multi-architecture Docker images that can be used by everyone in your team whose computers use AMD or ARM processors. Go ahead and add this environment variable back like so:

```
# in Dockerfile
FROM ${BUILDER_IMAGE} as builder
ENV ERL_FLAGS="+JPperf true"
```

Now let's proceed with building and running your release. To achieve this, you'll build a new Docker image and run the resulting Docker container. As you may remember, the command to build a Docker image is docker build. Run this command using a tag of your choice and . as the context, as we've done here:

```
$ docker build --tag kanban:latest .
...
 => exporting to image                                          0.0s
 => => exporting layers                                         0.0s
 => => writing image sha256:4748c46738dd921156809d376a02898...  0.0s
 => => naming to docker.io/library/kanban:latest                0.0s
```

Great. You've added a database to your Phoenix application and rebuilt your Docker image so that it includes these changes. In the next section, you'll manually run your application now that it has two services. While doing so, you'll find out if any extra configuration parameters are missing.

Run Your Multiservice Application Manually

A typical and effective approach for understanding an application's requirements before launching it is to first build the image and then run it. During this process, the application usually throws exceptions if certain requirements or external dependencies aren't met. So, now that your application includes a database, run your Docker container using the command docker run along with the same SECRET_KEY_BASE and port configuration as in Chapter 3. Let's see if your application still behaves in the same way.

```
$ docker run -e SECRET_KEY_BASE="$(mix phx.gen.secret)" \
             -p 4000:4000 \
             "kanban:latest"
ERROR! Config provider Config.Reader failed with:
** (RuntimeError) environment variable DATABASE_URL is missing.
For example: ecto://USER:PASS@HOST/DATABASE

    /app/releases/0.1.0/runtime.exs:26: (file)
    (elixir 1.16.0) src/elixir.erl:309: anonymous fn/4
...
```

As you can see, there is a runtime error telling you that you haven't specified the DATABASE_URL environment variable. You didn't encounter this error in Chapter 3 because you didn't have database support back then. When you omitted the --no-ecto flag and the Phoenix generator created your project, it added a few new configurations—an important one being the following database URL configuration code snippet found in the config/runtime.exs file:

```
# in config/runtime.exs

if config_env() == :prod do
  database_url =
    System.get_env("DATABASE_URL") ||
      raise """
      environment variable DATABASE_URL is missing.
      For example: ecto://USER:PASS@HOST/DATABASE
      """
```

So, you now know that you need to specify a database URL in the form ecto://USER:PASS@HOST/DATABASE for your project to run successfully. Let's create such a URL for a Postgres database. We'll do this in the next section by using the official Postgres Docker image.

Run a Postgres Container

As we mentioned in Chapter 3, there are hundreds of official Docker images that you can use. Before integrating a new technology into your stack, you should always check the official documentation in the Docker Hub for the recommended way to run that image as a container. In the case of Postgres, the docs[1] tell you that you can run a simple Postgres container using the following docker run command:

```
$ docker run --name postgres -e POSTGRES_PASSWORD=postgres -d postgres
```

This command runs a Postgres container, which is based on an image called postgres and determined by the last word of the code line. The container is also called postgres, specified by the --name flag. As the docs explain, this Postgres image, by default (unless you specify otherwise), creates a database called postgres with a user also called postgres. When running the command, it's essential to be explicit about the password, otherwise the container will fail to start and complain about the missing superuser password. In this example, the password given is also postgres. That's a lot of postgres, right? So, run the previous docker run command to start your own Postgres database container.

The exception raised in the previous section explained you need to specify a DATABASE_URL. This looks like ecto://USER:PASS@HOST/DATABASE, with USER, PASS, and DATABASE replaced by the parameters we just looked at. The HOST will be the container name. Your URL should look like the following:

ecto://postgres:postgres@postgres/postgres

Now run your Phoenix application container again using the same command and environment variables as in the previous section but this time adding the new DATABASE_URL environment variable:

```
$ docker run -e DATABASE_URL=ecto://postgres:postgres@postgres/postgres \
             -e SECRET_KEY_BASE="$(mix phx.gen.secret)" \
             -p 4000:4000 \
             kanban:latest
...
[error] Postgrex.Protocol (#PID<0.1819.0>) failed to connect: \
** (DBConnection.ConnectionError) tcp connect (postgres:5432):...
```

---

1. https://hub.docker.com/_/postgres

Uh oh! It appears that there is a problem connecting to the Postgres database from your Phoenix application. This is because, as we explained in Chapter 3, Docker containers run in isolation and aren't aware of the existence of other containers. Communication between containers isn't possible unless the containers belong to the same network. In the next section, we'll discuss what a network is, how to create a network, and how to attach containers to a network.

Before we move on, cancel your failing Phoenix application container. To do this, either press `^C` in your terminal or open another terminal and run `docker rm -f kanban:latest`.

Create a Network and Attach a Container

As we mentioned, Docker containers are isolated by default and are unable to talk to each other. In the case of your Phoenix application, it's unable to access the postgres container you specified as the HOST value in your database URL. For your application to be able to communicate with your Postgres database, you must use a Docker network.

You may be asking yourself why you can't just publish your postgres container to a port on your host machine and then use your laptop as the host for your database URL. Doing so is technically possible, but publishing container ports is insecure by default, meaning that when you publish a container's port, it becomes available not only to the Docker host but to the outside world as well. This means that your database would be accessible outside of Docker, which isn't ideal. A more secure way to access your database is via a Docker network. This way, your host machine won't have access to your database.

Before implementing your network, let's first discuss the different network types, or drivers, available to use. There are six main types of network drivers that Docker provides, but these are the three most commonly used:

- bridge: a private network that's only accessible to containers that use the same host. This is the default network used if you don't specify a driver with the --driver, or -d for short, option when you create the network.

- host: a network that removes network isolation between containers and the Docker host. Containers on this network will use the same network as the host. This provides the same effect as publishing all of the ports to the host machine.

- overlay: a network that connects multiple Docker daemons together and allows containers to communicate with each other across Docker hosts.

This network type is especially important to understand. In subsequent chapters, you'll deploy your application using Docker Swarm to create a distributed environment, and you'll use this type of network driver as it allows communication between containers in a distributed environment.

To create a Docker network, you must use the command `docker network create` followed by the network name. Create a bridge network, the default type, with the name `kanban_network` by running the following command:

```
$ docker network create kanban_network
```

Now, you just need to attach both of your containers to your network so that they can communicate. Let's start with your `postgres` container. To attach a running container, use the `docker network connect NETWORK_NAME CONTAINER_NAME` command. Run that command substituting in the appropriate values like so:

```
$ docker network connect kanban_network postgres
```

Great! Your Postgres database is running on your `kanban_network` network. Let's add your Phoenix application. You stopped running your Phoenix container after it threw an error at the end of the last section. You can attach a network to a nonrunning container at the moment you start running it by adding the `--network` flag followed by the network name to your `docker run` command. As you already have one container running with the name `postgres`, we suggest you also give your Phoenix application container a name when you run it by using the `--name` option. The name we've opted for is `elixir`. Run the `docker run` command with the `--network` option, remembering to add in all the previous environment variables and port configurations when you run the command like so:

```
$ docker run -e "DATABASE_URL=ecto://postgres:postgres@postgres/postgres" \
             -e SECRET_KEY_BASE="$(mix phx.gen.secret)" \
             --network "kanban_network" \
             -p 4000:4000 \
             --name elixir \
             kanban:latest
...
[info] Running KanbanWeb.Endpoint with cowboy 2.10.0 at :::4000
[info] Access KanbanWeb.Endpoint at https://example.com
```

Excellent. The connectivity error disappeared and your Phoenix application container is able to successfully connect to your database!

You may remember that we said you need to run your database migration scripts before starting your application. As you're first starting up the application, this isn't much of an issue, but imagine that you've just implemented a new feature that requires a new column in the database. When you boot your application, you need that column in the database to already exist.

Otherwise, your feature won't work. So, for that column to exist, you need to run the migration scripts before the application starts.

The database migration scripts sit in the application layer, so who should be in charge of running or maintaining these scripts? A backend developer who is able to understand Ecto and Elixir? Or someone from the operations team who is traditionally in charge of operational tasks? It should be someone who understands both of those concepts: a BEAMOps developer. We'll look at how you can run and maintain these migration scripts in the next section.

Release Tasks and Database Migrations

As we mentioned, to ensure your application runs smoothly, any unexecuted migration scripts must be manually run before your application starts. When Phoenix creates your release tasks in rel/overlays/bin, it provides two scripts: the server script to start your application and the migrate script to run your database migrations, as shown here.

```
$ tree rel
rel
└── overlays
    └── bin
        ├── migrate
        ├── migrate.bat
        ├── server
        └── server.bat
```

The tasks in this folder need to be manually run. In the Dockerfile of your project, the CMD value, which is the final binary that will be executed when your container is run, is "/app/bin/server", where /app is the working directory for your application:

```
# in Dockerfile
WORKDIR "/app"
RUN chown nobody /app

# set runner ENV
ENV MIX_ENV="prod"

# Only copy the final release from the build stage
COPY --from=builder --chown=nobody:root /app/_build/${MIX_ENV}/rel/kanban ./

USER nobody

# If using an environment that doesn't automatically reap zombie processes, it is
# advised to add an init process such as tini via `apt-get install`
# above and adding an entrypoint. See https://github.com/krallin/tini for details
# ENTRYPOINT ["/tini", "--"]

CMD ["/app/bin/server"]
```

In the same way that you need to execute the server script to run the application, you need to execute the migration script to perform the database migrations. The way to do this is to override the default CMD value of your Dockerfile. One option is to directly edit the Dockerfile. But we wouldn't recommend doing this as this Dockerfile was created by the Phoenix generator and any changes to this file would need to be maintained. If you were to edit this file directly, you'd not only have to add in the ERL_FLAGS environment variable each time you pulled the latest Docker image from the Phoenix generator using the --docker flag but also this CMD value.

Instead, we recommend that you override the CMD value for your Docker image by passing the migrate script to your docker run command. As the working directory for that container is app, the binary you need to execute is bin/migrate. First, exit out of your running container and remove it using the command docker rm -f elixir. Then rerun your elixir container using the same configuration as before but this time specifying the CMD executable to be the following bash command: bash -c 'bin/migrate && bin/server'. You can see how we've done so here:

```
$ docker rm -f elixir
elixir
$ docker run -e "DATABASE_URL=ecto://postgres:postgres@postgres/postgres" \
             -e SECRET_KEY_BASE="$(mix phx.gen.secret)" \
             --network "kanban_network" \
             --name elixir \
             -p 4000:4000 \
             kanban:latest bash -c 'bin/migrate && bin/server'
[info] Migrations already up
[info] Running KanbanWeb.Endpoint with cowboy 2.10.0 at :::4000
[info] Access KanbanWeb.Endpoint at https://example.com
```

Perfect! You'll see that the migrations are already up-to-date and your application is up and running on port 4000.

As you might have noticed, you've had to run a fair number of commands in this first part of the chapter to ensure your application is working properly. You had to do the following:

1. Create a Docker network.
2. Run a Postgres container and connect it to your network.
3. Run a container using your Phoenix application Dockerfile while attaching it to your network and overriding the CMD binary to execute your migration script before starting your application.

Your BEAMOps sense might be tingling. You might be thinking there's an easier way to do this that's simpler and more declarative. Well, you're right. This is where Docker Compose comes in. In the next section, you'll see how, with one short Docker Compose file, you can use one command to do everything we've done in this section in an easy-to-read and version-controlled manner.

Before moving on, make sure to clean up your current environment by exiting out of your running container, removing both your postgres and elixir containers using the command docker rm -f.

Get to Know Docker Compose

In the first part of this chapter, you needed to execute a lot of manual operations for your Phoenix application to work: you created a network, started your postgres container and attached it to the network, and then started your Phoenix application container, overriding the CMD binary and attaching it to the network. This isn't a huge deal for the time being, but it could become cumbersome when adding more services, or if at some point you need to add a volume to persist data, make changes to the network, and/or restart a policy of a particular container.

This is where Docker Compose comes in. It's a tool that allows you to define and run multi-container applications with Docker in a declarative way. So, what is a Docker Compose file, and how do you run one? We'll answer these questions in the next section.

Docker Compose 101

As we mentioned, Docker Compose, or Compose, is a tool for defining and running multi-container Docker applications. A Dockerfile, which you saw in Chapter 3, only defines the instructions to build and run a specific application. However, a Compose file is a single .yaml file that configures all of your application's services, whether they're images that you've defined in your own Dockerfiles or official public images. Then, with a single docker compose up command, you can create and start all of the services in your Compose configuration file at once.

Using Compose to start all of your application's services avoids the manual work that you saw in the previous section. More importantly, using Compose ensures integrity between environments as long as you use a single file for all of them. A Compose file defines the way in which your application's services relate to each other and the order in which they must be run. This ensures that every machine, and therefore every environment, runs your application in the exact same way. In the next section, we'll look at what a Compose file looks like and discuss its main components.

The Docker Compose File

A Docker Compose file is typically called compose.yaml. But you may see instances of Compose files called docker-compose.yaml, which was how files were named in previous versions of Docker Compose. A Compose file is made up of certain top-level elements, or directives, which each have their own subelement configurations. There are many top-level directives and subelement configurations that you can use in a Compose file, but in this book, we are only going to mention the ones that we'll focus on. If you want to learn more about Docker Compose directives and/or configurations, you can check the official documentation.[2]

Docker Compose Directives

There are six different top-level Docker Compose directives, but the ones we'll use in this chapter are version, services, and volumes.

- version: an optional number value that specifies the Docker Compose version. It should be aligned with the version of Compose you're running. For this book, it will be 3.9.

  ```
  version: "3.9"
  ...
  ```

- services: a required parameter that lists the different services that make up your application suite. Each service is a Docker container. Within each service, you can specify a different Docker image along with its unique configuration. The first top-level configuration for each service is always an ID string that will help you easily identify and differentiate each service. The ID is usually as simple as web or db.

  ```
  ...
  services:
    web:
  ...
  ```

- volumes: an optional parameter that lists the names of the different persistent data stores within your containers. By using volumes, you can ensure that important data remains accessible and persistent even after the containers are stopped or restarted. You may be asking yourself why you'd want to persist data of a Docker container given that one of the key benefits of containers is that they are stateless. Well, think about a database; you don't want to have to repopulate your database every time you start

---

2. https://docs.docker.com/compose/compose-file/

your application, and with volumes you don't have to. To create a volume, use the volumes directive followed by each volume on a new line. Each volume name must finish with a : .

```
...
volumes:
  db_data:
```

The most important and only obligatory directive in a Compose file is the services key. In the next section, we'll look at the most common subelement configurations you can use to customize each of your application services.

Docker Compose Service Configurations

As we mentioned, you can apply many different configurations to your Compose services, but we cannot list them all here. The ones we'll use in this chapter are: image, environment, volumes, ports, command, depends_on, and deploy. For a more comprehensive list, please see the services documentation.[3] Let's briefly define each of the configurations we mentioned.

- image: specifies the Docker image for a service. You can use an image from the Docker Hub, an image you've created yourself, or an image from a private remote repository.

  ```
  services:
    web:
      image: kanban:latest
  ```

- ports: enables communication between the host and the container through the specified ports. This has the same effect as using the --publish flag when running a Docker container.

  ```
  services:
    web:
      ports:
        - "4000:4000"
  ```

- environment: adds environment variables to your Docker service/container.

  ```
  services:
    web:
      environment:
        PHX_HOST: localhost
  ```

- command: overrides the default CMD executable for the container. This takes preference over whatever command was listed in the image Dockerfile:

---

3. https://docs.docker.com/compose/compose-file/05-services/

```
services:
  web:
    command: ls -la
```

- volumes: lists the volume names attached to your container and the path each volume corresponds to in your container. There are two main types of volumes: named volumes and bind mounts. A volume definition is written in the form VOLUME_NAME:CORRESPONDING_CONTAINER_PATH.

To attach a named volume called db_data to a folder named /container_db_data inside a db container, you'd write the following:

```
services:
  db:
    volumes:
      - db_data:/container_db_data
```

You can share volumes between containers, meaning that more than one container can have access to all of the data inside a volume. To do this, you'd define the volume in a second service in exactly the same way as the previous example. But the container path doesn't have to be the same: the folder could be named container_db_data in one container and my_db_data in another. Although the paths are different, the data in the specified folders will be the same in both containers.

If you're sharing a volume between containers, you must define the volume in the top-level volumes directive, as we saw earlier. But if you're only using a volume in one container, it's not strictly necessary to list the volume under the top-level volumes directive. Nonetheless, we recommend that you always define every volume in your Compose file under the top-level volumes directive so that it's clear to anyone reading the file which volumes your Compose file uses. This will also save you debugging time in the future if after using a volume in one container, you then decide to use that same volume for another.

Lastly, a bind mount volume is one that's shared with the host machine. This means that any changes made to the folder inside the Docker container will be reflected in a folder of the same name in the directory where the Compose file sits inside the host machine and vice versa. To create a host-container-shared bind mount volume, prepend the previous volume definition with ${PWD}/, like so:

```
services:
  db:
    volumes:
      - ${PWD}/db_data:/container_db_data
```

Unlike named volumes where you need to specify the volume name using the volumes top-level directive, bind mount volumes don't need to be referenced in the volumes top-level directive.

- depends_on: expresses a dependency between services. This has implications for the order in which services start up and shut down. If you add this configuration to a service, that service won't start until the service corresponding to the ID given as the depends_on value has successfully started.

  ```
  services:
    web:
      depends_on:
        - db
  ```

- deploy: specifies the runtime configuration requirements for the deployment and lifecycle of a service. This attribute and its subconfigurations will only be read when your services are started as part of a swarm. It will be ignored if you start your service with the docker compose up command, which we'll discuss later. A common subconfiguration of this attribute is the restart_policy, which we'll discuss next.

  ```
  services:
    web:
      deploy:
        restart_policy:
          condition: on-failure
  ```

- restart_policy: a subconfiguration of the deploy subelement that defines the restart policy for a service when it's started as part of a swarm. This is helpful in case of a service error/failure or when the Docker daemon restarts. There are three possible restart condition subconfiguration keys:

  - none: do not automatically restart the container.
  - on-failure: only restart the container if it exits with a non-zero exit status. As we'll see later in the chapter, you may also, optionally, limit the number of restart retries that the Docker daemon attempts.
  - any: always restart the container. This is the default restart_policy state.

  ```
  services:
    db:
      deploy:
        restart_policy:
          condition: on-failure
  ```

Now that you're familiar with what a Docker Compose file looks like, we'll look at four basic Docker Compose commands.

Docker Compose Commands

To interact with your Compose files, you'll use the Docker Compose CLI: docker compose. This CLI comes as part of the basic Docker Desktop installation and is followed by certain options and commands like so:

```
docker compose [OPTIONS] [COMMAND]
```

A common option used with docker compose is --file, or -f for short, to specify a certain Compose file for the given command. If you only have one Compose file in the path where you execute your command, the -f isn't necessary. It's possible to pass multiple -f flags to one docker compose command to build multiple configurations at once.

There are four main Compose commands that you'll regularly use to interact with your Compose file: docker compose up, docker compose stop, docker compose start, and docker compose down. There are of course more commands, and if you're curious, check out the Compose CLI documentation.[4]

The docker compose up command creates and starts all of the services listed in your Compose file. It follows this format:

```
docker compose up [OPTIONS] [SERVICE...]
```

It's possible to isolate certain services in your Docker Compose file and only start one service. To do this, you'd write docker compose up SERVICE_NAME. If you do this and the service has a depends_on configuration, the dependency services will also be started. If you run the command docker compose up without any arguments, all of the services in your application suite will start.

When you run docker compose up, the terminal in which the command was run outputs the logs of the containers that are run. If you wish to start your application suite without the terminal logs, you can use the --detach, or -d for short, option. This will run the suite in the background.

The docker compose stop command stops containers without removing them. It follows this format:

```
docker compose stop [OPTIONS] [SERVICE...]
```

If you choose not to run your containers in the background, it's also possible to stop your containers by executing Ctrl+C in the terminal in which they are running.

---

4. https://docs.docker.com/compose/reference/

The docker compose start command starts already created but stopped containers:

```
docker compose start [OPTIONS] [SERVICE...]
```

When you edit a Compose file and want to apply those changes, you can either use docker compose up or docker compose start.

The docker compose down command removes containers and networks. It follows this format:

```
docker compose down [OPTIONS] [SERVICE...]
```

This command does leave volumes intact, though, which is why volumes are persistent. Nonetheless, it's possible to forcibly delete all the volumes defined in a file by passing the --volumes, or -v for short, parameter.

> **The Power of down and up**
>
>  The docker compose down command is important because any time you make a change to your Compose file, you must stop your containers and rerun them for those changes to take effect. We recommend using the down and up commands instead of the stop and start ones in this scenario. This will allow you to start with a clean slate every time you make a change.

Internally, Compose caches the configuration used to create a container. If you start, or try to create, a service that hasn't changed, Compose reuses the existing container. This means that if you edit only one service in a Docker Compose file, stop all the containers, and then restart them again, Docker will use the cached version of all of the files, except the one you changed, which it will re-create.

Right, that's enough theory. Let's get to it and create your first Docker Compose file!

Create Your First Docker Compose File

You know that for your application to run properly, you need to have Postgres database before you start your application. So let's start by creating a Compose file that has a Postgres service. To do this, create a file called compose.yaml in the root of your project. In the next section, you'll define the Postgres service.

Create a Docker Compose Postgres Service

Let's add a service based on the same postgres Docker image you used in the first section of this chapter. As always, go to the Docker Hub and look for official documentation[5] for this image. There, you'll see that they have a Docker Compose example implementation that creates a db service and an adminer service; we'll only be creating the db service for now. To create your db service, copy the following code snippet into your compose.yaml file:

```yaml
# in compose.yaml
version: "3.9"
services:
  db:
    image: postgres
    healthcheck:
      test: ["CMD", "pg_isready", "--username=postgres"]
      interval: 10s
      timeout: 5s
      retries: 5
    deploy:
      restart_policy:
        condition: on-failure
    environment:
      POSTGRES_PASSWORD: postgres
```

In the previous code snippet, we've slightly edited the example given in the docs. Rather than using the version they specify, we are using the most up-to-date Compose version, as of the time of this writing. As you can see, this snippet defines one service, called db, which uses the official postgres image. We've added a pg_isready health check to this database, which checks if the Postgres server is accepting connections every ten seconds, waiting for five seconds for a response, and trying this a maximum of five times.

The container's restart policy is set to on-failure using the deploy and restart_policy configuration parameters. We haven't used the restart key given in the documentation as that configuration is ignored when you run your application as part of a swarm. Lastly, the POSTGRES_PASSWORD environment variable has been set to postgres. This variable is sensitive information and shouldn't be hard-coded; we'll look at how you can make this variable secret in Chapter 7. For now though, as you're developing locally, leave the example password in the file.

By default, this image also sets the user and database names to be postgres. This means that the previous example defines the exact same parameters, with the addition of the restart policy, to the ones you specified in your docker run --name postgres -e POSTGRES_PASSWORD=postgres -d postgres command in the first section of this chapter.

---

5. https://hub.docker.com/_/postgres

Now that your compose.yaml file is ready, start your db service using the command docker compose up:

```
$ docker compose up
[+] Running 2/2
 ✓ Network kanban_default   Created                                    0.0s
 ✓ Container kanban-db-1    Created                                    0.0s
kanban-db-1  | The files ... will be owned by user "postgres".
kanban-db-1  | This user must also own the server process.
kanban-db-1  |
kanban-db-1  | The db ... be initialized with locale "en_US.utf8".
kanban-db-1  | The default database encoding ... set to "UTF8".
...
```

Great! Your postgres container has started! You'll notice that a network was automatically created, even though you didn't specify one in your compose.yaml file. By default, Compose sets up a single network for your app. Each container for a service joins the default network and is reachable by other containers on that network. This means that when automating the manual steps that you followed in the first part of this chapter to run your application, you don't need to worry about attaching your containers to networks.

Try to connect to your database from your local machine in a new terminal using the psql command. You can see how we've done this in the following terminal interaction:

```
$ psql -h localhost -U postgres
psql: error: connection to server at "localhost" (::1), port 5432 failed:
        Connection refused
        Is the server running on that host and accepting TCP/IP
        connections?
connection to server at "localhost" (127.0.0.1), port 5432 failed:
        Connection refused
        Is the server running on that host and accepting TCP/IP
        connections?
```

Oops! The connection is being refused. Can you think of a reason why? That's right—it's because you never exposed the port. Remember that containers run in isolation, and if you want to access them from the host, you must explicitly expose the port. We'll look at how you can do that with Docker Compose in the next section.

Conditionally Expose Your Postgres Port

You weren't able to connect to your postgres database because you were trying to connect from your local machine but had not exposed any ports. Go ahead and check the status of your running containers by executing docker ps in a new terminal, as we've done here:

```
$ docker ps
CONTAINER ID     IMAGE        ...    CREATED      ...    PORTS        ...
e91bb95066c4     postgres     ...    41 hours     ...    5432/tcp     ...
```

If you look at the PORTS column, you'll see 5432/tcp. As there is no "->" in the port description, the postgres container is only running on port 5432 within Docker. This should always be the case in production, but when you're developing locally, you might want to access your database from your host. So, add a port configuration to your compose.yaml file to the end of your db service, using the ports key configuration. This way, your database will be available on port 5432 in your localhost. Have a go at doing so before looking at how we did it in the upcoming snippet:

```
# in compose.yaml
services:
  db:
    ports:
      - ${POSTGRES_PORT:-5432}
```

Now, apply these changes to your container and restart your db service by stopping your running container and executing docker compose down and then docker compose up like so:

```
$ docker compose down
  [+] Running 2/0
  ✓ Network kanban_default    Removed                    0.0s
  ✓ Container kanban-db-1     Removed                    0.0s
$ docker compose up
  [+] Running 2/2
  ✓ Network kanban_default    Created                    0.0s
  ✓ Container kanban-db-1     Created                    0.0s
......
```

Then try to connect to your database via psql again in another terminal. You'll see that there's no connection error and your database is prompting you for a password, as the following example indicates:

```
$ psql -h localhost -U postgres
Password for user postgres:
```

We won't access the database right now, so Ctrl+C that last command. Do the same in your running container.

Super! You were able to connect to your db service from your localhost! However, as this Compose file will be used for all environments, to ensure environment integrity and security, you don't want to have the exposed ports hard-coded. Instead, you should create a POSTGRES_PORT environment variable that you can optionally set when you run the docker compose up command to expose the ports. This POSTGRES_PORT should have a default value that does not expose the container to the host machine. To do this, edit the port assignation in your file to read like this:

```
# in compose.yaml
services:
  db:
    ports:
      - ${POSTGRES_PORT:-5432}
```

The ${POSTGRES_PORT:-5432} port assignation in the previous code snippet means that if the POSTGRES_PORT variable is defined, then that variable will be used; but if it doesn't exist, the default value is 5432. When assigning Docker ports, if you only specify one number, such as 5432, then you're only specifying the port in the Docker container. But if you specify two numbers, such as 5432:5432, then you're mapping the port to the host machine.

A handy way to check the configuration of the services in your Compose file is to use the command docker compose config. This command doesn't tell you the state of your current running container, but it reads the last saved version of your Compose file and tells you what the rendered result will be. So now that you've added the conditional POSTGRES_PORT variable, run the command docker compose config. This will tell you the state of a container were you to run the Compose file without specifying the POSTGRES_PORT variable. Your output should look like this (you might have to scroll down a bit in your terminal output):

```
$ docker compose config
...
services:
  db:
    ...
    ports:
    - mode: ingress
      target: 5432
      protocol: tcp
    ...
```

You can see that there's no published key in the previous code example. This means that your database is only running inside Docker.

Now, run the same docker compose config command again, but this time prepend the command with POSTGRES_PORT=5432:5432 to set the environment variable, as we've done here:

```
$ POSTGRES_PORT=5432:5432 docker compose config
...
services:
  db:
    ...
    ports:
    - mode: ingress
      target: 5432
      published: "5432"
      protocol: tcp
    restart: always
    ...
```

Now you can see that when you set that environment variable, the container port is published. Perfect! You now have a Compose file that you can use in any environment. In the next section, we'll look at how you can lock, or pin, an image version to preserve the integrity of your application.

Pin the Postgres Image Version

Because updates in new versions of Docker images may deprecate certain features that you use, it's important to pin the image version to your image definition in your Compose file. By pinning an image version, you ensure consistent deployment across all environments, maintaining system integrity. You can do this by adding a : to your Docker image definition followed by the image version number. Go ahead and update your postgres image definition so that your file uses version 15.2, like so:

```
# in compose.yaml
version: "3.9"
services:
  db:
    image: postgres:15.2

    healthcheck:
      test: ["CMD", "pg_isready", "--username=postgres"]
      interval: 10s
      timeout: 5s
      retries: 5
```

Now rerun your container by running docker compose down and then POSTGRES_PORT=5432:5432 docker compose up. You should see that when the image starts, the terminal output shows that the PostgreSQL version used is 15.2, like this:

```
$ docker compose down
[+] Running 2/0
 ✓ Container kanban-db-1       Removed ...
 ✓ Network kanban_default      Removed ...
```

```
$ POSTGRES_PORT=5432:5432 docker compose up
...
db    | 2023-07-21 12:24:34.135 UTC [1] LOG:    starting PostgreSQL 15.2 ...
...
```

Great! Now let's talk a bit more about volumes and how you can persist your database values. As Docker containers are stateless by default, if volumes are not used to explicitly retain files between container runs, any file system changes made in a previous container run are lost when the container restarts. In the case of your postgres database container, this would mean that each time your container starts after you run a docker compose down, your database would be empty and none of the values that you had previously saved would exist. That kind of defeats the point of a database, doesn't it? But with Docker volumes, you can persist file-system changes between container runs; you can save database values to a Docker volume and access them in subsequent container instances. Let's look at how they work in more detail.

Explicit Volumes

As we said earlier, volumes are used to persist container data even after the containers have been stopped with docker compose stop or removed with docker compose down. Let's see what happens with data in the postgres container after making changes to your database when you haven't specified a volume in your Compose file.

First, restart your db service in detached mode so that it runs in the background. Do this by canceling your running container and executing the commands docker compose down and POSTGRES_PORT=5432:5432 docker compose up -d. (We have suggested running the service in detached mode here because you've already tested that your database starts properly.)

Next, run the create task that's provided by the Ecto library in your current working directory by running mix ecto.create. This task will create a table in your database called schema_migrations and can only be run once. (We're using this particular task on its own now to easily create database changes, but you won't need to run this once you add your application to your Compose file because this is part of the migrations task.)

Next, *stop* your service using docker compose stop, restart it using POSTGRES_PORT=5432:5432 docker compose start -d, and run the ecto create task again. This task will output a message to your console saying the database has already been created. Now, *remove your service entirely* using the docker compose down command. Then restart it again and run the create task once more. You'll see that the create task was run without any issues. Here's the whole session:

```
$ docker compose down
  [+] Running 2/0
  ✓ Network kanban_default   Removed                          0.0s
  ✓ Container kanban-db-1    Removed                          0.0s
$ POSTGRES_PORT=5432:5432 docker compose up -d
  [+] Running 2/2
  ✓ Network kanban_default   Created                          0.0s
  ✓ Container kanban-db-1    Started                          0.0s
$ mix ecto.create
The database for Kanban.Repo has been created
$ docker compose stop
  [+] Stopping 1/1
  ✓ Container kanban-db-1    Stopped                          0.2s
$ POSTGRES_PORT=5432:5432 docker compose start
  [+] Running 1/1
  ✓ Container kanban-db-1    Started                          0.2s
$ mix ecto.create
The database for Kanban.Repo has already been created
$ docker compose down
  [+] Running 2/0
  ✓ Network kanban_default   Removed                          0.0s
  ✓ Container kanban-db-1    Removed                          0.0s
$ POSTGRES_PORT=5432:5432 docker compose up -d
  [+] Running 2/2
  ✓ Network kanban_default   Created                          0.0s
  ✓ Container kanban-db-1    Started                          0.0s
$ mix ecto.create
The database for Kanban.Repo has been created
```

The line that reads The database for Kanban.Repo has already been created in the previous terminal output (after you ran the mix ecto.create command for the second time) means that data, specifically the schema_migrations table created by the first mix ecto.create command, seems to have been persisted from your first service run after you stopped the container. How is this possible when you haven't specified a volume and we said that Docker containers are stateless? To be honest, there's a bit of behind-the-scenes magic going on here.

If you take a look at the Dockerfile[6] that the postgres image is created from, you'll see that it has its own volume defined in the /var/lib/postgresql/data directory. This means that the data that's stored in this directory will persist if the container is *stopped*. This is good, but you can see that when you *removed* the service by running docker compose down and restarted it again, the schema_migrations table was no longer there.

This is because volumes defined in a *Dockerfile* are assigned random names when they are created. So, when a container is *stopped* and then *started*

---

6. https://github.com/docker-library/postgres/blob/master/15/bullseye/Dockerfile#L189

again it uses the same volume. However, when the container is *removed*, even though the volume isn't deleted, the next time the image is used to create a new container a new random volume is created and attached.

On the other hand, when a volume is explicitly defined in a *Compose file*, Compose always creates a volume with the same name (if it hasn't been already created) and so attaches and unattaches containers to their volumes when they are created, stopped, and removed. This ensures the stateless principle of Docker containers while also allowing you to persist data across container runs, which is useful for scenarios such as databases.

The volume configuration for this postgres image is a bit confusing, and it's not immediately obvious that there's a volume in play when you look at the Compose file. The best way to deal with volumes, especially if you're using an image that implicitly creates them, is to always be explicit and define volumes directly in your Docker Compose file. Let's do just that.

Create a volume in your Docker Compose file called db_data that points to /var/lib/postgresql/data in the container and create an environment variable called PGDATA that points to the same directory—just as the Dockerfile for the postgres image does. Have a go at doing this yourself before looking at the next example to see our updated file:

```yaml
# in compose.yaml
version: "3.9"
services:
  db:
    image: postgres:15.2
    healthcheck:
      test: ["CMD", "pg_isready", "--username=postgres"]
      interval: 10s
      timeout: 5s
      retries: 5
    deploy:
      restart_policy:
        condition: on-failure
    environment:
      POSTGRES_PASSWORD: postgres
      PGDATA: /var/lib/postgresql/data
    ports:
      - ${POSTGRES_PORT:-5432}
    volumes:
      - db_data:/var/lib/postgresql/data
volumes:
  db_data:
```

Well done. You just defined your first volume! Now, restart your container and apply your new changes by running docker compose down to remove the temporary volume and then POSTGRES_PORT=5432:5432 docker compose up -d to start the service. Then, run the same mix ecto.create task as before to create the schema_migrations table. Now repeat the same process again. Restart your container, this time using the docker compose down command rather than docker compose stop, and then rerun the mix ecto.create task. You'll see that, unlike last time, the message saying that the schema_migrations table has already been created is still there, meaning that data is now being persisted even after the container is removed. We've pasted the example terminal interaction here:

```
$ docker compose down
  ✓ Network kanban_default   Removed                        0.0s
  ✓ Container kanban-db-1    Removed                        0.0s
$ POSTGRES_PORT=5432:5432 docker compose up -d
  ✓ Network kanban_default       Created                    0.0s
  ✓ Volume "kanban_db_data"      Created                    0.0s
  ✓ Container kanban-db-1        Started                    0.0s
$ mix ecto.create
  The database for Kanban.Repo has been created
$ docker compose down
...
$ POSTGRES_PORT=5432:5432 docker compose up -d
  [+] Running 2/2
  ✓ Network kanban_default       Created                    0.0s
  ✓ Container kanban-db-1        Started                    0.0s
$ mix ecto.create
  The database for Kanban.Repo has already been created
```

Your volume works! You can successfully save data to your container and access that same data even after removing the container. You've owned the volume creation and configured the postgres service to use it!

> **Aliases in mix.exs**
>
>  In this section, we've used mix ecto.create to show why you'd use explicit volumes. However, there are interesting aliases in your mix.exs like mix ecto.setup and mix ecto.reset. Setup will create the database, run the migrations, and seed the database. Reset will drop your database and then run mix ecto.setup.

Before we move on, let's sum up your progress so far. In this section, you've created a Compose file that allows you to run a Postgres service with a pinned version, ensuring the integrity of your service across environments. You've also added a variable to control the port exposure with a default value for production. Finally, you've added an explicit volume to the db service to ensure that data is persisted even if the container is removed.

When working in development, it isn't strictly necessary to have data persist between Docker container runs. However, we strongly suggest using the same file for both production and development to keep environment integrity. Being able to accurately replicate production scenarios in development will help you be sure of how your development features will behave in production and debug any errors that arise.

In the next section, you'll perform the final step in creating your Compose file: adding your Phoenix application as a service.

Add Your Phoenix Application

In the previous section, you saw how to add a Postgres service to your Compose file. Now it's time to turn your attention to your Phoenix application. This will be much simpler as you're using an image that you built, and no funny business is involved. All you need to do is replicate how you ran the application in the first section of the chapter. Recall that you had to go through these steps:

1. Create a Docker network.
2. Make sure your database is started (and added to your network).
3. Run a container using your Phoenix application Dockerfile while attaching it to your network and overriding the CMD binary to execute your migration script before starting your application.

You've already defined your database in your Compose file. You don't have to worry about creating a Docker network and attaching it to either your Phoenix app or your database. As you saw earlier, Compose implicitly creates a network for the services defined in a file and attaches all of the services to that network. If you take a look at the output of any of the docker compose up commands that you've run in this chapter so far, you'll see that they say this:

```
$ docker compose up
✓ Network kanban_default  Created
```

Unless you want to explicitly split up the services in your Compose file so that certain services use different networks, you don't need to use the networks top-level directive. So you don't have to worry about replicating that step.

To add your Phoenix application to your Compose file, you'll need to follow these steps:

1. Create a new service called web.
2. Specify the image name for your application. The image should be settable if the WEB_IMAGE variable is passed when running your Compose file. The

default value should be the latest image uploaded to the GitHub Docker registry. Defining your image in this way means that you'll be able to run any version of your application at will, but that the default image will always be the most updated and tested one in the registry.

3. Specify the DATABASE_URL environment variable.
4. Specify the SECRET_KEY_BASE environment variable.
5. Specify the PHX_HOST environment variable. This is a variable that will be needed for security when you deploy your application to your distributed production environment to control where incoming requests come from. For now, set this variable's value to be localhost.
6. Map the Docker port to your localhost.
7. Add an on-failure restart_policy that has a 20-second delay, a maximum attempt number of 3, and a window of 120 seconds.
8. Run the migrate script.
9. Start the server after the migration script has finished.

Let's start with the first seven items in the list: specifying your image, creating the three environment variables using the environment directive, mapping port 4000 using the ports directive, and adding the restart_policy. Try doing this yourself before looking at how we did it in here:

```yaml
# in compose.yaml
version: "3.9"
services:
  db:
    image: postgres:15.2
    healthcheck:
      test: ["CMD", "pg_isready", "--username=postgres"]
      interval: 10s
      timeout: 5s
      retries: 5
    deploy:
      restart_policy:
        condition: on-failure
    environment:
      POSTGRES_PASSWORD: postgres
      PGDATA: /var/lib/postgresql/data/pgdata
    ports:
      - ${POSTGRES_PORT:-5432}
    volumes:
      - db_data:/var/lib/postgresql/data
```

```
  web:
    image: ${WEB_IMAGE:-ghcr.io/beamops/kanban:latest}
    deploy:
      restart_policy:
        condition: on-failure
        delay: 5s
        max_attempts: 3
        window: 120s
    environment:
      DATABASE_URL: ecto://postgres:postgres@db/postgres
      SECRET_KEY_BASE: 9wORvLm5m1U0awC8RCj4ASIwXgcSzIYBiUqU8yzyF...
      PHX_HOST: "localhost"
    ports:
      - 4000:4000
volumes:
  db_data:
```

>  **Generate Your Own SECRET_KEY_BASE**
>
> You must generate your own SECRET_KEY_BASE value rather than copying ours. Remember you can do this using the mix phx.gen.secret command.

Great! Now you can create your web service by restarting your Compose file and executing docker compose down followed by docker compose up. When starting your application, set the WEB_IMAGE variable to be the local image you created in the "Installing Phoenix with Ecto" section of this chapter. You can't use the image stored in the GitHub Docker Registry yet as the CI you created in the previous chapter hasn't run yet and so your new image with your database configurations hasn't been pushed. Your terminal should look like this:

```
$ docker compose down
...
$ WEB_IMAGE="kanban:latest" docker compose up
...
web   | 14:20:08.184 [error] ... (#PID<0.1725.0>) failed to connect: \
** (DBConnection.ConnectionError) tcp connect (db:5432): connection refused
```

Oops, an error! The web service is unable to connect to the database. This is because the web service has started before the database is ready to accept connections. You may not have seen this error in your terminal because your host may have luckily finished creating your database before your web service booted. However, that's not a sure thing, and you need to always ensure that your web service doesn't start until your database is reachable. You can do this by adding the depends_on configuration, with the value db to the end of your web service like so:

```
# in compose.yaml
  web:
    depends_on:
      - db
```

Now, restart your Compose file again by doing a `docker compose down` followed by `docker compose up`. You should see that your application starts up without any issues.

There's only one step left to add to your Docker Compose file! The last thing you need to do is override the `CMD` value so the database migration script is run before the server is started. To do so, add the `command` directive to the end of your `web` service as we've done in the upcoming example, with the value set to the same `bash -c "bin/migrate && bin/server"` command you ran in the first section of this chapter. The end of your `web` service should now look like this:

```
# in compose.yaml
  web:
    depends_on:
      - db
    command: >
      bash -c "bin/migrate && bin/server"
```

Last step done! If you restart your Compose file for the final time, you'll see that your application is up and running and that the database migrations are up-to-date. Go ahead and admire your handiwork in port 4000 of your browser. Congratulations! That was hard work!

You've implemented a Docker Compose file that allows you to run your application which is made of a `web` service and a `postgres` service. Amazing!

Now that your application is composed of multiple services and your Phoenix application depends on a Postgres database, you must update your CI/CD workflow that you created in the previous chapter to include a Postgres database. Otherwise, the test step in your workflow won't run properly. You'll do this in the next section.

Update Your CI/CD Workflow to Include a PostgreSQL Database

If you left your current CI/CD workflow as is without starting a PostgreSQL database, your workflow wouldn't pass because your Phoenix application wouldn't be able to connect to a database. You'd see the following database connection error in the `Run tests` step of your `ci` job:

```
Error: ... [error] Postgrex.Protocol (#PID<0.303.0>) failed to connect:
** (DBConnection.ConnectionError) tcp connect (localhost:5432):
connection refused - :econnrefused
```

To solve this, you must add the following services configuration to the beginning of your ci job in your ci_cd.yaml file:

```yaml
# in workflows/ci_cd.yaml
jobs:
  ci:
    runs-on: ubuntu-latest
    name: Compile with mix test, format, dialyzer & unused deps check
    env:
      MIX_ENV: test
    services:
      postgres:
        image: postgres:15.2
        env:
          POSTGRES_PASSWORD: postgres
        ports:
          - 5432:5432
        options: >-
          --health-cmd pg_isready
          --health-interval 10s
          --health-timeout 5s
          --health-retries 5
```

The services key in a GitHub Action job creates a Docker container on the machine running your workflow with the name you specify. A service container provides a simple and portable way for you to host helper services that you might need to test or operate an application in a workflow. In this instance, you're using the postgres Docker image to run a Postgres database with its default configurations just as you did in the first section of this chapter. And as before, both the username and password values for this default database are postgres. This CI service uses version 15.2 of Postgres—the same version you used in your Compose file. This service has the same health checks as your db service in your Compose file.

Now that you've finished writing your first Compose file and you've updated your CI to accommodate the addition of a database to your Phoenix application, you can close the GitHub issue you created in Chapter 2 titled "Create a Docker Compose file." To do so, create a new branch, commit your file, and create and merge a pull request that includes the issue's ID in its description. When you open and merge your PR, you'll see your CI running (it may take a while as your 'mix.lock' file has changed and so not all your cache can be used).

With your Docker Compose file you can quickly start up a single instance of your multiservice application in any environment. But what if you want to make your application highly available and deploy it in a distributed environment that uses several nodes? The answer: use Docker Swarm! We'll look at Docker Swarm and its benefits in the next section.

Before moving on, remember to clean up your containers and volumes by running the `docker compose down -v` command.

Get to Know Docker Swarm

Docker Swarm is a container orchestration tool built and managed by Docker. It allows you to manage a distributed environment in which you can have multiple containers deployed across multiple host machines. There are other orchestration tools out there, such as Kubernetes (k8s) or AWS ECS, but we chose Docker Swarm because Docker is the most well-known tool for the majority of the developers out there—and we would love for them to jump over the fence into the operations domain. After all, this book is about bringing people together and stressing the importance of communication, collaboration, empathy, and environmental integrity.

When you use a Docker Compose file and do a `docker compose up`, you only have one instance of each service. However, if you use a Compose file in conjunction with Docker Swarm and execute the command `docker stack deploy`, you can have multiple container instances distributed across different host machines, or nodes. One of the key advantages of swarm services over standalone containers is that you can modify a service's configuration, including the networks and volumes it's connected to, without the need to manually restart the service. The Docker Swarm architecture is made up of four main concepts:

1. `swarm`: A swarm is a group of host machines running Docker that form a cluster. Each machine, or Docker instance, is referred to as a node.

2. `node`: A node is a Docker instance that participates in a swarm. A node can be either a manager node or a worker node. Manager nodes handle swarm management tasks, and worker nodes handle the running of services and tasks, which we'll look at next. All manager nodes are also workers, so services and tasks can also be run on manager nodes.

3. `service`: A service is the primary root of user interaction with the swarm. Like a service in a Docker Compose file, a swarm service defines the tasks that should be executed on a node.

4. `tasks`: a task is a running instance of a service. The output of a task being run on a node is a running container.

The following image demonstrates a visualization of a multinode swarm which runs your compose.yaml file with a few alterations. It has three replicas of your web service and one db service:

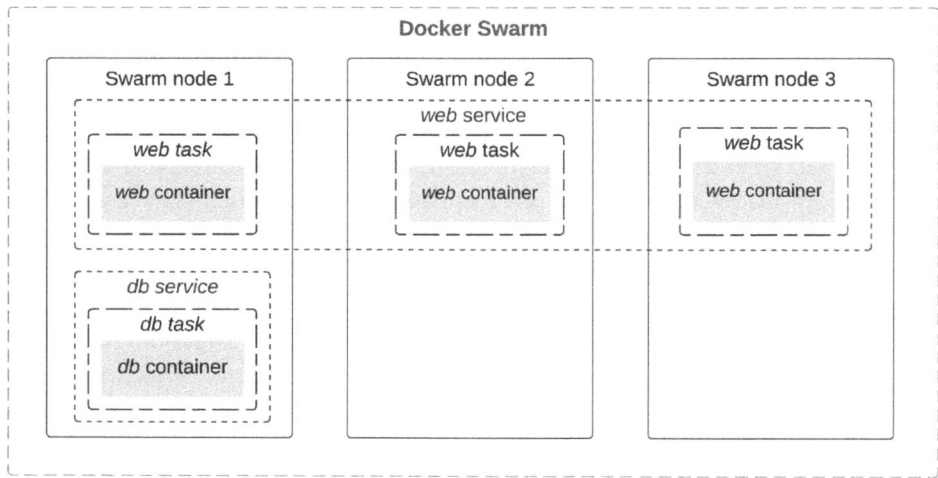

A container is the running instance of an application. A task is an instance of a service running on a specific swarm node. It's in charge of restarting a container if it fails. A service is a higher-level abstraction that defines how its tasks should be deployed. It's in charge of managing the task.

Now that you understand the four basic Docker Swarm concepts, we'll look at the different CLI commands that you can execute for each concept.

Docker Swarm CLI Commands

The Docker Swarm CLI, like the Docker Compose CLI, is part of the basic Docker Desktop installation. The CLI command is docker swarm and is followed by further subcommands, as you can see here:

```
docker swarm [COMMAND]
```

We've grouped the subcommands according to the key concepts that they relate to.

Docker Swarm Commands

The first command is to create a Docker Swarm, which you can do by executing docker swarm init. This command is formatted as follows:

```
docker swarm init [OPTIONS]
```

Running this command from a terminal makes the machine from where the command was run the swarm manager node. This command, as you'll see when you create your own swarm later in the chapter, outputs a command and token that you can use to add nodes to your swarm.

Next, let's look at the commands that nodes use to interact with a swarm.

Swarm Node Commands

The two commands that you'll use when adding or removing nodes from a Docker swarm are: docker swarm join and docker swarm leave. The first is formatted as follows:

```
docker swarm join [OPTIONS] HOST:PORT
```

In order for a node to join a swarm, you need to specify the swarm manager node's IP as well as the port. You also need to pass the --token option. This token is given to you when you initialize the swarm.

By contrast, to leave a Docker Swarm, the command is docker swarm leave. It is formatted as follows:

```
docker swarm leave [OPTIONS]
```

If the node you want to remove is a worker node, then you can execute this command without any options. However, if it's the last manager node, you will need to use the --force option.

The docker node ls Command

A helpful command to list all the nodes in a Docker Swarm is docker node ls. This command can only be run on the swarm manager node.

Now, let's move on to swarm service commands.

Swarm Service Commands

As we mentioned, services are the blueprints that create tasks, which then create Docker containers. They are the same as the services defined in a Compose file. All service commands must be executed from a swarm's manager node. Here are the five important commands, followed by their definitions:

- docker service create
- docker stack deploy
- docker service update
- docker service scale
- docker service ls

To manually create a swarm service, use the command docker service create. It is formatted as follows:

```
docker service create [OPTIONS] IMAGE [COMMAND] [ARG...]
```

While the previous command does create swarm services, it isn't the best way to create services for an application—doing things manually is never ideal. Instead, you should use the docker stack deploy command. This command enables you to deploy, or create, all the services listed in a Compose file. It's the very reason that we chose to use Docker Compose and Docker Swarm as the tools to run your application. They fit like a glove and make ensuring environment integrity among deployments incredibly easy. The docker stack deploy command is formatted as follows:

```
docker stack deploy [OPTIONS] STACK
```

As you can see, when you create all of your services, you allocate a name to the stack. This allows you to easily destroy your services all in one go if you wanted to. A common option added to the previous command is --compose-file, or -c for short, which specifies a Compose file to deploy.

One of the great things about Docker Swarm is that once you've created a service, you can perform zero-downtime updates, also known as rolling updates. After the update command is executed, all of the tasks related to that particular service will update their containers. The command to perform swarm service updates is docker service update, and it's formatted as follows:

```
docker service update [OPTIONS] SERVICE
```

There are many different service configurations that can be updated—volumes and ports are two examples.

The essence of Docker Swarm is the ability to scale your services and create replicas. These replicas create new tasks, which then create replica containers. The command to achieve this is docker service scale. It's formatted as follows:

```
docker service scale SERVICE=REPLICAS [SERVICE=REPLICAS...]
```

You can expand as many services as you wish at once, where the SERVICE in the previous example is the service name you wish to scale and the REPLICAS value is the total number of replicas you wish that service to have. We'll not expand on this command more in this chapter as you'll only deploy a single-node environment, but keep this command in mind as you'll use it in Chapter 8. Docker Swarm replicas are a great way to make your application highly available, as the swarm manager node constantly monitors the swarm's state and reconciles any differences between the desired state of the swarm and its current state. This means that if you set up a service to run ten replicas of a container and a machine hosting two of those replicas crashes, the manager automatically creates two new replicas to replace those that crashed.

Lastly, a helpful command to use to list out all of the services in a Docker swarm is docker service ls.

This is a lot of information to digest, but it's essential to have a basic understanding of the key concepts of Docker Swarm. As we mentioned, we'll delve into creating a distributed Docker Swarm environment later in the book. In the next and final section, you'll initialize a single-node swarm and deploy your application locally using the Compose file you created earlier.

Deploy Your Compose File with docker stack deploy

The first step is to initialize your swarm and make your localhost the manager node by using the docker swarm init command. Run this command and observe your terminal output, which should be similar to this next example:

```
$ docker swarm init
Swarm initialized: current node (z4nyuvim...) is now a manager.

To add a worker to this swarm, run the following command:

    docker swarm join --token SWMTKN-1-1ysgomgb ...

To add a manager to this swarm, run 'docker swarm join-token manager'...
```

You'll see in the code example that the init command outputs the command that you'd need to execute to join a worker node to the swarm. It also tells you how to see instructions on how to join a manager node to the swarm. We'll look at doing this later in the book, but for now, let's continue with the local single-node swarm.

Now that you've created your swarm, run docker node ls to inspect the different nodes in your swarm and docker service ls to list the services in your swarm. You can see the example terminal interaction here:

```
$ docker node ls
ID        HOSTNAME       STATUS   AVAILABILITY   MANAGER STATUS   ENGINE VERSION
ylx...    docker-de...   Ready    Active         Leader           20.10.24

$ docker service ls
ID        NAME           MODE     REPLICAS       IMAGE            PORTS
```

Notice that there's one node in your swarm: your machine. But no services are listed because you haven't created any yet. To do so, deploy both your postgres database and Phoenix application to your swarm by running the docker stack deploy command with a stack name of your choice. We've chosen the name kanban. Recall that the docker stack deploy command deploys a stack based on a Compose file, so use the -c option to specify your Compose file. Also remember that your Compose file takes the WEB_IMAGE environment variable. Your terminal should be similar to this:

```
$ WEB_IMAGE="kanban:latest" docker stack deploy -c compose.yaml kanban
Creating network kanban_default
Creating service kanban_db
Creating service kanban_web
```

Great. Your Docker network, database, and web application have been started. Now run the docker service ls command again like so:

```
$ docker service ls
ID         NAME          MODE     REPLICAS   IMAGE       PORTS
1k77...    kanban_db     rep...   1/1        postgr...   *:30001->5432/tcp
hyz5...    kanban_web    rep...   1/1        ghcr.i...   *:4000->4000/tcp
```

You did it! You now have a single-node Docker Swarm running your application. Although a single-node swarm doesn't take advantage of Docker Swarm's high availability and fault-tolerant benefits, you're off to a great start with the technology. You'll learn a lot more about Docker swarm in Chapter 8. This is just the beginning.

Visit http://localhost:4000 in your browser, and you'll see your Phoenix application running. You now know that any time you wish to start up your development environment, you can use the docker stack deploy command. This will deploy your application under the same conditions in any environment that you please. At any point, if you want to remove your stack from your Docker Swarm, you can execute the command docker stack rm STACK in your manager node. This leaves the swarm up and running, but it removes the services from your specific stack.

> **More Helpful Service Commands**
>
>  There are a few extra commands that are nice to have in your toolbox. The first is 'docker service inspect –pretty SERVICE', which gives detailed information on a certain service. You can also use 'docker service ps SERVICE' to see all of the tasks running in a service. If you want to see the logs of a particular service, you can use 'docker service logs SERVICE|TASK'. Alternatively, to see the logs for a specific container, use the 'docker logs CONTAINER'. Play around with the 'docker swarm', 'docker service', and 'docker logs' commands in the documentation[7] to see what you can find out.

---

7. https://docs.docker.com/engine/reference/commandline/service/

Before we summarize what you've learned in this chapter, the last step is to clean up and remove your local swarm. You can do that by executing the `docker swarm leave --force` command.

What Have You Learned?

In this chapter, you added a Postgres database to create a multiservice project. You practiced the BEAMOps principles of infrastructure-as-code and environment integrity by creating one Docker Compose file that includes your database and web application. This allows you to easily reproduce a development environment for your multiservice application with one simple `docker compose up` command. You began preparing your application to be deployed to production by equipping your Compose file to conditionally expose your database. Lastly, you learned the basics of Docker Swarm and are now able to create a single-node swarm and deploy your application to that swarm.

Now that you know how to easily deploy your application locally, you need to understand how to prepare your production environment in AWS. In the next chapter, you'll learn how to quickly spin up new AWS environments and deploy your application remotely with three simple commands.

> **The Extra Mile**
>
> If you wish to deepen your knowledge of the themes we've covered in this chapter and refine your BEAMOps developer super powers, we've created a few tasks for you to do:
>
> 1. Create a Docker Compose service for the adminer image that you saw in the Postgres documentation [a] in the Docker Hub. This will create a visual way for you to see your database.
>
> 2. Create a new Compose file and add your adminer service there, rather than in your main file, and then run your application, merging both files.
>
> ---
> a. https://hub.docker.com/_/postgres

CHAPTER 6

The Production Environment and Packer

BEAMOps is about owning each step of the software delivery process. By this point in the book, we've covered quite a bit of this process. You've gained confidence in project management by using the infrastructure-as-code tool Terraform. You've aced the abstraction of the building and packaging of your Phoenix application with Docker. You've become proficient in setting up CI pipelines with GitHub Actions. And you've learned how to create a reusable environment template for a multiservice application using Docker Compose that will ensure environment integrity. We've covered a lot of ground!

In this chapter, you'll set up your production environment and learn how to own another step of the software delivery process: configuring production compute resources. We'll teach you how to create the *minimum* computer resources required to deploy your application to production. Specifically, you will create an infrastructure-as-code template that will enable you to easily spin up new environments in AWS. This will offer you another opportunity to demonstrate the Kaizen principle of continuous improvement through small, ongoing changes.

As Joe Armstrong said: "Make it work, then make it beautiful." This chapter is about making it (your production environment) work in its most basic form: an AWS architecture that uses an EC2 instance and a Packer configuration to support the deployment of a single-node Docker Swarm. By the end of this chapter, you'll have your production environment up and running and be able to close two of the infrastructure milestones you created in Chapter 2.

Let's begin by creating an AWS EC2 resource using the AWS UI.

Create Your AWS Production Environment Manually

In the previous chapter, you initiated a Docker Swarm in a local development environment and deployed services to it using a Docker Compose file. Now, it's time to do this remotely in a production environment. The first step in achieving this is to set up your remote environment. To put this step in the context of the bigger picture, the following diagram shows you the production environment you'll ultimately have by the end of this book.

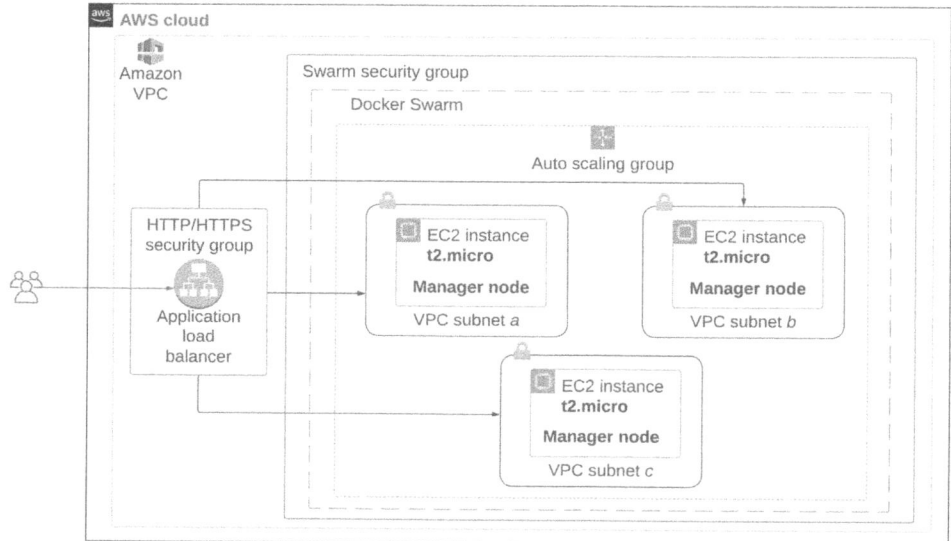

As you can see, the production environment targeted in this book consists primarily of two resources: an application load balancer and EC2 instances. An EC2 instance is a virtual machine (server) onto which you'll install the necessary tools and run your application. Each EC2 instance will be a node in the eventual multinode Docker Swarm that you'll create. The load balancer will then evenly distribute traffic among all of the EC2 instances within your swarm.

With this architecture blueprint in mind, let's start with the EC2 instances. To simplify things for now, you'll only create a single-node swarm (just as you did in the previous chapter). Because of this, you'll only launch one EC2 instance. You'll learn how to expand your AWS architecture for a multinode swarm in Chapter 8. As we said, this chapter is about making your production environment work in its most basic form. The next section will walk you through setting up an EC2 instance on AWS using the UI.

Launch Your First AWS Resource: An EC2 Instance

As we mentioned, an EC2 instance is a virtual machine you'll use to run your application remotely. In order for your application to run, you will need to install certain packages, such as Docker, onto your instance. You'll start off using the Amazon UI to create your instance. To reduce knowledge silos and embrace common shared knowledge, we always encourage you to use infrastructure-as-code tools to define your environment resources. In the next part of this chapter, you'll see how you can import resources created in the Amazon UI to Terraform code. We've separated our discussion of EC2 creation into two sections (manual and automated) because you may come into a project half-way through its implementation when remote resources have already been created. It's therefore beneficial for you to know how you can pull those already created resources into your infrastructure-as-code configuration.

Start by logging into your AWS account. Next, head to the EC2 dashboard. You can find this by typing "EC2" into the search bar and selecting the EC2 service option. Make sure that you're in the Ireland (eu-west-1) zone. The Ireland zone is one of AWS's oldest zones and so is well established. You can change your zone by clicking on the location drop-down next to your account name in the top right-hand corner. Once you're at the EC2 dashboard, click the Instances tab on the left-hand side and then press the orange Launch Instance button. This action presents an EC2 instance configuration form. Fill out the form according to the following instructions:

1. Name the Instance: Assign the name docker-swarm-manager to your instance.

2. Select the Base AMI: Choose "Amazon Linux" Amazon Machine Image (AMI).

3. Pick the Architecture: Ensure you choose the "64-bit(x86)" option for the AMI base architecture.

4. Select the Instance Type: Scroll down and select the "Free tier eligible" option. It's often a t2.micro option and is usually preselected for you. Although this option is free up to a certain resource usage limit, normally you would have to pay. For real-world production environments, we recommend that you use one of the t3.micro options as they have faster intel processors and are cheaper than t2.micro options (after you exceed the free limit). For learning purposes, select the free option.

5. Configure the Key Pair: In the "Key pair (login)" section, choose to "create a new key pair." Name it swarm-key, ensure that it uses the "RSA" algorithm, and select .pem as the file format. Upon creating the key pair, a .pem file will be automatically downloaded. This file is critical for secure access to your instance. You'll be using this file to SSH into your instance later on.

6. Set Up the Network Settings: There will be a default VPC selected, and a subnet and a public IP will be automatically assigned to your instance. A VPC is a private network dedicated to your AWS account that allows communication between resources on that network in a certain AWS region. A subnet is a smaller breakdown of a VPC, such as a group of IPs. Don't change these default VPC, subnet, or public IP settings. In this section, opt to create a new security group. A security group is a firewall that allows or rejects requests to certain ports depending on IP whitelists. Allow both SSH and HTTP traffic from anywhere for the time being. This ensures you can securely log in to your instance and access any web servers you'll set up.

7. Ignore the Storage & Advanced Settings: Skip over the "Configure storage" and "Advanced details" sections as you won't be making changes to the default settings at this moment.

8. Launch the Instance: Once all of these configurations are in place, make sure that "Number of instances" in the Summary section is set to 1. Then click the Launch Instance button to initialize your EC2 instance.

Your EC2 configuration form should look like the three figures starting on page 161.

Congratulations! You've just launched your first AWS EC2 instance. As part of this, you've selected the "Amazon Linux" Amazon Machine Image (AMI) to install the software on your instance. You've also created a security group with the default VPC and subnet, as well as a key pair. The next step is to connect to your instance via SSH using the key pair you just created.

Connect to Your EC2 Instance

To connect to your newly created EC2 instance, click the "Connect to instance" option on the Next Steps page, as shown in the second figure on page 163.

If you can't see that option, navigate back to the EC2 dashboard and click the Instances tab again on the left-hand side. Then, select the checkbox of your instance and click the Connect button, as shown in the third figure on page 163.

Launch an instance Info

Amazon EC2 allows you to create virtual machines, or instances, that run on the AWS Cloud. Quickly get started by following the simple steps below.

Name and tags Info

Name

| docker-swarm-manager | Add additional tags |

▼ Application and OS Images (Amazon Machine Image) Info

An AMI is a template that contains the software configuration (operating system, application server, and applications) required to launch your instance. Search or Browse for AMIs if you don't see what you are looking for below

🔍 Search our full catalog including 1000s of application and OS images

Recents | **My AMIs** | **Quick Start**

Amazon Linux	macOS	Ubuntu	Windows	Red Hat	SUSE Linux	Browse more AMIs
aws	Mac	ubuntu®	Microsoft	Red Hat	SUSE	Including AMIs from AWS, Marketplace and the Community

Amazon Machine Image (AMI)

Amazon Linux 2023 AMI   Free tier eligible
ami-00385a401487aefa4 (64-bit (x86), uefi-preferred) / ami-08c208c3af7f04012 (64-bit (Arm), uefi)
Virtualization: hvm   ENA enabled: true   Root device type: ebs

Description
Amazon Linux 2023 is a modern, general purpose Linux-based OS that comes with 5 years of long term support. It is optimized for AWS and designed to provide a secure, stable and high-performance execution environment to develop and run your cloud applications.

Architecture	Boot mode	AMI ID	Username ⓘ	
64-bit (x86) ▼	uefi-preferred	ami-00385a401487aefa4	ec2-user	Verified provider

Instance type Info | Get advice

Instance type

t2.micro	Free tier eligible
Family: t2 1 vCPU 1 GiB Memory Current generation: true	
On-Demand RHEL base pricing: 0.027 USD per Hour	
On-Demand Linux base pricing: 0.0126 USD per Hour	
On-Demand SUSE base pricing: 0.0126 USD per Hour	
On-Demand Windows base pricing: 0.0172 USD per Hour	

Additional costs apply for AMIs with pre-installed software

○ All generations

Compare instance types

Key pair (login) Info

You can use a key pair to securely connect to your instance. Ensure that you have access to the selected key pair before you launch the instance.

Key pair name - *required*

swarm-key

↻ Create new key pair

Network settings Info   [Edit]

Network Info
vpc-073bd07e

Subnet Info
No preference (Default subnet in any availability zone)

Auto-assign public IP Info
Enable

Additional charges apply when outside of free tier allowance

Firewall (security groups) Info
A security group is a set of firewall rules that control the traffic for your instance. Add rules to allow specific traffic to reach your instance.

- ● Create security group
- ○ Select existing security group

We'll create a new security group called '**launch-wizard-1**' with the following rules:

☑ **Allow SSH traffic from**
Helps you connect to your instance

Anywhere
0.0.0.0/0

☐ **Allow HTTPS traffic from the internet**
To set up an endpoint, for example when creating a web server

☑ **Allow HTTP traffic from the internet**
To set up an endpoint, for example when creating a web server

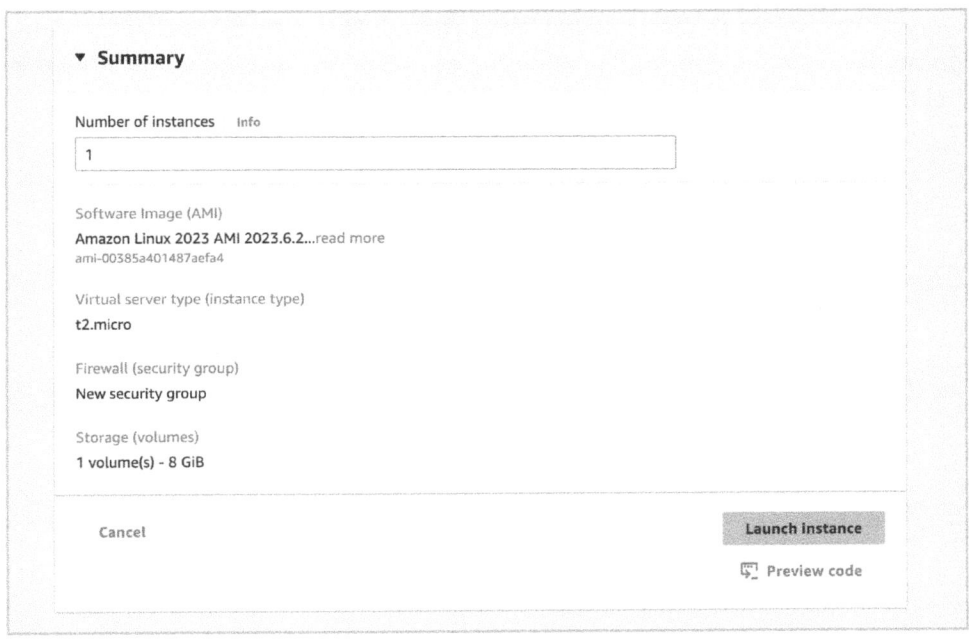

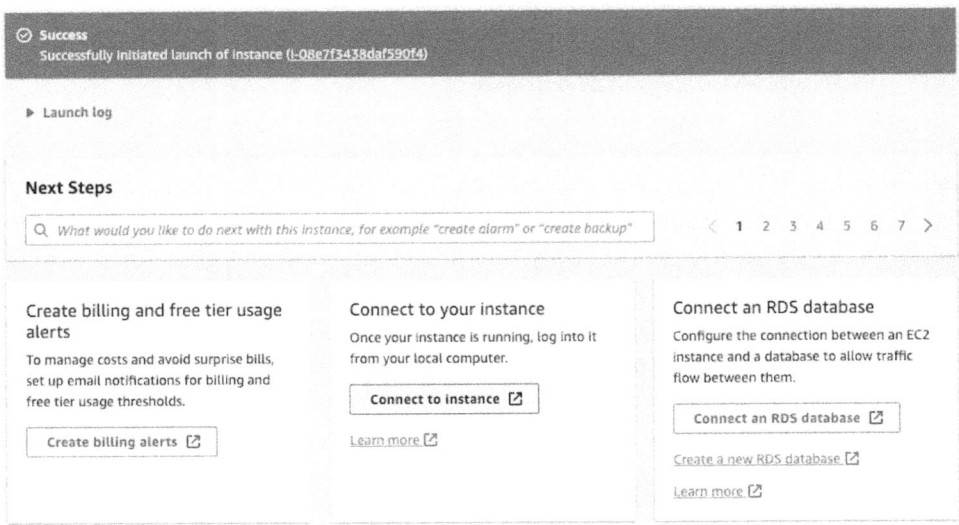

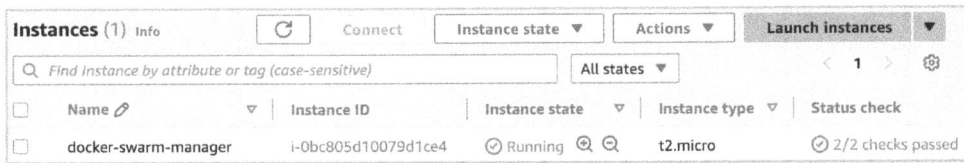

Once there, select the tab labeled "SSH client." There, you'll find an ssh command that you can copy and paste into your terminal, as shown in the following figure:

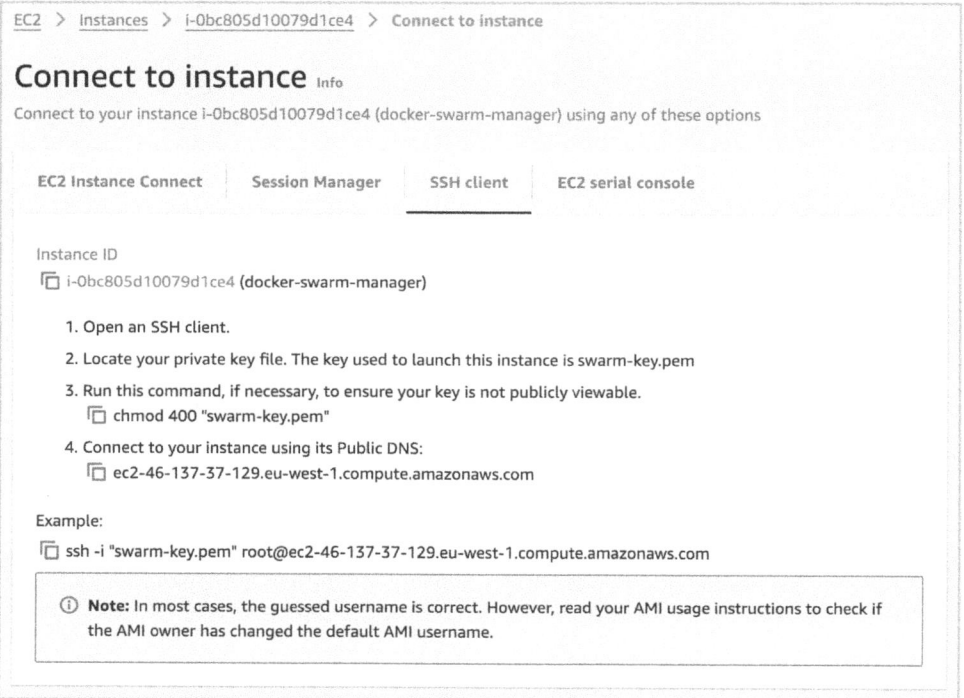

Before being able to run the ssh command, as the previous screenshot indicates, you'll need to alter the permissions of your .pem file that you downloaded in the previous section so that only the owner can read it. As the console tells you, you can do this by executing chmod 400 on the .pem file. After doing that, SSH into the instance using the command provided by Amazon, making sure that you replace the .pem placeholder with the actual path leading to the .pem file you downloaded earlier. When you execute the SSH command, write "yes" when prompted if you want to add the instance's IP to your list of known hosts. Do this throughout the chapter whenever asked. Once inside your instance, execute the docker ps command—you'll see the following error:

```
$ chmod 400 swarm-key.pem
$ ssh -i "swarm-key.pem" ec2-user@YOUR_INSTANCE_IP
The authenticity of host 'YOUR_INSTANCE_IP' can't be established.
ED25519 key fingerprint is SHA256:40Z2ASyRczR2RCYGkqVRCW2psRsFkQkj.
This key is not known by any other names
```

```
Are you sure you want to continue connecting (yes/no/[fingerprint])? yes
Warning: Permanently added 'YOUR_INSTANCE_IP' (ED25519) to the list of
known hosts.
       ,     #_
    ~\_   ####_        Amazon Linux 2023
   ~~  \_#####\
   ~~     \###|
   ~~       \#/ ___    https://aws.amazon.com/linux/amazon-linux-2023
    ~~       V~' '->
     ~~~         /
       ~~._.   _/
          _/ _/
        _/m/'
[ec2-user@YOUR_INSTANCE_IP ~]$ docker ps
-bash: docker: command not found
```

As you can see in the previous terminal output, you weren't able to execute any docker commands on your EC2 instance. This is because you created an instance based on Amazon Linux, which is a distribution based on Red Hat Enterprise Linux (RHEL) and doesn't come with Docker preinstalled. If you were to have used another Linux distribution, like Ubuntu or Debian, you could use the convenient get-docker script that Docker provides. However, as you chose to use the Amazon Linux AMI, you aren't able to run this script.

You chose the Amazon Linux AMI because it already has the AWS CLI and other tools that help you interact with AWS services preinstalled—you'll see how this is useful in Chapter 8. As the Amazon Linux AMI doesn't come with Docker preinstalled, you'll have to manually install it on your instance. As part of that Docker installation, you'll need to start the Docker daemon, enable the daemon as a service, and finally add the ec2-user into the Docker group. We've listed all of the commands that you need to run in the upcoming code snippet. At the end, to check that Docker has been installed, we ran the docker --version command. Run these same commands on your instance:

```
[ec2-user@YOUR_INSTANCE_IP ~] $ sudo dnf update -y && \
sudo dnf install -y docker && \
sudo systemctl start docker && \
sudo systemctl enable docker && \
sudo usermod -a -G docker ec2-user && \
newgrp docker
...
[ec2-user@YOUR_INSTANCE_IP ~] $ docker --version
Docker version 20.10.25, build b82b9f3
```

> **Set Up Rootless Mode**
>
>  We've added the ec2-user to the Docker group so that you can run Docker commands in your instance without having to prepend the commands with sudo. We recommend, however, that you set up rootless mode for real-world production environments. That's not something we'll go into in this book, but you can find out more by reading the Docker documentation.[1]

Great! You've successfully installed Docker and enabled the Docker daemon. However, your BEAMOps sense may be tingling. You might be a bit concerned about manually creating infrastructure resources in a UI. We've repeatedly emphasized the importance of having code representations for infrastructure resources. Doing so mitigates human error and makes the replication of environments and environment integrity extremely easy. In the next section, you will see how you can quickly import any AWS resource to your infrastructure-as-code configurations by using a new Terraform block.

Import an Existing Infrastructure Resource with Terraform

You might think that it would be extremely time-consuming to replicate already created remote resources in Terraform. Well, it's not. You can use one simple Terraform block (an import block) and two simple commands (terraform plan and terraform apply) to do so.

When we introduced Terraform in Chapter 2, we said when dealing with an infrastructure resource, you should always go to the Terraform registry and find the documentation of the provider and its specific resources. We also said each resource's docs give you import instructions. Keeping that in mind, the first resource you'll import is your EC2 instance. The Terraform resource related to EC2 instances is called aws_instance. Go to that resource's documentation,[2] and you'll find the import instructions at the bottom of the page.

You'll see that there are two different ways of importing a resource: either with an import block or by executing the terraform import command. We prefer using an import block as it allows you to see a plan of the import that you want to do before actually importing the resources. The terraform import command, on the other hand, imports the resource directly into your state without letting you see what it's importing first. Using an import block is safer and adheres to the Terraform work cycle discussed in Chapter 2, which includes planning your state modifications before you make them.

---

1. https://docs.docker.com/engine/security/rootless/
2. https://registry.terraform.io/providers/hashicorp/aws/latest/docs/resources/instance#import

In the aws_instance resource documentation, you'll see that the import block has the following structure:

```
import {
  to = RESOURCE_ADDRESS
  id = ID
}
```

The to argument refers to the address that will be used in your Terraform configuration/state for this resource. It expects a RESOURCE_ADDRESS as a value. The id argument refers to the ID of the remote resource that you're wanting to import. In this case, the ID will be the instance ID of your EC2 instance, which you can find in the Instances tab of the EC2 dashboard (shown in the following figure).

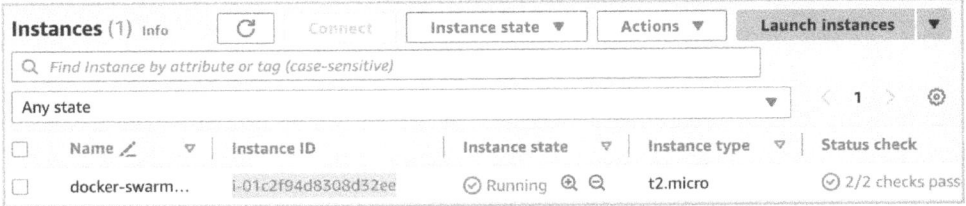

So, to import your EC2 resource into your Terraform configuration, you need to use an import block. To create this import block, you need a Terraform configuration file. You'll create one in the next section using Terraform modules.

Set Up Terraform and Import Your EC2 Instance

A Terraform module is a collection of .tf files kept together in a directory as a way to encapsulate and organize Terraform configurations into a self-contained and reusable unit. By defining your EC2 setup within a Terraform module, you can reuse that configuration to create the same resource across various different AWS environments. This is important in maintaining environment integrity because it ensures consistency when deploying resources. In this book, we'll only be showing you how to create your production environment, but in a real-world project, you'd likely have a staging environment also. You've actually already had some practice with modules without knowing it. The project management Terraform code you created in Chapter 2 is also a module.

To create your new AWS infrastructure module, create a new cloud/aws/compute /swarm nested directory (for example, where aws is inside cloud and so on) inside your modules folder. In that module, create a new main.tf file. This is where your EC2 configuration will live.

The first step in adding your EC2 instance to your Terraform configuration is to add the aws provider to your new main.tf file. As we mentioned in Chapter 2, there is a Use Provider button in the top right-hand corner of any resource's docs that gives you the installation instructions for that resource's provider. Copy the code that's shown when you click this button and paste it into your main.tf file. You don't need to copy over the provider block as you won't be adding any configuration options. Your main.tf file should look something like this:

```
# in modules/cloud/aws/compute/swarm/main.tf
terraform {
  required_providers {
    aws = {
      source  = "hashicorp/aws"
      version = "5.13.1"
    }
  }
}
```

Great. Any time you create a new Terraform configuration or add any new providers to your configurations, you need to run the command terraform init. Think of it like a mix deps.get. It's important that you run terraform init in a folder that's specific to your production environment. If you were to initialize your production Terraform configuration inside your cloud/aws/compute/swarm module, you couldn't then create a staging configuration in the same directory. In other words, your module wouldn't be reusable. To encapsulate your production environment configuration in one isolated place, create a new folder called environments in the root of your project and a subfolder called production inside environments. In this environments/production folder, create a new main.tf file and import your swarm module. You can do this using the module <BLOCK TYPE> and its source attribute. Your environments/production/main.tf file should look like this:

```
# in environments/production/main.tf
module "swarm" {
  source = "../../modules/cloud/aws/compute/swarm"
}
```

Now, cd into your new environments/production folder and run terraform init. Your initial provider configuration is complete!

But before you can try importing your EC2 instance, there's another crucial step to take: configuring your AWS access keys. Without configuring these, Terraform will throw an error because it won't know which AWS account to use when looking for the resource to import. To create your access keys, follow the Amazon documentation.[3]

Don't worry about the warning of not using root keys. Ideally, you'd use access keys that have IAM roles/permissions attached to them, but that's not something that we'll focus on in this book. Using the root access keys that don't restrict your permissions will simplify what we're doing in this chapter and throughout the book. You can find information on how to follow a more secure approach by assuming IAM roles.[4] Once you've created the keys, either add them to your shell profile or export them in your terminal like so:

```
$ export AWS_ACCESS_KEY_ID="YOUR_AWS_ACCESS_KEY_ID"
$ export AWS_SECRET_ACCESS_KEY="YOUR_AWS_SECRET_ACCESS_KEY"
$ export AWS_REGION=eu-west-1
```

To validate that you've exported the keys properly, you can run env | grep AWS. You should see the following result:

```
$ env | grep AWS
AWS_ACCESS_KEY_ID=*****************************
AWS_REGION=eu-west-1
AWS_SECRET_ACCESS_KEY=*****************************
```

Okay, you have configured your initial Terraform provider and have set your AWS keys. Now you must configure the import block. import blocks must be defined in the root module. Copy and paste the example import block given in the aws_instance documentation so that it sits under your current module block in your modules/environments/production/main.tf file. Change the value of the to argument to module.swarm.aws_instance.my_swarm to tell Terraform where you'll put the resource (inside your swarm module), and then change the value of the id argument to be the ID of your EC2 instance. Your modules/environments/production/main.tf file should now look something like this:

```
# in environments/production/main.tf

module "swarm" {
  source = "../../modules/cloud/aws/compute/swarm"
}
import {
  to = module.swarm.aws_instance.my_swarm
  id = "YOUR_EC2_INSTANCE_ID"
}
```

---

3. https://docs.aws.amazon.com/accounts/latest/reference/root-user-access-key.html
4. https://developer.hashicorp.com/terraform/tutorials/aws/aws-assumerole

We mentioned that import blocks allow you to plan your import before you do it. So, let's do just that. Run terraform plan inside your environments/production folder as we've done here:

```
$ terraform plan
Planning failed. Terraform encountered an error while generating this
plan.

  Error: Import block target does not exist

    on main.tf line 7:
    7: import {

  The target for the given import block does not exist. The specified
  target is within a module, and must be defined as a resource within
  that module before anything can be imported.
```

Oops! It didn't work. As you can see, the Terraform console is complaining that the block target (your module.swarm.aws_instance.my_swarm resource) hasn't been created. For Terraform to be able to import a resource, it has to know which resource address in your state to import the resource to.

-generate-config-out and Terraform Modules

You may see in the Terraform documentation that you can add the -generate-config-out option to the terraform plan command.[5] This option tells Terraform to automatically create a file called generated _resources.tf and configure the resource that you want to import in that file. However, this option doesn't work when using Terraform modules. Hashicorp have said that this is something they are working on. Remember that you need to use Terraform modules so that your AWS resource configurations can be reused across multiple environments to ensure environment integrity.

To create your resource that you want to import, add an empty aws_instance resource to your swarm module right after your current terraform block. Your modules/cloud/aws/compute/swarm/main.tf file should now look like this:

```
# in modules/cloud/aws/compute/swarm/main.tf
terraform {
  required_providers {
    aws = {
      source  = "hashicorp/aws"
```

---

5. https://developer.hashicorp.com/terraform/language/import/generating-configuration

```
      version = "5.13.1"
    }
  }
}
resource "aws_instance" "my_swarm" {
  # (resource arguments)
}
```

Great. Now replan the import of your EC2 instance by running terraform plan again. You should see a terminal response similar to ours here:

```
$ terraform plan

Error: Missing required argument

  with module.swarm.aws_instance.my_swarm,
  on ../../modules/cloud/aws/compute/swarm/main.tf line 14,
  in resource "aws_instance" "my_swarm":
  14: resource aws_instance my_swarm {

"launch_template": one of `ami,instance_type,launch_template` must be
specified

Error: Missing required argument

  with module.swarm.aws_instance.my_swarm,
  on ../../modules/cloud/aws/compute/swarm/main.tf line 14,
  in resource "aws_instance" "my_swarm":
  14: resource aws_instance my_swarm {

"instance_type": one of `instance_type,launch_template` must be
specified

Error: Missing required argument

  with module.swarm.aws_instance.my_swarm,
  on ../../modules/cloud/aws/compute/swarm/main.tf line 14,
  in resource "aws_instance" "my_swarm":
  14: resource aws_instance my_swarm {

"ami": one of `ami,launch_template` must be specified
```

More errors! What's happening this time?

The Terraform Core is indicating to you that to import your EC2 instance, you need to specify at least two of the following arguments: ami, instance_type, and/or launch_template. You'll specify the first two: ami and instance_type. Recall that when you created your EC2 instance manually using the AWS UI, the instance type you used was t2.micro. To find the AMI ID for your instance,

navigate back to the Instances tab of your EC2 dashboard in AWS, click on
your instance's ID in the "Instances" table to bring up more detail on your
instance and scroll down until you find the AMI ID:

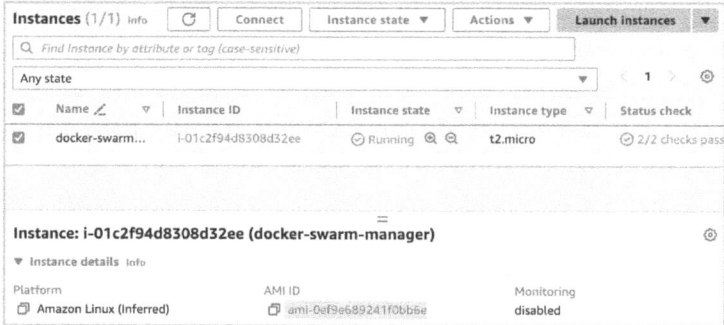

Add the ami and instance_type arguments and values to your aws_instance resource:

```
# in modules/cloud/aws/compute/swarm/main.tf

resource "aws_instance" "my_swarm" {
  ami           = "ami-0ef9e689241f0bb6e"
  instance_type = "t2.micro"
}
```

Now run terraform plan to replan your Terraform import again. You should see
something like this:

```
$ terraform plan
...
Terraform used the selected providers to generate the following execution
plan. Resource actions are indicated with the following symbols:
  ~ update in-place

Terraform will perform the following actions:

  # module.swarm.aws_instance.my_swarm will be updated in-place
  # (imported from "i-01c2f94d8308d32ee")
  ~ resource "aws_instance" "my_swarm" {
        ami                                  = "ami-0ef9e689241f0bb6e"
        ...
      ~ tags                                 = {
          - "Name" = "docker-swarm-manager" -> null
        }
      ~ tags_all                             = {
          - "Name" = "docker-swarm-manager"
        } -> (known after apply)
        tenancy                              = "default"
      + user_data_replace_on_change          = false
        ...

Plan: 1 to import, 0 to add, 1 to change, 0 to destroy.
...
```

Amazing, you have an import plan! You can see all of the attributes that the Terraform Core wants to import into your Terraform state for your resource.

However, if you look at the previous terminal output, you'll see that the Terraform Core wants to perform an update-in-place. It wants to remove the Name tag that you allocated to your resource. When importing resources, you want to import them as they are, rather than changing any attributes. To avoid this Name tag being removed, add it to your aws_instance resource in your modules /cloud/aws/compute/swarm/main.tf so that your resource looks like this:

```
# in modules/cloud/aws/compute/swarm/main.tf
resource "aws_instance" "my_swarm" {
  ami           = "YOUR_AMI_ID"
  instance_type = "t2.micro"

  tags = {
    "Name" = "docker-swarm-manager"
  }
}
```

And now run terraform plan again. You should no longer see that the Terraform Core will update your resource. Instead, its only plan is to import your resource. Run terraform apply to import your resource. Your terminal output should be similar to the following:

```
$ terraform plan
...
Plan: 1 to import, 0 to add, 0 to change, 0 to destroy.
...
$ terraform apply
...
Terraform will perform the following actions:

  # module.swarm.aws_instance.my_swarm will be imported
    resource "aws_instance" "my_swarm" {
        ami                                  = "ami-0ef9e689241f0bb6e"
        ...

Plan: 1 to import, 0 to add, 0 to change, 0 to destroy.

Do you want to perform these actions?
    ...
    Enter a value: yes

module.swarm.aws_instance.my_swarm: Importing... [id=i-01c2f9...]
module.swarm.aws_instance.my_swarm: Import complete [id=i-01c2f9...]

Apply complete! Resources: 1 imported, 0 added, 0 changed, 0 destroyed.
```

Excellent. Your EC2 instance resource has been imported into your Terraform state. Although it is your state, it is not yet in your Terraform configuration file and so is not part of your infrastructure-as-code.

To add the resource to your configuration, run the terraform state show command that you saw in Chapter 2 on page 27. Remember that this command takes a resource address as an argument. Run this command with the appropriate resource address, and you'll be able to see the configurations you imported:

```
$ terraform state show module.swarm.aws_instance.my_swarm
# module.swarm.aws_instance.my_swarm:
resource "aws_instance" "my_swarm" {
    ami                          = "ami-0ef9e689241f0bb6e"
    arn                          = "arn:aws:ec2:eu-west-1..."
    associate_public_ip_address  = true
    availability_zone            = "eu-west-1b"
...
```

Copy the output of the terraform state show command and replace your current aws_instance resource with those configurations. Now run terraform plan again as we have in the following terminal interaction to make sure there are no changes if you were to apply your new configuration:

```
$ terraform plan

  Error: Value for unconfigurable attribute

    with module.swarm.aws_instance.my_swarm,
    on ../../modules/cloud/aws/compute/swarm/main.tf line 16,
    in resource "aws_instance" "my_swarm":

    16:     arn = "arn:aws:ec2:eu-west-1..."

  Can't configure a value for "arn": its value will be decided
  automatically based on the result of applying this configuration.

  Error: Conflicting configuration arguments

    with module.swarm.aws_instance.my_swarm,
    on ../../modules/cloud/aws/compute/swarm/main.tf line 19,
    in resource "aws_instance" "my_swarm":

    19:     cpu_core_count                              = 1

  "cpu_core_count": conflicts with cpu_options.0.core_count
...
```

More errors! This time for unconfigurable and conflicting attributes. This is because the terraform state show command shows you all of the details for that resource, almost as if it was running a GET request for that resource. However, the AWS API (and the Terraform provider that's based off of it) doesn't allow you to specify all of those fields, such as the arn or id. To resolve these errors and ensure you aren't setting any nonconfigurable/conflicting metadata arguments, remove the erroring attributes and run the terraform plan command again. Repeat this process until there are no errors in the console.

We also suggest that you remove all of the attributes that you didn't select in the UI so that you're left with just the following values: ami, availability_zone, instance_type, key_name, subnet_id, tags, and vpc_security_group_ids. You don't need to specify any of the other arguments as they are either duplications of the same configurations and/or use default values that you don't need to set. Removing these "extra" attributes will make your configuration file much cleaner without changing the state of your resource. Your aws_instance resource should now look like this:

```
# in modules/cloud/aws/compute/swarm/main.tf

resource "aws_instance" "my_swarm" {
  ami                 = "ami-0ef9e689241f0bb6e"
  availability_zone   = "eu-west-1a"
  instance_type       = "t2.micro"
  key_name            = "swarm-key"
  subnet_id           = "subnet-699da921"
  tags = {
    "Name" = "docker-swarm-manager"
  }
  vpc_security_group_ids = [
    "sg-0fdcee06ed70d0116",
  ]
}
```

Now, run terraform plan for the last time. You'll see output similar to the following:

```
$ terraform apply
No changes. Your infrastructure matches the configuration.

Terraform has compared your real infrastructure against your
configuration and found no differences, so no changes are needed.

Apply complete! Resources: 0 added, 0 changed, 0 destroyed.
```

Fantastic! You've imported your AWS EC2 instance into your Terraform state, and you can now handle it with Terraform. You now know how to use an import block. The diagram on page 176 shows the import process you just executed. You should implement this any time you want to import an already existing resource. We've also included the import process for when you aren't working with Terraform modules.

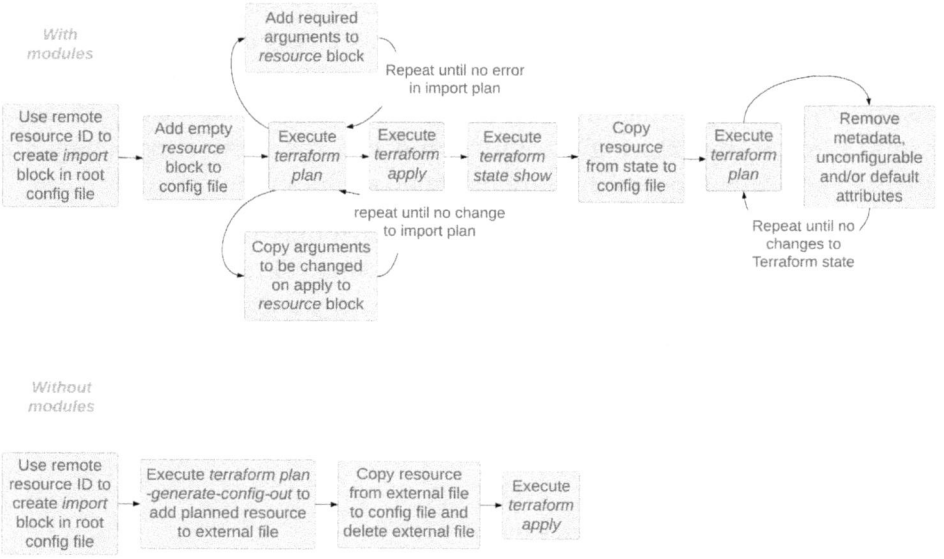

Now that you've imported your EC2 instance, it's time to import the rest of the resources that you implicitly created when you created the EC2 instance in the UI: the security group, VPC, and key pair. We'll start with the security group in the next section.

> **import Blocks: Should They Stay or Should They Go?**
>
>
> import blocks in Terraform are idempotent, meaning that after you import a resource, running another plan won't generate another import action as long as that resource remains in your state. For this reason, you can either choose to leave the import block in your environments/production/main.tf file or remove it. In our implementation, we've removed it so that the production environment module stays clean.

Import Your Security Group and Link It to Your EC2 Instance

You've successfully imported your EC2 instance resource that you created via the UI into your Terraform state. However, since you haven't imported all of the resources you created via the UI, you're not yet at the stage where you can create your remote resources instantly and implement the BEAMOps development workflow we discussed in Chapter 2 on page 40. Remember the CREATE–DESTROY–IMPROVE–REPEAT sequence? You're on your way, but you're not there yet.

Recall that when you set up your EC2 instance in the UI, you had to create a security group and a key pair and choose an AMI and a VPC. You now need to import all of these resources into your Terraform state. The first step will be to import the security group.

To import the security group, you'll follow the same import process you used for importing the EC2 instance: creating an import block and then running terraform plan followed by terraform apply.

The Terraform resource for security groups is aws_security_group. Return to the AWS provider documentation and locate that resource. Scroll to the bottom of the page and find the import block. It follows the familiar pattern:

```
import {
  to = RESOURCE_ADDRESS
  id = SECURITY_GROUP_ID
}
```

To obtain your security group ID, refer to the vpc_security_group_ids attribute of your EC2 instance resource in your modules/cloud/aws/compute/swarm/main.tf configuration file where it's hard-coded. Add this, as well as the resource address module.swarm.aws_security_group.swarm_sg, to a new import block inside your environments/production/main.tf file as we've done here:

```
# in environments/production
module "swarm" {
  source = "../../modules/cloud/aws/compute/swarm"
}
import {
  to = module.swarm.aws_security_group.swarm_sg
  id = "YOUR_SECURITY_GROUP_ID"
}
```

Now, run terraform plan like so:

```
$ terraform plan
module.swarm.aws_instance.my_swarm: Refreshing state...

Planning failed. Terraform encountered an error while generating this
plan.

  Error: Import block target does not exist

    on main.tf line 7:
     7: import {

  The target for the given import block does not exist. The specified
  target is within a module, and must be defined as a resource within
  that module before anything can be imported.
```

Oops! You're seeing the same error as before. You know what to do. Add the empty resource to the end of your modules/cloud/aws/compute/swarm/main.tf configuration file and then run the plan command again:

```
$ terraform plan
module.swarm.aws_security_group.swarm_sg: Preparing import...
module.swarm.aws_security_group.swarm_sg: Refreshing state...
module.swarm.aws_instance.my_swarm: Refreshing state...
...
Terraform will perform the following actions:

  # module.swarm.aws_security_group.swarm_sg must be replaced
  # (imported from "sg-0fdcee06ed70d0116")
  # Warning: this will destroy the imported resource
-/+ resource "aws_security_group" "swarm_sg" {
      ~ arn                    = "arn:aws:ec2:eu-west-1..." ->
                                  (known after apply)
      ~ description            = "launch..." -> Managed by Terraform"
                                  # forces replacement
      ~ egress                 = [
          - {
              - cidr_blocks      = [
                  - "0.0.0.0/0",
                ]
              - description      = ""
              - from_port        = 0
              - ipv6_cidr_blocks = []
              - prefix_list_ids  = []
              - protocol         = "-1"
              - security_groups  = []
              - self             = false
              - to_port          = 0
            },
        ] -> (known after apply)
      ~ id                     = "sg-0fdcee..." -> (known after apply)
...
Plan: 1 to import, 1 to add, 0 to change, 1 to destroy.
```

As before, you need to clean up the import plan by adding those attributes that will be removed/changed if you were to apply this current plan to your aws_security_group resource. The attributes you need to add are description, ingress, and egress. Once you've added these, rerun terraform plan to see that your import won't change the state of your security group.

When you see that the only plan the Terraform Core has is to import the resource (and not modify its state), run terraform apply to import the resource.

After you've done this, run terraform state show and copy the resulting configuration into your swarm module. Switch between eliminating any attributes that cannot be configured and running terraform plan command again until no errors appear.

Once you've done this, change one of the ingress objects so that the port exposed by your security group is 4000 rather than 80. This is because your application runs on port 4000, and to be able to access your application once you deploy it later in this chapter, your security group needs to expose that port. Using the same port in both development and production is key in ensuring environment integrity. Now run terraform apply and apply your configuration. You should see an output similar to this:

```
$ terraform apply
...
Terraform will perform the following actions:
  # module.swarm.aws_security_group.swarm_sg will be updated in-place
  resource "aws_security_group" "swarm_sg" {
    ...
      - from_port          = 80
      - to_port            = 80
      + from_port          = 4000
      + to_port            = 4000
    ...
  }
...
Do you want to perform these actions?
...
  Enter a value: yes

module.swarm.aws_security_group.swarm_sg: Modifying...
module.swarm.aws_security_group.swarm_sg: Modifications complete...

Apply complete! Resources: 0 added, 1 changed, 0 destroyed.
```

Well done! You've successfully imported two resources into your Terraform configuration! However, these two resources aren't connected yet. While you're aware that the EC2 instance cannot be created without the security group, you haven't told Terraform. Recall our discussion on implicit dependencies from Chapter 2. To create a dependency between two resources, you can use an attribute from one resource as an argument value when defining a different resource. In this particular case, you can link your security group to your EC2 instance by replacing the hard-coded security group ID in the vpc_security _group_ids attribute of the aws_instance resource with the ID exported by your aws_security_group resource. The modification you need to make is shown on the next page.

```
# in modules/cloud/aws/compute/swarm/main.tf
resource "aws_instance" "my_swarm" {
  vpc_security_group_ids = [
    aws_security_group.swarm_sg.id
  ]
}
```

Now apply your configuration using the terraform apply command. Ideally, you shouldn't observe any modifications to your infrastructure. If the apply command indicates that an instance will be replaced—where one resource will be added and another will be destroyed—there may be an error in your Terraform file. Revisit your configurations to ensure you've used the correct attributes.

Great! You've successfully imported and linked your EC2 instance and your security group. The next step is to address the VPC and subnet, after which you'll manage the key pair and then look at the AMI. We'll discuss setting up the VPC and subnet in the next section.

Use a Data Source to Get the Default VPC and Subnet

So far, you've imported your EC2 instance and your security group into your Terraform state. When you first created your EC2 instance in the UI, there was a default VPC and a subnet selected for you. It's now time to make that selection part of your infrastructure-as-code and add it to your Terraform configuration file.

> **Maximize Security with Custom VPC**
>
>  To keep things straightforward in this chapter, you're using the default VPC that AWS sets up in your chosen region (Ireland) when you establish an AWS account. This isn't recommended for long-term use as it's not the most secure option but it's sufficient for our current needs. Ideally, you should always aim to set up a custom VPC. This isn't something we'll cover in this book, but you can find more information in the documentation on the Amazon site.[6]

You already have two attributes related to VPCs and subnets in your current Terraform configuration file. The first, subnet_id, is part of your EC2 instance resource block and determines the subnet for the instance when it's created. The second is the vpc_id parameter in the security group resource block, which designates the VPC for your security group. As you selected the default options

---

6. https://docs.aws.amazon.com/vpc/latest/userguide/vpc-security-best-practices.html

provided by AWS for both of these resources, both of these attributes are just an ID. As you didn't create them manually yourself, you don't need to import them into your Terraform state in the same way you did for the EC2 instance and security group. Nonetheless, since they are a dependency of your EC2 instance and security group, you shouldn't have them as hard-coded IDs, but rather you should retrieve them programmatically and add them explicitly to your configuration file. To do this, you'll use a new Terraform <BLOCK TYPE>: a data source.

In Chapter 2 on page 16, we briefly mentioned that, besides offering resources, Terraform offers data sources, which are one of the main <BLOCK TYPES>. A data source is a special type of resource that allows you to fetch information from existing resources managed by the provider. Data sources are defined in the same way as a resource, with a <BLOCK TYPE> (data), <BLOCK INSTANCE> (the resource name), and a <BLOCK LABEL> (the ID for that resource in your Terraform state). You'll create two new data sources: one using the aws_vpc resource[7] (to get the VPC ID) and the aws_subnets resource[8] (to get the subnet ID).

When using data sources, you must provide a filter so that Terraform knows which data you want. You can do this using the filter argument. To get the VPC ID programmatically, you need to search for the VPC whose isDefault attribute is true. Then, to search for the automatically assigned subnet, you can search for all of the subnets whose vpc-id is the default VPC's ID. You'll cycle through the subnets later on to find the automatically assigned one. Have a go at implementing the aws_vpc and aws_subnets data sources in your modules/cloud/aws/compute/swarm/main.tf file above your EC2 instance resource before looking at the next code snippet for our implementation:

```
# in modules/cloud/aws/compute/swarm/main.tf
data "aws_vpc" "main" {
  filter {
    name   = "isDefault"
    values = ["true"]
  }
}
data "aws_subnets" "main_subnets" {
  filter {
    name   = "vpc-id"
    values = [data.aws_vpc.main.id]
  }
}
```

---

7. https://registry.terraform.io/providers/hashicorp/aws/latest/docs/data-sources/vpc
8. https://registry.terraform.io/providers/hashicorp/aws/latest/docs/data-sources/subnets

In the previous code snippet, the first data source, aws_vpc, retrieves the ID of the region's default VPC. The second construct, aws_subnets, uses the id attribute exported by the first data source to fetch all of the subnets of the default VPC. Now that you've fetched these two IDs, you can replace the hard-coded subnet_id and vpc_id values in your configuration file. You can see how we have done so here:

```
# in modules/cloud/aws/compute/swarm/main.tf
resource "aws_instance" "my_swarm" {
  subnet_id = data.aws_subnets.main_subnets.ids[2]
}

resource "aws_security_group" "swarm_sg" {
  description = "launch-wizard-1 created 2024-03-05T16:16:27.800Z"
  vpc_id = data.aws_vpc.main.id
}
```

You may notice in the previous code snippet that, when setting the subnet_id, we chose the third one at index 2. This is because when you created the instance via the UI, you didn't select a subnet and were automatically assigned one of the three default subnets that Amazon creates. As you didn't select it, you may have to cycle through the IDs at indexes 0, 1, or 2 until you find the ID that was assigned to your instance; run terraform plan after each one to know whether that index gives you the same ID or not.

Great job! You've added the VPC and subnet to your Terraform configuration. To make sure everything you selected in the UI is in your Terraform file, there's only one step left: creating your key pair. After that, we'll discuss installing Docker on your EC2 and configuring your AMI.

Create a Key Pair with Local and TLS Providers

So far, you've created two resources and imported them into your Terraform state. You've also fetched the default VPC and subnets of the region where you placed the resources using a data source. In this section, you're going to add a key pair to your Terraform configuration so that you can SSH into your EC2 instance. It's not possible to import a key pair as is (without replacing the existing one) using Terraform.[9] So, rather than fiddling around with the key pair that you've already created, it's better to be explicit about the creation of your SSH key pair and add it to your Terraform file so that it also forms part of your infrastructure-as-code. First, you will create your new key pair.

---

9. https://registry.terraform.io/providers/hashicorp/aws/latest/docs/resources/key_pair#import

Next, you'll save the private key locally in your environments/production folder. Finally, you'll attach this new key pair to your instance.

> **Securely Connect with AWS Instance Connect**
>
>  Throughout this book, we're using a generated key pair to connect to EC2 instances. In a real-world production environment, you'd use instance connect to connect to your instances. This is an AWS feature that allows you to connect to your instances by pushing the SSH public key of a key pair that's generated every time you connect to an instance. This is a more secure way of connecting to your instances but is less straightforward, so we won't go into this method in detail. You can find more information on instance connect in the Amazon documentation.[10]

To create the key pair, you'll use the tls provider,[11] which lets you create private keys and certificates. As always, the first thing to do is go to the docs and press the Use Provider button. Do this and then copy the provider instantiation given in the required providers section at the top of your modules/cloud/aws/compute/swarm/main.tf file. The beginning of your file should now look like this:

```
# in modules/cloud/aws/compute/swarm/main.tf

terraform {
  required_providers {
    aws = {
      source  = "hashicorp/aws"
      version = "5.13.1"
    }
    tls = {
      source  = "hashicorp/tls"
      version = "4.0.4"
    }
  }
}
```

To create the key pair, you'll use the tls_private_key resource.[12] This resource takes the algorithm and rsa_bits attributes. Use the RSA algorithm and 4096 key size the same way you did when you created the EC2 instance in the UI. Add this tls_private_key resource to your modules/cloud/aws/compute/swarm/main.tf with the aforementioned configurations just before your aws_instance resource like so:

---

10. https://docs.aws.amazon.com/AWSEC2/latest/UserGuide/ec2-instance-connect-methods.html
11. https://registry.terraform.io/providers/hashicorp/tls/latest/docs
12. https://registry.terraform.io/providers/hashicorp/tls/latest/docs/resources/private_key

```
# in modules/cloud/aws/compute/swarm/main.tf
# RSA key with 4096 rsa bits
resource "tls_private_key" "rsa" {
  algorithm = "RSA"
  rsa_bits  = "4096"
}
```

Once you apply the configuration, this tls_private_key resource will create the key pair in your Terraform state. It exports a private_key_pem attribute (your private key) and a public_key_openssh attribute (your public key). However, this resource doesn't create the .pem file you'll need to pass when SSH-ing into your instance. To create that file, you need to use the local provider, which exposes a local_sensitive_file resource. Look for the local provider[13] in the registry and add its configuration to the required providers section of your modules/cloud/aws/compute/swarm/main.tf file as we've done here:

```
# in modules/cloud/aws/compute/swarm/main.tf
terraform {
  required_providers {
    local = {
      source  = "hashicorp/local"
      version = "2.4.0"
    }
  }
}
```

Then add the local_sensitive_file resource block to your configuration file specifying the content, file_permission, and filename attributes for your .pem file. Use the 0400 permission for your file. This is the same permission you gave your .pem file that you created in the UI when you ran chmod 400. As for the content, use the private_key_pem attribute that's exported by your tls_private_key resource.

When specifying the filename, use an input variable rather than a hard-coded filename. This is so your main.tf file is reusable. Remember that you are applying your configuration from your environments/production folder. As your module is reusable, the SSH key location must depend on where your swarm module is being imported. Otherwise, your key will be overwritten each time you apply your module from a different folder.

An input variable is a way of defining dynamic configurations that are set when you import that module. To create your variable, create a new variables.tf file in your modules/cloud/aws/compute/swarm folder and define a variable block. This variable should be called private_key_path of type string and with a description of

---

13. https://registry.terraform.io/providers/hashicorp/local/latest/docs/resources/sensitive_file

your choice. Splitting out your variables from your main.tf file is beneficial as it makes your configuration easier to read. Even though your variable is defined in a separate file, your Terraform configuration will still be able to read it. This is because when applying a configuration, the Terraform Core looks for any and all files with the .tf suffix in a module folder and squashes them all together into one big file. After you've created your variable, set the filename attribute of your local_sensitive_file resource in your main.tf file accordingly. You can see the additions you need to make to each file here:

```
# in modules/cloud/aws/compute/swarm/variables.tf

variable "private_key_path" {
  description = "The path to the private key file."
  type        = string
}

# in modules/cloud/aws/compute/swarm/main.tf

resource "local_sensitive_file" "private_key" {
  filename        = var.private_key_path
  content         = tls_private_key.rsa.private_key_pem
  file_permission = "0400"
}
```

Now you must instantiate your variable in the import of your swarm module in your environments/production file. The file path should be such so the SSH key is saved inside your environments/production folder. To do this, use the ${path.module} function and a name of your choice to define the filename. ${path.module} is a built-in function that returns the path of the module where the function is called. In this case, the path will be the same as where your environments/production/main.tf file is defined. To instantiate your variable, add the private_key_path variable as an attribute under the source attribute of your swarm module. Your swarm module should now look like this:

```
# in environments/production/main.tf

module "swarm" {
  source           = "../../modules/cloud/aws/compute/swarm"
  private_key_path = "${path.module}/private_key.pem"
}
```

Terrific! Now apply your configuration to create your key pair locally. You must run terraform init in your environments/production folder before you do so because you've added two new providers to your swarm module file in this section. Once you apply your configuration, you'll see that a private_key.pem file has been added to your environments/production folder.

The last step is to replace your current key pair in AWS with the one you just created. You can do this by adding an import block to your environments/production/main.tf file that references your remotely created key pair, and the aws_key_pair resource[14] to your modules/cloud/aws/compute/swarm/main.tf file. The aws_key_pair resource expects the key_name and public_key arguments. Add swarm-key as the key name, and set the public_key value to be the public_key_openssh attribute exported by your tls_private_key resource. Then, link your new key pair to your EC2 instance by replacing the key_name value of your aws_instance resource with the public key you just created. You can see the changes you have to make here:

```
# in environments/production/main.tf
import {
  to = module.swarm.aws_key_pair.deployer_key
  id = "swarm-key"
}

# in modules/cloud/aws/compute/swarm/main.tf
resource "aws_key_pair" "deployer_key" {
  key_name   = "swarm-key"
  public_key = tls_private_key.rsa.public_key_openssh
}

resource "aws_instance" "my_swarm" {
  key_name = aws_key_pair.deployer_key.key_name
}
```

Great! Your Terraform configuration is complete! You have added almost everything you did via the UI in the first section of this chapter to your infrastructure-as-code. Plan the replacement of your UI key pair with the one that you've created using Terraform by running terraform plan. You'll see a warning that Terraform will destroy the imported resource—it will plan to import one resource, add one, and destroy one. Ignore the warning. This is exactly what you want to happen. Run terraform apply to replace the key. You can see an example terminal interaction here:

```
$ terraform plan
...
Terraform will perform the following actions:

  # module.swarm.aws_key_pair.deployer_key must be replaced
  # (imported from "swarm-key")
  # Warning: this will destroy the imported resource
-/+ resource "aws_key_pair" "deployer_key" {
```

---

14. https://registry.terraform.io/providers/hashicorp/aws/latest/docs/resources/key_pair

```
            ...
        + public_key       = "ssh-rsa AA..." # forces replacement
            ...
    }
Plan: 1 to import, 1 to add, 0 to change, 1 to destroy.
...
$ terraform apply
...
Do you want to perform these actions?
  Terraform will perform the actions described above.
  Only 'yes' will be accepted to approve.

  Enter a value: yes
module.swarm.aws_key_pair.deployer_key: Importing... [id=swarm-key]
module.swarm.aws_key_pair.deployer_key: Import complete [id=swarm-key]
module.swarm.aws_key_pair.deployer_key: Destroying... [id=swarm-key]
module.swarm.aws_key_pair.deployer_key: Destruction complete after 0s
module.swarm.aws_key_pair.deployer_key: Creating...
module.swarm.aws_key_pair.deployer_key: Creation complete after 1s...

Apply complete! Resources: 1 imported, 1 added, 0 changed, 1 destroyed.
```

Nice work! It's time to move on to the DESTROY part of the CREATE–DESTROY–IMPROVE–REPEAT motto. As we said in Chapter 2, don't be afraid to destroy things. Before you do that, there's one last handy little trick. When dealing with Terraform configurations that include SSH key pairs, it's a good idea to add a Terraform output <BLOCK TYPE> that prints the SSH command that you need to connect to your EC2. This means that every time you apply your configuration, the Terraform console will print the SSH command so that you can easily copy and paste it in your terminal. Alternatively, if you already have a configuration applied, you can run the command terraform output and the Terraform Console will print any outputs defined in your configuration.

An output should consist of a value and a description. For the value, you'll need the private_key_path variable that you created in this section and the IP address to your EC2 instance in the format ec2-user@PUBLIC_IP. The public_ip value is exported by your aws_instance resource. Have a go at creating the output yourself in a new outputs.tf file inside your modules/cloud/aws/compute/swarm folder before looking at our implementation here:

```
# in modules/cloud/aws/compute/swarm/outputs.tf

output "ssh_command" {
  value       = <<-EOF
    ssh -i ${var.private_key_path} \
    ec2-user@${aws_instance.my_swarm.public_ip}
  EOF
  description = "The SSH command to connect to the instance."
}
```

> **Remove the heredoc**
>
>  In the previous example, we used heredoc in the value attribute to split its content over multiple lines. We did this so that the text doesn't exceed the margin of the page in this book. When adding this output to your file, put the whole value on one single line. This will make the output in your CLI easier to read.

When using Terraform modules, any outputs defined in a child module need to be forwarded to their parent module. Currently, if you were to apply your configuration, your output wouldn't be shown. So, to include the SSH command output in your environments/production module, you must also define the output there. When doing this, create a new output block and set the value to be the ssh_command output exported from your swarm module. The end of your environments/production file should now look as follows:

```
# in environments/production/main.tf
output "swarm_ssh_command" {
  value = module.swarm.ssh_command
}
```

Start the terraform lifecycle by running terraform destroy as we've done:

```
$ terraform destroy
...
Plan: 0 to add, 0 to change, 5 to destroy.
...
Do you really want to destroy all resources?
  Terraform will destroy all your managed infrastructure, as shown above.
  There is no undo. Only 'yes' will be accepted to confirm.

  Enter a value: yes
...
Destroy complete! Resources: 5 destroyed.
```

> **Update the Name and Description for Your Security Group**
>
>  After you destroy your infrastructure, we recommend that you update the name of your security group to be swarm_pool_ports so that it's more descriptive than the default AWS name. You should also remove the description argument for your security group resource before applying it again. This way, when you apply your configuration, Terraform will automatically assign your security group a "Managed by Terraform" description so that it's clear to you in the UI that this resource should only be edited by Terraform.

As you've destroyed your infrastructure, make sure you've removed all of the import blocks in your environments/production/main.tf file. If not, you'll get a "Cannot import nonexistent remote object" error when trying to apply your configuration. Run terraform apply to re-create your resources like so:

```
$ terraform apply
...
Apply complete! Resources: 5 added, 0 changed, 0 destroyed.
Outputs:
ssh_command = "ssh -i ./private_key.pem ec2-user@18.168.205.215"
```

As you can see, the Terraform Core has added the SSH command to the terraform apply terminal output. Copy and paste the SSH command, and you'll see that you can connect to the EC2 instance in the same way as when you created it using the UI. Once you SSH into the instance, you'll notice that, like before, you aren't able to execute any Docker commands straight away. But don't fret; we'll look at this in the upcoming section.

Before you proceed, make sure to terminate your EC2 instance using the terraform destroy command.

Bootstrap Your EC2 Instance Using the user_data Attribute

So far, you've re-created your EC2 instance using Terraform. However, after SSH-ing into it, you discovered that Docker was not installed on the instance. Recall that this happened after you created the instance in the UI as well and you had to manually install it. In this section, you'll automate the Docker installation. To achieve this, you'll use the user_data attribute provided by the aws_instance resource. This attribute lets you define a script or sequence of commands to run when your EC2 instance is initially launched. The commands you executed in the first section to install Docker were the following:

```
$ sudo dnf update -y && \
sudo dnf install -y docker && \
sudo systemctl start docker && \
sudo systemctl enable docker && \
sudo usermod -a -G docker ec2-user && \
newgrp docker
```

To add these commands to your Terraform file, assign them to a new user_data attribute of your aws_instance resource like so:

```
# in modules/cloud/aws/compute/swarm/main.tf
resource "aws_instance" "my_swarm" {
  user_data = <<-EOF
            #!/usr/bin/env bash
            sudo dnf update -y && \
            sudo dnf install -y docker && \
```

```
            sudo systemctl start docker && \
            sudo systemctl enable docker && \
            sudo usermod -a -G docker ec2-user && \
            newgrp docker
            EOF
}
```

Now, execute the terraform apply command. Upon completion, you may observe that adding the user_data did not increase the time it took for the Terraform Core to apply your configuration. This is because Terraform doesn't wait for the user_data commands to finish executing before completing its own execution. If you SSH into your EC2 instance immediately after the apply command finishes, you may notice that the docker command isn't available yet. But if you exit the instance and a few minutes later you SSH back in, the docker command will be accessible.

As you can tell, this scenario isn't optimal. If you're expanding the number of instances in your production cluster, you'd want each instance to be immediately ready for the tasks at hand, with all necessary requirements already installed. We'll look at how you can achieve this in the next section, where we'll discuss Packer and Amazon Machine Images (AMIs).

Get to Know Packer

In the previous section, you saw that the user_data attribute of the aws_instance resource isn't reliable enough to install software onto your EC2 instance when it starts up. Using Packer to create a machine image with all necessary requirements already installed and using that machine image as a base for your EC2 instance is a great way to solve this. Before delving into Packer, let's recap what a machine image is.

A machine image is a static unit that contains a preconfigured operating system and installed software, which you can use to quickly create new running machines. Some prominent examples are Amazon EC2 AMIs, Docker images, and virtual machine OVA files.

So, how does Packer factor into this? Packer is a tool that allows you to automate the creation of machine images for multiple platforms from a single source configuration. Let's review Packer's main benefits and explore its constructs written in HCL.

Why Use Packer?

There are numerous benefits to using Packer. The following list highlights the four most important ones:

- *Consistency*: Packer allows you to create identical images across different cloud providers or platforms. It's a helpful tool when your goal is to ensure environment integrity.

- *Versioning*: Just like code, machine images can be versioned. This allows you to ensure that your deployments use the correct configurations.

- *Immutability*: Once you've built an image, it doesn't change. This gives you confidence and stability when deploying.

- *Speed*: Using pre-baked images that have all the necessary software already installed means you can launch an instance far quicker than you could if you were configuring it manually from scratch.

Just like Terraform, Packer is a Hashicorp product. The advantage of this is that Packer is also written using HCL. In the next section, we'll take a look at two important Packer concepts and introduce the HCL Packer template that you'll use to build your AMI.

Packer 101

Packer has two important concepts: a builder and a provisioner. A *builder* reads in some configuration and uses it to run and generate a machine image. Examples include VirtualBox, VMware, and Amazon EC2. A *provisioner* is used to install and configure software within a running machine before it's turned into a static image. It performs the major work of making the image contain useful software. Examples include shell scripts, Ansible, Chef, and Puppet.

> **Post-Processor**
>
> Related to this discussion is the concept of a *post-processor*. But we won't talk about this in the book. If you want to know more about it, you can read the Packer documentation.[15]

To create a machine image, the Packer builder reads a template file and creates a temporary EC2 instance based on the base AMI you specify. It enables SSH access to this temporary EC2 instance via a new security group, and then the provisioner installs the commands specified in the template onto the EC2 instance. Packer then creates a static image of the instance, after which it destroys the temporary EC2 instance and the associated security group that it created. Cool, right? You'll see this in action later on when you build your first AMI using Packer. First, you need to create your template.

---

15. https://developer.hashicorp.com/packer/docs/templates/hcl_templates/blocks/build/post-processor

As we mentioned, Packer is written in HCL. We've pasted the Packer configuration you'll use in this chapter in the upcoming code snippet. Create a new folder called packer in the root of your project and inside a file called aws-docker.pkr.hcl. Then paste in the Packer configuration and give it a read. We'll discuss the main components afterward:

```
# in packer/aws-docker.pkr.hcl
packer {
  required_plugins {
    amazon = {
      version = ">= 0.0.2"
      source  = "github.com/hashicorp/amazon"
    }
  }
}
source "amazon-ebs" "base" {
  ami_regions   = ["eu-west-1"]
  source_ami    = "YOUR_AMI_ID"
  instance_type = "t2.micro"
  ssh_username  = "ec2-user"
  ami_name      = "amazon-linux-docker_{{timestamp}}"
}
build {
  sources = ["source.amazon-ebs.base"]

  provisioner "shell" {
    inline = [
      "sudo dnf update -y",
      "sudo dnf install -y docker",
      "sudo systemctl start docker",
      "sudo systemctl enable docker",
      "sudo usermod -a -G docker ec2-user",
      "sudo dnf install -y nmap"
    ]
  }
}
```

As you can see, the previous Packer example has three main sections: a packer block, a source block, and a build block. Let's go through each one.

The packer block is used to specify the required plugins that Packer will use to create the machine. Think of it in the same way as the terraform block that Terraform uses to specify the required providers that Terraform will use to create its infrastructure.

The source block is used to specify the base machine image that Packer will use to create the new machine image. This block has the same information that you entered in the UI to create your instance. The resource being used is the amazon-ebs resource.[16] This is the storage artifact used to build EC2 instances. Replace the source_ami value with the ami attribute that you have in your aws_instance resource in your main.tf file. This source_ami is the base AMI that Packer uses when it creates its temporary instance: an Amazon Linux distribution. The instance_type value is also the same. The region has been specified, as well as the SSH username. The SSH username is implicitly created by the AWS UI when you created your key pair and is what you've been entering in your SSH commands. Lastly, the AMI has been assigned a unique name so that when you have multiple AMIs, you can tell them apart.

Finally, the build block is used to specify the builder source to use, as well as the provisioners that Packer will use to install and configure software on the machine prior to turning it into a machine image. In this case, it's a shell provisioner that will execute the commands specified in the inline attribute; the same commands you executed in the first section of this chapter after creating the instance using the UI. You may notice, however, that we've removed the newgrp docker command. This is because after installing Docker on your EC2 instance at the beginning of this chapter, you needed to refresh your EC2 instance before you're able to run any docker commands.

If you hadn't run this command on your instance after you created it via the UI, then you wouldn't have been able to run docker --version with prefixing the command with sudo. However, as these commands are being run on an AMI that'll be installed anew on an EC2 instance when it's booted, this command isn't needed in the Packer configuration. Besides removing this command, we have added a sudo dnf install -y nmap command. This is so that you can execute network scanning tasks later in the book. Don't worry about this for now, we'll discuss it in more detail in Chapter 8.

Perfect. You have your Packer template defined. But how do you actually build your machine image? We'll discuss this in the next section where we'll look at the Packer CLI.

Basic Packer Commands

There are four important Packer CLI commands that you'll use in this chapter: packer init, packer validate, packer build, and packer inspect. Let's go through each one.

The packer init command is like terraform init and is used to initialize a Packer template or download any new plugins. It has the following format:

```
packer init .
```

---

16. https://developer.hashicorp.com/packer/integrations/hashicorp/amazon/latest/components/builder/ebs

The packer validate command, as its name suggests, validates the syntax and configuration of a Packer template. Any errors found when this command is run are output to your terminal. The command has the following format:

```
packer validate FILE
```

The packer inspect command takes a template and outputs the various components it defines without actually building them. It has the following format:

```
packer inspect FILE
```

The packer build command is what actually builds a machine image based on a template you pass. The various builds specified within the template are executed in parallel unless otherwise specified. The command has the following format:

```
packer build FILE
```

When running any of the last three commands, you can either specify a certain file path or you can pass the . context. If you pass . , Packer will look for the first .pkr.hcl file it finds in your current working directory and use that file as its input.

Alright, you've created your Packer configuration template and you know the necessary Packer CLI commands to initialize, validate, and inspect it, as well as build a machine image. In the next section, you'll get your hands dirty by doing just that.

Build Your First Amazon Machine Image (AMI)

You've written your template, and you know the necessary CLI commands. Let's now validate and build your Packer template. To do this, cd into the packer directory where your template is located. As you only have one Packer template created, you can use . as the context in your Packer commands rather than specifying the filename. Go ahead and run packer init and packer validate, followed by packer inspect to validate and then inspect your Packer template. Your terminal output should look similar to this:

```
$ cd ../../packer
$ packer init .
$ packer validate .
The configuration is valid.
$ packer inspect .
Packer Inspect: HCL2 mode
> input-variables:
> local-variables:
```

```
> builds:
  unnamed build 0:
    sources:
      amazon-ebs.example
    provisioners:
      shell
    post-processors:
      no post-processor
```

As you can see from the output of the `packer validate` command, your Packer template has the correct syntax and configuration. Moreover, the `packer inspect` command output shows you an overview of the template's components. You can see that you have one build source (an Amazon EBS) and one provisioner (a shell script).

Now that you've validated your template and know what to expect once you build the machine image, let's build it. To do so, you need to export your AWS credentials onto your machine. You already did this in the second section of this chapter. Run the `packer build .` command and we'll observe the output afterward. We've pasted the terminal output in the next code snippet, but you might want to get a coffee while the image is building; it could take around five minutes:

```
$ packer build .
amazon-ebs.example: output will be in this color.

==> amazon-ebs.example: Prevalidating any provided VPC information
==> amazon-ebs.example: Prevalidating AMI Name: \
    amazon-linux-docker_1693054715_v0.0.1
    amazon-ebs.example: Found Image ID: ami-0ef9e689241f0bb6e
==> amazon-ebs.example: Creating temporary keypair: \
    packer_64e9f6fb-a37b-d6ea-e270-767288ff492f
==> amazon-ebs.example: Creating temporary security group for this \
    instance: packer_64e9f6fd-2e74-9311-cef0-4ffe602127d1
==> amazon-ebs.example: Authorizing access to port 22 from [0.0.0.0/0] \
    in the temporary security groups...
==> amazon-ebs.example: Launching a source AWS instance...
    amazon-ebs.example: Instance ID: i-0e0f95009ea733e5d
...
```

You may see a warning message that there is a more recent Amazon Linux AMI that you can use. Ignore that for now. You'll solve that in the next section.

So, what's happening while the image is being built? As we mentioned earlier, Packer has created a temporary EC2 instance, a temporary key pair, and a temporary security group. Once it has done this, it has SSH-ed into the instance and the provisioner has run the commands you specified in the provisioner block of your Packer template. It has then created a static image—an

AMI—of the configured EC2 instance and saved it to your AWS account, before clearing up the temporary resources. If you go to the EC2 dashboard in your Amazon account and click the AMIs tab on the left-hand side, you'll be able to see your AMI (as shown in the following figure).

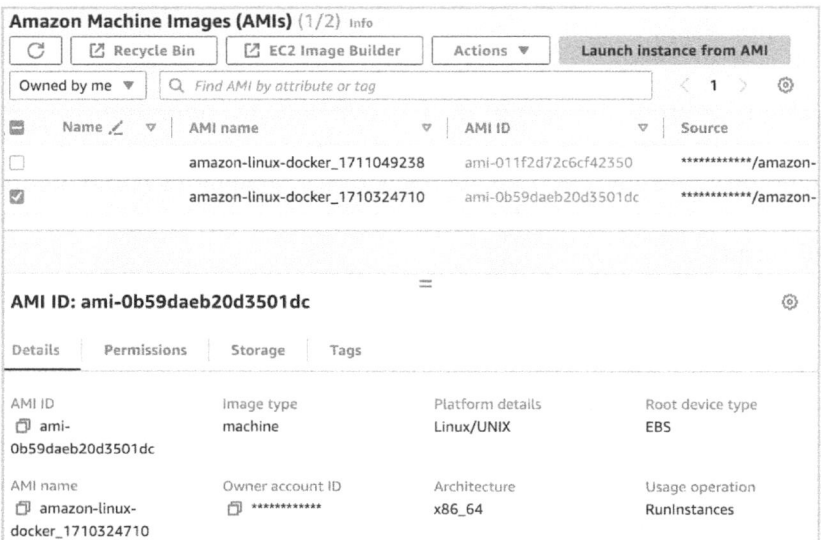

Amazing, right? Now that you've seen Packer in action and you've built your first AMI, you can add it to your Terraform file so that your EC2 instance uses it. However, let's first refactor your template a bit to tidy it up and make it more reliable.

Refactor Your Packer Template

The Packer template you created already builds an image that works. But there are some small improvements that you can make such as parameterizing the AWS region, using the most up-to-date base AMI, and making your Docker installation not interfere with any default setup scripts that are running on your AMI base. You'll start by making your AWS region a Packer variable.

Packer Variables

To tidy up your Packer implementation, we suggest you parameterize your ami_regions parameter. This way, if you need to update the regions that your AMI should be available in, you don't have to update your core configuration file. To do this, you can use variables. Given that Packer is written in HCL, there's no need to delve into how the variable construct functions; it operates identically to Terraform. To parametrize the AWS region, create a variable called ami_regions. Just like with Terraform, when using variables, you have to create a variable type. To do so, create a new file called variables.pkr.hcl inside your packer folder and paste in the following code snippet:

```
# in packer/variables.pkr.hcl
```

```
variable "ami_regions" {
  type        = list(string)
  description = "A list of regions where the AMI will be copied to."
}
```

Once you've defined your variable's structure, you can incorporate it into your template in the same way Terraform does, using dot notation. Try updating your amazon-ebs construct yourself before looking at the next code snippet for our implementation:

```
# in packer/aws-docker.pkr.hcl
source "amazon-ebs" "base" {
  ami_regions  = var.ami_regions
}
```

OK, you've defined your variable structure and incorporated it into your main file, but you haven't instantiated it. Unlike Terraform, which will prompt you to input any undefined variables at runtime, Packer will fail. If you want to see this, run the packer validate command. So, how can you specify your ami _regions variable? There are two ways to do it. Either by specifying the parameter in the CLI by using the --var option when running the build command, or using a dedicated variables file. To specify the parameter via the CLI, you'd run the build command like this: packer build -var 'ami_regions=[eu-west-1]' ..

However, we don't suggest using this method. You want to be explicit with your variable instantiation to be able to version-control your variables and make your configuration open and easy. In the same way that Terraform allows variable auto-loading with the .auto.tfvars file, you can enable variable auto-loading with Packer by creating a .auto.pkrvars.hcl file. Create this file inside your packer folder and copy in the following code snippet:

```
# in packer/.auto.pkrvars.hcl
```

```
ami_regions = ["eu-west-1"]
```

Now run the packer validate . command and you'll see that the template doesn't have any errors. Great! You've parametrized your AWS region. What about the hard-coded AMI version? With AMIs, you always want to use the latest version to make sure your instance is as secure as possible. We'll look at this in the next section.

Use the Latest Version of Your Base AMI

In your current Packer template, you're using a hard-coded AMI ID. Using hard-coded IDs for AMI versions isn't pragmatic, though. Whenever that ID changes or is no longer available, the Packer build will fail. To update it, you would need to go to the AMI marketplace and search for the latest AMI ID. You could always search for the latest AMI version using the AWS CLI, but you'd still have to update the file manually.

As a BEAMOps developer, automating things should always be on your mind. This is why you're going to fetch the latest AMI of the Amazon Linux image programmatically. To do this, you will use the source_ami_filter attribute of the amazon-ebs builder, which lets you filter through the base AMIs that AWS offers and select a certain one. Replace your current source_ami attribute with the source_ami_filter block below into your amazon-ebs source block, and then we'll go through its attributes:

```
# in packer/aws-docker.pkr.hcl
source "amazon-ebs" "base" {
  source_ami_filter {
    filters = {
      name         = "al2023-ami-2023*"
      architecture = "x86_64"
    }
    most_recent = true
    owners      = ["amazon"]
  }
}
```

The previous code snippet filters the AWS AMIs by the same architecture type and AMI name as you selected in the AWS UI at the beginning of this chapter: x86_64 and al2023-ami-2023, which stands for Amazon Linux 2023. Then, because of the most_recent attribute, this filter will only select the latest version of those Amazon Linux images. Great. You've ensured you're using the most up-to-date version of that base AMI! Now, let's make your Docker installation more robust and not interfere with the initial setup of the temporary EC2 that Packer creates when building your machine image.

Provision Your AMI with cloud-init

cloud-init[17] is a setup assistant for cloud servers that is already preinstalled in many cloud images, such as the Amazon Linux image you're using. When you start a new virtual server in the cloud, cloud-init automatically configures

---

17. https://cloud-init.io/

that server the first time it boots up. This includes setting up users, updating software, and configuring network settings. One important feature is that it ensures all configurations are completed before the server is considered "ready." To make sure that there are no conflicts between the cloud-init run and your own installation script, you should wait for the cloud-init setup to finish before installing Docker. To do this, you must follow these steps:

1. Extract the commands that you have in your current provisioner block into a separate file called setup.sh.

2. Update your current provisioner block to wait for cloud_init to finish and then run your new setup.sh file.

Let's begin with step 1. Create a new file in your packer directory called setup.sh. Then move all of the commands currently in the inline attribute of your shell provisioner block to this new file. Your setup.sh file should look like this:

```bash
#!/usr/bin/env bash

# in packer/setup.sh

set -ex
sudo dnf update -y
sudo dnf install -y docker nc
sudo systemctl start docker
sudo systemctl enable docker
sudo usermod -a -G docker ec2-user
sudo dnf install -y nmap
```

For step 2, refactor your provisioner block to run the setup.sh script after having checked that the cloud-init has finished executing. To do this, replace the content of your current provisioner block configuration with the script attribute and set your new file as its value. Then copy and paste the execute_command attribute specified in the following code snippet. Update your aws-docker.pkr.hcl file, and then we'll discuss what's happening:

```
# in packer/aws-docker.pkr.hcl

build {
  provisioner "shell" {
    script = "setup.sh"
    # run script after cloud-init finishes to avoid race conditions
    execute_command = "cloud-init status --wait && sudo -E sh '{{ .Path }}'"
  }
}
```

Let's break down the execute_command value in the previous example:

- cloud-init status --wait: The --wait option tells Packer to wait until cloud-init has finished its tasks. This is important because if cloud-init is still doing things on the machine and you try to run your script at the same time, they might interfere with each other.

- &&: This is a shell operator that says that the proceeding command will only be run if the previous command succeeds.

- sudo -E sh '{{ .Path }}': This is the command that actually runs your setup.sh script. sudo runs commands as the superuser (root). The -E option preserves the user's environment. sh is the shell that will execute the script. {{.Path}} is a placeholder that Packer will replace with the working directory of your Packer file. Packer will then add that path to the file in the script attribute and execute that file.

And that's it! Now run the packer validate command and see that it passes. After this, create your new AMI by running packer build.

Once the command finishes, go to the AMIs tab of the EC2 dashboard in your AWS account, and you'll see your brand-new AMI alongside the one you created earlier.

> **Build Local Images Using Virtualization Software**
>
>
> Rather than directly creating your machine images in AWS, you could build local versions of your images using a virtualization software provider like VirtualBox or Parallels, and then build a Vagrant box with the Vagrant post-processor. Vagrant is another Hashicorp tool that lets you create and manage virtualized development environments. Creating local versions of your images would allow you to replicate your multinode environment locally. We won't delve into this in any more detail, but if you're curious to know more, check out the Hashicorp docs.[18]

Great. Your Packer file is now tidy and robust. You now have a Packer template that builds an AMI with Docker installed and saves it to your Amazon account! Your last task for this chapter is to put Packer and Terraform together so that your EC2 instance defined in your main.tf file uses the AMIs you create with Packer. Let's get to it.

Putting Packer and Terraform Together

So far, you've created a Terraform configuration file that creates an EC2 instance and a security group that pulls the default VPC and subnet in AWS. You then defined a Packer file, which creates an AMI with Docker already

---

18. https://developer.hashicorp.com/packer/tutorials/aws-get-started/aws-get-started-post-processors-vagrant

installed on it. In this final section, you will update your swarm Terraform module so that your EC2 instance uses your new AMI created by Packer. Just as your Packer file uses the most recent version of the Amazon Linux base AMI, your Terraform file should use the most recent version of your AMI. To fetch the most recent AMI, you'll create another data source, this time using the aws_ami resource.[19] Recall that your AMI names follow this format: amazon-linux-docker_{{timestamp}}. This means that you can easily pull the most recent image by using the filter attribute to filter all of the AMIs in your account by the name amazon-linux-docker. You can then use the most_recent flag to pull the most recent version. Try implementing this data source in your modules/cloud/aws/compute/swarm/main.tf file on your own before looking at the upcoming snippet for our answer:

```
# in modules/cloud/aws/compute/swarm/main.tf
data "aws_ami" "amazon_linux_docker" {
  most_recent = true

  filter {
    name   = "name"
    values = ["amazon-linux-docker*"]
  }
  owners = ["YOUR_AWS_ACCOUNT_ID"]
}
```

> **Replace owners Value**
>
>  You must replace the owners value in the snippet with your AWS account owner ID. It's important to be explicit with the owner in this data source to ensure that Terraform only searches for AMIs in your account. You can find your account owner ID in the AWS console if you click on your name in the top right-hand corner.[20] Alternatively, if you have the AWS CLI installed, you can run aws sts get-caller-identity.

The filter in the previous code snippet uses a wildcard to match the AMI name before the timestamp. This will query all of the machine images that include that name, and then, thanks to the most_recent attribute, the most recent AMI will be used. You've now located the AMI you want to use, but you haven't told your EC2 instance to use it yet. To link your new aws_ami data source to your EC2 instance, you must set the ami attribute of your aws_instance resource to be the ID attribute exported by the aws_ami data source you created. You

---

19. https://registry.terraform.io/providers/hashicorp/aws/latest/docs/data-sources/ami
20. https://console.aws.amazon.com/

can also remove the user_data attribute as your AMI will now take care of the Docker installation. Have a go at setting the ami attribute yourself before looking at our implementation:

```
# in modules/cloud/aws/compute/swarm/main.tf
resource "aws_instance" "my_swarm" {
  ami = data.aws_ami.amazon_linux_docker.id
}
```

Amazing! Now cd into your environments/production directory, run terraform apply, SSH into your EC2 instance, and check that Docker is installed by running a docker ps. Your terminal should look something like this:

```
$ cd ../environments/production
$ terraform apply
module.swarm.tls_private_key.rsa: Refreshing state...
module.swarm.local_sensitive_file.private_key: Refreshing state...
...
  # module.swarm.aws_instance.my_swarm must be replaced
-/+ resource "aws_instance" "my_swarm" {
      ~ ami = "ami-0cfd0973d..." -> "ami-0ae7f..." # forces replacement
...
Plan: 1 to add, 0 to change, 1 to destroy.
Changes to Outputs:
  ~ swarm_ssh_command = "ssh -i ./private_ke..." -> (known after apply)
Do you want to perform these actions?
  Terraform will perform the actions described above.
  Only 'yes' will be accepted to approve.

  Enter a value: yes
module.swarm.aws_instance.my_swarm: Destroying...
module.swarm.aws_instance.my_swarm: Destruction complete after 30s
module.swarm.aws_instance.my_swarm: Creating...
module.swarm.aws_instance.my_swarm: Creation complete after 24s

Apply complete! Resources: 1 added, 0 changed, 1 destroyed.

Outputs:

ssh_command = "ssh -i ./private_key.pem ec2-user@YOUR_INSTANCE_IP"
...

$ ssh -i ./private_key.pem ec2-user@YOUR_INSTANCE_IP
The authenticity of host 'YOUR_INSTANCE_IP' can't be established.
ED25519 key fingerprint is SHA256:40Z2ASyRczR2RCYGkqVRCW2psRsFkQkj.
This key isn't known by any other names
Are you sure you want to continue connecting (yes/no/[fingerprint])? yes
Warning: Permanently added 'YOUR_INSTANCE_IP' (ED25519) to the list of known hosts.
```

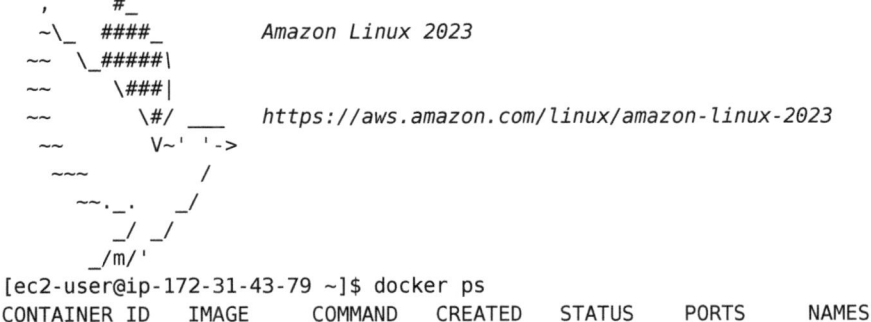

```
[ec2-user@ip-172-31-43-79 ~]$ docker ps
CONTAINER ID    IMAGE     COMMAND     CREATED     STATUS     PORTS     NAMES
```

Fantastic, you did it! You programmatically created an EC2 instance that uses your own AMI with Docker preinstalled. You also created a security group for your instance and programmatically selected a default VPC and subnet. Your production environment is ready!

You can close the issue called "Create the EC2 AMI" that you created in Chapter 2. To do so, update your .gitignore file to include unwanted Packer files. You can find the files that should be ignored in the gitignore repository on GitHub—[21]copy and paste them into your .gitignore. Then create a new branch, commit your .gitignore file packer folder, open a pull request with closes #ISSUE_ID in the description, and merge it. There's only one thing left to do: deploy your application. To achieve this, you'll initialize a remote Docker Swarm and replicate your local application from the previous chapter in your new production environment.

Initialize Your Remote Docker Swarm

Recall that in the previous chapter, when you deployed your application locally, you first executed the docker swarm init command to initiate your swarm and then you ran the docker stack deploy command. Deploying your application to production is no different. First, you must initialize your swarm on your EC2 instance after it has finished booting.

As you saw earlier, to run commands on your EC2 instance once it has started, you should use the user_data attribute of your aws_instance resource. So, to start your swarm on your EC2 after it starts up, re-add the user_data attribute and set it to be a bash script that runs the command docker swarm init like so:

---

21. https://github.com/github/gitignore/blob/main/Packer.gitignore

```
# in modules/cloud/aws/compute/swarm/main.tf
resource "aws_instance" "my_swarm" {
  user_data = <<-EOF
              #!/usr/bin/env bash

              docker swarm init
              EOF
}
```

You may be asking yourself why you have to add this user_data attribute again since we told you earlier to get rid of it. When you added the user_data attribute last time, you used it to install Docker. However, you saw that installing Docker on your EC2 instance in that way, after it has already finished booting, means that you run the risk of your production environment not being ready quickly enough (for example, if you SSH into it straight away, Docker hasn't yet been installed). To mitigate that issue, you created the AMI that already has Docker installed so that when your instance starts up, it already has Docker installed and is ready to go.

This time around, rather than installing Docker using the user_data attribute, you'll start your swarm. The starting of the swarm must be done using the user_data attribute and not on the AMI configuration itself, as adding the docker swarm init command to the AMI setup makes that AMI not as reuseable (what if you wanted an EC2 that had Docker installed but wasn't a Docker swarm).

Nice! Now apply your new configuration by running terraform destroy followed by terraform apply. You must destroy your configuration and then apply it again as any code in the user_data attribute is only run when an EC2 instance first starts up. If you were to run terraform apply without destroying the instance first, as the instance wouldn't be booting up for the first time, your docker swarm init command wouldn't be run.

Let's double-check that your swarm started properly in your instance. To do this, you could just SSH into your instance and then run the docker node ls command once inside. However, that would mean that any time you want to run a Docker command in your instance, you would have to SSH inside and then run the command—that's too many steps for us. It would be easier if you could just run the Docker command directly from your terminal. And, you can. But how?

You can do this by specifying the DOCKER_HOST environment variable when running your Docker command. This environment variable allows you to run your command on a different host than your host machine. In order to run Docker commands on your EC2 instance, the DOCKER_HOST value must be the

SSH address of your instance. To configure this, there are three simple steps you can follow:

1. Adding your EC2 instance's IP to the list of known hosts on your computer.
2. Adding the private key for your instance to your ssh-agent.
3. Running a Docker command in your computer's terminal while specifying your EC2 instance's SSH address as the DOCKER_HOST.

When connecting to a host via SSH, there is a ~/.ssh/known_hosts file that keeps track of the IPs that you connect to and their public keys. There is also an ssh-agent to which you can add a private key. Once you add a private key to your SSH agent, provided the IP has already been added to your known hosts, you won't have to specify the private key for that IP when SSH-ing into it. This is because the SSH client will apply the private key itself for you.

To add an IP to the known hosts of your computer, you can either SSH into an instance and write "yes" when asked if you want to add it to your known hosts (as you've been doing throughout this chapter), or you can run the command ssh-keyscan -H YOUR_INSTANCE_IP >> ~/.ssh/known_hosts (the -H option hashes the hostname). Then to add a private key to your ssh-agent, you'd run the command ssh-add PRIVATE_KEY_FILE.

How about running the docker command? When running a docker command, you can specify the DOCKER_HOST environment variable to run the command on a different host than your local computer. To run commands on your instance from your terminal, you'd set this DOCKER_HOST variable to be the SSH address of your instance. The following code snippet walks you through adding your private key to your ssh-agent, adding your instance's IP to your known hosts, and then running the docker node ls command on your instance from your own terminal with the SSH authentication being done automatically in the background by the SSH client. Run these commands:

```
$ ssh-add private_key.pem
Identity added: private_key.pem (private_key.pem)
$ ssh-keyscan -H YOUR_INSTANCE_IP >> ~/.ssh/known_hosts
# 13.42.45.160:22 SSH-2.0-OpenSSH_8.7
...
$ DOCKER_HOST=ssh://ec2-user@YOUR_INSTANCE_IP docker node ls
ID        HOSTNAME      STATUS   AVAILABILITY   MANAGER STATUS   ENGINE VER
xkq...    ip-172-3...   Ready    Active         Leader           20.10.25
```

Great. You can see that your swarm is active and ready for your application to be deployed. You'll do this in the next section.

Deploy Your Application to Production

Now that you can execute commands in your instance directly from your terminal, you don't even have to save your Docker Compose file on your instance. You can do everything from your own terminal! Amazing, isn't it?

To deploy your application, all you need to do is run a `docker stack deploy` of the Docker Compose file that you created in the previous chapter. Recall that the default image in your Compose file is the one saved to the remote GitHub Docker registry. Remember that because of the CI pipeline you implemented in Chapter 4, the Docker image for the application with database support that you built and deployed locally in the previous chapter was saved to the GitHub Docker registry when you merged your PR. That means that to deploy your web service defined in your Docker Compose file, you must be able to pull your remote `ghcr.io/YOUR_GITHUB_USERNAME/kanban:latest`. In order to do this, you must log in to the GitHub Docker registry. You can do this the same way that you did in Chapter 4: by running `echo "$GITHUB_TOKEN" | docker login ghcr.io -u USERNAME --password-stdin`.

Then, to deploy your application, just run `docker stack deploy`, remembering to specify your Compose file with the command and your EC2 instance SSH address as the `DOCKER_HOST`. You'll also have to pass the `--with-registry-auth` flag so that the Docker daemon can authenticate itself with the GitHub Docker registry and pull the image. Once you've deployed your application, check that it has been deployed properly by running the `docker service ls` command on your instance from your terminal. You should see both your `web` and `db` services in the output. Your terminal interaction should look like this:

```
$ echo "$GITHUB_TOKEN" | docker login ghcr.io -u USERNAME --password-stdin
Login Succeeded
$ DOCKER_HOST=ssh://ec2-user@YOUR_INSTANCE_IP \
    docker stack deploy -c ../../compose.yaml kanban --with-registry-auth
Creating network kanban_default
Creating service kanban_db
Creating service kanban_web
$ DOCKER_HOST=ssh://ec2-user@YOUR_INSTANCE_IP docker service ls
ID     NAME         MODE       REPLICAS   IMAGE              PORTS
tup    kanban_db    repl...    1/1        postgres:15.2      *:30000->5432/tcp
tw3    kanban_web   repl...    1/1        ghcr.io/beamops    *:4000->4000/tcp
```

Now visit port 4000 of your EC2 instance's IP and you'll see your application running. Congratulations! You just deployed your application to production! That was hard work.

You can now close the "Create production env in AWS for a single-node swarm" issue you created in Chapter 2. To do so, add your .pem file to your .gitignore, create a new branch, commit your remaining files, and make and merge a pull request, being sure to include closes #ISSUE_ID in your PR description. Lastly, clean up and remove your production environment by running terraform destroy.

What Have You Learned?

In this chapter, you created your production environment in AWS—consisting of an EC2 instance, a security group, a VPC, a subnet, and an AMI—and deployed your application to it. Having your AWS resources defined by Terraform and Packer in infrastructure-as-code means that they are under version control and you can replicate your environment easily with one terraform apply command and ensure environment integrity. You now have a template to create a remote environment in AWS and deploy your application with two simple commands: terraform apply and docker stack deploy. You can officially own the "creation and reproducibility of remote environments" part of the software delivery process!

It's now time to hide any sensitive data in your code and automate the deployment of your application with a continuous deployment (CD) pipeline. In doing so, you will gain even more practice demonstrating the Kaizen principle. You'll see how deploying smaller features more often makes your application more robust and makes you more confident when deploying.

> **The Extra Mile**
>
> If you wish to deepen your knowledge of the themes we've covered in this chapter and refine your BEAMOps developer super powers, we've created a few tasks for you to do:
>
> 1. You know that you can validate your Packer template with the command packer validate. There's also a separate command that checks whether your template is properly formatted. Create a GitHub Action that uses these two commands to validate your Packer template and check that's properly formatted. This GitHub Action should be triggered on a pull request in which a Packer template is part of the diff.
>
> 2. You've seen that you can execute remote commands in a Docker host using the DOCKER_HOST environment variable. Docker has a cool concept called contexts.[a] Create a new Docker context for your production environment that references your instance's IP. Then run commands in your EC2 instance using this context without specifying the DOCKER_HOST variable.
>
> ---
> a. https://docs.docker.com/engine/context/working-with-contexts/

CHAPTER 7

Continuous Deployment and Repository Secrets

As applications evolve, so too should their security and efficiency. Once your application is out of the development phase and being deployed to production, two important things need to happen: you must maintain the confidentiality and integrity of sensitive data (such as passwords, API keys, and certificates), and you must implement an automated continuous deployment (CD) pipeline to easily identify issues and ensure your application always deploys in the same way.

In order to practice the Kaizen principle in your work as a developer, you should aim to ship less code more often and be sure that it works. Your CI pipeline covers the "be sure that it works" part. Your CD pipeline will help you "ship less code more often." It'll ensure that any feature that passes your CI checks and is merged into your main branch will automatically deploy to production. This means you'll be more careful about what you ship and how you ship it. It'll also encourage you to submit smaller features and babysit a deployment to ensure that it works as expected. Then, if a bug arises, you'll immediately submit a new PR to fix the concrete issue—which is far better than dropping everything on a different task and switching your focus to fix the issue. Implementing a CD pipeline will boost your confidence in the stability of your application and speed up the delivery time of new features. John C. Maxwell said: "Fail early, fail often, but always fail forward." A CD pipeline will help you to fail forward.

This chapter will show you how to secure your application using secrets—a Docker feature—and how to construct an efficient CD pipeline using these secrets. By the end of this chapter, you'll be able to close two of the CI/CD issues you created in Chapter 2.

Let's get down to business!

Handle Sensitive Data with Docker Secrets

Docker secrets are a crucial feature of Docker and are essential in enhancing the security of your application. The primary goal of Docker secrets is to prevent sensitive data from being exposed in plain text inside a Docker Swarm or stored hard-coded in an application's codebase. Recall that to run your web application and database services, you need to specify three separate environment variables that have sensitive values: your POSTGRES_PASSWORD, your DATABASE_URL, and your SECRET_KEY_BASE. With Docker secrets, you can safely handle and share such data in a Docker Compose or Docker Swarm environment.

A common way to define secret environment variables is to use a standard .env file. However, Docker secrets are a better way to do so. These are the three main advantages to using Docker secrets over a standard .env file:

- *Scope of Access*: Docker secrets are only accessible to services running in your stack. Moreover, not all of your services have access to all of your secrets—only the ones allocated to them in their service description. This allows for fine-grained control over which processes access certain secret data.

- *Security*: Docker secrets are stored encrypted in a swarm's RAFT logs, and they're only decrypted when they're allocated to a service. RAFT is an algorithm that ensures consensus among swarm nodes so that they can work together in a consistent and replicated state even if there is a failure. The RAFT logs record changes and transactions within the swarm. For more information, check out the Docker docs.[1]

- *Lifecycle Management*: Docker secrets allow for robust lifecycle management—they can be created, used, rotated, and revoked without the need for service downtime.

When using an .env file, environment variables are not encrypted and are globally available, but with Docker secrets, your data is encrypted and only shared with the parts of your infrastructure that need it.

---

1. https://docs.docker.com/engine/swarm/raft/

Now that you know why you should use Docker secrets, let's have you practice how to use them to hide your POSTGRES_PASSWORD, DATABASE_URL, and SECRET_KEY_BASE variables.

Use Docker Secrets with the postgres Image

Incorporating Docker secrets into your application is relatively straightforward. There are two ways you can work with Docker secrets, either using the docker secrets command[2] or defining your secrets in secret files and adding these files to your Compose file. As a BEAMOps developer, you should always prefer the declarative option and include your secret management in your infrastructure-as-code. Doing so makes your application more legible and easier to replicate. For that reason, you will declare your secrets in secret files and then inject those secrets into your Docker architecture by referencing them in your Compose file. Docker secrets work with both docker compose and docker stack commands, so you can keep environment integrity and run your application in the same way locally and remotely.

To define a Docker secret, you use the secrets top-level key in your Compose file. Under this key, you'll write a list of IDs that will be the names of the secret variables that you'll create. Each of these IDs will have the file sub-attribute to specify which file each of those secrets is defined in. Each Docker secret you create will be in a separate file. This is done to make the updating of secrets more explicit. To update a secret, you cannot just update the value in the file; you must create a whole new secret. We'll not cover the topic of updating secrets in this book, but if you want to know more then check out the Docker docs.[3]

In the first instance, you'll create a secret for the POSTGRES_PASSWORD environment variable listed in your compose.yaml file. The convention is to name secrets without spaces or special characters, all lowercase. This means the secret that will eventually be set to your POSTGRES_PASSWORD environment variable would be named postgrespassword. This convention also affects the name of the file that contains the secret value, which is the same as the secret name but with a dot at the beginning, for example, .postgrespassword. To define your postgrespassword secret, add the secrets top-level key to the Compose file you created in Chapter 5. Then add postgrespassword as a sub-ID and add the file attribute beneath this. The bottom of your compose.yaml file should now look like this:

---

2. https://docs.docker.com/engine/swarm/secrets/
3. https://docs.docker.com/engine/swarm/secrets/#example-rotate-a-secret

```
# in compose.yaml
secrets:
  postgrespassword:
    file: ./secrets/.postgrespassword
```

Now that you have defined where your secret will come from, you need to add your secrets attribute to the db service. This attribute specifies a list of secret names that are the secrets that will be exposed to that service. Add this attribute so that the beginning of your db service looks like this:

```
# in compose.yaml
services:
  db:
    image: postgres:15.2
    secrets:
      - postgrespassword
```

Adding this secrets key to your service mounts the files where your secrets are defined into your service container. Each file is mounted to the path /run/secrets/<SECRET_NAME>. In this case, your postgrespassword secret will be mounted to the file /run/secrets/postgrespassword. This is important to note for when you define the environment variable.

Now that your service has access to the file in which your postgrespassword secret is defined, set your POSTGRES_PASSWORD environment variable as the value inside that file. You may be thinking that you could just set the filename to be equal to your POSTGRES_PASSWORD environment variable. But if you do so, the secret won't be loaded properly. This is because your secret is defined in a file and the contents of this file aren't automatically exported for you. The content of the file must be extracted manually. Because of this, the convention is to use the _FILE suffix in the environment variable name to indicate that the value should be read from a file. After you define your variable with the _FILE suffix, we'll look at how to adapt your db service to read its contents.

This may seem like a lot of effort to hide an environment variable, but remember it's much more secure than using a .env file. So, remove the POSTGRES_PASSWORD environment variable from db service and add a new POSTGRES_PASSWORD_FILE variable that's set to your mounted /run/secrets/postgrespassword filei:

```
# in compose.yaml
services:
  db:
    image: postgres:15.2
    environment:
      POSTGRES_PASSWORD_FILE: /run/secrets/postgrespassword
```

So, how does the Postgres image know that the POSTGRES_PASSWORD_FILE variable that you just defined corresponds to the POSTGRES_PASSWORD? Well, if you look at that image's docs[4] and scroll down to the Docker secrets section, you'll see that this image automatically does the association for you. That might seem like a bit of dark magic, but you can see why this happens if you go to the entrypoint.sh file of the image.[5] There you'll see that if the name of a variable doesn't exist, but there is a variable of the same name with the _FILE suffix, then the contents of the file will be read and exported to the name of the variable without the _FILE suffix. In this case, the contents of the file in the variable POSTGRES_PASSWORD_FILE will be exported to the variable POSTGRES_PASSWORD.

Well done. You've defined your postgrespassword secret in your Compose file, mounted it in your db service, and instantiated your environment variable. The only thing left is to create the actual secret file. To do this, create a directory called secrets and inside it a file called .postgrespassword whose contents is postgres. You can achieve this by running the following command in the root of your application:

```
$ mkdir secrets && echo "postgres" > secrets/.postgrespassword
```

Great! Now let's make sure that your database password has been properly set by running your application. You can build a local version of your web service image and run it by passing the WEB_IMAGE environment variable to the docker compose up command. Or, instead, you can run docker compose up without the WEB_IMAGE environment variable and use the default image in your Compose file: the :latest tag of your image that your CI pushes to the remote GitHub Docker registry. If you choose to run the remote image, be sure to add the --pull=always option to the docker compose up command. This ensures that you're in fact running your remote image and not any potential stale images in your local machine with the same name. In the following terminal example, we've chosen to use the remote image:

```
$ docker compose up --pull=always
[+] Running 8/8
 ✓ web 6 layers [██████]      0B/0B Pulled                          2.1s
   ✓ 85e50d2242ce Already exists                                    0.0s
   ...
 ✓ db Pulled                                                        1.3s
 ...
 ✓ Network kanban_default     Created                                0.0s
 ✓ Volume kanban_db_data      Created                                0.0s
 ✓ Container kanban-db-1      Created                                0.1s
```

---

4. https://hub.docker.com/_/postgres
5. https://github.com/docker-library/postgres/blob/master/docker-entrypoint.sh#L9

```
✓ Container kanban-web-1    Created                                    0.1s
Attaching to kanban-db-1, kanban-web-1
..db-1    | The files belonging to this database system will be owned ...
...
... web-1 | 04:50:37.189 [info] Migrations already up
... web-1 | 15:12:41.214 [info] Running ...Endpoint... at :::4000 (http)
... web-1 | 15:12:41.216 [info] Access ...Endpoint at https://localhost
```

Nice work! You've successfully used Docker secrets to inject your POSTGRES_PASSWORD environment variable into your db service and avoid it being hard-coded in your Compose file. You've taken the first step in securing your application so that it can be part of an efficient CD pipeline.

To recap, the steps to adding a Docker secret to your Compose file are the following:

1. Use the secrets top-level key to define your secrets.

2. Add the secrets attribute to your services to mount specific secret files in that particular service and give access to specific secrets.

3. Set the secret file path as the value of an environment variable whose name is the environment variable you wish to use with the _FILE suffix at the end.

4. Adapt your application to be able to read secrets from the filesystem and set them equal to the environment variable name without the _FILE suffix.

In this instance, you haven't done step 4, as the postgres image does this for you automatically. But what happens when you're using a custom image that doesn't handle the _FILE association for you? We'll look at this in the next section.

Before moving on, make sure to clean up your current environment by running docker compose down.

Load Secrets from _FILE Environment Variables with env.sh.eex

In the previous section, you dipped your toes into Docker secrets. You learned that secrets are mounted as files in a service container and that the postgres image is able to read the password from a file. Let's recap the steps that the postgres entrypoint executes to set the environment variable:

1. It looks for any environment variable that ends with _FILE.

2. It reads the value of the environment variable, which will be a file path in the form /var/run/<SECRET_NAME>.

3. It reads the content of the file in the path of the previous step.

4. It exports the file content and sets it to an environment variable that's the same as the environment variable read in step 1 but without the _FILE suffix.

The postgres image does these four steps for you automatically. But how will you handle the environment variables for your Phoenix application in your web service? The answer lies in your Release configuration. Earlier in the book, you ran two commands to create your releases:

1. phx.gen.release: to create the migrate and server Phoenix release helper scripts.
2. mix release: to build the release itself.

There is another Elixir mix command that you can use alongside the Phoenix release generator command to create more release configuration files: mix release.init. This new command generates four new .eex template scripts that allow you to fine-tune your release configuration. It doesn't interfere with the phx.gen.release command but rather adds extra configurations. Run this command in the root of your project as we've done in the following example, and we'll observe the output:

```
$ mix release.init
* creating rel/vm.args.eex
* creating rel/remote.vm.args.eex
* creating rel/env.sh.eex
* creating rel/env.bat.eex
```

As you can see, this command generated four new files in your rel directory: two vm.args scripts (which allow you to specify flags that control how the Erlang VM and its runtime operate) and two env scripts.

We're interested in the env scripts. The env.sh.eex script is for Unix-like systems and the env.bat.eex is for Windows machines. You'll use one of these files to specify the setting of your environment variables—you'll have to choose the appropriate file based on your machine. In this book, we'll be using the env.sh.eex file.

These env files are eex[6] templates that are used to generate an env.sh file when you build your release. You can see this in action now if you generate your release by executing the MIX_ENV=prod mix release command. Run this command. You may be asked if you want to overwrite your current release, type "Y" and press Enter. Do this whenever you're asked this question again during the rest of the chapter. You can see an example terminal interaction at the top of the next page.

---

6. https://hexdocs.pm/eex/1.15.6/EEx.html

```
$ MIX_ENV=prod mix release
...
Release kanban-0.1.0 already exists. Overwrite? [Yn] Y
...
* creating _build/prod/rel/kanban/releases/0.1.0/vm.args
* creating _build/prod/rel/kanban/releases/0.1.0/remote.vm.args
* creating _build/prod/rel/kanban/releases/0.1.0/env.sh
...
```

Your release now includes an env.sh file. If you look at the contents and compare it with the env.sh.eex file, you'll see that the content is the same.

In Chapter 3, you saw that the two ways to run a release are to either run the release script itself (_build/prod/rel/kanban/bin/kanban) followed by the start command or to run the server helper script created by the Phoenix generator (which in turn runs that release script while setting the PHX_SERVER environment variable). If you look at this release script, you'll see that the env.sh is sourced whenever this script is run. We've pasted the part of the file that specifies this here:

```
# in _build/prod/rel/kanban/bin/kanban
REL_VSN_DIR="$RELEASE_ROOT/releases/$RELEASE_VSN"
. "$REL_VSN_DIR/env.sh"
```

As the previous code snippet shows, the env.sh file will be sourced every time a release is run. This means that any logic to do with environment variables that must be applied on every run should be included in this file. You could write the logic directly in this env.sh file. However, as you saw earlier, every time you run the mix release command, this file is re-created based on the contents of the .eex template file. Therefore, the logic itself must be written in the .eex file, otherwise it would be overwritten the next time you build a release. In the next section, you'll edit this file so that your Phoenix application can properly interpret your DATABASE_URL once you add the value as a Docker secret to the environment variable DATABASE_URL_FILE.

The Bourne Shell and Logic in env.sh.eex

 Pay attention to the first line of the _build/prod/rel/kanban/bin/kanban script. It's written in #!/bin/sh—the bourne shell, and not the bash shell. This has been done to make the release more portable and compatible with as many distributions as possible. So, when implementing any logic in the env.sh.eex file, take into account that not all bash functions will be available. You must only use functions that the bourne shell can interpret.

Load your DATABASE_URL Environment Variable from a Secret File

In the previous section, you learned that in order to prepare your Phoenix application to be able to load Docker secrets, you must edit the env.sh.eex file. It may seem that using Docker secrets and having to edit this file to be able to interpret them is a lot of effort for hiding environment variables. But remember that Docker secrets are more secure than using a standard .env file as they are encrypted by default and are only exposed to the services that you specify.

To set your DATABASE_URL variable, you'll start by adapting your Phoenix application and editing your env.sh.eex file. In your current Compose file, the DATABASE_URL value is hard-coded as ecto://postgres:postgres@db/postgres. Remove this hard-coded value from this file, and let's make it secret. To do so, follow the same steps as you did in the previous section with your postgrespassword secret, adhering to the lowercase and no-space convention. Create a new file called .databaseurl in your /secrets folder whose content is ecto://postgres:postgres @db/postgres. You can do so with the following command:

```
$ echo "ecto://postgres:postgres@db/postgres" > secrets/.databaseurl
```

Nice! In the previous section, you practiced handling secrets in your Compose file using the secrets top-level and subkey attributes. The part that you didn't implement yourself was the transforming of the environment variable name to read a secret file and then set the contents to be a new environment variable without the _FILE suffix. We, therefore, recommend that before you add the secrets key to your Compose file, you start with this transformation of the data to make sure that the data in your secret files is being properly read. So, let's start by implementing a simple if case in your env.sh.eex file that states that if the DATABASE_URL_FILE environment variable is present, read the file and set the contents as the value of a new environment variable called DATABASE_URL. You can see how we've done that using cat here:

```
# in rel/env.sh.eex
if [ "${DATABASE_URL_FILE}" ]; then
    DATABASE_URL="$(cat "$DATABASE_URL_FILE")"
    echo "Loading dabatase URL secret: ${DATABASE_URL}"
    export DATABASE_URL="$DATABASE_URL"
fi
```

As we mentioned, the code snippet checks if there is a DATABASE_URL_FILE environment variable. If there is one, it reads the content of the file and assigns it to the DATABASE_URL variable. There is also a log message to show the value has been properly read from the file.

Now that you've edited the env.sh.eex template file, you need to rebuild your release by running the mix release command. Any time you change any release configuration files, you must always rebuild your release to apply these changes. So, run this command while specifying the MIX_ENV variable as usual to overwrite your current release to create a new env.sh file. After this, run the release script without the start command. This will source the env.sh script that you just updated and print out your DATABASE_URL variable. Run these two commands. Your terminal should look similar to this:

```
$ MIX_ENV=prod mix release
Release kanban-0.1.0 already exists. Overwrite? [Yn] Y
...
* creating _build/prod/rel/kanban/releases/0.1.0/env.sh
...
$ DATABASE_URL_FILE=secrets/.databaseurl \
  ./_build/prod/rel/kanban/bin/kanban
Loading dabatase URL secret: ecto://postgres:postgres@db/postgres
Usage: kanban COMMAND [ARGS]
...
```

> **Run Binary Script Alone to Simplify Debugging**
>
>  We're running the release script alone, rather than running it with the start command or the server script because we don't want to actually start the application. If you were to start the application, you would receive database connection errors as you don't have a Postgres database running. Running the binary script alone allows you to avoid those errors but still debug the env.sh script.

As you can see from the code snippet, the log was printed and the database value was successfully read from your file. Well done! However, your BEAMOps sense may be tingling because this environment variable transformation is coupled to the DATABASE_URL secret. This means that every time you add a new secret, you have to update the template. This isn't sustainable, and it's not a good use of time. So, how can you dynamically load all secrets that follow the pattern *_FILE? We'll look at this in the next section.

Load All Environment Variable Secrets Dynamically

In the previous section, you saw that to transform the way environment variables are set, you need to edit the env.sh.eex template file. You saw how to do this with the DATABASE_URL_FILE environment variable. In this section, you'll replace that if clause with a dynamic for loop that's able to transform *all* environment variables that end with _FILE.

We noted that the env.sh script uses the bourne shell to perform its commands. This means that you can run common sh commands like env and grep. Combining these two commands, you can loop through the environment variables that end in _FILE, extract the variable name and filename value, and set the environment variable accordingly. To do this, replace your current if clause in your env.sh.eex file with the following code snippet. (We'll walk through what is happening afterward.)

```
# in rel/env.sh.eex
for key in $(env | grep "_FILE" ); do
    var_name="${key%%_FILE=*}"
    secret_file="${key#*=}"
    file_words=$(wc -w < "$secret_file")
    if [ -e "$secret_file" ] && [ "$file_words" -eq 1 ]; then
        echo "Exporting $secret_file so $var_name is $(cat "$secret_file")"
        export "$var_name=$(cat "$secret_file")"
    fi
done
```

Let's walk through the for loop in the previous example line by line to understand what is going on:

1. for key in $(env | grep "_FILE"); do: This line uses the env command to list all environment variables and uses grep to filter only those containing _FILE. It then iterates over these variables using a for loop. The key iteratee is a string of both the variable name and the file name value, for example, "DATABASE_URL_FILE=secrets/.databaseurl".

2. var_name="${key%%_FILE=*}": This line extracts the variable name from the key iteratee by setting the var_name variable to be everything before _FILE, for example, DATABASE_URL.

3. secret_file="${key#*=}": This line extracts the secret filename from the key iteratee by setting the secret_file variable to be everything after the "=" sign, for example, secrets/.databaseurl.

4. file_words=$(wc -w < "$secret_file"): This line works out the number of words in your secret file.

5. if [-e "$secret_file"] && ["$file_words" -eq 1]; then: This line checks if the secret_file variable exists and that it only contains one word (secret).

6. echo "Exporting secret......": This line is a helper log that indicates that the script is exporting a value from file X and setting it to be environment variable Y. This is just for debugging purposes. You'll remove this line later on once you know that the code snippet works.

7. `export "$var_name=$(cat "$secret_file")"`: This line exports the secret stored in the secret_file file to be an environment variable that has the same name as the var_name value. It uses cat to read the content of the file and export to make the variable available.

Now that you've written your dynamic for loop, rebuild your release and then run the release script again in the same way as before, specifying the DATABASE_URL_FILE environment variable. Your terminal should look like this:

```
$ MIX_ENV=prod mix release
...
$ DATABASE_URL_FILE=secrets/.databaseurl \
  ./_build/prod/rel/kanban/bin/kanban
...
Exporting secrets/.databaseurl so DATABASE_URL is
ecto://postgres:postgres@db/postgres
Usage: kanban COMMAND [ARGS]
...
```

> **You May See Many Export Logs**
>
> If you have other environment variables in your PATH that end in _FILE, you may find that your log shows those other environment variables. Don't worry! This won't affect the variables injected into your swarm, as your swarm will only have access to the variables you specify in your Compose file. If you wish to only see the log for your DATABASE_URL variable, put your echo statement inside another if clause where ["$var_name" == "DATABASE_URL"].

It worked! Your secrets/.databaseurl was successfully read and the environment variable name was transformed correctly! Go ahead and remove the echo log in your env.sh.eex file and rebuild your release, specifying the MIX_ENV variable. The next step is to add a secret file for your SECRET_KEY_BASE environment variable. After this, you'll update the secrets top-level key in your Compose file as well as the secrets and environment sub-attributes of your web service to include these secrets programmatically. To create the secret key base file, run the following command:

```
$ echo $(mix phx.gen.secret) > secrets/.secretkeybase
```

Now update your Compose file so your secrets top-level key includes your two new databaseurl and secretkeybase secrets. Then add these secrets to your web service using the secrets and environment attributes. Remember to remove your hard-coded DATABASE_URL and SECRET_KEY_BASE variables in the process. Your Compose file should now look like this:

```yaml
# in compose.yaml
  web:
    image: ${WEB_IMAGE:-ghcr.io/beamops/kanban:latest}
    deploy:
      restart_policy:
        condition: on-failure
        delay: 5s
        max_attempts: 3
        window: 120s
    environment:
      DATABASE_URL_FILE: /run/secrets/databaseurl
      SECRET_KEY_BASE_FILE: /run/secrets/secretkeybase
      PHX_HOST: "localhost"
    ports:
      - 4000:4000
    command: >
      bash -c "bin/migrate && \
               bin/server"
    depends_on:
      - db
    secrets:
      - databaseurl
      - secretkeybase
secrets:
  postgrespassword:
    file: ./secrets/.postgrespassword
  secretkeybase:
    file: ./secrets/.secretkeybase
  databaseurl:
    file: ./secrets/.databaseurl
```

>
> **Load Secret Values Dynamically**
>
> It's extremely easy to load secret values dynamically, depending on your environment (for example, staging vs. production). To do so, you'd create separate environment subfolders inside your .secrets directory and then make your file name references in your Compose file dynamic, for example, ./secrets/${ENVIRONMENT}/.secretkeybase.

Great! You've successfully removed the hard-coded values for the DATABASE_URL, SECRET_KEY_BASE, and POSTGRES_PASSWORD variables from your Compose file! Feel free to run your stack by building a new Docker image for your web service and then executing docker compose up, remembering to specify the WEB_IMAGE environment variable. In this instance, you cannot use your remote image created by the CI to run your application as you've changed the release configuration and your remote image doesn't include these changes. If you build a new local image and run it, you'll see that your secrets are applied properly and your application runs without any errors.

You're off to a great start with Docker secrets. But, if you run git status, you'll see that git is tracking all of the files in your secrets folder. If you were to add these files to GitHub in plain text, this would defeat the point of not having the values hard-coded.

You could always put those files in the .gitignore and then share the files manually with your team. But there's a better and more programmatic way to do this where your secret files are under version control and cannot be updated by accident: by using SOPS, a tool that encrypts and decrypts the content of sensitive files. We'll look at this in more detail in the next section. Clean up your environment by running docker compose down before you move on.

Encrypt Secret Data with SOPS

It's a good practice to ensure secrets are version-controlled, just like your infrastructure configurations or application code. Version-controlling your secrets means that they cannot be easily, or accidentally, changed. However, you must *never version-control your secrets in plain text*. Doing so isn't secure and leaves your application exposed to a security breach. Instead, you should encrypt your data at rest in your version-control repository—and this is something that you can achieve with SOPS.

SOPS (Secrets OPerationS)[7] is an open-source tool developed by Mozilla for managing and storing secrets in a secure and manageable way. It allows you to encrypt sensitive information—such as passwords, tokens, or API keys—directly within configuration files. The tool uses public key cryptography to ensure secrets are encrypted and that only authorized users or systems can decrypt them. SOPS integrates seamlessly with version-control systems like Git, enabling the safe storage and sharing of secrets among team members or automated systems. It also supports various backends for key management, such as AWS KMS, GCP KMS, Azure Key Vault, and PGP, meaning that it can be used for different cloud environments and workflows. The primary aim of SOPS is to provide a method for managing secrets that aligns with modern requirements for operating applications and infrastructure.

With SOPS, you create and update decrypted data in your terminal using text editors provided by running sops commands. You give SOPS the data you want to encrypt, and SOPS encrypts the data and creates a file in your working

---

7. https://github.com/getsops/sops

directory with that encrypted data. When you want to update your encrypted values, you use a sops command, and SOPS will regenerate your encrypted file. When encrypting and decrypting data, SOPS uses a symmetric key, which is provided by a backend that you choose.

>
> **vault: Another Tool for Managing Secrets**
>
> While SOPS is a powerful tool for encrypting files within Git repositories, vault[8] by Hashicorp is another excellent tool you might consider for managing secrets. It provides a broader set of features for secret management and is widely adopted in the industry. We chose to use SOPS in the book for simplicity and ease of use, but we encourage you to explore both options to find the best fit for your needs.

So, how will you use SOPS to make your application more robust and build an efficient CD pipeline? You'll first create a .sops.yaml file in the root of your project that will specify the backend that you want to use (age) and the public age key that SOPS will use for encryption. You'll then use SOPS to encrypt the .postgrespassword, .secretkeybase, and .databaseurl values that you've created so far in this chapter into a single secrets.enc.yaml. This will allow you to push your secret values to GitHub in one centralized file. As your secrets.enc.yaml file is encrypted, its contents won't be visible–only users with a key will be able to unlock its content.

In the next section, we'll look at two CLI commands you'll use to handle the encryption and decryption of your secrets: one from age and another from sops.

age and sops Commands

The first command that you'll use is: age-keygen. It has the following format:

```
age-keygen -o PATH_TO_KEY
```

The age-keygen command generates a new age key pair and saves the private key to the file specified by the -o flag. When the key pair is generated, the public key is printed to the terminal like so:

```
$ age-keygen -o key.txt
Public key: age1nve8m26qrwzqd62gt4q78smgfhwh2rexeqh9fmjgjp93nw65c3squl9377
```

The second command you'll use is sops. It'll do different things depending on the options you do or don't pass. The command has the following format:

```
sops [OPTIONS] FILENAME
```

---

8. https://www.vaultproject.io/

The `FILENAME` is the name of the file that will hold your encrypted data. You can pass *no* options to the command like this:

```
$ sops my_secret_file.yaml
```

In this case, SOPS will open a text editor in your terminal that, once saved, will be the contents of the file path you specified.

The first time you run this command, you specify the data that you want to encrypt. Once you write in your data and save the file that the text editor gives you, SOPS encrypts the contents with the backend specified in your .sops.yaml file (which in this case will be age), creates the my_secret_file.yaml in your working directory, and saves the encrypted data to that file.

If you ever want to edit your encrypted values, you can rerun the same sops my_secret_file.yaml command again, but this time specifying the `SOPS_AGE_KEY_FILE` environment variable whose value should be the path of the private key that you're using for encryption. Running this command will open up a SOPS editor in your terminal again, and you can edit the file as you wish. When you save and exit the terminal editor, SOPS will automatically re-encrypt your my_secret_file.yaml file with the new values.

To decrypt the contents of your secret file, pass the `--decrypt` option to the `sops` command. When you do this, you need to specify the `SOPS_AGE_KEY_FILE` environment variable, like so:

```
$ SOPS_AGE_KEY_FILE=key.txt sops --decrypt my_secret_file.yaml
```

SOPS will then decrypt the contents of your file and output the decrypted values to your terminal.

If you're working with a team, you'll need to save the private age key in a safe place that everyone can access. A secure way to share the file would be to either use a password manager application like 1password[9] or onetimesecret.[10]

In the next section, you'll create your .sops.yaml file and add your three environment variables to a secrets.enc.yaml file to encrypt their data.

Create Your .sops.yaml File

Now that you know the general lay of the land, generate your key pair by running the age-keygen -o key.txt command inside your environments/production folder. This will output the public key, which you'll add in your .sops.yaml file. You can see an example terminal interaction here:

---

9. https://1password.com/
10. https://onetimesecret.com/

```
$ cd environments/production
$ age-keygen -o key.txt
Public key: age197tlltzcpsag02kz56dqch9kaal4y3htucjwvm90essuf7y5rd2s0np
```

Now create a .sops.yaml file in the root of your project and put the public key that was output in your terminal into it, like so:

```
# in .sops.yaml
creation_rules:
  - path_regex: secrets/.*$
    key_groups:
      - age:
        - "age1rpt4347r8xkhlk68cl402drfdm5q29ajw8q76l6hlvsguf6u0u6sl2k3ld"
```

This .sops.yaml file indicates to SOPS that when encrypting and decrypting files in the path specified in the regex_path value (your secrets folder), it should use the age key that you created.

Now that you've done this, run sops ../../secrets/secrets.enc.yaml from your environments/production folder to create your encrypted secrets file inside your secrets folder. Running this command will open up a text editor in your terminal. Edit the contents of the file in your text editor to include your .postgrespassword, .secretkeybase, and .databaseurl variables. Look at the next two terminal interactions to see how to do this:

```
$ sops ../../secrets/secrets.enc.yaml
    hello: Welcome to SOPS! Edit this file as you please!
    example_key: example_value
    # Example comment
    example_array:
        - example_value1
        - example_value2
    example_number: 1234.56789
    example_booleans:
        - true
        - false
```

Replace the placeholders with the contents of your .postgrespassword, .secretkeybase, and .databaseurl files so that the editor looks something like this (remember to replace the secret key base value with the value of *your* secrets/.secretkeybase file and not what we have in the code snippet):

```
$ sops ../../secrets/secrets.enc.yaml
    .databaseurl: ecto://postgres:postgres@db/postgres
    .postgrespassword: postgres
    .secretkeybase: 9w0RvLm5m1U0awC8RCj4ASIwXgcSzIYBiUqU8yzyFl11xfsFqy/X
```

Now save the file in the editor and exit. You'll see that a new secrets.enc.yaml file has been added to your secrets folder. If you open this file, you'll see that your three environment variables are there, but their contents are encrypted. The beginning of your secrets.enc.yaml file will look something like this:

```
# in secrets/secrets.enc.yaml
.databaseurl: ENC[AES256_GCM,data:b7...,iv:0e...,tag:Gf...Q==,type:str]
.postgrespassword: ENC[AES256_GCM,data:lY...,iv:T...,tag:1...g=,type:str]
.secretkeybase: ENC[AES256_GCM,data:jG...,iv:C5...,tag:zK...g=,type:str]
```

If you want to see the decrypted version of your secrets/secrets.enc.yaml file, run the command SOPS_AGE_KEY_FILE="key.txt" sops --decrypt secrets/secrets.enc.yaml, and you will see the decrypted values in your terminal like so:

```
$ SOPS_AGE_KEY_FILE="key.txt" sops --decrypt ../../secrets/secrets.enc.yaml
.databaseurl: ecto://postgres:postgres@db/postgres
.postgrespassword: postgres
.secretkeybase: 9wORvLm5m1UOawC8RCj4ASIwXgcSzIYBiUqU8yzyFl1lxfsFqy/X
```

Now add your .databaseurl, .postgrespassword, .secretkeybase, and key.txt files to your .gitignore file by appending the following line to your file:

```
# in .gitignore
secrets/.*
**/key.txt
```

You've officially removed all the hard-coded sensitive values from your Compose file and placed them into one centralized secret file. You've encrypted these secrets so that they can be under version control and no one can know their contents unless they have the key. Great!

Now, create a new branch and commit all of the changes that you've made so far to this branch. Then push this commit to your remote repository and create a PR. You're now able to close the "Hide any sensitive data using Docker secrets" issue that you created in Chapter 2. Add closes #ISSUE_ID in the description of your PR and merge it. Go back to your main branch and pull your changes.

It's time to deploy your stack and create a CD script. This will give you the basis from which you can confidently employ the Kaizen principle and deploy small but effective changes to your application. First, though, you'll take the usual approach of manually running the steps before automating them. This way, you'll get very familiar with each step. In the next section, you'll manually deploy your application both locally and remotely to understand the deployment requirements.

Deploy Manually to Understand Requirements

Now that you've replaced your hard-coded environment variables with Docker secrets, let's recap the necessary steps to manually deploy your application both locally and remotely. After this, you'll create a streamlined script that automates the deployment of your application for you. We'll look first at deploying to a local swarm.

Manually Deploy Your Stack with Your Secrets to a Local Swarm

Let's deploy your stack to a local swarm. You have added the secrets functionality to your env.sh.eex file and generated a new release script. To make sure you deploy these new changes locally, rebuild your image locally and use the rebuilt image rather than the image stored in the remote repository. cd to the root of your repository and run the docker build command as we have done here, remembering to specify a tag:

```
$ cd ../../
$ docker build -t "kanban:latest" .
...
 => exporting to image                                          0.0s
 => => exporting layers                                         0.0s
 => => writing image sha256:caf094246d9ba47d6ba009292531ff870...  0.0s
 => => naming to docker.io/library/kanban:latest               0.0s
```

Remember that to deploy your application locally, as you did at the end of Chapter 5, you must run two commands: docker swarm init and docker stack deploy.

Before initiating your swarm, be sure that your host isn't already part of a swarm by running docker swarm leave --force. Then initiate your swarm and deploy your stack, remembering to specify the WEB_IMAGE environment variable to use your local image and not the remote one. We've done this here:

```
$ docker swarm leave --force
...
$ docker swarm init
Swarm initialized: current node (v5u992nwu...) is now a manager.
...
$ WEB_IMAGE=kanban:latest docker stack deploy -c compose.yaml kanban
...
Creating network kanban_default
Creating secret kanban_postgrespassword
Creating secret kanban_secretkeybase
Creating secret kanban_databaseurl
Creating service kanban_db
Creating service kanban_web
```

It worked! You can also see that the secrets you added to your Compose stack have been created as secrets in the swarm. You can verify this by inspecting your web service with docker service inspect, passing the prettier option and scrolling down to the Env and Secrets parts of the terminal output. You should see something similar to this:

```
$ docker service inspect --pretty kanban_web
...
 Env:            DATABASE_URL_FILE=/run/secrets/databaseurl
                 SECRET_KEY_BASE_FILE=/run/secrets/secretkeybase
Secrets:
 Target:         databaseurl
  Source:        kanban_databaseurl
 Target:         secretkeybase
  Source:        kanban_secretkeybase
...
```

Your secrets were defined and applied successfully. Now check that the services are up and running by executing docker service ls and then visiting http://localhost:4000 to see your application. There you have it, your application deployed locally! Once you're done with this, you can leave the swarm with docker swarm leave --force.

To recap, in order to deploy your stack locally, you need to go through the following steps:

1. Define the secrets for your application.
2. Initialize your local swarm.
3. Specify an image and run docker stack deploy.

Now that you know the three steps required to deploy your application locally after you added Docker secrets, let's recap how to deploy your application to production.

Manually Deploy to Production

We covered how to deploy to production in the previous chapter. Recall that you ran two commands: terraform apply and docker stack deploy. After running terraform apply to create your AWS resources and your remote Docker Swarm, you added the private key to your ssh-agent and the IP address of your EC2 instance to your list of known hosts. You then specified the IP address as the DOCKER_HOST and ran docker stack deploy. Let's see if anything has changed now that you've added Docker secrets.

To start, cd into environments/production where your main.tf file is located and run terraform apply as we've done in the upcoming example. This will re-create your

EC2 instance, security group, VPC, and subnets, as well as create your remote Docker Swarm:

```
$ cd environments/production
$ terraform apply
...
Apply complete! Resources: 5 added, 0 changed, 0 destroyed.
Outputs:
swarm_ssh_command = "ssh -i ./private_key.pem ec2-user@18.168.205.215"
```

Terrific. To deploy to your remote swarm, you'll need the private key for the EC2 instance as well as its IP address. Recall that when your Terraform configuration is applied for the first time, a new private key is created and stored in a file called private_key.pem. The next step is to add this to your ssh-agent. Just as you did in the previous chapter, you can do this by running ssh-add private_key.pem like so:

```
$ ssh-add private_key.pem
Identity added: private_key.pem (private_key.pem)
```

Now you're ready to deal with the IP address of the EC2 instance. You could use the IP address in the ssh command that was output to your terminal after you ran terraform apply. However, think about the fact that you'll be creating a script to do this deployment process for you in a few moments time, and that script won't have access to your Terraform outputs. You therefore need another way of obtaining the IP address of your EC2 instance. You can do this using the AWS CLI—a tool that you *will* be able to use in a script.

The AWS CLI has an ec2 describe-instances command that, as its name suggests, returns information for an EC2 instance. In this case, you want to know the IP address for the EC2 instance that has the tag docker-swarm-manager and the status running. To filter this information, use the --filters option where you can filter by the Name of an attribute and its Values. Once you have the IP, save it to an environment variable called IP. We've pasted the CLI command you need to run here:

```
$ IP=$(aws ec2 describe-instances \
    --filters "Name=tag:Name,Values=docker-swarm-manager" \
    "Name=instance-state-name,Values=running" \
    --query "Reservations[0].Instances[0].PublicIpAddress" \
    --region eu-west-1 --output text)
```

If you want to check that the IP has been exported properly, run echo $IP, you'll notice that its the same as what was in your Terraform output. Now that you have the IP address, add the IP to your list of known hosts using the ssh-keyscan command you used in the previous chapter. Run this command as we've done here, specifying the $IP environment variable that you just created:

```
$ ssh-keyscan -H "$IP" >> ~/.ssh/known_hosts
\# YOUR_EC2_IP:22 SSH-2.0-OpenSSH_8.7
...
```

Now that you've added the IP address to your list of known hosts, you're ready to rebuild your secrets from your secrets/secrets.enc.yaml. You already have the .databaseurl, .postgrespassword, and .secretkeybase secrets files in your secrets folder, but recall these files are in your .gitignore file, so they won't be available in GitHub to use in the CD pipeline you'll create later. You therefore need a way to create these files on the fly. It's important you regenerate your secret files each time that you want to deploy your application as your encrypted secret file should be the source of truth for your secrets. To regenerate your secrets, you'll create a script that decrypts your encrypted file, reads its content and then creates the necessary secret files in your secrets folder.

Create a new file in your scripts folder called decrypt.sh and copy in the following code, we've added comments above each line to help you understand what is going on:

```
#!/usr/bin/env bash

# in scripts/decrypt.sh

# get path of secrets/ folder relative to current script
# so script can be run from anywhere
CURRENT_SCRIPT_DIRECTORY=$(dirname "$0")
SECRETS_DIRECTORY="$CURRENT_SCRIPT_DIRECTORY/../secrets"

# decrypt the file and store the output in a variable
decrypted_content=$(sops --decrypt $SECRETS_DIRECTORY/secrets.enc.yaml)

# read each line of decrypted content -
# the text before the ":" is the filename and the text after is the secret
echo "${decrypted_content}" | while IFS=: read -r filename value; do
    # trim any leading space from value
    content=$(echo "$value" | xargs)
    # write the content to the corresponding file in the secrets folder
    echo "${content}" > "$SECRETS_DIRECTORY/${filename}"
done
```

Recall that when running the sops --decrypt command, you need to set the SOPS_AGE_KEY_FILE environment variable. Set this environment variable, cd back to the root of your project, make your new decrypt.sh script executable, and then delete the .databaseurl, .postgrespassword, and .secretkeybase files inside your secrets folder. Now run your new decrypt.sh script as we've done here to regenerate your secret files:

```
$ export SOPS_AGE_KEY_FILE="$(pwd)/key.txt"
$ cd ../../
$ chmod +x scripts/decrypt.sh
$ ./scripts/decrypt.sh
```

Perfect! You are set up to run commands in your EC2 instance. In the previous section, when you were deploying locally, you used your local image. However, as you'll be deploying your stack remotely, you'll use the remote image saved in the registry. Recall that this image was updated with your secret configuration when you committed your code earlier in the chapter. Because of this, you need to ensure that you're logged into the GitHub Docker registry. Do this with the same docker login command that you used in the previous chapter, as we've done here:

```
$ echo "$GITHUB_TOKEN" | docker login ghcr.io -u USERNAME --password-stdin
Login Succeeded
```

Okay, you're ready to deploy your application to production using the docker stack deploy command. Run this command, remembering to specify the DOCKER _HOST environment variable as we've done here (you don't have to specify the WEB_IMAGE as the image specified by default in your Compose file is your remote one):

```
$ DOCKER_HOST=ssh://ec2-user@"$IP" \
  docker stack deploy -c compose.yaml kanban --with-registry-auth
Creating network kanban_default
Creating secret kanban_postgrespassword
Creating secret kanban_secretkeybase
Creating secret kanban_databaseurl
Creating service kanban_web
Creating service kanban_db
```

You may notice that the docker stack deploy terminal output is slightly different than it was in the previous chapter. This is because the secrets you specified in your Compose file have been created.

You've done it! You've deployed your application with its secrets to production! Run docker service ls inside your EC2 to ensure your services are running and then visit port 4000 of your EC2's IP address. You'll see your application up and running!

Let's quickly recap what you've done in this section. You'll notice that the steps you took to deploy your application haven't changed since you added Docker secrets to your application. You first created your AWS resources and initiated your remote swarm by running terraform apply. Then, to deploy your application, you follow the five steps at the top of the next page (notice that this is a longer process than deploying your application locally):

1. You added your EC2 instance's private SSH key to your ssh-agent.
2. You found the IP address of the EC2 instance using the AWS CLI.
3. You added the IP address of the EC2 instance to your known_hosts file.
4. You regenerated your .databaseurl, .postgrespassword, and .secretkeybase secret files using a decrypt.sh file that decrypts your encrypted secrets.enc.yaml file.
5. You logged into the GitHub Docker registry.
6. You deployed your application using docker stack deploy while specifying the DOCKER_HOST environment variable.

We've recapped all of the necessary deployment steps, and you can see that your secrets are being properly applied. Now it's time to add these six deployment steps to a convenience script (meaning, a script that's convenient). Creating a convenience script is handy because it allows you to consolidate all of the deployment steps in one place. Not only will you use this script in a CD pipeline, but you can also use it to easily deploy your application from your local machine, which can be useful when debugging the deployment process or manually deploying to non-production environments.

Turn Deploy Commands into a Convenience Script

In the previous section, we went through the six steps required to manually deploy your application. Now it's time to turn those steps into a script. Doing so ensures that your application will always be deployed using the same commands. Not only does that help ensure environment integrity, but it's convenient for everyone working on your application and it allows you to run your CD locally. We would always encourage you to turn any repetitive tasks into code—it's a real time-saver!

First, create a new script in your scripts folder called deploy.sh. we've pasted the entire script in the upcoming code snippet and added some comments along the way to help you understand what is going on in each block. When this script is run, it requires the file path of the private key to your EC2 instance to be passed as an environment variable called PRIVATE_KEY_PATH. It also requires the AWS_ACCESS_KEY_ID, AWS_SECRET_ACCESS_KEY, GITHUB_TOKEN, GITHUB_USER, and SOPS_AGE_KEY_FILE environment variables. Copy and paste the script, and then we'll go through each of the sections one by one:

```bash
#!/usr/bin/env bash
# in scripts/deploy.sh

# set exit and logging rule for script
set -ex
```

```bash
# check for required tools (AWS CLI and Docker) and exit if not found
command -v aws >/dev/null 2>&1 || {
  echo "Error: AWS CLI not found. Please install it."; exit 1;
}
command -v docker >/dev/null 2>&1 || {
  echo "Error: Docker not found. Please install it."; exit 1;
}
# check that the necessary env variables have been passed and exit if not
if [ -z "$SOPS_AGE_KEY_FILE" ]; then
  echo "Error: Please set the SOPS_AGE_KEY_FILE environment variable."
  exit 1
fi

if [ -z "$PRIVATE_KEY_PATH" ]; then
  echo "Error: Please set the PRIVATE_KEY_PATH environment variable."
  exit 1
fi

if [ -z "$AWS_ACCESS_KEY_ID" ] || [ -z "$AWS_SECRET_ACCESS_KEY" ]; then
  echo "Error: Please set the AWS_ACCESS_KEY_ID and AWS_SECRET_ACCESS_KEY."
  exit 1
fi

if [ -z "$GITHUB_TOKEN" ] || [ -z "$GITHUB_USER" ]; then
  echo "Error: Please set both the GITHUB_TOKEN and GITHUB_USER."
  exit 1
fi

# set default variables
IMAGE=${1:-"ghcr.io/beamops/kanban:latest"}
AWS_REGION="eu-west-1"
INSTANCE_TAG_NAME="docker-swarm-manager"
STACK_NAME="kanban"

# get EC2 IP address
MANAGER_IP=$(aws ec2 describe-instances \
    --filters "Name=tag:Name,Values=$INSTANCE_TAG_NAME" \
              "Name=instance-state-name,Values=running" \
    --query "Reservations[0].Instances[0].PublicIpAddress" \
    --region "$AWS_REGION" --output text)

# exit if no running EC2 found
if [ -z "$MANAGER_IP" ]; then
  echo "Error: No instance found with tag name $INSTANCE_TAG_NAME."
  exit 1
fi

# decrypt secrets and create secret files
CURRENT_SCRIPT_DIRECTORY=$(dirname "$0")
"$CURRENT_SCRIPT_DIRECTORY/decrypt.sh"

# add SSH key to ssh-agent
eval "$(ssh-agent -s)"
```

```
chmod 600 "$PRIVATE_KEY_PATH"
mkdir -p ~/.ssh/
ssh-add "$PRIVATE_KEY_PATH"

# add EC2 IP to list of known hosts
ssh-keyscan -H "$MANAGER_IP" >> ~/.ssh/known_hosts

# log in to the GitHub Docker registry
echo "$GITHUB_TOKEN" | docker login ghcr.io \
  -u "$GITHUB_USER" --password-stdin

# deploy the application
DOCKER_HOST="ssh://ec2-user@$MANAGER_IP" \
WEB_IMAGE="$IMAGE" \
docker stack deploy -c compose.yaml --with-registry-auth "$STACK_NAME"

echo "Deployment completed."
```

This script may seem complicated at first glance, but we promise you it's not. It implements each of the six steps you went through in the previous section with a few extra checks and conditionals to make it more robust. Let's go through each of the blocks that start with a comment:

1. set -ex: This line sets two shell options that edit the way the script is run. -e makes the script exit if any command it runs exits with a non-zero status (indicating an error), and -x makes the shell print each command and its arguments to the standard error output before executing it.

2. command -v aws... and command -v docker...: This 6-line block checks if the AWS CLI and Docker are installed. If either isn't found, it prints an error and exits with a status of 1.

3. if [-z "$SOPS_AGE_KEY_FILE"]...if [-z "$PRIVATE_KEY_PATH"]...if [-z "$AWS_ACCESS_KEY_ID"]... if [-z "$GITHUB_TOKEN"]... : This block checks the SOPS_AGE_KEY_FILE, PRIVATE_KEY_PATH, AWS_ACCESS_KEY_ID, AWS_SECRET_ACCESS_KEY, GITHUB_TOKEN, and GITHUB_USER environment variables have been passed to the script. If any of them haven't been passed, the script prints an error and exits with a status of 1

4. IMAGE=...AWS_REGION=...INSTANCE_TAG_NAME=...STACK_NAME=...: This block sets four default re-usable variables for the script. The IMAGE variable has a default value—the :latest version of your remote image—but has been configured so that it can be set when the script is run so that you can deploy a certain Docker image. Remember to replace the default image value to be your remote image.

5. MANAGER_IP=$(aws ec2 describe-instances...: This command uses the AWS CLI in the same way that you did in the previous section to get your EC2 IP address and saves its value to the MANAGER_IP variable.

6. CURRENT_SCRIPT_DIRECTORY=..."$CURRENT_SCRIPT_DIRECTORY/decrypt.sh": These two lines run your decrypt.sh script to decrypt the secrets.yaml.enc file and create the .databaseurl, .postgrespassword, and .secretkeybase files in your secrets folder. We've made the decrypt.sh path relative to your deploy.sh script so that this script can be run from any path (for example, the root of your folder, or inside your scripts folder, and so on).

7. if [-z "$MANAGER_IP"]; then...: These four lines print an error message and exit the script if no EC2 IP address is found.

8. eval "$(ssh-agent -s)"...ssh-add "$PRIVATE_KEY_PATH": These four lines add the private key that you passed when running the script to the SSH agent of the machine in which the script is being run. The first line, eval "$(ssh-agent -s)", makes sure the ssh-agent is running. The second line, chmod 600... sets the right permissions for the private key so that it can be added to the ssh-agent. The third line mkdir -p ~/.ssh/ makes sure that the .ssh/ folder exists—the -p option ensures that if it does exist, an error is not thrown. The final line ssh-add "$PRIVATE_KEY_PATH" adds the private key file to the ssh-agent in the same way that you've been doing.

9. ssh-keyscan -H "$MANAGER_IP" >> ~/.ssh/known_hosts: This adds the EC2's IP to the known_hosts file of the machine where it's run, just as you did in the previous section.

10. echo "$GITHUB_TOKEN" | docker login...: This line logs in to the GitHub Docker registry in the same way as you've been doing.

11. DOCKER_HOST=...WEB_IMAGE=...docker stack deploy...: This command deploys your application to your remote swarm in the same way as you've been doing: by setting the DOCKER_HOST and WEB_IMAGE environment variables and running docker stack deploy.

And that's it! You now have a script that will deploy your application in the same way that you did earlier. Execute chmod +x deploy.sh to make your script executable, and let's try to run it. You'll need to set the PRIVATE_KEY_PATH, GITHUB_USER, and SOPS_AGE_KEY_FILE environment variables. You won't need to set the AWS_ACCESS_KEY_ID, AWS_SECRET_ACCESS_KEY, or GITHUB_TOKEN environment variables as you already have these exported to your PATH. cd to the root of your project and run the script, setting the required environment variables as we've done here:

```
$ cd ../../
$ PRIVATE_KEY_PATH=./environments/production/private_key.pem \
SOPS_AGE_KEY_FILE=./environments/production/key.txt \
GITHUB_USER=YOUR_GITHUB_USERNAME ./scripts/deploy.sh
```

```
...
+ IMAGE=ghcr.io/beamops/kanban:latest
+ AWS_REGION=eu-west-1
+ INSTANCE_TAG_NAME=docker-swarm-manager
+ STACK_NAME=kanban
...
+ ssh-add ./environments/production/private_key.pem
Identity added: ./environments/production/private_key.pem
(./environments/production/private_key.pem)
+ ssh-keyscan -H 13.40.179.240
...
+ DOCKER_HOST=ssh://ec2-user@13.40.179.240
+ WEB_IMAGE=ghcr.io/beamops/kanban:latest
+ docker stack deploy -c compose.yaml --with-registry-auth kanban
Updating service kanban_db (id: zcvwfdkxqqfuxvyeqbzx7imqp)
Updating service kanban_web (id: vr97mibij9vnn9zd4p3pw8dqf)
+ echo 'Deployment completed.'
Deployment completed.
```

Great! You have a working script that deploys your stack to a Docker Swarm in AWS. The script allows you to specify which image tag you want to deploy, but if no image is specified, it deploys the latest remote image.

Now, that you have this script, the next step is to add it to a CD pipeline so that your image is automatically deployed when a pull request is merged into main. After you do this, you'll be able to fail fast, fail often, and fail forward. We want to emphasize that failing when deploying isn't a bad thing! Enabling continuous deployment will give you confidence in the code you submit and will streamline your software delivery cycle. We'll look at how to create your CD pipeline using a GitHub Action in the next and final section.

Enable Continuous Deployment

In the previous section, you created a script that deploys your application. Now it's time to add this script to a GitHub Action. When doing this, you need to make sure that GitHub has access to all the information required to run your script.

When you ran the script, you explicitly specified three environment variables: PRIVATE_KEY_PATH, SOPS_AGE_KEY_FILE, and GITHUB_USER. You also implicitly specified your AWS_ACCESS_KEY_ID and AWS_SECRET_ACCESS_KEY and GITHUB_TOKEN environment variables, which were already exported to your PATH. For GitHub to be able to run your script in an action, it needs to have access to these six variables. Not only that, it needs to be able to decrypt your secrets.enc.yaml file properly. For it to do this, you need to give GitHub Actions access to the age key that you used to encrypt your secrets.

So, how can you give GitHub Actions access to all of this information? You must use GitHub secrets. You must use GitHub secrets over Docker secrets here, as it is good practice to separate your application and deployment configurations. Besides, you'll need your SSH private key to be a GitHub secret anyway. If your private key was a secret within your secrets folder, you'd need to commit your new SSH key every time that you destroy and re-create your AWS Terraform infrastructure. Making it a GitHub secret will mean your private key will be instantly available in GitHub right after it's created.

You'll create your GitHub secrets using Terraform. You could create some of the GitHub secrets, such as the AWS credentials, manually but it's always better to define such resources in your infrastructure-as-code.

Let's add these six deployment configurations as GitHub secrets in your Terraform code. To do so, you'll use the github_actions_secrets resource[11] from the GitHub provider.[12] As always, when using a provider, the first thing to do is to copy the code snippet given to you when you press the Use Provider button. Create a new main.tf file in a new module folder called modules/integrations/github/secrets and paste in the following code snippet. Again, you don't need to copy over the provider section. Your file should look like this:

```
# in modules/integrations/github/secrets/main.tf
terraform {
  required_providers {
    github = {
      source  = "integrations/github"
      version = "5.41.0"
    }
  }
}
```

This modules/integrations/github/secrets module folder is where the template code related to GitHub secrets will live. Now that you've added the provider configuration, it's time to add the configurations that your github_actions_secrets resource and your GitHub provider will need—a list of secrets, your GitHub username, and your GitHub repository—where these secrets should be created. You'll create these configurations as variables. Remember that when creating Terraform variables, you need to define their shape first before instantiating them. To create these variable templates, create a new variables.tf file inside your modules/integrations/github/secrets folder and copy in the following snippet:

---

11. https://registry.terraform.io/providers/integrations/github/latest/docs/resources/actions_secret
12. https://registry.terraform.io/providers/integrations/github/latest/docs

```
# in modules/integrations/github/secrets/variables.tf
variable "secrets" {
  description = "A map of secrets to be created for a certain repository"
  type        = map(string)
}
variable "github_owner" {
  description = "The name of the GitHub organization."
  type        = string
}
variable "repository" {
  description = "The name of the GitHub repository."
  type        = string
}
```

As you can see, the secrets variable will be a map where each item of the map will be a different secret; each of the map keys will be a secret name; and each key's value will be the secret value.

Now that you've created these variable definitions, update your github/secrets/main.tf file to use these variables and create your secrets. To do so, create a github_actions_secret resource. If you look at the documentation for that resource,[13] you'll see that each secret expects three attributes: repository, secret_name, and plaintext_value.

As your secrets variable will be a map, use the for_each meta-argument in your resource definition to loop over each item in the secrets variable and set the secret_name and plaintext_value attributes to be the key and value attributes of each item. You can see how to do this here:

```
# in modules/integrations/github/secrets/main.tf
resource "github_actions_secret" "main" {
  for_each = var.secrets

  repository      = var.repository
  secret_name     = each.key
  plaintext_value = each.value
}
```

You should also update your GitHub provider configuration options to use your github_owner variable like so:

```
# in modules/integrations/github/secrets/main.tf
provider "github" {
  owner = var.github_owner
}
```

---

13. https://registry.terraform.io/providers/integrations/github/latest/docs/resources/actions_secret#argument-reference

Great! You have the structure of your GitHub secrets all set up. Now it's time to create the secrets themselves. Because these secrets are environment-specific, you'll create them inside the environments/production folder rather than in the github/secrets folder you just created. And because these secrets are, well, secret, you must create them as variables. That way, you can instantiate them in an .auto.tfvars file, which won't be committed to your repository.

> **.auto.tfvars Limitations When Using Terraform Modules**
>
>
>
> You may be wondering why the age key and GitHub token are being instantiated in your environments/production folder when they are general GitHub configurations that aren't environment-specific. This is a Terraform issue: when using modules you cannot have an .auto.tfvars file in a module if that module will be imported somewhere else. If you were to put these two GitHub configurations in a separate general module, their values would have to be hard-coded. You could use a tool like Terragrunt[14] to get around this issue but we'll not cover that here.

We'll first focus on creating your AWS_SECRET_ACCESS_KEY, AWS_ACCESS_KEY_ID, AGE_KEY, and GITHUB_TOKEN secrets before discussing the SSH private key and the GitHub user. As usual, when defining variables, you need to establish their structure first, so create a new variables.tf file inside your environments/production folder and copy in the following code:

```
# in environments/production/variables.tf
variable "aws_access_key_id" {
  description = "The AWS access key ID."
  type        = string
}
variable "aws_secret_access_key" {
  description = "The AWS secret access key."
  type        = string
  sensitive   = true
}
variable "age_key" {
  description = "The age key for sops encryption tool"
  type        = string
  sensitive   = true
}
variable "gh_pat" {
  description = "A GitHub personal access token. Used to log into ghcr.io."
  type        = string
  sensitive   = true
}
```

---

14. https://terragrunt.gruntwork.io/

Nice! You have your first four variable structures defined. Now it's time to instantiate them. To do this, create an .auto.tfvars file in your environments/production folder and add in the values for the two AWS variables, your personal GitHub access token that you created in Chapter 4, as well as your age key. When specifying your age key, you only need to copy the last line of your key.txt file that starts AGE-SECRET-KEY. Your file should look like this:

```
# in environments/production/.auto.tfvars
aws_access_key_id     = "YOUR_AWS_ACCESS_KEY_ID"
aws_secret_access_key = "YOUR_AWS_SECRET_ACCESS_KEY"
gh_pat                = "YOUR_GITHUB_PERSONAL_ACCESS_TOKEN"
age_key               = "AGE-SECRET-KEY-XXXX"
```

Let's look at your SSH private key. The logic for creating your private key is in your cloud/aws/compute/swarm module. To be able to access this key in your environments/production module (which is where you'll import your secrets module), you must make your SSH key an output of your swarm module. To do this, create a new private_key output inside your modules/cloud/aws/compute/swarm/outputs.tf file and set the value to be local_sensitive_file.private_key.content. Remember that outputs require a description, and since the value is sensitive data, you must add the sensitive attribute as well.

Add this new output so that the end of your modules/cloud/aws/compute/swarm/outputs.tf file looks like this:

```
# in modules/cloud/aws/compute/swarm/outputs.tf
output "private_key" {
  value       = local_sensitive_file.private_key.content
  sensitive   = true
  description = "The SSH private key to connect to the instance."
}
```

Your key is now an output of your swarm module! It's now time to put everything together and instantiate your swarm and github/secrets modules in your environments/production/main.tf file. First, import your github/secrets module and add in the three variables that you created earlier: secrets, repository, and github_owner. The secrets map should have the PRIVATE_KEY, AWS_ACCESS_KEY_ID, AWS_SECRET_ACCESS_KEY, AGE_KEY, and GH_PAT values. Use the variables from your environments/production/.auto.tfvars file to set their values.

You may be wondering about the GITHUB_USER variable and why you haven't added this value as a GitHub secret in your Terraform code. This variable isn't a secret and is actually available by default when running GitHub Actions so you don't need to explicitly create this value. As for your PRIVATE_KEY secret, use the private_key swarm module output that you just created. You'll need to import your swarm module first. Try doing this yourself before looking at how we did it in the upcoming code snippet:

```
# in environments/production/main.tf
module "swarm" {
  source           = "../../modules/cloud/aws/compute/swarm"
  private_key_path = "${path.module}/private_key.pem"
}
module "repository_secrets" {
  source = "../../modules/integrations/github/secrets"
  secrets = {
    "PRIVATE_KEY"           = module.swarm.private_key,
    "AWS_ACCESS_KEY_ID"     = var.aws_access_key_id,
    "AWS_SECRET_ACCESS_KEY" = var.aws_secret_access_key,
    "AGE_KEY"               = var.age_key,
    "GH_PAT"                = var.gh_pat
  }
  repository   = "kanban"
  github_owner = "YOUR_GITHUB_USERNAME"
}
```

Your Terraform code is now ready to create all of the necessary variables that GitHub will need to be able to deploy your application in an action. Let's apply these changes so that you can see the secrets. cd into your environments/production folder. As you've created new Terraform modules, you need to run terraform init first. Then to create the secrets, run terraform apply. After this, run terraform state list, and you'll be able to see your secrets in the Terraform state. You can see an example terminal interaction here:

```
$ cd environments/production
$ terraform init
...
$ terraform apply
...
$ terraform state list | grep secret
module.repository_secrets.github_actions_secret.main["AGE_KEY"]
module.repository_secrets.github_actions_secret.main["AWS_ACCESS_KEY_ID"]
module.repository_secrets.github_actions_secret.main["AWS_SECRET_ACCESS_KEY"]
module.repository_secrets.github_actions_secret.main["GH_PAT"]
module.repository_secrets.github_actions_secret.main["PRIVATE_KEY"]
```

Awesome! Your repository now has all of the secrets needed to run your deploy.sh script. If you want to see them, go to the Settings tab of your GitHub repository and select Security > Secrets and variables > Actions.

The next step is to add your script to a GitHub Action. You'll do this in the next section, where you'll create a composite deployment action.

Create a Composite Deployment Action

In this section, you'll add a composite deployment action to the CI/CD workflow that you created in Chapter 4 that will use your deploy.sh script to deploy your application. A composite action is a way to separate certain logic of a GitHub Action workflow into its own easy-to-read file. Composite actions are beneficial because they help you avoid having really large GitHub Action files and allow you to reuse logic in multiple workflows, keeping your workflows DRY. Adding your deployment script to your CI/CD pipeline means that each time any code is merged into main, it will be fully tested and then deployed to production. Having this deployment logic be a composite action allows you to easily create a separate workflow that you can use to deploy your application manually, if you ever want to.

When using composite GitHub Actions, you need to understand something important. The context of an action's steps doesn't have access to the wider GitHub Action context that's available in the parent workflow. This means that any variables that your composite action will need must be passed explicitly as inputs. In this case, this will be the six environment variables we discussed earlier, your five GitHub Secrets, and your GitHub user. You'll also pass an image tag as an input to your action so that it knows which image to deploy. Although there's a default image specified in the script itself, it's better to be explicit about the version.

Composite actions must always be defined in a file called action.yaml. So, the first step is to create a new file called action.yaml in a new actions/deploy folder inside your .github directory. Then, copy in the code in the upcoming snippet, which sets up everything that your composite action will need to run:

```yaml
# in .github/actions/deploy/action.yaml
name: "Continuous Deployment to Remote Docker Swarm"
description: "Deploys into a Docker Swarm when given a certain image tag"
inputs:
  image_tag:
    description: "Image tag to update the web service in the swarm"
    required: true

  github_user:
    description: "Owner of the package used by the registry login step"
    required: true
  gh_pat:
    description: "GitHub token used to log in the registry"
    required: true
  aws_access_key_id:
    description: "An AWS access key ID"
```

```
    required: true
  aws_secret_access_key:
    description: "The AWS secret key"
    required: true
  age_key:
    description: "The age key used by SOPS"
    required: true
  ssh_private_key:
    description: "The SSH key used to run docker commands on the remote host"
    required: true
```

This composite action has both a `name` and a `description`. It then lists the six different secret variables required to run your deploy.sh script and an image tag. Although your secrets are defined in uppercase, the convention for composite actions is that inputs are always defined in lowercase.

Now that you've defined the inputs, you need to define the action itself. To do this, use the `runs` top-level key. Then add the `using: "composite"` subkey. After this, define the `steps` of your action. This action will have five steps:

1. Check out the code, as always.

2. Install `sops` in your runner's environment.

3. Install `age` in your runner's environment.

4. Create the `age` key and the `ssh` private key files available in your runner's environment.

5. Deploy your application by running your deploy.sh script. Use the action's inputs to set the environment variables that your script requires: GITHUB _TOKEN, GITHUB_USER, AWS_ACCESS_KEY_ID, AWS_SECRET_ACCESS_KEY, PRIVATE_KEY_PATH, and SOPS_AGE_KEY_FILE. The first four can be specified in the `env` attribute of the step. However, to set the PRIVATE_KEY_PATH and SOPS_AGE_KEY_FILE variables, they need to be relative file paths. When passing these files to your script, remember to use PWD in the file path so that the path is valid. Lastly, pass the `image_tag` input as a script argument.

Try adding these five steps to your workflow on your own. (Our version is on the next page.)

Once you've added these steps, your workflow should look like this:

```yaml
# in .github/actions/deploy/action.yaml
runs:
  using: "composite"
  steps:
    - uses: actions/checkout@v4

    - name: Setup SOPS
      uses: nhedger/setup-sops@v2
      with:
        version: 3.7.3

    - uses: alessiodionisi/setup-age-action@v1.3.0
      with:
        version: ^1.1.0

    - name: Create age and SSH key files
      shell: bash
      run: |-
        echo "${{ inputs.age_key }}" > ./key.txt
        echo "${{ inputs.ssh_private_key }}" > ./private_key.pem

    - name: Deploy
      shell: bash
      env:
        GITHUB_TOKEN: ${{ inputs.gh_pat }}
        GITHUB_USER: ${{ inputs.github_user }}
        AWS_ACCESS_KEY_ID: ${{ inputs.aws_access_key_id }}
        AWS_SECRET_ACCESS_KEY: ${{ inputs.aws_secret_access_key }}
      run: |-
        SOPS_AGE_KEY_FILE=$(pwd)/key.txt \
        PRIVATE_KEY_PATH="$(pwd)/private_key.pem" \
        ./scripts/deploy.sh ${{ inputs.image_tag }}
```

Perfect! You've created your composite action that deploys your application stack. The last step is to add it to your CI/CD workflow that you created in Chapter 4. You'll do this in the next section.

Add Your Composite Action to Your CI/CD Workflow

Adding a composite action to a GitHub workflow is super easy. All you need to do is use the uses key and specify the inputs that the action expects using the with key like so:

```yaml
- uses: PATH_TO_COMPOSITE_ACTION
  with:
    LIST OF INPUTS
```

As you know, one of the inputs that the workflow expects is an image tag so the deploy script knows what image to deploy. Before adding the composite action, first determine the unique image tag that was created in the build-push job of your CI/CD workflow and set it as an output of that job. Recall that your CI workflow uses the docker/metadata-action@v4, which creates image tags for the Docker image that it builds. You'll need to access those tags and extract the unique one to be able to pass it to your composite action. Remember that you can access the tags that are output by the docker/metadata-action@v4 step through the steps.meta.output.tags output. When this step is run in your main branch, which is the only time when you'll deploy your application, this variable is a three-line string that contains three different tags: the generic :main and :latest tags, as well as a unique commit sha tag in the form :sha-xxx.

You'll use the :sha-xxx tag to avoid any confusion regarding which specific version of your image the :latest tag refers to. Using the exact commit sha will help you if you were needing to debug the deployed image. To extract the unique tag from the steps.meta.output.tags variable, use grep to search for any line containing 'sha', tr to trim any whitespace characters, and then awk to get the first word from that line. Finally, echo that value and save it to the GITHUB_OUTPUT (the output configuration of your job). Lastly, use the outputs key to create an output of your build-push job called unique_docker_tag so that you can use this tag in the new deploy job of your workflow that you'll create.

Now that you have a unique tag, you can add your new deploy job. When doing this, remember to check out the code first. Then add your composite action using the uses key, specifying the seven necessary inputs: the five environment variables, the SSH key, and the image tag. The image tag should be the unique_docker_tag output of your build-push step. Since you only want to deploy your application when this CI workflow is run in your main branch, both the step that gets the unique Docker tag and your deploy job must use the if key to specify that they are only to be run if the github.ref is equal to your refs/heads/main. Have a go at implementing these new steps before looking at how we did in this code snippet:

```yaml
# in ci_cd.yaml
  build-push:
    outputs:
      unique_docker_tag: ${{ steps.get-unique-docker-tag.outputs.sha_tag }}
    steps:
      - name: Gets unique image tag
        id: get-unique-docker-tag
        if: github.ref == 'refs/heads/main'
        run: |-
          IMAGE_TAG=$(echo "${{ steps.meta.outputs.tags }}" \
                      | grep 'sha' \
                      | tr '\n' ' ' \
```

```
                      | awk '{print $1}')
          echo "sha_tag=$IMAGE_TAG" >> $GITHUB_OUTPUT
deploy:
  if: github.ref == 'refs/heads/main'
  runs-on: ubuntu-latest
  needs: build-push
  name: Deploy application
  steps:
    - uses: actions/checkout@v4

    - uses: ./.github/actions/deploy
      with:
        github_user: ${{ github.repository_owner }}
        gh_pat: ${{ secrets.GH_PAT }}
        aws_access_key_id: ${{ secrets.AWS_ACCESS_KEY_ID }}
        aws_secret_access_key: ${{ secrets.AWS_SECRET_ACCESS_KEY }}
        age_key: ${{ secrets.AGE_KEY }}
        ssh_private_key: ${{ secrets.PRIVATE_KEY }}
        image_tag: ${{ needs.build-push.outputs.unique_docker_tag }}
```

Alright! You've successfully created a composite GitHub Action that deploys your application, and you've added it to your CI/CD workflow. Now, any code that's merged into your main branch is fully tested and then automatically deployed! You're officially operating by the Kaizen principle. You can now close the "Create a Continuous Delivery pipeline" issue you created in Chapter 2. Create a new branch and commit the code you've written in this section and open a PR. Remember to include closes #ISSUE_ID in your PR description. You'll see that your two CI jobs run as they did before. Now merge your PR, and you'll see that your new deploy job also runs. Amazing!

We'd like to show you one last thing. We recommend you protect your main branch to maintain transparency in your team and to make sure no one can add any sneaky commits to that branch that haven't been approved by the team.

Add Branch Protection to Your main Branch

Now that you have a CD workflow in place, it's time to protect your main branch. This is a very important step as it'll prevent anyone pushing directly to it.

Unfortunately, given that your repository is private, you'll only be able to complete this section if you have a GitHub Pro, GitHub Team, or GitHub Enterprise account. Alternatively, you can make your repository public. This restriction exists as branch protection is a feature that's only offered under certain GitHub plans. You can see their documentation[15] for more information.

---

15. https://docs.github.com/en/repositories/configuring-branches-and-merges-in-your-repository/managing-protected-branches/about-protected-branches

Protecting your main branch is a must in real-world applications—it ensures that only well-tested and approved changes make their way into the core codebase, which improves the stability of your application. You could add this option via the GitHub UI, but infrastructure resources should always be defined as code. For that reason, you'll add this branch protection using Terraform. You'll also use another resource from the GitHub provider, the github_branch_protection resource.[16]

First, create a new main.tf file inside a new contributing_workflow module within your modules/integrations/github directory. We've pasted the code Terraform provides when you press on the Use Provider button in the upcoming code snippet. We've also populated the github_branch_protection resource for you. Copy this code into your modules/integrations/github/contributing_workflow/main.tf file, and then we will go through the different github_branch_protection resource configurations we have added:

```
# in modules/integrations/github/contributing_workflow/main.tf
terraform {
  required_providers {
    github = {
      source  = "integrations/github"
      version = "5.41.0"
    }
  }
}
provider "github" {
  owner = var.github_owner
}
resource "github_branch_protection" "main" {
  repository_id = var.repository

  pattern        = "main"
  enforce_admins = true

  required_status_checks {
    strict   = true
    contexts = var.status_checks
  }

  required_pull_request_reviews {
    require_code_owner_reviews      = false
    required_approving_review_count = 1
  }
}
```

---

16. https://registry.terraform.io/providers/integrations/github/latest/docs/resources/branch_protection.html

As you can see, we've added various configurations to the github_branch_protection resource. We'll go through each one:

1. The enforce_admins option also prevents the repository administrators from pushing directly to the main branch. We don't want any sneaky commits.

2. The required_status_checks option has two configurations:

   - The strict attribute has been set to true. This requires branches to be up-to-date before merging.

   - The contexts specifies a list of status checks that need to pass before merging is allowed. You can see that it has been set to a variable. You'll create this variable in a moment.

3. The required_pull_request_reviews option has two configurations:

   - The require_code_owner_reviews attribute has been disabled. This means that a review from the owner of the repository isn't necessary. This helps shorten the feedback loop. Imagine that a CTO created the repository. If this option were set to true, that CTO would have to manually review every single pull request, which is unrealistic.

   - The required_approving_review_count attribute has been set to 1. This means for a PR to be merged, at least one other person has to approve it.

Now that you've added your github_branch_protection resource, define the three variables that it uses: the github_owner, the repository, and the status_checks. As always, you must define the variable structure first. Create a new variables.tf file in your contributing_workflow module and paste in the following snippet:

```
# in modules/integrations/github/contributing_workflow/variables.tf
variable "repository" {
  description = "Name of the GitHub repository."
  type        = string
}
variable "github_owner" {
  description = "Owner/organization where the GitHub repository resides."
  type        = string
}
variable "status_checks" {
  description = "List of required status checks that must pass."
  type        = list(string)
  default     = []
}
```

Lastly, instantiate these variables and include this module in your environments/production/main.tf file so that the branch protection is applied when you next run terraform apply. To do this, import your module and specify the three variables you just created like so, remembering to replace the repository and username variables with your own values:

```
# in environments/production/main.tf
module "contributing_workflow" {
  source         = "../../modules/integrations/github/contributing_workflow"
  repository     = "kanban"
  github_owner   = "YOUR_GITHUB_USERNAME"
  status_checks  = [
    "Compile with mix test, format, dialyzer & unused deps check"
  ]
}
```

You'll notice that the status check that we've specified is the ci job from your CI/CD workflow. Great! Now, apply your Terraform configuration file. You'll have to run terraform init before you can run terraform apply. You'll see that once you apply your configuration, you'll no longer be able to commit directly to your main branch. To test this, commit your new branch protection configuration files and try to push them to your main branch. You'll see that your commit is rejected. Your terminal should look something like this:

```
$ git add .
$ git commit -m "test: protection" && git push
...
 ! [remote rejected] main -> main (protected branch hook declined)
error: failed to push some refs to ...
```

You see? You weren't able to push your commit. From now on, your main branch is protected and you'll need to create a feature branch and submit a PR to merge your code. Do just that with your most recent commit.

Congratulations! You've done it! You have created a CI/CD pipeline and have protected your main branch. Well done. That was hard work! Let's sum up what you have learned in this chapter. Before we move on, remember to clean up your production environment by running terraform destroy.

What Have You Learned?

In this chapter, you've taken the final step in preparing your application so that you can employ the Kaizen principle of continuous improvement. You've also made your application more secure.

As you now know, two core characteristics of BEAMOps developers are confidence and ownership. That is, *empowering yourself to take responsibility for the code you submit*. Having an efficient CD pipeline in place gives you the confidence that all code that's committed into your main branch is tested and deployed automatically. And protecting your main branch makes the code-submittal process in your repository transparent and more collaborative.

Now that your application is up and running with a CD pipeline that's protected, it's time to look at the fault tolerance of your application. In the next chapter, you'll review your AWS resources to create a multinode swarm, rather than a single-node one, and you'll distribute your different swarm nodes in multiple locations. Doing this will make your application more stable, robust, and highly available.

The Extra Mile

If you wish to deepen your knowledge of the themes we've covered in this chapter and refine your superpowers as a BEAMOps developer, we've created a few tasks for you to do:

1. You may have noticed that adding ARM support has slightly incremented the build time of your CI/CD pipeline. Now that you know how to create a composite action, create a new composite action that builds your Docker image. Once you have this, build just the AMD image for the deploy step. Build the ARM image in parallel while deploying the AMD image. This will ensure that your deployment isn't delayed by the ARM build.

2. SOPS and age both have a Terraform provider. Create a new Terraform module that manages your age keys. This module should create the key.txt in your environments /production folder and should also create the .sops.yaml file in your root directory. Use the outputs of this module to set the AGE_KEY for your secrets.

CHAPTER 8

Revise Your AWS Stack to Create a Multinode Swarm

In Chapter 6, you created the minimum infrastructure required to deploy your application to production: a single-node swarm hosted in AWS. We stressed the importance of delivering the minimum viable product and starting with something "basic" that works without getting bogged down trying to implement too many features at once. Recall what Joe Armstrong, one of the co-creators of Erlang, said: "Make it work, then make it beautiful, then if you really, really have to, make it fast. 90 percent of the time, if you make it beautiful, it will already be fast. So really, just make it beautiful!"

The BEAMOps philosophy embraces this idea. You've already made your production environment work. In this chapter, you'll make your application beautiful by progressing beyond the basics and creating a multinode Docker Swarm that's distributed across different AWS availability zones.

Why would a multinode Docker Swarm make your application beautiful? Well, having multiple nodes in a Docker Swarm allows you to take advantage of a swarm's best features: fault tolerance and resource optimization. Distributing the nodes of your Docker Swarm across different availability zones is an important part of deployment because it makes the application highly available and resilient. Distributing the nodes means that there's almost no chance that your application will go down due to an AWS server fault in a specific zone within a region.

By the end of this chapter, you'll be confident in the stability of your production environment, and you'll have a robust and highly available application. You'll also be able to close one of the infrastructure issues that you created in Chapter 2.

Let's dive right in and edit your Terraform configuration to create multiple EC2 instances rather than just one.

Create and Distribute Multiple EC2 Instances

In Chapter 6, you used Terraform to create the minimum computer resources required to deliver your application: a single EC2 instance that uses an AWS AMI, which has Docker preinstalled. You assigned your EC2 instance to the default VPC and randomly selected one subnet. This means that your application is only being deployed to a single-node swarm in one subnet, and therefore one availability zone. An availability zone (AZ) is a distinct location within an AWS region that's isolated from failures in other availability zones.

Your first task in this chapter is to prepare your AWS infrastructure for your multinode swarm. The first step in achieving this is to create the multiple EC2 instances that will become the different nodes in your swarm. To make your application more robust, you'll tell your Terraform configuration to create three EC2 instances rather than just one. You'll then edit the subnet allocation of your EC2 instances so they are located in different AWS AZs. Spreading your EC2 instances across multiple AZs will make your application highly available and more reliable as there will be no single point of failure, meaning that your application won't be susceptible to data center outages in a specific AZ. Let's get started and increase the number of EC2 instances in your AWS stack.

Increase the Number of EC2 Instances in Your AWS Stack

To increase the number of EC2 instances that your Terraform configuration creates, you'll add the count attribute to your aws_instance resource. Rather than hard-coding this value into your modules/cloud/aws/compute/swarm/main.tf file, you'll use a variable. This means that anytime you wish to scale up or down the number of EC2 instances when you apply your configuration, you'll not have to change your main configuration file directly.

Create a new variable inside your modules/cloud/aws/compute/swarm/variables.tf file called number_of_nodes. It should be a number and have a default value of 3. The default is 3 because there are typically three AZs in a region and each AZ must have a manager node. This means that if one of the AZs crashes, your swarm won't be left without a manager. You can see the variable you must add here:

```
# in modules/cloud/aws/compute/swarm/variables.tf
variable "number_of_nodes" {
  description = "The number of nodes to create."
```

```
  type        = number
  default     = 3
}
```

Now add the count attribute to your aws_instance resource in your main.tf file like so:

```
# in modules/cloud/aws/compute/swarm/main.tf
resource "aws_instance" "swarm_node" {
  count = var.number_of_nodes
}
```

Note that we've updated the name of the resource to be swarm_node so that it is more representative of what the EC2 instance is.

Great! Your Terraform configuration now creates three EC2 nodes. Easy, right?

The next step is to update the SSH command output. This output is located in your modules/cloud/aws/compute/swarm/outputs.tf file and currently only expects one EC2 instance. Now that you have three instances, you must loop through your instances in the output and create an output for each one. You can see how to do this here:

```
# in modules/cloud/aws/compute/swarm/outputs.tf

output "ssh_commands" {
  value = {
    for idx, instance in aws_instance.swarm_node :
    format("node_%d", idx + 1) =>
    format("ssh -i ./private_key.pem ec2-user@%s", instance.public_ip)
  }
  description = "The SSH commands to connect to the instances."
}
```

Note that we've pluralized the name of the output to be ssh_commands. Remember to update the import of that output in your environments/production/main.tf file to stop your configuration from erroring when you apply it in a moment. Nice! The next step is to distribute your EC2 instances so that they are each created in different AZs.

Distribute Your EC2 Instances Across Multiple Availability Zones

Now that your Terraform configuration creates three EC2 instances, the next step is to distribute these instances across different subnets, and therefore AZs. This will make your application highly available and less susceptible to data center outages.

To do this, delete the availability_zone attribute of your aws_instance resource and edit its subnet_id attribute to allocate the subnets for your instances in a round-robin fashion, rather than randomly as you're doing now. To assign the subnet, loop through all of the main subnet IDs and select the subnet using the index attribute exported by the count variable you used in the previous section like so: count.index % length(data.aws_subnets.main_subnets.ids). As you can see, this uses the % operator to get the remainder of dividing the count.index value by the length of the main subnets. This will be a number between 0 and the number of subnets, which will allow you to select a subnet at a certain index of the subnet list.

For example, there are three main subnets, and you have three instances. On the creation of the first EC2 instance, count.index will have a value of 0. The first EC2 instance will be allocated to the subnet at index 0 of the subnet list because 0 % 3 is 0. The second EC2 instance will then be allocated to the subnet at index 1 of the subnet list because 1 % 3 is 1. The third EC2 instance will be allocated to the subnet at index 2 of the subnet list because 2 % 3 is 2.

In the hypothetical case that you were creating more EC2 instances, the fourth would be assigned to the subnet at index 0 of the subnet list because 3 % 3 is 0, then the fifth to the subnet at index 1 because 4 % 3 is 1, and so on.

So, delete the availability_zone attribute of your aws_instance resource and edit the subnet_id attribute so that it takes the remainder of dividing the current count.index by the length of the data.aws_subnets.main_subnets value as we have done here:

```
# in modules/cloud/aws/compute/swarm/main.tf
resource "aws_instance" "swarm_node" {
  subnet_id = data.aws_subnets.main_subnets.ids[
    count.index % length(data.aws_subnets.main_subnets.ids)
  ]
}
```

Great! Now cd into your environments/production folder and run terraform apply to apply your configuration. Once you apply your configuration, run terraform state show 'module.swarm.aws_instance.swarm_node[0]' | grep availability_zone three times, swapping the [0] for [1] and [2]. When you do this, you'll see that each output shows a different AZ.

Well done. You've successfully distributed your EC2 instances across multiple AZs. However, as the user_data attribute of each of your EC2 instances still runs docker swarm init, you're in fact currently creating three single-node Docker Swarms. In the next section, we'll discuss how to create just one swarm using one EC2 instance and have the other two instances join that swarm.

Create a Multinode Swarm

The user_data attribute for your aws_instance resource is currently set to docker swarm init. This means that each of your EC2 instances will start their own single-node swarm once they've finished booting. This isn't what you want because this means that your application isn't benefitting from the orchestration advantages that a multinode swarm brings. Specifically, a multinode swarm is more fault-tolerant and optimizes resource utilization because, if one node fails, others can continue the work. Multinode swarms ensure higher availability and reliability, both of which are crucial for maintaining uninterrupted services and minimizing downtime. In this section, you'll edit the user_data field of your aws_instance resource to be a conditional so that only one of your EC2 instances will start the swarm and the other two instances will join that swarm, becoming swarm nodes.

As we mentioned in Chapter 5 on page 149, there are two types of nodes in a swarm cluster: manager nodes and worker nodes. Worker nodes are responsible for running the tasks (containers) that are part of your stack. Manager nodes are responsible for the orchestration of the swarm—they receive the stack deployment commands and are responsible for the state of the cluster. Manager nodes also have the ability to run tasks. In this book, each of your swarm nodes will be a manager. This is because worker nodes join swarms using different tokens and adding that extra functionality to your configuration is out of the scope of this book.

You've given a default value of 3 to your number_of_nodes variable, as it's essential that each of your AZs has a manager node. This is so that your swarm won't be left without a manager if one of the AZs crashes. It's also important because if there's a communication issue between nodes and a network partition, or brain split, the manager nodes will be divided into isolated groups. Docker will then use a consensus algorithm to ensure that a majority of manager nodes agree on decisions. Having an odd number of manager nodes is crucial in this context, as it helps to avoid situations where an equal split leads to a lack of consensus. If you'd like more information, check the Docker docs.[1]

To ensure that your number_of_nodes variable is always an odd number, add the following validation to your variable definition:

---

1. https://docs.docker.com/engine/swarm/join-nodes/#join-as-a-manager-node
   https://docs.docker.com/engine/swarm/raft/
   https://docs.docker.com/engine/swarm/admin_guide/#maintain-the-quorum-of-managers

```
# in modules/cloud/aws/compute/swarm/variables.tf
variable "number_of_nodes" {
  description = "The number of nodes to create."
  type        = number
  default     = 3

  validation {
    condition     = var.number_of_nodes % 2 == 1
    error_message = "The number_of_nodes value must be an odd number."
  }
}
```

So, how will two of your EC2 nodes join the swarm that the other node creates? You may recall that when you run the docker swarm init command, the terminal output prints the docker swarm join command populated with the token that you need to use to join that swarm as a *worker node*. It also includes instructions on how to print the command that you need to join the swarm as a *manager*. We've pasted the terminal output for your reference. We have also run the command that prints the command needed to join the swarm as a manager:

```
$ docker swarm init
Swarm initialized: current node (i1mhklcu...) is now a manager.

To add a worker to this swarm, run the following command:

    docker swarm join --token SWMTKN-1-3pdik ... 192.168.65.4:2377

To add a manager to this swarm, run 'docker swarm join-token manager'
and follow the instructions.
$ docker swarm join-token manager
To add a manager to this swarm, run the following command:

    docker swarm join --token SWMTKN-1-0ozc ... 192.168.65.4:2377
```

As you can see, the docker swarm join-token manager command prints the command, and token, that you need to execute to join the swarm as a manager node. It has the following format:

```
docker swarm join --token <MANAGER_TOKEN> <MANAGER_IP:MANAGER_LISTENING_PORT>
```

This is the command that two of your three EC2 instances will have to run to join the Docker Swarm that was created by the other instance. These two "secondary" EC2 instances will need to have access to three things: the swarm's manager token, the IP of the EC2 instance that started the swarm (which we'll now refer to as the "primary node"), and the port on which this primary node is listening for swarm orchestration commands. Let's look at how your two secondary nodes will gain access to these three pieces of information. We'll start in the next section by discussing the manager token.

Use the SSM Parameter Store to Save Swarm Tokens

How can your two secondary nodes obtain the manager token they need to join the swarm created by your primary node? Since each of your nodes are different EC2 instances, they'll need to get the token from an external store that they can all access. This is where the AWS Systems Manager Agent (SSM Agent)[2] comes in. The SSM Agent is a service that allows you to update, manage, and configure EC2 instances. It has a product called the Parameter Store, which is a cloud-based secrets manager. You may be thinking, wow another secrets manager? Weren't SOPS, Docker secrets, and GitHub secrets enough? In this case, you cannot use any of those options because your Docker Swarm is being created remotely, directly in AWS. AWS doesn't have access to your GitHub repository so it wouldn't be able to read the token from there. You, therefore, must use a secret store that your instances will have access to: the SSM Parameter Store.

The first step in enabling your two secondary nodes to get the manager token they need is to save the token itself in the Parameter Store. This will be done by the primary node right after it creates the swarm. As you saw in the previous section, you can run docker swarm join-token manager to obtain the command needed to join the swarm as a manager node. If you add the -q option to this command, the output will be the token itself, like so:

```
$ docker swarm join-token manager -q
SWMTKN-1-0ozc39ehnz6kc90aubadkubjjvb...
```

The role of your *primary* node will be to do the following:

1. Initialize the Docker Swarm.

2. Save the swarm's manager token to the SSM Parameter Store so your secondary nodes can access it.

3. Ensure that port 22 is open so that you know that the node is ready to receive swarm commands (Docker Swarm sends/receives commands using this port).

4. Assign itself a SwarmReady tag to indicate to the secondary nodes that the swarm has been created and your primary node is ready to receive swarm commands.

---

2. https://docs.aws.amazon.com/systems-manager/latest/userguide/ssm-agent.html

The role of your *secondary* nodes will be to do the following:

1. Get the token that's needed to join the swarm as manager from the SSM Parameter Store.

2. Get the primary node's IP address by searching for EC2 instances that have the SwarmReady tag.

3. Get the port that the primary node uses to listen to swarm orchestration commands.

4. Join the swarm.

5. Ensure that port 22 is open so that you know that the node is ready to receive swarm commands.

6. Assign itself a SwarmReady tag to indicate that the node has successfully joined the swarm and is ready to receive swarm commands.

But before you can implement this logic, you must allocate certain permissions to your EC2 instances. They currently don't have the permissions to access the SSM Parameter Store or the information about other EC2 instances, or create tags and assign them to themselves outside of the initial creation process. These permissions are something that you must specify when you create the instance. You'll learn how to do this in the next section.

IAM Roles, Policies, and Instance Profiles

For your primary node to store the swarm's manager token in the SSM Parameter Store and for your two secondary nodes to be able to access it, all of these nodes will need to have read and write access to the Parameter Store. This is not something that they have by default. You need to give your EC2 instances permission to do this by using identity and access management (IAM) roles, policies, and instance profiles.

IAM roles are a feature of AWS that allows you to grant specific permissions to entities (like EC2 instances or AWS users themselves) without having to manually assign API access keys. When a role is assumed, temporary security credentials are provided behind the scenes by AWS to the service/user for the action they wish to perform. These temporary access keys are continually rotated to reduce security risks. In essence, IAM roles give an entity permission to execute certain operations.

The policies are the permissions themselves. They are attached to an IAM role.

An IAM instance profile is the way that IAM roles are assigned to EC2 instances.

Let's create an IAM role for the four permissions that your EC2 instances need: reading and writing from the SSM Parameter Store, getting information about other EC2 instances, and assigning tags. The first step in doing this is to create an IAM policy.

Create an IAM Policy

To give your EC2 instances the ability to read and write values into the SSM Parameter Store, describe other instances, and assign tags, add the aws_iam _policy resource[3] to your Terraform configuration. Using this resource to create an IAM policy, you will grant your EC2 instances four permissions: ssm:PutParameter, ssm:GetParameter, ec2:DescribeInstances, and ec2:CreateTags.

So far, you've been defining your Terraform configuration in one single main.tf file. However, when dealing with large configurations, it's a good idea to split up your Terraform configuration into multiple files within the same root folder, where each file handles a certain domain. When you then apply your configuration, the Terraform Core will look for any and all files with the .tf suffix in the folder where you execute terraform apply (or all of the .tf files in a child module as is your current case) and squash them all together into one big file.

So, let's define your IAM configurations in their own file. Create a new file inside your modules/cloud/aws/compute/swarm folder called iam.tf. Then copy in the following code:

```
# in modules/cloud/aws/compute/swarm/iam.tf
locals {
  ssm_arn = "arn:aws:ssm:${var.region}:${var.account_id}:parameter/docker/*"
}
resource "aws_iam_policy" "ssm_policy" {
  name        = "DockerSwarmSSMPolicy"
  description = "Policy to PUT and GET parameters from SSM for Docker Swarm"

  policy = jsonencode({
    Version = "2012-10-17",
    Statement = [
      {
        Sid      = "SSMPutParameter",
        Effect   = "Allow",
        Action   = "ssm:PutParameter",
        Resource = local.ssm_arn
      },
      {
        Sid      = "SSMGetParameter",
        Effect   = "Allow",
```

---

3. https://registry.terraform.io/providers/hashicorp/aws/latest/docs/resources/iam_policy

```
          Action    = "ssm:GetParameter",
          Resource  = local.ssm_arn
      },
      {
        Sid       = "EC2DescribeInstances",
        Effect    = "Allow",
        Action    = "ec2:DescribeInstances",
        Resource  = "*"
      },
      {
        Sid       = "EC2CreateTags",
        Effect    = "Allow",
        Action    = "ec2:CreateTags",
        Resource  = "*"
      }
    ]
  })
}
```

This code snippet creates an IAM policy with four permissions. Each policy has four attributes. The Sid attribute is the statement ID.

The Effect attribute states whether you allow or explicitly deny access to the permission. (By default, access to resources is denied.)

The Action attribute describes the action or permission that you're wanting to allocate. The ssm:PutParameter permission allows your instances to write to the SSM Parameter Store. The ssm:GetParameter permission allows your instances to retrieve values from the Parameter Store. The ec2:DescribeInstances permission allows your instances to fetch data about other instances. This is what you'll use in the secondary nodes to get the IP of the primary node. And the ec2:CreateTags permission allows your instances to create/assign tags after they've been created.

Finally, the Resource attribute expects an Amazon Resource Name (ARN), which is an ID of a resource, and specifies the object that this statement applies to. The Resource attribute for the SSMPutParameter and SSMGetParameter policies uses a reusable ssm_arn local variable, which has the value arn:aws:ssm:${var.region}:${var.account_id}:parameter/docker/*. This means that those two permissions will only give your EC2 instances permission to read and write a Parameter Store variable with the name /docker/*. On the other hand, the Resource for the EC2DescribeInstances and EC2CreateTags policies is *. This means that your instances will have the ability to describe and create tags for any and all of the EC2 instances in your AWS account.

In the example, the local variable refers to two variables: region and account_id. You must add these variables to the variables.tf file of your swarm module. They

should both be strings. The region variable should have a default value of
eu-west-1. Add these variables as follows:

```
# in modules/cloud/aws/compute/swarm/variables.tf
variable "account_id" {
  type        = string
  description = "AWS account ID"
}
variable "region" {
  type        = string
  description = "AWS region"
  default     = "eu-west-1"
}
```

Now that you've created the IAM policy, the next step is to create an IAM role and attach this policy to that role.

Create an IAM Role and Attach an IAM Policy

To be able to assign your four permissions to your EC2 instances, you need to create an IAM role. To do this, you'll use the aws_iam_role resource.[4] This resource simply creates a new role inside AWS but doesn't attach any policies. To attach your four IAM policies, you will need to use the aws_iam_role_policy _attachment resource and specify the policy_arn and role attributes. The policy_arn will be the arn attribute exported by your aws_iam_policy resource and the role will be the name attribute that will be exported from your aws_iam_role resource. The upcoming code snippet shows you what you need to add to the end of your iam.tf file:

```
# in modules/cloud/aws/compute/swarm/iam.tf
resource "aws_iam_role" "ssm_role" {
  name = "DockerSwarmSSMRole"

  assume_role_policy = jsonencode({
    Version = "2012-10-17",
    Statement = [
      {
        Action = "sts:AssumeRole",
        Effect = "Allow",
        Principal = {
          Service = "ec2.amazonaws.com"
        }
      }
    ]
  })
}
```

---

4. https://registry.terraform.io/providers/hashicorp/aws/latest/docs/resources/iam_role

```
resource "aws_iam_role_policy_attachment" "ssm_role_policy_attachment" {
  policy_arn = aws_iam_policy.ssm_policy.arn
  role       = aws_iam_role.ssm_role.name
}
```

As you can see, the aws_iam_role resource has been given the name DockerSwarm SSMRole. It uses the assume_role_policy attribute to state the service that this role will be applied to. In this case, it has been specified as an EC2 instance. The aws_iam_role_policy_attachment resource then attaches the policies that you created earlier that has your four permissions to this DockerSwarmSSMRole.

Now that you've created your IAM role and attached your permissions, the next step is to create an IAM instance profile and attach it to your aws_instance resource.

Create an IAM Instance Profile and Attach It to Your EC2 Instances

An IAM instance profile is what AWS uses to assign IAM roles to EC2 instances. To create this instance profile, you'll use the aws_iam_instance_profile resource.[5] This resource takes a name attribute to give it a descriptive name, and the role attribute to specify the role that you wish to attach to the profile. For the role, you'll use the name attribute that's exported by your aws_iam_role resource. Add the following code snippet to the end of your iam.tf file to create the instance profile:

```
# in modules/cloud/aws/compute/swarm/iam.tf
resource "aws_iam_instance_profile" "main_profile" {
  name = "DockerSwarmSSMInstanceProfile"
  role = aws_iam_role.ssm_role.name
}
```

Great! The last step is to attach this instance profile to your aws_instance resource.

To do this, add the iam_instance_profile attribute to your aws_instance resource in your main.tf file and set it equal to the name attribute exported by your aws_iam_instance_profile resource, as we've done here:

```
# in modules/cloud/aws/compute/swarm/main.tf
resource "aws_instance" "swarm_node" {
  iam_instance_profile = aws_iam_instance_profile.main_profile.name
}
```

---

5. https://registry.terraform.io/providers/hashicorp/aws/latest/docs/resources/iam_instance_profile

>  **You Can Access Attributes Defined in Other Files**
>
> Even though you've defined your aws_iam_instance_profile resource in your iam.tf file and your aws_instance resource in your main.tf file, you can still access the exported attributes of resources created in different files. This is because of what we mentioned earlier, that when the Terraform Core applies your configuration, it will merge all of the .tf files in your module into one big file.

And that's it! You've configured your EC2 instances so that they can read and write values in the Parameter Store (as long as the value starts with /docker/), retrieve information about other EC2 instances, and create/assign tags. You're one step further in being able to configure your secondary nodes to join the swarm that your primary node creates.

Now let's apply your configuration and test that the configurations have been successfully added to your instances.

To be able to run terraform apply, you'll have to pass account_id as an input variable to your module. To do this, create a new account_id variable in your environments/production/variables.tf file identical to your swarm module one, and then instantiate that variable in an .auto.tfvars file. Then add the var.account_id variable to the import of your swarm module.

When you apply your configuration, you'll see that Terraform wants to add four new resources (your IAM role, policy, policy attachment, and profile) and update your three instances in place to attach your IAM profile.

After your configuration has been applied, SSH into one of the instances given in your terminal output as we've done in the upcoming terminal interaction. (Since you still haven't edited the user_data field of your aws_instance resource, all three of your instances will create their own swarm, so it doesn't matter which one you pick.):

```
$ terraform apply
...
Outputs:
swarm_ssh_commands = {
  "node_1" = "ssh -i ./private_key.pem ec2-user@18.170.119.35"
  ...
}
$ ssh -i ./private_key.pem ec2-user@18.170.119.35
# ... instance banner and prompt
```

Now run the four commands that your primary EC2 instance would execute:

1. Get the manager token by running `docker swarm join-token manager -q` and save it to a variable called SWARM_TOKEN like so:

   ```
   [ec2...~]$ SWARM_TOKEN=$(docker swarm join-token manager -q)
   ```

2. Write your swarm token to the SSM Parameter Store using the `ssm put-parameter` AWS CLI command. The secret should have the name /docker/swarm_manager_token, be of type SecureString, and have a value that's the manager token saved in step 1 like so:

   ```
   [ec2...~]$ aws ssm put-parameter \
                --name "/docker/swarm_manager_token" \
                --value "$SWARM_TOKEN" --type "SecureString"
   {
       "Version": 1,
       "Tier": "Standard"
   }
   ```

3. Ensure that port 22 of your EC2 instance is open using `nc` so that you know that your node is ready to receive swarm commands. `nc` is a utility tool for reading from and writing to network connections. You must pass the IP of your EC2 instance as an argument to `nc`. Add the -z option to make `nc` operate in scanning mode (meaning that it will check for open ports without sending any data), the -v option to enable verbose mode and provide a more detailed output, and finally the -w5 option to set a timeout of five seconds for the connection attempt like so:

   ```
   [ec2...~]$ nc -z -v -w5 "YOUR_EC2_INSTANCE_IP" 22
   Ncat: Version 7.93 ( https://nmap.org/ncat )
   Ncat: Connected to YOUR_EC2_INSTANCE_IP.
   Ncat: 0 bytes sent, 0 bytes received in 0.04 seconds.
   ```

4. Assign a SwarmReady tag that has a value of true to your instance using the `ec2 create-tags` AWS CLI command. You'll need to pass the ID of your instance to this command using the --resources option.

   You can obtain the ID of your instance through instance metadata.[6] Instance metadata gives you access to internal data about your instance such as its hostname, instance ID, AMI ID, IP, and so on. Instance metadata can be obtained using a link-local IP address in each instance (169.254.169.254) that's only available to query from inside that instance.

---

6. https://docs.aws.amazon.com/AWSEC2/latest/UserGuide/ec2-instance-metadata.html

To be able to query that IP, you need an authentication token. You can get this token by sending a PUT request to the local IP at the path latest/api/token and adding the TTL (Time To Live) header X-aws-ec2-metadata-token-ttl-seconds:3600. This will give the token a validity time of 3600 seconds. Get the authentication token and save it as a variable called AWS_TOKEN like so:

```
[ec2...~]$ AWS_TOKEN=$(curl -X PUT \
            "http://169.254.169.254/latest/api/token" \
            -H "X-aws-ec2-metadata-token-ttl-seconds: 3600")
```

Then, call the latest/meta-data/instance-id endpoint of that local IP to get the instance ID and save that ID to a variable called INSTANCE_ID. Lastly, execute the ec2 create-tags command using that variable. You can see an example terminal interaction here:

```
[ec2...~]$ INSTANCE_ID=$(curl -H "X-aws-ec2-metadata-token: $AWS_TOKEN" \
            http://169.254.169.254/latest/meta-data/instance-id)
[ec2...~]$ aws ec2 create-tags \
            --resources "$INSTANCE_ID" \
            --tags "Key=SwarmReady,Value=true" \
            --region "eu-west-1"
```

Great! You've successfully tested the commands that your primary node will execute. You know that your instances can write to the Parameter Store and create tags.

It's time to test the commands that your secondary instances would execute minus the swarm joining (as we'll go through that in the next section), the port 22 check, and the creation of the SwarmReady tag (because you've just tested both of those):

1. Use the ssm get-parameter AWS CLI command to get the /docker/swarm_manager _token secret that you created in step 2 of the previous list for the primary EC2 instances, remembering to add the --with-decryption option to decrypt the secure string like so:

```
[ec2...~]$ aws ssm get-parameter \
            --name "/docker/swarm_manager_token" \
            --with-decryption
{
    "Parameter": {
        "Name": "/docker/swarm_manager_token",
        "Type": "SecureString",
        "Value": "SWMTKN-1-6hf4a...",
        "Version": 6,
        "LastModifiedDate": "2023-10-29T20:12:07.033000+00:00",
        "ARN": "arn:aws:ssm:eu-west-1:90153392...",
        "DataType": "text"
```

        }
}

2. Use the ec2 describe-instances AWS CLI command to get the private IP address of your primary EC2 instance using the SwarmReady tag like so:

```
[ec2...~]$ aws ec2 describe-instances \
              --filters "Name=tag:Name,Values=docker-swarm-manager" \
                        "Name=instance-state-name,Values=running" \
                        "Name=tag:SwarmReady,Values=true" \
              --query "Reservations[0].Instances[0].PrivateIpAddress" \
              --region "eu-west-1" --output text
172.31.4.169
```

Amazing, it worked! You've successfully given your EC2 instances the permissions they need to be able to save the swarm's manager token, create a tag, read the manager token, and get information about other EC2 instances.

Now it's time to edit the user_data attribute of your aws_instance resource so that your Terraform configuration only creates one Docker Swarm using one primary instance and joins the other two secondary instances to the swarm as manager nodes. You'll do this in the next section.

> **Amazon Linux Provides AWS CLI Out-of-the-Box**
>
>  You may have noticed that you were able to use the AWS CLI in your EC2 instances without having to install it first. This is why you selected *Amazon Linux* as the base AMI for your Packer image in Chapter 6. Amazon Linux comes with helpful tools, such as the AWS CLI, already installed by default.

Use Separate Initialize and Join Swarm Scripts in Your user_data Attribute

In the previous section, you gave your EC2 instances permission to read and write values in the SSM Parameter Store, describe other EC2 instances, and create tags. This gave your secondary instances a way to access the join token for the swarm created by the primary node and retrieve the private IP of other nodes. It also allowed each node to assign themselves the SwarmReady tag. And you manually executed those commands after SSH-ing into one of your instances.

In this section, you'll automate this process and create two different scripts, one for the primary node and another foe the secondary nodes. The initialization script for your primary node, which starts your swarm, saves the token in the Parameter Store, ensures port 22 is open, and creates the SwarmReady tag. The second script for your secondary nodes gets the token from the Parameter Store, gets the primary node's IP, joins the swarm, checks port 22 is open, and assigns itself the SwarmReady tag.

After creating these scripts, you'll add a conditional to the user_data attribute of your aws_instance so only one of your instances runs the initialization script and the other two run the join script. Adding these commands to a script will help keep the configuration in your main.tf file neat and tidy.

Let's start by creating the initialization script.

Create the Initialization Script

To create the initialization script, create a new folder called scripts inside your modules/cloud/aws/compute/swarm directory. Then create a file called initialize.sh and copy in the following code snippet. We'll go through it afterward:

```bash
#!/usr/bin/env bash

# in modules/cloud/aws/compute/swarm/scripts/initialize.sh
get_aws_api_token() {
  curl -X PUT "http://169.254.169.254/latest/api/token" \
       -H "X-aws-ec2-metadata-token-ttl-seconds: 3600"
}
get_instance_meta_data() {
  local API_TOKEN=$1
  local META_DATA_ATTRIBUTE_NAME=$2
  curl -H "X-aws-ec2-metadata-token: $API_TOKEN" \
       "http://169.254.169.254/latest/meta-data/$META_DATA_ATTRIBUTE_NAME"
}

# create swarm
docker swarm init

# save swarm token to parameter store
MANAGER_TOKEN=$(docker swarm join-token manager -q)
aws ssm put-parameter --name "/docker/swarm_manager_token" \
                     --value "$MANAGER_TOKEN" \
                     --type "SecureString" --overwrite

# ensure port 22 is open
AWS_API_TOKEN=$(get_aws_api_token)
CURRENT_INSTANCE_IP=$(get_instance_meta_data "$AWS_API_TOKEN" "public-ipv4")

while ! nc -z -v -w1 "$CURRENT_INSTANCE_IP" 22; do
  echo "Waiting for SSH to be available..."
  sleep 2
done
```

```
# add "SwarmReady" tag
CURRENT_INSTANCE_ID=$(get_instance_meta_data "$AWS_API_TOKEN" "instance-id")
aws ec2 create-tags \
    --resources "$CURRENT_INSTANCE_ID" \
    --tags "Key=SwarmReady,Value=true" \
    --region "eu-west-1"
```

The script includes the docker swarm init command followed by steps 1, 2, 3 and 4 that you executed in the previous section. The node that runs this script will create a Docker Swarm, save the swarm's manager token to a value in the Parameter Store called /docker/swarm_manager_token, check that port 22 is open, and then assign itself the SwarmReady tag.

You may notice we've created a get_instance_meta_data function. We parametrized the curl execution that calls the instance metadata endpoint of the link-local IP address into the get_instance_meta_data function because you need to call this command twice—each time using a different sub-path. First, you need to query the public-ipv4 endpoint and get the IP of the instance that the script is being run on. This is so that you can ensure that port 22 is open. When you tested this command earlier, you passed the IP for your instance directly to that command as you had just SSH-ed in and so knew the IP. But this script will be agnostic to the instance it's being run on and so you need to retrieve that IP programmatically. And secondly, you need to query the same instance-id path as earlier to get the ID of the instance running the script so that you can create the SwarmReady tag.

Notice that to ensure that port 22 of the node is open, we've run the nc command inside a while loop that will only exit once the nc command returns a successful result.

Let's now test this script, as well as the joining logic, by having one of your three EC2 instances run it. For now, the other two instances will do nothing.

You need to create a local value called init_script in your main.tf file so that your Terraform configuration can read your initialization script. Then, use the built-in file Terraform function to import the initialize.sh script you just created. After this, update the user_data attribute so that only the EC2 instance where the count.index is 0 runs this script. You can see how to do this here:

```
# in modules/cloud/aws/compute/swarm/main.tf
locals {
  init_script = file("${path.module}/scripts/initialize.sh")
}
resource "aws_instance" "swarm_node" {
  user_data = count.index == 0 ? local.init_script : ""
}
```

Great! Now apply your configuration by running terraform destroy followed by terraform apply. You must destroy your configuration before applying it, because the user_data attribute is only run when an EC2 instance starts up. After your configuration has finished applying, test the swarm join logic by SSH-ing into the *second* ssh_command output, repeating the last 2 steps in the previous section and running docker swarm join. (You aren't testing the port 22 check or the SwarmReady tag creation because you already know that logic works). The commands you have to run are as follows:

1. Use the AWS CLI to get the manager join token from the SSM Parameter Store.
2. Use the AWS CLI to get the primary node's IP and then save it to a variable called MANAGER_IP.
3. Run the docker swarm join --token <TOKEN> <MANAGER_IP:LISTENING_PORT> command to join that EC2 instance as a manager node on your swarm. The default port that Docker uses to listen to orchestration requests is 2377.

You can see an example terminal interaction of this whole process here:

```
$ terraform destroy
...
$ terraform apply
...
$ ssh -i ./private_key.pem ec2-user@YOUR_SECOND_EC2_INSTANCE
...
[ec2...~]$ TOKEN=$(aws ssm get-parameter \
            --name "/docker/swarm_manager_token" \
            --query "Parameter.Value" --output text \
            --with-decryption)
...
[ec2...~]$ MANAGER_IP=$(aws ec2 describe-instances \
    --filters "Name=tag:Name,Values=docker-swarm-manager" \
              "Name=instance-state-name,Values=running" \
              "Name=tag:SwarmReady,Values=true" \
    --query "Reservations[0].Instances[0].PrivateIpAddress" \
    --region "eu-west-1" --output text)
...
[ec2...~]$ docker swarm join --token "$TOKEN" "$MANAGER_IP:2377"
Error response from daemon: Timeout was reached before node joined. The
attempt to join the swarm will continue in the background. Use the
"docker info" command to see the current swarm status of your node.
```

Oops, a timeout error! What has happened? Joining a Docker Swarm relies upon port 2377 being open on the primary node, and you haven't yet configured the security group for your EC2 instances to permit traffic through this port. To do this, move your current aws_security_group resource out of your main.tf file to a new sg.tf file. This separates out the logic and makes your main configuration file easier to read. Then add the last four ingress objects in the following code snippet so that your sg.tf file looks like this:

```
# in modules/cloud/aws/compute/swarm/sg.tf
resource "aws_security_group" "swarm_sg" {
  name   = "swarm_pool_ports"
  vpc_id = data.aws_vpc.main.id

  ingress {
    description = "Elixir Phoenix app"
    from_port   = 4000
    to_port     = 4000
    protocol    = "tcp"
    cidr_blocks = ["0.0.0.0/0"]
  }
  ingress {
    description = "SSH port"
    from_port   = 22
    to_port     = 22
    protocol    = "tcp"
    cidr_blocks = ["0.0.0.0/0"]
  }
  ingress {
    description = "Docker swarm management"
    from_port   = 2377
    to_port     = 2377
    protocol    = "tcp"
    cidr_blocks = [
      data.aws_vpc.main.cidr_block,
    ]
  }
  ingress {
    description = "Docker container network discovery"
    from_port   = 7946
    to_port     = 7946
    protocol    = "tcp"
    cidr_blocks = [
      data.aws_vpc.main.cidr_block,
    ]
  }
  ingress {
    description = "Docker overlay network"
    from_port   = 4789
    to_port     = 4789
    protocol    = "udp"
    cidr_blocks = [
      data.aws_vpc.main.cidr_block,
    ]
  }
```

```
  egress {
    from_port  = 0
    to_port    = 0
    protocol   = "-1"
    cidr_blocks = ["0.0.0.0/0"]
  }
}
```

The ingress objects allow inbound traffic and the egress objects allow outbound traffic. The four new ingress rules in the previous snippet include all of the ports that Docker uses for various communications in a swarm. You can find more detailed information on these ports in the official documentation.[7] You'll notice we've updated the name of the security group and added descriptions to the existing ingress and egress objects. We've also removed the ipv6_cidr_blocks, prefix_list_ids, security_groups, and self parameters. This is because these are all optional parameters which you haven't set.

Now that you've updated your security group, plan your Terraform configuration by running terraform plan. When you do this, you'll notice that Terraform wants to remove your SwarmReady tag from your first EC2 instance. This is because this tag isn't part of your Terraform configuration and was added by your initialize.sh script after the instance was created. To avoid Terraform wanting to delete this tag, add the following lifecycle attribute to your aws_instance resource, which will tell Terraform to ignore any changes to the tags of your EC2 instances:

```
# in modules/cloud/aws/compute/swarm/main.tf
resource "aws_instance" "swarm_node" {
  lifecycle {
    ignore_changes = [tags]
  }
}
```

You might be thinking that using the ignore_changes lifecycle meta-argument goes against the declarative principles of Terraform according to which you define the state of a resource and Terraform figures out how to achieve/maintain that state, and you'd be right. Adding this meta-argument will make it harder for you to track the state of your resource, but there are some scenarios, like this one, where this meta-argument is needed. If you weren't to ignore the adding of this SwarmReady tag, each time you try to update your configuration, Terraform would want to delete the tag. Without this tag, your secondary nodes wouldn't know whether they could send swarm requests

---

7. https://docs.docker.com/engine/swarm/swarm-tutorial/#open-protocols-and-ports-between-the-hosts

to your primary node. We'd recommend using this ignore_changes meta-argument sparingly though, and only when absolutely necessary.

Now run terraform apply again. You'll see that Terraform will replace your security group (by destroying your current security group and creating a new one) and update your EC2 instances in place to update the security group they each use. Once you've applied your configuration, SSH back into your second EC2 instance and run the three steps you executed earlier to try to join one of your secondary EC2 instances as a manager node in your swarm. To check whether the join was successful, run docker node ls in either of the connected nodes to list the nodes of your swarm. You can see an example terminal interaction here:

```
$ terraform apply
...
$ ssh -i ./private_key.pem ec2-user@18.170.119.36
...
[ec2...~]$ TOKEN=$(aws ssm get-parameter \
           --name "/docker/swarm_manager_token" \
           --query "Parameter.Value" --output text \
           --with-decryption)
...
[ec2...~]$ MANAGER_IP=$(aws ec2 describe-instances \
    --filters "Name=tag:Name,Values=docker-swarm-manager" \
              "Name=instance-state-name,Values=running" \
              "Name=tag:SwarmReady,Values=true" \
    --query "Reservations[0].Instances[0].PrivateIpAddress" \
    --region "eu-west-1" --output text)
...
[ec2...~]$ docker swarm join --token "$TOKEN" "$MANAGER_IP:2377"
This node joined a swarm as a manager.
[ec2-user@ip-172-31-40-63 ~]$ docker node ls
ID       HOSTNAME               STATUS   AVAIL...  MANAGER...  ENGINE...
hbl...   ip-172...eu-west-1...  Ready    Active    Leader      24.0.5
tfx...   ip-172...eu-west-1...  Ready    Active    Reachable   24.0.5
```

Great! You've successfully joined one of your secondary instances as a manager node to the swarm that your primary instance created! Well done. The next step is to automate this joining process by creating a join script and editing the user_data attribute of your secondary instances.

Create the Join Script

You know that to join an EC2 instance to your Docker Swarm as a node, you need to know the swarm's manager token and the primary node's IP address. To retrieve the primary node's IP, you need to know two things: the tag assigned to that instance and the region it's created in. Once you know both of these pieces of information (the token and the IP), run the command docker swarm join, check that port 22 is open, and assign the node the SwarmReady tag. To put this into a join script, create a new file called join.sh inside your modules /cloud/aws/compute/swarm/scripts directory and paste in the following code:

```bash
#!/usr/bin/env bash

# in modules/cloud/aws/compute/swarm/scripts/join.sh
get_aws_api_token() {
  curl -X PUT "http://169.254.169.254/latest/api/token" \
      -H "X-aws-ec2-metadata-token-ttl-seconds: 3600"
}
get_instance_meta_data() {
  local API_TOKEN=$1
  local META_DATA_ATTRIBUTE_NAME=$2
  curl -H "X-aws-ec2-metadata-token: $API_TOKEN" \
      "http://169.254.169.254/latest/meta-data/$META_DATA_ATTRIBUTE_NAME"
}

# get swarm token
while true; do
  TOKEN=$(aws ssm get-parameter \
          --name "/docker/swarm_manager_token" \
          --query "Parameter.Value" --output text \
          --with-decryption)
  echo "Waiting for Swarm Manager token..."
  sleep 2
done

# get primary node's IP
MANAGER_IP=$(aws ec2 describe-instances \
    --filters "Name=tag:Name,Values=${manager_tag}" \
              "Name=instance-state-name,Values=running" \
              "Name=tag:SwarmReady,Values=true" \
    --query "Reservations[0].Instances[0].PrivateIpAddress" \
    --region "${region}" --output text)

# join swarm
docker swarm join --token "$TOKEN" "$MANAGER_IP:2377"

# ensure port 22 is open
AWS_API_TOKEN=$(get_aws_api_token)
CURRENT_INSTANCE_IP=$(get_instance_meta_data "$AWS_API_TOKEN" "public-ipv4")

while ! nc -z -v -w1 "$CURRENT_INSTANCE_IP" 22; do
  echo "Waiting for SSH to be available..."
  sleep 2
done
```

```
# add "SwarmReady" tag
CURRENT_INSTANCE_ID=$(get_instance_meta_data "$AWS_API_TOKEN" "instance-id")
aws ec2 create-tags \
    --resources "$CURRENT_INSTANCE_ID" \
    --tags "Key=SwarmReady,Value=true" \
    --region "eu-west-2"
```

This script has a while loop that waits for the existence of the /docker/swarm_manager _token variable in the Parameter Store. This avoids any potential race conditions in which the secondary nodes are trying to access the join token before it has been properly saved. You may also have noticed that the manager_tag and region variables have been parametrized. This is because they are both reusable values that are used in many different places in your configuration. After joining the swarm, the script ensures that port 22 is open and then assigns itself the SwarmReady tag in the exact same way as your initialize.sh script does. We know that it's not ideal to have the same logic replicated in different files, but don't worry about this for now, you'll refactor this in Chapter 10. Remember that the first step is always to make it work. You can make it beautiful afterward.

Since this script needs arguments to be run, you cannot use the same built-in file() function that you used when including your initialize.sh script in your main.tf file. Instead, you need to use the templatefile function,[8] which expects two arguments: the path to the script and an object with variables that will be interpolated when the script is run.

To add this join script to your configuration, create a local value called join_script whose first argument is the path to your join.sh script and whose second argument is an object that specifies the manager_tag and region script arguments. Then replace the "" clause in the if statement of the user_data attribute of your aws_instance resource to be your new local join_script value. You can see the modifications you have to make here. Note that we've parametrized the tag applied to your EC2 instances to keep your code DRY:

```
# in modules/cloud/aws/compute/swarm/main.tf
locals {
  init_script = file("${path.module}/scripts/initialize.sh")
  manager_tag = "docker-swarm-manager"
  join_script = templatefile("${path.module}/scripts/join.sh", {
    manager_tag = local.manager_tag,
    region      = var.region
  })
}
```

---

8. https://developer.hashicorp.com/terraform/language/functions/templatefile

```
resource "aws_instance" "swarm_node" {
  user_data = count.index == 0 ? local.init_script : local.join_script
  tags = {
    Name = local.manager_tag
  }
}
```

Great! Your join script is ready to go.

In theory, you could go ahead and apply your configuration straight away and create your multinode swarm. However, your BEAMOps sense might be tingling. While your initialize and join scripts create a secret in the Parameter Store, this value isn't handled by Terraform. This means that your configuration isn't idempotent. You'll rectify this in the next section.

Add Your SSM Parameter Resource to Your Terraform Configuration

Currently, if you were to apply your Terraform configuration and destroy it, your Parameter Store secret would remain in your AWS account. This could lead to your join script trying to join your swarm with an incorrect and outdated token. It's important that your swarm module is idempotent and allows you to apply the Terraform cycle as many times as you want. To ensure this, add your /docker/swarm_manager_token to your Terraform configuration using the aws_ssm_parameter resource.[9]

As you know, you can import resources into your Terraform configuration using import blocks. However, you shouldn't import your current swarm token as it is now. This is because your swarm token will be different every time you destroy and apply your configuration. When you create your /docker/swarm _manager_token value using Terraform, you must create it with a *placeholder* value of NONE. You must then update the while loop in your join.sh script that waits for the /docker/swarm_manager_token variable to be set and tell it to keep looking for a value if the value of /docker/swarm_manager_token is NONE (that is, the placeholder value). If you don't add this if clause, the while loop would exit on its first GET execution and would try to join your Docker Swarm with a token value of NONE.

By handling the initial token creation in Terraform, you can make sure the token is destroyed when your infrastructure is destroyed. We have created the aws_ssm_parameter resource for you in the upcoming code snippet. Copy this resource into your main.tf file, add it as a dependency to your aws_instance

---

9. https://registry.terraform.io/providers/hashicorp/aws/latest/docs/resources/ssm_parameter

resource, and then add the necessary import block to your environments/production/main.tf file:

```
# in modules/cloud/aws/compute/swarm/main.tf
resource "aws_ssm_parameter" "swarm_token" {
  name        = "/docker/swarm_manager_token"
  description = "The swarm manager join token"
  type        = "SecureString"
  value       = "NONE"
  lifecycle {
    ignore_changes = [value]
  }
}
resource "aws_instance" "swarm_node" {
  depends_on = [aws_ssm_parameter.swarm_token]
}

# in environments/production/main.tf
import {
  to = module.swarm.aws_ssm_parameter.swarm_token
  id = "/docker/swarm_manager_token"
}
```

You'll notice that the aws_ssm_parameter resource includes the ignore_changes lifecycle meta-argument. This is because your EC2 instances will update the Parameter Store value outside of your Terraform configuration and you need to be sure that the token isn't updated in subsequent configuration applications.

As we mentioned, you need to update the while loop in your join script to keep waiting for a join token if the token value is NONE:

```
# in modules/cloud/aws/compute/swarm/scripts/join.sh
  if [ -n "$TOKEN" ] && [ "$TOKEN" != "NONE" ]; then
    break
  fi
```

And that's it! Your join script is ready to go, and your Terraform configuration is idempotent.

Import your Parameter Store token into your Terraform configuration by running terraform apply. You'll see that Terraform will also update the user_data field of your instances. But as you know, the join script won't be run because user_data scripts are only run when an instance first boots. Once you've imported your Parameter Store token, remove your import object from your environments/production/main.tf file and then destroy and re-create your configuration by running terraform destroy followed by terraform apply.

If you go to the Parameter Store page in the AWS UI, you'll see that your parameter has been re-created. Then, SSH into one of your EC2 instances and run the command docker node ls. You'll see that your Docker Swarm includes three nodes!

Feel free to apply and destroy your configuration as many times as you want. You'll see that each time, a placeholder Parameter Store token will be created with a value of NONE and, once your swarm is initiated, this value will change and your two secondary EC2 instances will join the swarm using that token.

You did it! You've successfully created a multinode swarm. Congratulations! Once you deploy your application, it will no longer be vulnerable to data center outages and the swarm will distribute the load of requests more efficiently, helping reduce the risk of your application becoming overwhelmed.

The last step in this chapter is to add the deployment script that you created in the previous chapter to your Terraform configuration. This way, after you create your AWS resources, your application will be automatically deployed without you having to manually interfere. You'll do this in the next section using a new Terraform resource.

Automate the Initial Deployment of Your Application

Well done! You've done a lot of work to get here! You've implemented a Terraform module to create a reproducible swarm cluster that's distributed across three AZs. The last step in your AWS revision is to add the deployment script that you created in the previous chapter for your CD pipeline to your Terraform configuration. Once you do that, any time you run terraform apply to create all of your AWS resources, your application will automatically be deployed.

Right now, even though you have a multinode swarm, you still only have one instance of your Phoenix application. To make your application highly available in your swarm, you have to make one small change to your Compose file and ensure you can deploy multiple instances of your web service rather than just one. To do this, add the replicas attribute to the deploy key. The replicas value should be settable if a WEB_REPLICAS environment variable is passed, but should have a default value of 1. Try doing this yourself before looking at the following example:

```
# in compose.yaml
web:
  image: ${WEB_IMAGE:-ghcr.io/beamops/kanban:latest}
  deploy:
    replicas: ${WEB_REPLICAS:-1}
```

Great! Now, any time you deploy your application suite, you can specify how many instances of your web service you want to create. These instances will then be spread across your swarm nodes automatically by Docker in a round-robin fashion.

When deploying your instances, you only need to send the docker stack deploy command to *one* of your manager nodes. No matter which manager node receives the deploy request, it will forward the request to the LEADER node. The leader node is often the one that creates the swarm, that is, the primary node (unless it has gone down or failed and another node has taken over its responsibilities). The leader node is responsible for issuing commands to all the other nodes in the cluster, which will then update the various tasks that are running the containers that need to be updated.

Virtual IP Enables All Nodes to Access Your Database

 In this book, you'll only deploy multiple instances of your web service, not your db service. Distributing your Postgres database is out of the scope of this book. But don't worry. Even if one of your web service instances is located in a different EC2 instance, in a different availability zone, than your database, it won't have any issues accessing the database. This is because the DATABASE_URL variable that you're passing to your Phoenix application references the db service name rather than a specific IP. When you do this, your Phoenix application will access the Virtual IP (VIP), or entry-point, of your db service, which balances traffic across different tasks in your swarm. The VIP isn't a running instance of your database but a load balancer that will forward traffic onto your database, even if it comes from a different node.

To deploy the multiple instances of your Phoenix application when you apply your Terraform configuration, you'll use a new Terraform resource from a new provider: the null_resource.[10] This resource implements the standard resource lifecycle but takes no further action. It's useful for running local or remote commands, when used with the local-exec provisioner.[11]

Remember that to deploy your application, you need to provide your deploy.sh script with six environment variables (GITHUB_TOKEN, GITHUB_USER, AWS_ACCESS_KEY_ID, AWS_SECRET_ACCESS_KEY, PRIVATE_KEY_PATH, and SOPS_AGE_KEY_FILE) and one optional argument (the image tag to be deployed). Your script then gets the IP of your

---

10. https://registry.terraform.io/providers/hashicorp/null/latest/docs/resources/resource
11. https://developer.hashicorp.com/terraform/language/resources/provisioners/local-exec

manager node, SSH-es into that node, logs into the GitHub Docker registry, and runs the docker stack deploy command, specifying the DOCKER_HOST.

As you'll be adding this script to your Terraform configuration, which now creates a *multinode* swarm rather than a single one, there are a few tweaks you must make to your deploy.sh script:

1. Update the aws ec2 describe-instances query that searches for the MANAGER_IP that your script will use when deploying the application so that it includes your SwarmReady tag. This is important as this tag is only added once you know that port 22 is open and can receive connections.

2. Add a COMPOSE_FILE_PATH variable to your script that can be passed as an argument but that has a default value of compose.yaml. This will allow you to specify the compose file in your Terraform configuration to a file that lives outside of your Terraform modules.

The changes that you have to make to your deploy.sh script are as follows:

```
# in scripts/deploy.sh

# set default variables
IMAGE=${1:-"ghcr.io/beamops/kanban:latest"}
AWS_REGION="eu-west-1"
INSTANCE_TAG_NAME="docker-swarm-manager"
STACK_NAME="kanban"
COMPOSE_FILE_PATH=${COMPOSE_FILE_PATH:-"compose.yaml"}

# get EC2 IP address
MANAGER_IP=$(aws ec2 describe-instances \
    --filters "Name=tag:Name,Values=$INSTANCE_TAG_NAME" \
              "Name=instance-state-name,Values=running" \
              "Name=tag:SwarmReady,Values=true" \
    --query "Reservations[0].Instances[0].PublicIpAddress" \
    --region "$AWS_REGION" --output text)

# deploy the application
DOCKER_HOST="ssh://ec2-user@$MANAGER_IP" \
WEB_IMAGE="$IMAGE" \
docker stack deploy -c "$COMPOSE_FILE_PATH" --with-registry-auth \
"$STACK_NAME"

echo "Deployment completed."
```

OK, your deploy.sh script is ready to be added to your Terraform configuration. For the null_resource, you'll create two different instances of this resource. The first one waits for your first EC2 instance to have the SwarmReady tag. And the second, a null_resource, runs your deploy.sh script.

As we mentioned, you'll use the local-exec provisioner. This provisioner can take two attributes: environment (to specify environment variables) and command (to specify the command to be run). Your first null_resource will have two environment variables: the AWS region and the tag for your EC2 instance. The value of the command attribute will be a new script that runs the same aws ec2 describe-instances command that your deploy.sh script runs every two seconds until your first EC2 instance has the SwarmReady tag.

This is a necessary step because, as you saw in Chapter 6, Terraform doesn't wait for the user_data attribute to finish executing before it finishes its own execution. This means that when you tell Terraform to run your deploy script after having created the EC2 instances, if you didn't wait for your first instance to have a SwarmReady tag, your deploy script could fail as it may not be able to find a MANAGER_IP. We've written the first null_resource for you in the upcoming code snippet. Copy it into your modules/cloud/aws/compute/swarm/main.tf file. Remember that you also need to install the null plugin:

```
# in modules/cloud/aws/compute/swarm/main.tf
terraform {
  required_providers {
    null = {
      source  = "hashicorp/null"
      version = "3.2.1"
    }
  }
}
resource "null_resource" "wait_for_swarm_ready_tag" {
  provisioner "local-exec" {
    environment = {
      AWS_REGION          = var.region
      INSTANCE_MANAGER_TAG = local.manager_tag
    }
    command = "../../scripts/wait_for_swarm_ready_tag.sh"
  }
  depends_on = [aws_instance.swarm_node]
}
```

As you can see, we've added the aws_instance resource as a dependency to the null_resource so that the script isn't executed until the EC2 instances have been created. This resource references a script called wait_for_swarm_ready_tag.sh. Create a script in the scripts folder at the root of your project with that name and paste in the following code that'll search for EC2 instances with the SwarmReady tag every two seconds until it finds one. Once you've created the script, make it executable by running chmod +x scripts/wait_for_swarm_ready_tag.sh:

```bash
#!/usr/bin/env bash
# in scripts/wait_for_swarm_ready_tag.sh
while true; do
    MANAGER_IP=$(aws ec2 describe-instances \
        --filters "Name=tag:Name,Values=$INSTANCE_MANAGER_TAG" \
                  "Name=instance-state-name,Values=running" \
                  "Name=tag:SwarmReady,Values=true" \
        --query "Reservations[0].Instances[0].PublicIpAddress" \
        --region "$AWS_REGION" --output text)
    if [ -n "$MANAGER_IP" ] && [ "$MANAGER_IP" != "None" ]; then
        break
    fi
    echo "No instances with SwarmReady tag yet. Retrying in 2 seconds..."
    sleep 2
done
```

The second null_resource that runs your deploy.sh script should include an environment block that specifies the six environment variables your script requires as well as the new WEB_REPLICAS environment variable that your Compose file needs. You'll also need to pass the image tag as an argument to the script. We recommend using a Terraform variable to do this so that you can deploy any image you wish when applying your configuration. This variable should have a default value of the :latest tag of your Docker image. The upcoming example shows you the new null_resource you need to add to your main.tf file:

```
# in modules/cloud/aws/compute/swarm/main.tf
resource "null_resource" "swarm_provisioner" {
  provisioner "local-exec" {
    environment = {
      GITHUB_USER            = var.gh_owner
      GITHUB_TOKEN           = var.gh_pat
      AWS_SECRET_ACCESS_KEY  = var.aws_secret_access_key
      AWS_ACCESS_KEY_ID      = var.aws_access_key_id
      PRIVATE_KEY_PATH       = var.private_key_path
      SOPS_AGE_KEY_FILE      = var.age_key_path
      COMPOSE_FILE_PATH      = var.compose_file
      WEB_REPLICAS           = length(aws_instance.swarm_node)
    }
    command = "../../scripts/deploy.sh ${var.image_to_deploy}"
  }
  depends_on = [null_resource.wait_for_swarm_ready_tag]
}
```

As you can see, we've added your first null_resource as a dependency so that the script is only run once your wait_for_swarm_ready_tag.sh script has finished executing. We've also added various variables, the same ones that you have in your environments/production folder. The WEB_REPLICAS variable has been set to be the same as the number of nodes in your swarm. As variables can only be auto-loaded when they are defined in the same root folder, you'll have to copy these variables over to the variables.tf file in your swarm module folder. We've pasted the variables that you need to add here:

```
# in modules/cloud/aws/compute/swarm/variables.tf
variable "aws_access_key_id" {
  description = "The AWS access key ID."
  type        = string
  sensitive   = true
}
variable "aws_secret_access_key" {
  description = "The AWS secret access key."
  type        = string
  sensitive   = true
}
variable "gh_pat" {
  description = "The GitHub Personal Access Token (PAT)."
  type        = string
  sensitive   = true
}
variable "gh_owner" {
  description = "The GitHub owner of the repo."
  type        = string
}
variable "age_key_path" {
  description = "The path to the SOPS age key file."
  type        = string
}
variable "compose_file" {
  type        = string
  description = "Docker Compose file"
  default     = "../../compose.yaml"
}
variable "image_to_deploy" {
  type        = string
  description = "Image to deploy"
  default     = "ghcr.io/YOUR_GITHUB_USERNAME/kanban:latest"
}
```

And you're done! Remember to instantiate your variables in the swarm module import in your environments/production/main.tf file. Make sure you hide the secret variables (the AWS keys and GitHub token) by using the variables in your environments/production/.auto.tfvars file. Your swarm module import should look like this:

```
# in environments/production/main.tf
module "swarm" {
  source                = "../../modules/cloud/aws/compute/swarm"
  private_key_path      = "${path.module}/private_key.pem"
  account_id            = var.account_id
  age_key_path          = "${path.module}/key.txt"
  compose_file          = "../../compose.yaml"
  aws_access_key_id     = var.aws_access_key_id
  aws_secret_access_key = var.aws_secret_access_key
  gh_pat                = var.gh_pat
  gh_owner              = "BeamOps"
  image_to_deploy       = "ghcr.io/YOUR_GITHUB_USERNAME/kanban:latest"
}
```

You can now destroy and re-create your multinode Docker Swarm, and your application will be automatically deployed! You'll have to run terraform init before you do so to install the null provider that you added. Once you re-create your configuration, it might take a minute for the stack to be up and running (even after your deploy script finishes executing), so take a break and make a coffee or tea. When you get back, SSH into any one of your EC2 instances and run docker service ls. This will show you that your stack is up and running. Now visit port 4000 of all of your EC2 instances, and you'll see your application!

You did it! You created a multinode swarm that has been distributed over multiple AZs. You also added a WEB_REPLICAS environment variable that allows you to deploy multiple instances of your web service to make your Phoenix application highly available. Finally, you added your deployment script to your Terraform configuration so that any time you create your AWS resources from scratch, your application suite will be automatically deployed. You're really owning your infrastructure-as-code configuration and should be confident in automating your resource configuration and deployment. You're looking more like a BEAMOps developer with every chapter!

You can now close the "Update Terraform Configuration for a multinode swarm" issue that you created in Chapter 2. To do this, create a new branch, commit your code from this chapter, and create a PR. Add closes #ISSUE_ID to the description of your PR and merge it.

Before moving on, be sure to destroy your AWS infrastructure. Make sure that your CD has finished running before you do this, otherwise, the deployment step will fail.

What Have You Learned?

In this chapter, you adapted your Terraform configuration to create a multinode swarm rather than a single node one. You made your application highly available by distributing the different nodes in different AZs. And you added the deploy script that you created in the previous chapter to your Terraform configuration so that every time you apply your configuration for the first time, your application suite is automatically deployed. Your application can now make full use of Docker Swarm's orchestration capabilities.

You're becoming a master in infrastructure-as-code, having successfully deployed your application in a remote and distributed AWS environment.

In the next chapter, you'll learn how to use distributed Erlang to make the multiple instances of your web service communicate and share data in real time. You'll take advantage of one of Elixir's and Erlang's best features: the ability to join multiple Erlang nodes into a cluster so that each node is aware of processes running in other nodes.

> **The Extra Mile**
>
> If you wish to deepen your knowledge of the themes we've covered in this chapter and refine your BEAMOps developer superpowers, we've created a task for you to do:
>
> 1. Play around with destroying different resources and seeing how your infrastructure behaves when you apply your configuration again. What happens if you destroy one of your secondary nodes (EC2 instances) and then apply again? What happens if you destroy the primary node and apply again? Have a play with the number of replicas and see how the swarm behaves. You can destroy one specific resource in your configuration by using the --target option when running terraform destroy.

CHAPTER 9

Distributed Erlang

In the previous chapter, you created a multinode Docker Swarm that included multiple replica instances of your application. In this chapter, you'll enable those instances to communicate and share data in real time by making each one part of a distributed Erlang cluster. Distributed Erlang clusters are sort of like the cool kids at school—everyone knows they're cool but no one really knows why.

You might already be aware that Elixir runs on top of the Erlang VM, which is designed to be distributed, fault-tolerant, and resilient from the ground up. In this chapter, you will use an out-of-the-box Erlang functionality—connecting all of the instances of your application as part of a distributed Erlang cluster—to leverage some original features such as Pub/Sub message communication and real-time user-connection statistics. Using Pub/Sub messaging in conjunction with connected Erlang nodes allows you to easily share information between your nodes and ensures that your application will work in the same way when scaled and new nodes join the cluster. We'll also introduce you to the application that we wrote with our friend Ricardo García Vega to show you the benefits of distributed Erlang in action.

After reading this chapter, you'll be able to deploy your application to a multinode swarm in production where each node is part of a distributed Erlang cluster. Being able to do this will allow you to ensure the scalability of your application. You'll also be able to close one of the infrastructure issues that you created in Chapter 2.

So, let's dive right in and discuss what distributed Erlang actually is.

Get to Know Distributed Erlang

As an Elixir developer, you've probably heard about *distributed Erlang* but you might not understand what it means. As we mentioned, distributed Erlang is like the cool kid at school. You know it's cool but you're not sure why.

Distributed Erlang simply means connecting different Erlang nodes to form a cluster. A node in this context is an executing Erlang runtime system that's given a name when started. You'll see this in action in a few pages.

So, how do different Erlang nodes connect? How exactly does the "distributed" part work? Distributed Erlang works by creating TCP connections between nodes. For a connection to be successful, both of the nodes have to share, or use, the same authentication token. This authentication token is referred to as a cookie.

Now that you have a general sense of what distributed Erlang is, the next section will look at its benefits.

Why Use a Distributed Erlang Cluster?

As we mentioned, distributed Erlang is the joining of Erlang nodes into a cluster. The main advantage of doing this is that it allows whatever is running in your Erlang nodes, which in your case will be instances of your web service, to share data and be aware of changes made in other nodes. Think of a Google Doc: When multiple people are editing the same document, each person can see the changes made by others. Although Google Doc technology is written in Java, a similar type of live replication can occur when Erlang nodes are joined. That is, any changes made on one node are reflected in the other.

Here is a list of the advantages of distributed Erlang and the ways in which it harnesses the power of the Erlang VM (BEAM) to give you benefits that other languages don't offer out of the box:

1. *Fault Tolerance*: One of the key features of the BEAM is its ability to provide fault-tolerant systems. By connecting multiple nodes, you can build systems where if one node fails, another can take over its responsibilities while the failing node is restarted.

2. *Load Distribution*: If you have an application with varying workloads, you can distribute the workload across different nodes to ensure that no single node is overwhelmed.

3. *Data Replication*: For applications that require a high availability of data, having multiple connected nodes allows for data to be replicated across

them. This ensures that even if one node goes down, the data is still accessible from another node. An example of this might be an e-commerce platform where you can't afford to lose access to user data or transactions.

4. *Global Process Registry*: By using modules like :global, you're able to register a process under a given name across nodes. This allows for processes to be uniquely addressed across a distributed system. Processes can be started in one node and accessed from another node. An example of this could be a chat room that's started in one node but users can join it even if they're connected to another node.

5. *Shared Caching*: It's possible to create a shared, distributed cache between Erlang nodes using caching solutions like Cachex or Nebulex. This means that if you cache certain data in node A, node B will be able to access this information. This is beneficial for scenarios where you have a high volume of repetitive requests, such as a news site where multiple users are accessing the same articles.

6. *Better Usage of Resources*: Having multiple connected nodes allows for better usage of available resources by distributing tasks across nodes. This is different from load distribution in the sense that you can allocate certain tasks to certain nodes. Think of a cloud-based video-processing application. Different nodes can be assigned tasks like video transcoding, thumbnail generation, and metadata extraction.

7. *Message Passing*: Erlang's message-passing model makes it easy to build distributed systems by sending messages between processes running on different nodes. This asynchronous communication style simplifies the development of concurrent and distributed applications, similar to the Google Docs example we gave earlier.

As you can see, there are multiple advantages to using connected Erlang nodes. You could write a whole book on distributed Erlang. (Maybe someday we will!) In this book, however, we'll only focus on two benefits: data replication and message passing. We'll show you two examples of cool features that these benefits enable without you having to use any packages outside the world of Erlang/Elixir: real-time user connection statuses using Phoenix's Presence[1] module and real-time user notifications using Phoenix's Pub/Sub[2] module.

Now that you know some of the theory, let's get to work and create a local distributed Erlang cluster.

---

1. https://hexdocs.pm/phoenix/Phoenix.Presence.html
2. https://hexdocs.pm/phoenix_pubsub/Phoenix.PubSub.html

Manually Implement a Local Distributed Erlang Cluster

In this section, we'll show you four different ways of creating a distributed Erlang cluster: with iex, by using your Phoenix application, with Docker Compose, and finally in a Docker Swarm.

The next section will look specifically at connecting Erlang nodes using iex.

Manually Connect Erlang Nodes Using iex

In Chapter 2 on page 29, you saw how to initiate an iex session when you used Elixir's kernel Date module to calculate the due dates for your issues. While we haven't delved deeply into using the Elixir interactive console, you'll soon see that it's invaluable in debugging and testing applications.

To begin an iex session, cd into the root of your Kanban folder where your Phoenix application lives. You'll first connect two basic nodes that are simply an Elixir shell. You'll move on to connecting two instances of your Phoenix application shortly. To create your two basic nodes, open two separate terminal shells.

As we mentioned, an Erlang node is simply an instance of the Erlang runtime system that was given a name when started. The format of a node name is an atom in the form name@host. There are two ways of naming an Erlang node: using names and short names. What are the differences between names and short names? Short names are used for *local* Erlang nodes (that is, nodes that will be on the same network), whereas names are used for global *distributed* Erlang clusters/systems.

Name Node and Short Name Node Cannot Connect

 You can also use names for local Erlang nodes, but be aware that you cannot connect a name node to a short name node.

To give an Erlang node a *short name*, pass the --sname parameter when starting the process. With a short name, you don't need to specify the host as it will be automatically added using the hostname of the machine where the BEAM process is started. This means that to create an iex session that's a local Erlang node called node1, you'd run the command iex --sname node1. Even though you didn't specify the host, the resulting node name would be node1@your-host-name. It would only be able to connect with other nodes that have been created in your host.

To give an Erlang node a *name*, add the --name parameter and then specify the fully qualified domain name. This means that to create an iex session that could be connected with other Erlang nodes that have been started on different machines, you'd run the command iex --name node1@your-host-name.

> **Naming Nodes**
>
>  If you don't specify a node name when starting the Erlang runtime system, then it will be assigned a :node@nohost name. This node won't be able to form part of a distributed Erlang cluster until it's given a name. Giving names to nodes after they've already started is possible using the Node.start function.[3]

If you ever want to check the name of a node, you can call the node() function. In iex shells, this isn't needed, however, because the node name is always printed, as you'll see in a moment.

OK, let's get to work. Create two local nodes using the --name option: one node in each of your open terminals. In your first terminal, run the command iex --name n1@127.0.0.1, and in the second one, run iex --name n2@127.0.0.1. In your second terminal, run the command Node.list/0. This command returns the list of nodes that are connected to the node in which the command is run. You'll see that it returns an empty list. To connect your nodes, you'll use the Node.connect/1 function. This function expects one argument, a node name. To connect the node you created in your first shell to the one you created in the second shell, run Node.connect(:"n1@127.0.0.1") in your second shell. Lastly, rerun the Node.list/0 command and you'll see that the list now contains one entry.

You can see an example terminal interaction here:

```
# in 1st shell
$ iex --name n1@127.0.0.1
Erlang/OTP 26 [erts-14.2.1] [source] [64-bit] [smp:8:8] [ds:8:8:10]
[async-threads:1] [jit]

Interactive Elixir (1.16.0) - press Ctrl+C to exit (type h() ENTER for
help)
iex(n1@127.0.0.1)1>

# in 2nd shell
$ iex --name n2@127.0.0.1
Erlang/OTP 26 [erts-14.2.1] [source] [64-bit] [smp:8:8] [ds:8:8:10]
[async-threads:1] [jit]

Interactive Elixir (1.16.0) - press Ctrl+C to exit (type h() ENTER for
help)
iex(n2@127.0.0.1)1> Node.list
```

---

3. https://hexdocs.pm/elixir/1.12/Node.html#start/3

```
[]
iex(n2@127.0.0.1)2> Node.connect(:"n1@127.0.0.1")
true
iex(n2@127.0.0.1)3> Node.list
[:"n1@127.0.0.1"]
```

Congratulations! You've just connected two basic Erlang nodes and created a local Erlang cluster. We mentioned earlier that Erlang nodes use cookies to establish their connections, but you never specified a cookie. So, how was this connection possible? We'll look at this in the next section.

The Erlang Cookie

When Erlang nodes connect, they use a cookie as an authentication token. It may seem that because you didn't specify any cookie when you created your nodes, any node that knows your host domain name could join your Erlang cluster. However, this isn't the case unless they explicitly specify the same cookie that you used. Cookies are assigned to nodes when they're created. It's possible to create a node with a predefined cookie by specifying the --cookie option. However, when you don't specify a cookie, the first time you create a node on your machine, Erlang will automatically create a cookie for you and store it in a file called ~/.erlang.cookie. Erlang will then use that cookie for all subsequent nodes that you create on your machine, provided that you don't pass the --cookie option. If you'd like to know how Erlang does this, you can find the implementation in the official Erlang repository on GitHub.[4] To see the contents of the ~/.erlang.cookie file on your machine, run the command cat ~/.erlang.cookie in a new terminal.

The connection between the two nodes you created in the previous section was successful as they both used the same default cookie. If you were to create a third node that uses a different cookie, it wouldn't be allowed to join the cluster.

Let's put this to the test. Open a third terminal and create a third node, but this time, specify the --cookie option to create this node with a cookie called ANOTHER_COOKIE. Then run the Node.connect/1 command from your second terminal and specify your third node's name. You'll see that the connection fails just as it does in the following terminal interaction. We've run the :auth.cookie Erlang function in both of the shells so that you can check the cookie contents at each step:

```
# in 3rd shell
$ iex --name n3@127.0.0.1 --cookie ANOTHER_COOKIE
```

---

4. https://github.com/erlang/otp/blob/master/lib/kernel/src/auth.erl#L382zq

```
...
iex(n3@127.0.0.1)1> :auth.cookie
:ANOTHER_COOKIE

# in 2nd shell
iex(n2@127.0.0.1)1> :auth.cookie
:ZANNJGLIVSUVXKLHZTIV
iex(n2@127.0.0.1)2> Node.connect(:"n3@127.0.0.1")
false
```

As you can see, the connection of your third node failed as that node uses a different cookie and so the authentication handshake wasn't possible.

Now that you know how to connect basic nodes and what the Erlang cookie is, let's see how to manually start multiple instances of your Phoenix application, each as a different Erlang node. Before we move on, exit out of your three iex shells that you currently have open.

Manually Create and Connect Multiple Elixir Releases as Erlang Nodes

So far, we've explored launching the interactive Elixir shell as a named Erlang node. You might be wondering, "How can I apply this to my Phoenix application and start it as an Erlang node to harness distributed Erlang's message-passing and data-replication powers?"

To create an instance of your Phoenix application locally as an Erlang node, start a new iex shell using the same command as before, but this time adding the -S flag and the mix phx.server command. The -S flag instructs the interactive Elixir shell to incorporate your application and its dependencies in its scope. This means that you'll be able to reference any of the modules in your application in the iex shell. However, before you do this, you must ensure that a PostgreSQL database is running, and then run mix ecto.create to set up the database. You must do this before creating your iex session because without it, when you start your Phoenix application in your iex shell, it will fail when trying to connect to your database.

To start the PostgreSQL database, run POSTGRES_PORT="5432:5432" docker compose up db -d. Adding the db argument to the docker compose up command tells Docker to only start the db service in your Compose file. You don't need to start the web service because you'll do this later on in the iex shell. After this, run mix ecto.create. You can see an example terminal interaction here:

```
$ POSTGRES_PORT="5432:5432" docker compose up db -d
 ✓ Network kanban_default    Created                                    0.0s
 ✓ Container kanban-db-1     Started                                    0.0s
$ mix ecto.create
The database for kanban.Repo has been created
```

Now start the iex shell by running: iex --name n1@127.0.0.1 -S mix phx.server.

This command will start your application as a node on port 4000. To be able to run two instances of your application and connect these nodes together, however, your application must have the ability to run on different ports. The port for Phoenix applications is hardcoded as 4000 by default. So, in order to run your application on different ports, you need to enable the port to be passed when the application is started. You can do this by changing your config/dev.exs file slightly. Here are the modifications that you need to make:

```
# in config/dev.exs
import Config
port = String.to_integer(System.get_env("PORT") || "4000")
config :kanban, KanbanWeb.Endpoint,
  # Binding to loopback ipv4 address prevents access from other machines.
  # Change to `ip: {0, 0, 0, 0}` to allow access from other machines.
  http: [ip: {127, 0, 0, 1}, port: port],
```

Now, open up a second terminal and run the command PORT=4001 iex --name n2@127.0.0.1 -S mix phx.server. This will create your second node. After you've done this, run Node.connect/1 in your second terminal and join your two nodes together. Like before, run Node.list/0 to see that the connection is successful. You can see an example terminal interaction here:

```
# in 1st terminal
$ iex --name n1@127.0.0.1 -S mix phx.server
...
# in 2nd terminal
$ PORT=4001 iex --name n2@127.0.0.1 -S mix phx.server
...
iex(n2@127.0.0.1)1> Node.connect(:"n1@127.0.0.1")
true
iex(n2@127.0.0.1)2> Node.list
[:"n1@127.0.0.1"]
```

Great! You did it! You ran two instances of your project in development as Erlang nodes and connected them. Now, how can you apply this to your release so that it's always started as a named Erlang node?

Before you continue, exit out of your two iex shells.

Now regenerate your release by running MIX_ENV=prod mix release and set up your database by running MIX_ENV=prod DATABASE_URL=ecto://postgres:postgres@localhost/kanban SECRET_KEY_BASE=$(mix phx.gen.secret) mix ecto.setup.

Recall that initiating a release involves executing the _build/prod/rel/kanban/bin/kanban script with an argument. So far, you've been running this script with the start argument or using the server release script, which also runs that script using the start argument. But there are other arguments that you can pass to this script. Run the _build/prod/rel/kanban/bin/kanban command without any arguments inside your Phoenix project and you'll see the full list of arguments you can add. You'll see that there's a start_iex option that starts your release and opens an iex shell. Run the command again, this time with the start_iex argument. Remember that when running your application, you have to specify the SECRET_KEY_BASE and DATABASE_URL environment variables. Do this like so:

```
$ DATABASE_URL=ecto://postgres:postgres@localhost/kanban \
  SECRET_KEY_BASE=$(mix phx.gen.secret) \
  MIX_ENV=prod \
  _build/prod/rel/kanban/bin/kanban start_iex
Erlang/OTP 26 [erts-14.2.1] [source] [64-bit] [smp:8:8] [ds:8:8:10] ...
...
iex(kanban@your_host_name)1>
```

As you can see, the interactive Elixir shell is already started as a node with the name kanban@your_host_name. As the node name uses your hostname, you can deduce that Elixir releases are always started as a local node with a short name where the name follows the pattern: APP_NAME@YOUR_HOST_NAME. Since you'll eventually connect Erlang nodes inside your Docker Swarm, where each swarm node is in a different AZ, you need to start your release with a name, not a short name. As we discussed in Chapter 7 on page 215, you can add extra configuration to your release by editing the rel/env.sh.eex template file that's created after running mix release.init. In this file, you'll see the following commented lines:

```
# in rel/env.sh.eex

# # Set the release to work across nodes.
# # RELEASE_DISTRIBUTION must be "sname" (local), "name" (distributed)...
# export RELEASE_DISTRIBUTION=name
# export RELEASE_NODE=<%= @release.name %>
```

The RELEASE_DISTRIBUTION variable enables the choice between using names or short names, and the RELEASE_NODE variable specifies the actual node name. To control the node name and type of node, you need to edit these two variables. You also need to add in some logic to determine the IP address of the process running your release so that you can add that to the node name. You can achieve this by replacing the last three lines of the previous code snippet with the following:

```
# in rel/env.sh.eex
# sets a default host IP
IP_ADDR=$(hostname -i 2>/dev/null || echo "127.0.0.1")
RELEASE_NODE_NAME="${RELEASE_NODE_NAME:-$RELEASE_NAME}"

# use "name" (distributed) rather than "sname" (local) as release will be
# distributed accross multiple AZs
export RELEASE_DISTRIBUTION=name
export RELEASE_NODE="$RELEASE_NODE_NAME@$IP_ADDR"
```

This code snippet works out the IP of the machine running the release. It then defines a variable called RELEASE_NODE_NAME, which has a default value of RELEASE_NAME, a variable with the value of the project name (in this case kanban). The RELEASE_NODE_NAME can also be passed as an argument when the release is run, which you'll do in a moment.

Once you've updated your env.sh.eex file, rebuild your release files and then start your release again in the same way as before. This time, however, add in the RELEASE_NODE_NAME environment variable, setting it to n1 as we've done:

```
$ MIX_ENV=prod mix release
...
$ DATABASE_URL=ecto://postgres:postgres@localhost/kanban \
  SECRET_KEY_BASE=$(mix phx.gen.secret) \
  MIX_ENV=prod \
  RELEASE_NODE_NAME=n1 \
  _build/prod/rel/kanban/bin/kanban start_iex
...
iex(n1@YOUR_IP)1>
```

Terrific! You just started your Phoenix application as an Erlang node. Now, open another terminal and start another release, but this time specifying the RELEASE_NODE_NAME environment variable with the value n2. After you've done this, run the Node.connect/1 function from that second terminal to join your two nodes together. Check whether the connection has been successful by running Node.list/0. An example terminal interaction is as follows:

```
# in 2nd terminal
$ DATABASE_URL=ecto://postgres:postgres@localhost/kanban \
  SECRET_KEY_BASE=$(mix phx.gen.secret) \
  MIX_ENV=prod \
  RELEASE_NODE_NAME=n2 \
  _build/prod/rel/kanban/bin/kanban start_iex
...
iex(n2@YOUR_IP)1> Node.connect(:"n1@YOUR_IP")
true
iex(n2@YOUR_IP)2> Node.list
[:"n1@YOUR_IP"]
```

Amazing! You've just started two separate versions of your Phoenix application using releases and linked them together so that they form part of an Erlang cluster. Good work! You're one step closer to understanding how to link the instances of Phoenix applications together so that you can harness Erlang's inherent message passing and see how amazing features such as Phoenix's Pub/Sub behave in the same way when you scale. This will allow you to make your application more robust and share live data between your different nodes so that you can update multiple UIs at the same time.

> **Enhance Security with Custom RELEASE_COOKIE**
>
>  In this section, you haven't specified a cookie when creating your Erlang nodes. This is because Elixir releases create cookies automatically and saves them to the releases folder of your application in a file called COOKIE. To be more secure, however, you should create this cookie as a secret and inject it into your application using an environment variable called RELEASE_COOKIE. Phoenix applications are configured to automatically read the value of the RELEASE_COOKIE environment variable and use it when starting your application. We'll not go through the implementation of this step by step, but if you want to implement this yourself, emulate the Docker secrets creation process that you did in Chapter 7 and create a new secret in your secrets.enc.yaml file in your /secrets folder and rerun your decrypt.sh script. Then, create a new environment variable in the env section of your web service in your Compose file.

In the next section, we'll look at how you can manually start a distributed Erlang cluster in a Docker network using your Docker Compose file. Before we move on, remember to exit out of your interactive shells.

Manually Connect Elixir Release Erlang Nodes Using Docker Compose

So far, you've been able to start and connect two iex shells as Erlang nodes as well as two instances of your Phoenix application. The next step is to replicate the same process but inside a Docker network. We could go directly and see this in action in a Docker Swarm, but we want you to see all the possible options for testing and connecting nodes and how the Docker DNS behaves in both scenarios. To start your Phoenix application using your Compose file, you'll need to rebuild the image that your web service uses so that it incorporates your new env.sh.eex changes. Do this by running docker build -t kanban:latest . in the root of your project as we have done here:

```
$ docker build -t kanban:latest .
```

Now you must comment out the port assignment of your web service in your Compose file, as we've done in the following example. This is an important step because you'll create two instances of your web service, but your machine only has one port 4000. If you keep the port assignment there, when Docker tries to expose the second web instance to your machine, an error will be thrown as your machine cannot run two applications on the same port.

```
# in compose.yaml
services:
  web:
    # ports:
    #   - 4000:4000
```

Start your web service by running the docker compose up command, remembering to specify the WEB_IMAGE environment variable to make sure you're running the local version of your image. When you run the command, add the --scale option with the value web=2. This will create two instances of your web service. You can see how we've done this here:

```
$ WEB_IMAGE=kanban:latest docker compose up --scale web=2
...
kanban-web-2  | 10:38:00 [info] ... cowboy 2.10.0 at :::4000 (http)
kanban-web-1  | 10:38:00 [info] ... cowboy 2.10.0 at :::4000 (http)
```

OK, your two web instances are up and running as Erlang nodes. Now it's time to connect them. In Chapter 3 on page 65, you saw that you could run containers interactively and open a bash shell inside the container by adding the -ti options to the docker run command. When you already have your containers running, to open an interactive bash shell inside the container, you can use the docker exec command, again with the -ti options, but this time passing the command /bin/bash as an argument. The docker exec command expects a container name/ID as an argument, as well as the command you wish to execute. In this instance, you want to open up a bash shell, which is why you need to pass the /bin/bash command.

To get the ID of your two web services, run docker ps in a new terminal. After you have your two IDs, run the docker exec -ti CONTAINER_ID /bin/bash command in two separate terminals, changing the ID each time. Then, open up an interactive Elixir shell in both terminals by running bin/kanban remote. You must open up a remote shell as your application is already running as a node. Once you do all of this, you'll see both of the names of your Erlang nodes. From one of your shells, connect your two nodes by running the Node.connect/1 command and then check that the nodes have successfully connected with Node.list/0. You can see an example terminal interaction here:

```
# in 1st shell
$ docker ps
CONTAINER ID    IMAGE            ...    PORTS        NAMES
24944c01c8d3    kanban:latest    ...                 kanban-web-1
d2f0ac5ba18a    kanban:latest    ...                 kanban-web-2
...
$ docker exec -ti 24944c01c8d3 /bin/bash
nobody@24944c01c8d3:/app$ bin/kanban remote
...
Interactive Elixir (1.16.0) - press Ctrl+C to exit (type h() ENTER for
help)
iex(kanban@192.168.0.4)1>

# in 2nd shell
$ docker exec -ti d2f0ac5ba18a /bin/bash
nobody@d2f0ac5ba18a:/app$ bin/kanban remote
...
Interactive Elixir (1.16.0) - press Ctrl+C to exit (type h() ENTER for
help)
iex(kanban@192.168.0.3)1> Node.connect(:"kanban@192.168.0.4")
true
iex(kanban@192.168.0.3)2> Node.list
[:"kanban@192.168.0.4"]
```

Congratulations! You've manually connected two Docker web services in a Docker network. Your Phoenix applications in your Docker containers are now connected and can share information, pass messages, and distribute workload.

If you look at the two IP addresses in the iex shells of both of your Erlang nodes inside your Docker containers, you'll notice that they're different. This is because, when you start a container inside Docker, it's assigned its own IP in the internal Docker network. Rather than assigning the IP of your machine to containers, the Docker DNS assigns its own internal IPs to containers so that the IP of each container is different. To understand why this is important, we'd like to introduce you to the :inet_res.lookup/3 function.

The :inet_res.lookup/3 Function

The :inet_res.lookup/3 function[5] is an Erlang function that resolves DNS names. It expects three arguments: a DNS name, a DNS class, and a DNS type. The DNS name that you'll use is web (the name of your service), the class you'll use is :in (internet), and the DNS type will be a (an IPv4 address). Execute the function :inet_res.lookup(:"web", :in, :a) in one of the interactive Elixir shells that you opened in the previous section like so:

---

5. https://www.erlang.org/doc/man/inet_res#lookup-3

```
# in 2nd shell
iex(kanban@192.168.0.3)3> :inet_res.lookup(:"web", :in, :a)
[{192, 168, 0, 4}, {192, 168, 0, 3}]
```

As you can see, when you search for the domain name web, there are two results: the two replicas of your Phoenix application that you started when you ran docker compose up. You've already manually connected your instances so you don't have a use for this function right now. However, it will come in handy in the next section when you start multiple web instances as Erlang nodes inside a Docker Swarm and want to connect them. Now, let's see if the :inet_res.lookup/3 function behaves differently when it's executed inside a Docker Swarm. Before we move on, exit out of your interactive shells and Docker containers and run docker compose down.

Programmatically Retrieve the IP of Your Docker Swarm Nodes

In the previous section, you learned how to manually scale your web service, creating replicas and starting them as Erlang nodes and then connecting the different nodes. You also saw how to use the :inet_res.lookup/3 function while inside one of your web service Docker containers to search for the IPs of the other web service containers. In this section, you'll learn how to start multiple versions of your web service in a local single-node Docker Swarm where each web instance is also an Erlang node, and how to search for each instance's IP programmatically. This will help you understand how you can apply your distributed Erlang knowledge to an environment that replicates your desired production infrastructure.

Initialize a local Docker Swarm and then deploy your stack with two replicas of your web service. You can do this by specifying the WEB_REPLICAS environment variable that you added to your Compose file in the previous chapter. You can see the commands that you have to run here:

```
$ docker swarm init
Swarm initialized: current node (g0r2vjktqf...) is now a manager.
...
$ WEB_IMAGE=kanban:latest \
WEB_REPLICAS=2 docker stack deploy -c compose.yaml kanban
...
```

OK, your application suite is up and running in a single-node swarm with two instances of your web service, where each instance is an Erlang node. To get the IPs of your web services, run the :inet_res.lookup/3 function again. We've opened up an interactive Elixir shell and run the inet_res.lookup/3 function twice in the following code snippet. Have a read of it without trying to execute the commands, and then we'll discuss it:

```
iex(kanban@10.0.1.4)5> :inet_res.lookup(:"web", :in, :a)
[{10, 0, 1, 2}]
iex(kanban@10.0.1.4)6> :inet_res.lookup(:"tasks.web", :in, :a)
[{10, 0, 1, 4}, {10, 0, 1, 3}]
iex(kanban@10.0.1.4)7>
```

As you can see, when we looked up the DNS name web, there was only one IP address, but when we looked for tasks.web, there were two different addresses. What's happening here?

When we fetched the IPs by searching for the DNS name web, we were in fact retrieving the Virtual IP (VIP). This is how a Docker Swarm service load-balances requests across multiple tasks (containers) to distribute incoming traffic and provide high availability. On the other hand, when we searched using the DNS name tasks.web, we retrieved the IP addresses of the individual service tasks, each of which corresponds to a running container and therefore a running instance of your Phoenix application. The number of IP addresses returned in this case corresponds to the number of replicas you specified using the WEB_REPLICAS environment variable - 2.

Now run this :inet_res.lookup/3 function in one of your swarm containers to connect your different nodes. To do this, follow these steps:

1. Enter into a bash shell of one of your swarm containers following the same method as last time: running docker ps and then docker exec.

2. Open an iex shell by running bin/kanban remote.

3. Run the :inet_res.lookup(:"tasks.web", :in, :a) function to retrieve the IPs of your nodes inside the Docker network.

4. Connect your Erlang node to the other node in your swarm using Node.connect/1 and then list the nodes to see the successful connection.

Great! You've just started multiple instances of your Phoenix application that are Erlang nodes in a local, single-node Docker Swarm, connecting these nodes to form an Erlang cluster. Not only are your Phoenix application instances connected via Docker (and so will be orchestrated and monitored by Docker), they will also be able to pass messages to each other in real time.

In the final section of this chapter, you'll put what you've learned about Erlang nodes together with a remote Docker Swarm to create a remote distributed Erlang cluster in AWS. Rather than manually connecting the Erlang nodes, as you have been doing so far, you'll learn how to automate this. Before we move on, un-comment your port assignation in your compose.yaml file and exit out of your interactive shell.

Automate the Creation of a Distributed Erlang Cluster in a Remote Docker Swarm

In this section, you'll update your Phoenix application so that it can automatically create and join a distributed Erlang cluster and then re-create your remote Docker Swarm in AWS and deploy your application.

To automate the connection of Erlang nodes in your Phoenix application, you'll use the DNSCluster library.[6] DNSCluster is a library that allows you to create a cluster of Erlang nodes in a distributed system by automatically handling the connection of nodes to that cluster by periodically polling DNS addresses (using the same strategy used by the :inet_res.lookup/3 function you saw earlier) without you having to manually interfere.

As a first step, find the latest DNSCluster release with mix hex.search and then add it to your mix.exs file, like so:

```
# in mix.exs
  defp deps do
    [
      {:dns_cluster, "~> 0.1.3"},
    ]
  end
```

Now start the DNSCluster module in the supervision tree of your application. The module has certain options that you can pass. The query option specifies the DNS name to look for. You should set it to tasks.web. There's also an interval option that you can pass to specify how often DNSCluster should search for IPs. But you don't need to set this because it has a default value of 5000. Add the DNSCluster module to your project like so:

```
# in lib/kanban/application.ex
    children = [
      {DNSCluster, query: "tasks.web"}
    ]
```

Amazing! You've finished setting up DNSCluster. Easy, right? Let's first deploy this change locally to see that the nodes connect successfully. After that, you'll deploy your application remotely. To deploy your application locally, rebuild your local Docker image so that it includes your DNSCluster changes. After this, remove your kanban stack by running docker stack rm kanban and then rerun the docker stack deploy command. Then reopen an iex shell in one of your

---

6. https://hexdocs.pm/dns_cluster/DNSCluster.html

containers by running docker ps, docker exec and bin/kanban remote. Once inside, run Node.list/0 and you'll see that the Erlang nodes are successfully connected, just like ours:

```
$ docker build -t kanban:latest .
...
$ WEB_IMAGE=kanban:latest \
  WEB_REPLICAS=2 docker stack deploy -c compose.yaml kanban
...
$ docker ps
8514gh560dh2    kanban:latest    ...
6dja342hkg41    kanban:latest    ...
....
$ docker exec -ti 8514gh560dh2 /bin/bash
nobody@8514gh560dh2:/app$ bin/kanban remote
iex(kanban@10.0.1.8)1> Node.list
[:"kanban@10.0.1.6"]
```

It worked! Now deploy your stack remotely. To do this, we'll show you a new way of testing PR changes. Run terraform apply to create all of your infrastructure resources. Then create a PR with your changes from this chapter. Once your CI finishes running, find the image tag that was created—it should look something like this: ghcr.io/beamops/kanban:pr-8. You can find it in the Docker Meta section of the CI run under the Docker tags label. Then cd to the root of your project and run your deploy script, specifying the image created by your PR as an argument to the script. Remember that you'll have to set the PRIVATE_KEY_PATH, SOPS_AGE_KEY_FILE, GITHUB_USER, and WEB_REPLICAS environment variables as well. The command you run should look something like this:

```
$ cd ../..
$ PRIVATE_KEY_PATH="environments/production/private_key.pem" \
  SOPS_AGE_KEY_FILE=environments/production/key.txt \
  GITHUB_USER=YOU_GITHUB_USERNAME \
  WEB_REPLICAS=3 \
  ./scripts/deploy.sh ghcr.io/beamops/kanban:pr-8
...
```

Now, SSH into one of your EC2 nodes and run the command Node.list/0 in an iex shell inside one of your web service containers to see that your node connection was successful. You'll see a list of two nodes as shown on the next page:

```
$ ssh -i ./environments/production/private_key.pem ec2-user@3.249.245.223
....
$ docker ps
....
$ docker exec -ti fha6384ga /bin/bash
...
$ bin/kanban remote
...
iex(kanban@10.0.1.25)1> Node.list
[:"kanban@10.0.1.23", :"kanban@10.0.1.24"]
```

Do you see how easy it is to test your PRs? Well done! You know how to create a multinode swarm using Terraform and connect your web service Phoenix application instances in a distributed Erlang cluster! You now have a resilient and highly available application that's able to pass real-time messages in between its Erlang nodes to provide your site with some amazing, original features such as Pub/Sub message passing. You'll see these benefits in action in the next section.

See the Benefits of Distributed Erlang in Action

We mentioned that one important benefit to a distributed Erlang cluster is message passing. In this section, to demonstrate this benefit and show you how great distributed Erlang is, you'll deploy two different versions of the application we wrote with our friend Ricardo—a Kanban project management board. You'll deploy one nondistributed version of the application and one distributed version. In doing this, you'll see the impact of creating and connecting nodes in an Erlang cluster.

First, you'll deploy a version of our Kanban application that's *not* part of a distributed Erlang cluster. The image you'll use in your deployment doesn't start the Phoenix application as an Erlang node. Therefore, it's not aware of any other application instances and cannot pass any messages. To deploy this application, rerun your deploy script with the same environment variables as before, specifying the following `ghcr.io/beamops/kanban:non-distributed` Docker image like so:

```
$ PRIVATE_KEY_PATH=environments/production/private_key.pem \
  SOPS_AGE_KEY_FILE=environments/production/key.txt \
  GITHUB_USER=YOUR_GITHUB_USERNAME \
  WEB_REPLICAS=3 \
  ./scripts/deploy.sh ghcr.io/beamops/kanban:non-distributed
```

Great. You've just deployed the non-distributed version of our application. You might have to wait half a minute or so for all of your containers to be updated with the new image. To check whether the images have been updated, SSH into one of your EC2 instances and run docker ps until you see that the deployed image column has changed from your PR image to this new image.

For you to be able to see the advantages of distributed Erlang, you need to populate data for this application so that the Kanban board must have a few tasks. To do this, seed your db service by running the bin/seed script that we've included for you inside your web image containers. Do this by running the same docker exec -ti command that you've been doing so far, replacing /bin/bash for bin/seed.

Now open port 4000 of two of your EC2 instances in two different windows. Have these windows arranged side by side so that you can see them both at the same time. Make sure that you're using HTTP rather than HTTPS. In one window, sign in to the application using one of the default emails (beamops@example.com) and password ("password password") that were created when you seeded the database. In the other window, sign in with the email admin@example.com and password "password password." Your windows should look something like this:

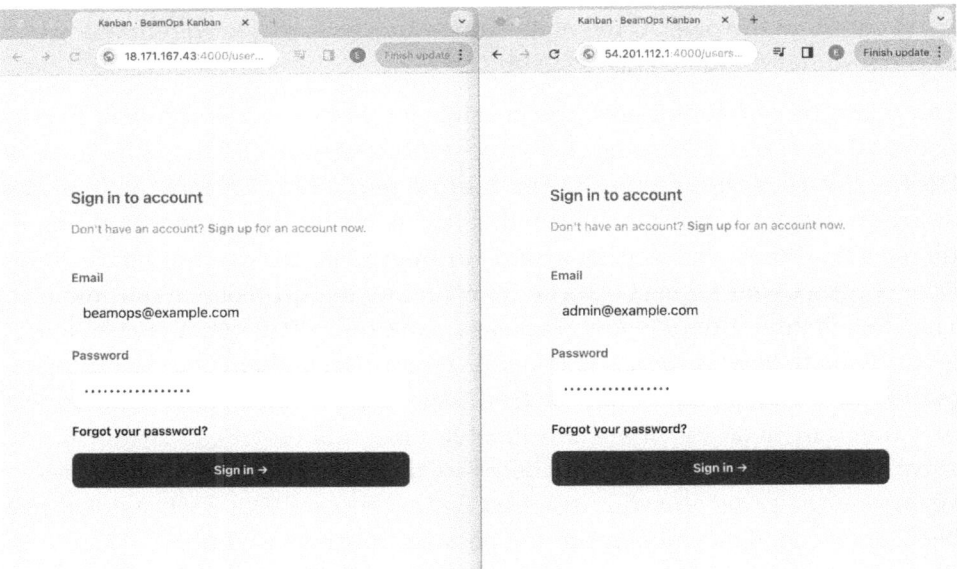

Press the sign in button. Both of your windows should now be logged in with a different user and you should see a basic Kanban board with eight tasks in the Backlog column and only one avatar next to the user icon in the top right-hand corner (this represents the number of users that are online), as shown in the figure on page 304.

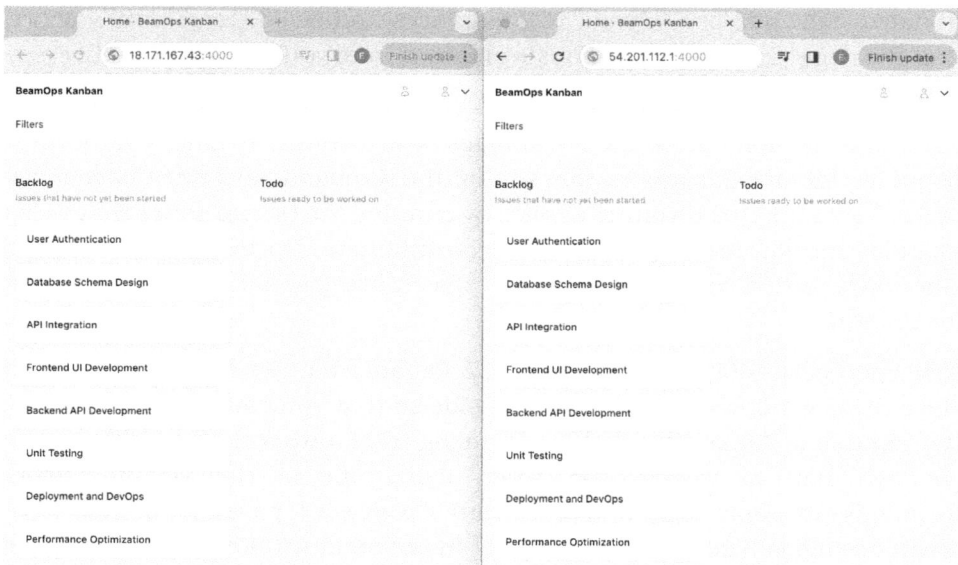

Make sure that both of your windows are accessing different Erlang nodes. You can see the Erlang node name in the drop-down menu in the top right-hand corner of the page. If the node names are the same, keep refreshing one of your windows until they're different.

You might be wondering how it is possible for you to access *different* Erlang nodes when you're accessing the *same* IP (EC2 instance). This is because of Docker Swarm's routing mesh. The routing mesh enables each node in the swarm to accept connections on published ports for any service running in the swarm. When you access a port on any node, for example port 4000, Docker routes your request to an active container to load-balance your request. This means that although you're accessing the same EC2 instance, you aren't guaranteed to be accessing the Phoenix application (Erlang node) running on port 4000 of that EC2 instance. Instead, the swarm could reroute your request to a different node in the swarm (hosted on a different EC2 instance) and serve you the container (Erlang node) in that swarm node. You can see a visualization of this shown in the first figure on page 305; each request has been color-coded so you can see the possible routings available.

Rerouting requests to different containers ensures that the load is distributed evenly so the system remains responsive as the number of containers or nodes in the swarm changes. You'll see this in action in the next chapter where you'll deploy an image that lets you visualize your remote infrastructure.

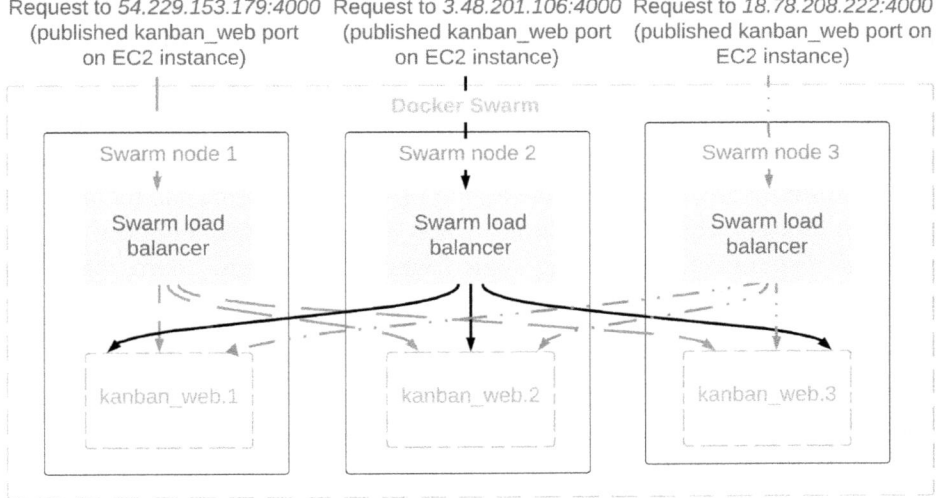

Now that you're accessing different Erlang nodes, in only one of your open windows, move one of the tasks from the Backlog column into the Todo column so that there are only seven tasks in the Backlog column and one task in the Todo column, like so:

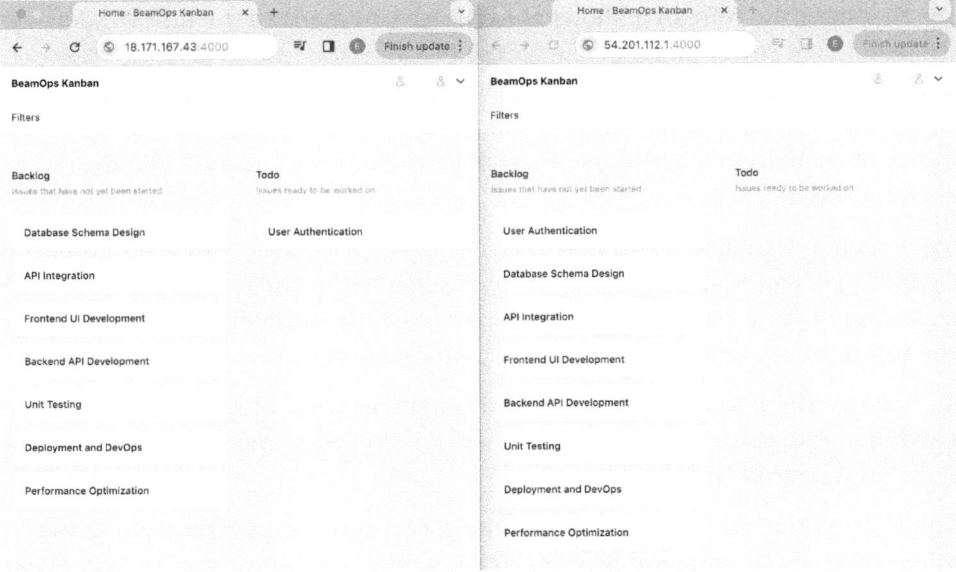

You'll notice that nothing happened in your second window. Your second window still has eight tasks in the Backlog column. You didn't see any changes in your second window because the two different running instances of your Phoenix application haven't been connected and so aren't aware of each other. This means that changes made to one instance aren't reflected in the other.

Now, let's see what happens if you deploy the exact same application, but a version that *does* start the Phoenix application as an Erlang node and forms a distributed Erlang cluster. This version of our application has followed the exact same steps that you've done in the last half of this chapter: it uses DNSCluster to connect the Erlang nodes whose DNS name corresponds to tasks.web.

To deploy this application, rerun your deploy script, this time using the ghcr.io/beamops/kanban:distributed image like so:

```
$ PRIVATE_KEY_PATH=environments/production/private_key.pem \
  SOPS_AGE_KEY_FILE=environments/production/key.txt \
  GITHUB_USER=YOU_GITHUB_USERNAME \
  WEB_REPLICAS=3 \
  ./scripts/deploy.sh ghcr.io/beamops/kanban:distributed
```

OK, you've just deployed the distributed version of our application. Again, you might have to wait half a minute or so for the containers to finish updating. Now go back to your two UI windows. Refresh your second window and make sure it shows a different Erlang node than your first window. You'll see that after the refresh it shows the change you made in the first window—it will also have seven tasks in the Backlog column and one task in the Todo column. You'll also see that in the top right-hand corner of the page, there are two avatars next to each other. This is because both of your windows are aware of each other's existence. Both of your windows will look like the figure shown on page 307.

Move as many tasks as you like in either of the windows. You'll see that any update that you make in one window is reflected in the other window. Now, close one of your windows, and you'll see that the number of avatar icons in the top right changes from two to one. Amazing, right?

To achieve the live issue updates and demonstration of online users, we've used the Pub/Sub library[7] and Phoenix's Presence module[8] (which uses Pub/Sub) behind the scenes.

The Pub/Sub library is used for handling real-time communication between different parts of your application. It uses topics to allow you to broadcast

---

7. https://hexdocs.pm/phoenix_pubsub/Phoenix.PubSub.html
8. https://hexdocs.pm/phoenix/Phoenix.Presence.html

messages, which different parts of your application can subscribe to. The Pub/Sub library is included out-of-the-box in Phoenix applications and is part of their default supervision tree. We won't go through a step-by-step guide to using the Pub/Sub library, but we'll give you a brief introduction into how it works.

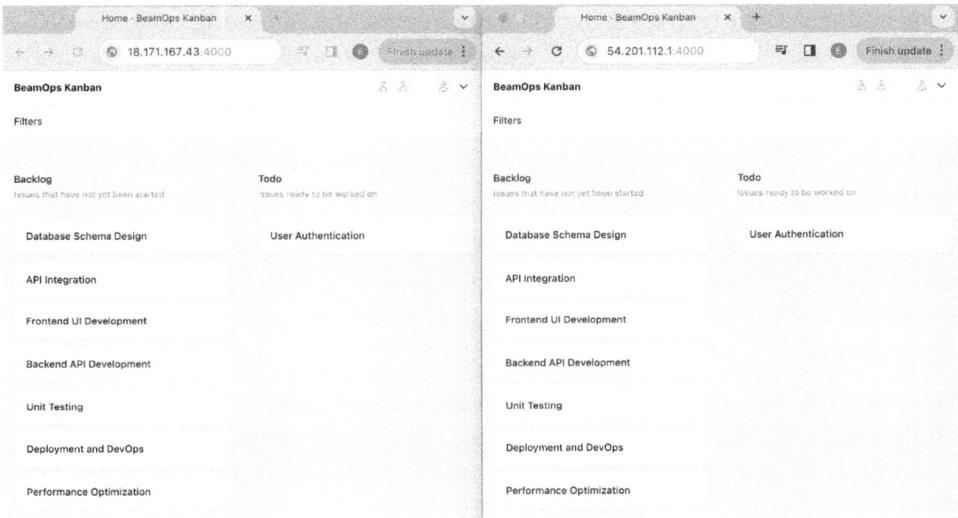

To create and subscribe to a topic in a part of your application you write this:

```
Phoenix.PubSub.subscribe("my-topic")
```

And then to send a message to that topic, you write:

```
Phoenix.PubSub.broadcast(PubSub.Kanban, "my-topic", {
  :user_update,
  %{id: 123, name: "Sasha"}
})
```

Then, any of your LiveView pages or GenServers that are subscribed to this topic and implement a handle_info/2 callback, similar to that in the following code snippet, will be able to handle that published message and rerender its components with this new information or perform any other tasks:

```
def handle_info({:user_update, user_data}, state) do
  # logic to update user

  {:noreply, state}
end
```

Phoenix's Presence module uses Pub/Sub behind the scenes to enable the tracking of users in real time. It allows you to see who is currently online in your application and provides information about their current status. We've simply used Presence in our application to list the users that are online by listing the number of users that have subscribed to a presence:users topic that we created. This is why when you closed your window, the users list went from 2 to 1.

And that's the beauty of message passing in distributed Erlang nodes! Thanks to the Phoenix Pub/Sub library, changes made in one Erlang node are published and all the other Erlang nodes in that cluster subscribe to the change and execute it in their node. This means that your nodes can communicate in real time and make updates as they happen. We hope you think this is as cool as we do!

We encourage you to read *Programming Phoenix LiveView*[9] by Bruce A. Tate and Sophie DeBenedetto for more information about both Pub/Sub and Presence. They give some great examples of how to pass messages in Elixir applications.

Now that you've seen distributed Erlang in action, you can close the "Make Elixir app part of a Distributed Erlang cluster" issue that you created in Chapter 2. To do this, add closes #ISSUE_ID with the issue ID for that issue in the description of your PR and merge it.

Before we summarize what you've learned in this chapter, be sure to destroy your AWS infrastructure after your CI has finished running.

What Have You Learned?

You now know what a distributed Erlang cluster is and how to create one—simply join two Erlang nodes together. You're able to do this locally on the same machine, as well as with nodes that are distributed across multiple machines like in your AWS configuration. You've seen the benefits of a distributed Erlang cluster firsthand—connecting Erlang nodes and using Phoenix's Pub/Sub and Presence libraries enables your Erlang nodes to share live updates with one another. Applying what you've learned in this chapter, you can now deploy a highly available Phoenix application and take full advantage of the interesting features that the BEAM offers.

In the next chapter, you'll further amend your Terraform configuration to automatically scale your application depending on the EC2 instances' CPU usage. You'll also learn how to improve your deployment strategy by implementing an automatic rollback policy and including house-keeping tasks in

---

9. https://pragprog.com/titles/liveview/programming-phoenix-liveview/

your deploy.sh script. Autoscaling your application will make it more robust and prevent it from getting overwhelmed by too much workload. Automatic rollbacks and house-keeping tasks will minimize the downtime your application experiences upon a failed deployment and will maintain the health and performance of your EC2 instances.

Onward!

> **The Extra Mile**
>
> If you wish to deepen your knowledge of the themes we've covered in this chapter and refine your BEAMOps developer superpowers, we've created a few tasks for you to do:
>
> 1. Now that you have a remotely distributed cluster, you can open a remote iex shell to it. Find a way to do this in a single command with the help of the DOCKER_HOST variable, docker exec -ti and bin/kanban remote.
>
> 2. Open an interactive iex shell inside two of your SSH instances and play around with the Node.spawn() function. Get the PID of one of the instance shells and send a message to that instance using Node.spawn(). You'll be able to see that message in your other terminal using the flush() function.

CHAPTER **10**

Autoscaling and Optimizing Your Deployment Strategy

Your current Terraform configuration creates a multinode Docker Swarm in AWS and three replicas of your Phoenix application. Right now, you're able to manually scale your application up or down in three ways. First, you can increase or decrease the number of EC2 instances in your infrastructure by changing the number_of_nodes variable in your swarm module and applying your configuration. This will affect the WEB_REPLICAS environment variable in your deploy script and increase/decrease the number of web service replicas in your swarm. Second, you can directly increase the number of web service replicas by directly increasing the WEB_REPLICAS environment variable value in your deployment script and redeploying your application. Third, you can run docker service scale web=<NUMBER>. But all of these commands have to be run by a human—and BEAMOps is all about automating processes wherever possible.

In this chapter, we'll discuss the elasticity of your infrastructure and how you can automate the scaling of your application. Enabling your application to scale up or down at will is an essential part of practicing the BEAMOps philosophy—it makes your application more efficient and reliable. Not only does autoscaling give you confidence in your application's performance, but it's also a cost-effective way to manage your production infrastructure. Autoscaling ensures you're not overpaying for resources you don't need during periods of low demand, but it also prevents service disruptions during peak times when your application needs to scale up.

By the end of this chapter, you'll have an infrastructure-as-code implementation that has a robust deployment strategy. You'll have confidence that your application will behave appropriately when it experiences a surge in demand. And you'll also be able to close two of the infrastructure issues that you created in Chapter 2.

Let's get started with autoscaling!

Autoscale Your Phoenix LiveView Application

Autoscaling is a feature that's offered by most major cloud providers. It allows you to automatically scale your infrastructure up or down based on certain conditions called triggers. A few common examples of triggers include CPU usage, the number of requests per second, and the number of messages in a queue. Your application's ability to scale is referred to as its elasticity—your infrastructure will grow and shrink depending on the triggers you set.

In AWS, you can set up autoscaling by creating an *Auto Scaling group*. This is a group of EC2 instances that share the same configuration and are managed by the same autoscaling policies. When creating an Auto Scaling group, you don't actually define the EC2 instances themselves. Instead, you create the Auto Scaling group rules—such as the minimum and maximum size (number of EC2 instances)—and then attach a launch template to the EC2 instances. The Auto Scaling group will then take responsibility for creating the EC2 instances. This means that you'll no longer be using the aws_instance resource to define your EC2 instances. You'll instead use the aws_launch_template resource.[1]

To make your application autoscale, you'll follow these steps:

1. Replace your EC2 resource with a launch template. As part of this, you'll revisit your initialize.sh and join.sh swarm scripts.

2. Create the AWS Auto Scaling group, link your launch template to it, and update the user_data script value.

3. Create two alarms for when the average CPU of your Auto Scaling group is above or below certain percentages, and then add a policy to your Auto Scaling group that reacts to that alarm.

4. Create an SSM document that will be run on your EC2 instances when your application scales down to remove any out-of-date swarm nodes.

After completing these four steps, you'll apply your configuration and deploy an image that we've preprepared. This will allow you to see how your

---

1. https://registry.terraform.io/providers/hashicorp/aws/latest/docs/resources/launch_template

autoscaling application behaves during a CPU spike—specifically, you'll see how both the nodes and the containers in your swarm adjust.

OK, you know the plan. Get started by creating the launch template for the EC2 instances that your AWS Auto Scaling group will use.

Create Your Autoscaling Group and EC2 Launch Template Resources

To add your autoscaling resources to your Terraform configuration, create a new file in your modules/cloud/aws/compute/swarm folder called autoscaling.tf. This file will contain all the autoscaling configuration that will make your infrastructure elastic. Start by creating your Auto Scaling group. To do this, use the aws_autoscaling_group resource.[2] This resource configures the minimum and maximum size of your group, the availability zones for your group, any dependencies, and so on. Copy the following code snippet into your autoscaling.tf file, and then we'll discuss it:

```
# in modules/cloud/aws/compute/swarm/autoscaling.tf
locals {
  asg_name = "swarm-asg"
}
resource "aws_autoscaling_group" "main" {
  name = local.asg_name

  vpc_zone_identifier = data.aws_subnets.main_subnets.ids
  max_size            = var.number_of_nodes + 4
  min_size            = var.number_of_nodes
  health_check_type   = "EC2"

  termination_policies = ["NewestInstance"]

  tag {
    key                 = "Name"
    value               = local.manager_tag
    propagate_at_launch = true
  }

  depends_on = [aws_ssm_parameter.swarm_token]
}
```

The previous code snippet gives the name swarm-asg to your Auto Scaling group and specifies the availability zones that your group should use when creating EC2 instances using the vpc_zone_identifier attribute. It uses the number_of_nodes variable that you created in Chapter 8 on page 252, to set the minimum default number of instances in the group to be 3 and sets the maximum default to be 7. When an Auto Scaling group is created, it is initially empty and begins

---

2. https://registry.terraform.io/providers/hashicorp/aws/latest/docs/resources/autoscaling_group

to scale to the min_size value. The health checks for this group have been set to EC2, which means that the group will rely on the EC2 service to report the health status of each instance. The EC2 service performs checks on the underlying hardware and software to ensure the instance is running as expected.

The termination_policies attribute has been set to NewestInstance. This means when a descaling event occurs, the newest instances will be terminated first. Setting this value avoids a situation where your Auto Scaling group terminates one of your original instances in which your database is running.

The manager_tag local value from your main.tf has been reused to add a tag to the group that will be propagated to the EC2 instances when they launch.

Lastly, a dependency on the SSM Parameter Store has been created. The dependency is the same as your aws_instance dependency because the Auto Scaling group will be responsible for creating the instances, and you need the Parameter Store token to be created and set to NONE before any instance is created so that the swarm can be created and joined properly.

OK, you've created the AWS Auto Scaling group, but you haven't told it what the instances that it creates should look like. As we mentioned, you can do this using the aws_launch_template resource, which will replace your aws_instance resource. Have the aws_instance resource open in one window and your autoscaling.tf file open in another. Then add the launch_template attribute to your aws_autoscaling_group resource as shown:

```
# in modules/cloud/aws/compute/swarm/autoscaling.tf
locals {
  launch_node_script = templatefile("${path.module}/scripts/initialize.sh", {
    manager_tag = local.manager_tag,
    region      = var.region
  })
}

resource "aws_launch_template" "swarm_node" {
  image_id               = data.aws_ami.amazon_linux_docker.id
  instance_type          = "t2.micro"
  key_name               = aws_key_pair.deployer_key.key_name
  name_prefix            = "swarm-node-"
  vpc_security_group_ids = [aws_security_group.swarm_sg.id]
  user_data              = base64encode(local.launch_node_script)

  iam_instance_profile {
    name = aws_iam_instance_profile.main_profile.name
  }
}
```

```
resource "aws_autoscaling_group" "main" {
  launch_template {
    id      = aws_launch_template.swarm_node.id
    version = "$Latest"
  }
}
```

As you can see, there's a new attribute added to your locals block, an aws_launch_template resource, and finally an addition to your aws_autoscaling_group resource.

If you compare the aws_launch_template to the aws_instance in your main.tf file, you'll see that they share almost all of the same information (even though some of the attribute names are different). Just like your aws_instance resource, your aws_launch_template resource specifies the following:

- the AMI image ID
- the instance type
- the SSH key name
- the security group IDs for your instances
- the IAM instance profile (that gives your instances the ability to describe other instances, read/write values in the Parameter Store, and create tags)
- a base64-encoded user_data script

You may notice that your aws_launch_template only has *one* user_data script this time rather than two. This is because your aws_instance resource explicitly specified the number of instances to create using the count value, and so you were able to apply a different script depending on the count.index value. However, your launch template is unaware of the number of instances it is being used on. It's the auto_scaling_group resource that will define the number of instances, and although you have linked the aws_launch_template to your aws_autoscaling_group using an implicit dependency, the aws_launch_template doesn't have access to its "parent" (the aws_autoscaling_group) attributes. This means that you cannot specify a different script for your EC2 instances depending on the order in which they were created. Because of this, you'll need to combine the join and initialization logic of your swarm into a new, single script. You'll create this script in a moment. For now, leave the user_data script value as your initialize.sh script.

Unlike your aws_instance resource, your aws_launch_template doesn't have the subnet_id attribute. This is because your Auto Scaling group will assign a random subnet within the vpc_zone_identifier list to the EC2 instances that it launches so that they are evenly distributed across those availability zones. Lastly, your aws_launch_template doesn't have the lifecycle attribute. This is because the EC2 instances themselves won't directly be part of your Terraform state. Instead, your Terraform configuration will rely on your Auto Scaling group to manage the EC2 instances it creates. For this reason, you don't have to worry about your configuration removing the SwarmReady tag that's added to your instances by the user_data script any time you run terraform apply after first creating your configuration.

Now that you've defined your aws_launch_template, remove both the aws_instance resource from your main.tf file as well as the init_script and join_script values from your locals block. Then, comment both of your null_resource blocks. (They won't work until you finish this section.)

You're now in a place where you can apply your changes. Remember that the CREATE–DESTROY–IMPROVE–REPEAT process is your friend—it allows you to make small changes. The "ship less, more often, and check that it works" philosophy should be applied to anything that you do in your project. cd into your environments/production folder, apply your changes, and see what happens:

```
$ cd environments/production
$ terraform apply
```

```
Error: Reference to undeclared resource

  on ../../modules/cloud/aws/compute/swarm/outputs.tf line 3, in
        output "ssh_commands":
  26:       for idx, instance in aws_instance.swarm_node :

A managed resource "aws_instance" "swarm_node" hasn't been declared in
module.swarm.
```

Oh no! What happened? You've removed the aws_instance resource in favor of the aws_launch_template resource, but the output you implemented in Chapter 8 that was based on your aws_instance is still there.

As we mentioned, when you create a launch template and an Auto Scaling group, you're telling AWS what you want (a template for an EC2 instance) and how you want it (in an Auto Scaling group with X number of instances). But you aren't actually creating the instances; the Auto Scaling group will create the instances "behind the scenes." Because of this, the EC2 instances won't directly be part of your configuration, and so you can't access the instances themselves that are created by the Auto Scaling group using

Terraform. Instead, in order to query the instances to get their IPs, you'll need to use an external tool—the AWS CLI.

Replace your current ssh_commands output in your outputs.tf file with the following:

```
# in modules/cloud/aws/compute/swarm/outputs.tf
output "ssh_commands" {
  value       = <<-EOT
    aws ec2 describe-instances \
      --query "Reservations[*].Instances[*].{IP:PublicIpAddress}" \
      --filters \
        "Name=tag:aws:autoscaling:groupName,Values=${local.asg_name}" \
        "Name=instance-state-name,Values=running" \
      --region ${var.region} \
      --output text | \
      awk '{print "ssh -i ./private_key.pem ec2-user@"$1}'
  EOT
  description = "AWS CLI command to print the EC2 instance SSH commands."
}
```

This output will print the command that you can run, once your configuration has been applied, to retrieve the IPs of the instances in your Auto Scaling group.

Nice. Now reapply your Terraform configuration. When you do this, your Auto Scaling group will be created as well as three EC2 instances (the min_size) inside this group. The Terraform Console will then output the command you can run to get the three different SSH commands for your instances. Run this command, SSH into one of your instances, and then run docker node ls. You can see an example terminal interaction here:

```
$ terraform apply
...
Plan: 17 to add, 0 to change, 0 to destroy.
Do you want to perform these actions?
  Terraform will perform the actions described above.
  Only 'yes' will be accepted to approve.

  Enter a value: yes
...
module.swarm.aws_launch_template.swarm_node: Creating...
module.swarm.aws_launch_template.swarm_node: Creation complete after 0s
module.swarm.aws_autoscaling_group.main: Creating...
...
module.swarm.aws_autoscaling_group.main: Creation complete after 41s
...
$ aws ec2 describe-instances ...
...
ssh -i ./private_key.pem ec2-user@52.56.45.235
ssh -i ./private_key.pem ec2-user@18.133.171.79
ssh -i ./private_key.pem ec2-user@18.171.54.128
```

```
$ ssh -i ./private_key.pem ec2-user@52.56.45.235
...
       ,     #_
    ~\_   ####_        Amazon Linux 2023
   ~~  \_#####\
   ~~      \###|
   ~~      \#/  ___   https://aws.amazon.com/linux/amazon-linux-2023
    ~~    V~'  '->
     ~~~         /
       ~~._.   _/
          _/ _/
        _/m/'
[ec2-user@ip-172-31-34-208 ~]$ docker node ls
ID                         HOSTNAME                    STATUS ...
zenhymjnc4etp6ow74o9r2r5q * ip-172-31-34-208.eu-west- ... Ready  ...
```

Wait a minute. Why is there only one node in the swarm? Remember that, due to your aws_launch_template not having any knowledge of the EC2 instance it's being used on, you're only allowed to set one user_data script. This user_data script is currently set to your initialize.sh script, which runs docker swarm init, adds your swarm token to the AWS Parameter Store, and creates the SwarmReady tag. This means that your current Auto Scaling group is in fact creating a group of three instances that each start their own swarm. This sounds familiar, right? Think back to Chapter 8 before you introduced the conditional in your user_data attribute and each of your EC2 instances were running docker swarm init once booted.

In the next section, you'll create a new single script that combines the initialization and join logic for your swarm so that you can properly set the user_data attribute of your aws_launch_template.

One Script to Rule Them All

You've successfully created the two basic resources for your Auto Scaling group in your swarm Terraform module: the aws_autoscaling_group and the aws_launch_template. But due to the dynamics of the Auto Scaling group and its associated launch template, the init_swarm and join_swarm scripts need to be combined into one unified script that considers both the logic for initializing the swarm and the logic for joining an existing swarm. Create a new file called launch_node.sh inside your modules/cloud/aws/compute/swarm/scripts folder.

Just like your current implementation, when the value of your token in your AWS Parameter Store is NONE, your primary node will initialize your swarm and update the Parameter Store token. Then, your secondary nodes will get that token and use it to join the swarm.

To achieve this, your new script will need to do the following:

1. Build an ordered list of your EC2 instances to distinguish your primary and secondary nodes.
2. Initialize the swarm and update the Parameter Store token value if the token value is NONE and the instance on which the script is being run is the first in the ordered list made in step 1 (that is, the primary node).
3. Wait for the swarm token not to be NONE (because it has been updated by the primary node) and join the swarm if the instance on which the script is being run is not the first in the ordered list (that is, a secondary node).
4. Make sure port 22 of the instance in which the script is being run is open, and set the "Swarm Ready" tag to indicate that the instance is ready to receive swarm commands.

Start, as always, with step 1: building an ordered list of the EC2 instances in your Auto Scaling group to distinguish the primary and secondary nodes.

Distinguishing Between Primary and Secondary Nodes

To determine whether an EC2 instance should be the primary node or secondary node in your swarm, build an ordered array of your instances by copying the following code into your launch_node.sh script. The primary node will be the first instance in the array, and the rest will be secondary nodes:

```bash
#!/usr/bin/env bash

# in modules/cloud/aws/compute/swarm/scripts/launch_node.sh

# get all of the running EC2 instances
get_running_instance_ids() {
  aws ec2 describe-instances \
    --filters "Name=tag:aws:autoscaling:groupName,Values=$ASG_NAME" \
              "Name=instance-state-name,Values=running" \
    --query "Reservations[*].Instances[*].[InstanceId,LaunchTime]" \
    --output text \
    --region "$REGION" | sort -k2 | awk '{print $1}'
}

# constants
REGION="${region}"
ASG_NAME="${asg_name}"
SORTED_INSTANCE_IDS_STRING=$(get_running_instance_ids)
SORTED_INSTANCE_IDS_ARRAY=($(echo "$SORTED_INSTANCE_IDS_STRING" \
  | tr ' ' '\n' \
  | tr '\n' ' '))
```

To get all of the EC2 instances inside your swarm, this code snippet has a get_running_instance_ids function that uses the same ec2 describe-instances AWS

CLI command as your outputs.sh file. However, rather than looking for the public IP address, it looks for the instance ID. It also uses two variables that you'll need to pass to your script: the AWS region and the name of your Auto Scaling group, saving them as variables. The snippet then calls this get_running_instance_ids functions and saves the instance IDs string output to a variable called SORTED_INSTANCE_IDS_STRING. It creates a new variable called SORTED_INSTANCE_IDS_ARRAY that's the result of converting the string list to an array.

It's time for the next step: initializing the swarm.

Initialize Your Docker Swarm

Remember, you only want to initialize your swarm if the instance on which this script is being run is the first in the SORTED_INSTANCE_IDS_ARRAY and if the token value is NONE.

First, you need to get the swarm token. To do this, create a new function called get_swarm_token and inside paste the aws ssm get-parameter command you use in your join.sh script. Then, get the token and save it to a variable called SWARM_TOKEN.

After this, you need to know the ID of the instance running this script, which you'll get by querying the local instance metadata IP in the instance. Copy over the get_aws_api_token function from your join.sh script that creates the authentication token for the metadata endpoint. Then, copy over your get_instance_meta_data function that requires two arguments: the API token and the metadata attribute that you want to search for. Just like in your join.sh script, use these two functions to create two variables, AWS_API_TOKEN and CURRENT_INSTANCE_ID, that are the API token and the ID of the instance that your script is being run on. You can see the additions you need to make here:

```
# in modules/cloud/aws/compute/swarm/scripts/launch_node.sh

# get swarm token from parameter store
get_swarm_token() {
  aws ssm get-parameter \
      --name "/docker/swarm_manager_token" \
      --query "Parameter.Value" \
      --output text \
      --with-decryption 2>/dev/null
}

# get API token to be able to query EC2 instance data
get_aws_api_token() {
  curl -X PUT "http://169.254.169.254/latest/api/token" \
      -H "X-aws-ec2-metadata-token-ttl-seconds: 3600"
}
```

```bash
# get a meta-data value of an EC2 instance given the API token and
# attribute name
get_instance_meta_data() {
  local API_TOKEN=$1
  local META_DATA_ATTRIBUTE_NAME=$2
  curl -H "X-aws-ec2-metadata-token: $API_TOKEN" \
       "http://169.254.169.254/latest/meta-data/$META_DATA_ATTRIBUTE_NAME"
}

SWARM_TOKEN=$(get_swarm_token)
AWS_API_TOKEN=$(get_aws_api_token)
CURRENT_INSTANCE_ID=$(get_instance_meta_data $AWS_API_TOKEN "instance-id")
```

Now, add a conditional that states that if the CURRENT_INSTANCE_ID value is the same as the first value in the SORTED_INSTANCE_IDS_ARRAY and if the SWARM_TOKEN value is NONE, call a function that initializes the swarm. You can see how we've done this here:

```bash
# in modules/cloud/aws/compute/swarm/scripts/launch_node.sh

# initialize the docker swarm
initialize_swarm() {
  docker swarm init
  local MANAGER_TOKEN=$(docker swarm join-token manager -q)
  aws ssm put-parameter --name "/docker/swarm_manager_token" \
                        --value "$MANAGER_TOKEN" \
                        --type "SecureString" --overwrite
}

# if there is no swarm token and the current instance is the first in
# the list
if [ "$SWARM_TOKEN" == "NONE" ] && \
   [[ $CURRENT_INSTANCE_ID == "$${SORTED_INSTANCE_IDS_ARRAY[0]}" ]]; then
    initialize_swarm
else
    break # you'll fill this in in the next section
fi
```

> **Terraform Escape Characters**
>
>
> We've included an extra $ when referencing SORTED_INSTANCE_IDS_ARRAY[0] to escape the variable interpolation. This prevents your Terraform configuration from complaining about an undefined Terraform variable. Check the Terraform docs for more information on escape characters.[3]

Nice! Now, complete the next step in building your unified script: joining the swarm.

---

3. https://developer.hashicorp.com/terraform/language/expressions/strings#escape-sequences

Join Your Swarm

You'll add the join logic into the else clause of the if that you just created.

Create a function called join_swarm that expects the swarm token as an argument, gets the manager IP address, and then runs the docker swarm join command. This function will use two constants called MANAGER_TAG and SWARM_READY_TAG which will be passed to the script.

You can see the function and constants you have to add here:

```
# in modules/cloud/aws/compute/swarm/scripts/launch_node.sh

# join the current EC2 as a node to the docker swarm given its swarm
# token
join_swarm() {
  local TOKEN=$1
  local MANAGER_IP=$(aws ec2 describe-instances \
      --filters "Name=tag:Name,Values=$MANAGER_TAG" \
                "Name=instance-state-name,Values=running" \
                "Name=tag:$SWARM_READY_TAG,Values=true" \
      --query "Reservations[0].Instances[0].PrivateIpAddress" \
      --region "$REGION" --output text)
  docker swarm join --token "$TOKEN" "$MANAGER_IP:2377"
}

MANAGER_TAG="${manager_tag}"
SWARM_READY_TAG="SwarmReady"
```

Now you need to create the join logic in this else statement. You must consider both of these scenarios:

1. When the node is a secondary node but the primary node hasn't finished initializing the swarm and setting the token yet (which means the token still has a value of NONE).

2. When the token is *not* NONE because it has already been changed by the primary node.

To satisfy both of these scenarios, copy the following code into your script and then we'll go through it:

```
# in modules/cloud/aws/compute/swarm/scripts/launch_node.sh

# if there is no swarm token and the current instance is the first in
# the list
if [ "$SWARM_TOKEN" == "NONE" ] \
   && [[ $CURRENT_INSTANCE_ID == "$${SORTED_INSTANCE_IDS_ARRAY[0]}" ]]; then
   initialize_swarm
else
# get the swarm token until it is not NONE and then join the swarm
   while [ "$SWARM_TOKEN" == "NONE" ]; do
```

```
  SWARM_TOKEN=$(get_swarm_token)
    sleep 2
  done

  join_swarm "$SWARM_TOKEN"

  INSTANCE_COUNT=$(echo "$SORTED_INSTANCE_IDS_STRING" | wc -l)
    docker service update --replicas="$INSTANCE_COUNT" kanban_web
fi
```

In the else statement, there's a while loop that keeps getting the swarm token every two seconds until the SWARM_TOKEN value is not NONE. After this while loop, the join_swarm function is called, and then the number of kanban_web replicas in the swarm is updated to be the total number of instances in the SORTED_INSTANCE_IDS_STRING using a new INSTANCE_COUNT variable that calculates the length of the list using wc -l. This ensures that once your application is deployed and it autoscales, any new EC2 instances that are created and join your swarm as nodes, will also host a web service replica.

> **Update Multiple Services with docker service scale**
>
>  We've chosen to run docker service update to update the number of kanban_web replicas in the swarm rather than using docker service scale. We've done this because we want to ensure that only the web service is updated. With docker service update, you can only update one service at a time. But docker service scale lets you update multiple services at once.

On to the last step: ensuring that your instance is prepared to receive SSH commands.

Prepare Your Instance to Receive Swarm Commands

The final step in creating your unified script is to make sure that the instance running the script can receive SSH commands on port 22 and add the "SwarmReady" tag to that instance so that your deploy script can send commands to it.

You've already implemented this logic in both your initialize.sh or join.sh scripts. Copy it over to your launch_node.sh script as follows:

```
# in modules/cloud/aws/compute/swarm/scripts/launch_node.sh

# make sure port 22 of the current instance is open so that SSH is possible
CURRENT_INSTANCE_IP=$(get_instance_meta_data "$AWS_API_TOKEN" "public-ipv4")
while ! nc -z -v -w1 "$CURRENT_INSTANCE_IP" 22; do
  echo "Waiting for SSH to be available..."
  sleep 2
done
```

```
# indicate that this instance is ready to receive docker commands
aws ec2 create-tags \
    --resources "$CURRENT_INSTANCE_ID" \
    --tags "Key=$SWARM_READY_TAG,Value=true" \
    --region "$REGION"
```

And that's it! You've successfully unified the swarm initialization and join logic into one launch_node.sh script. Before you can apply your changes and use your new script, you must update the name and the variables passed to the script in the launch_node_script local value in your autoscaling.tf file. Your launch_node_script variable should now look like this:

```
# in modules/cloud/aws/compute/swarm/autoscaling.tf
locals {
  launch_node_script = templatefile("${path.module}/scripts/launch_node.sh",
    {
      manager_tag = local.manager_tag,
      region      = var.region,
      asg_name    = local.asg_name
  })
}
```

Fantastic! Now change the depends_on attribute of your wait_for_swarm_ready_tag null_resource in your main.tf to be aws_autoscaling_group.main and update the WEB_REPLICAS environment variable from your swarm_provisioner null_resource to be your number_of_nodes variable. You still need to pass this variable to your deploy.sh script the first time you apply your AWS configuration because, although your launch_node script does update the number of web service replicas in your swarm, this script will be run before your deploy.sh script, and it's your deploy.sh script that creates your kanban stack.

After you've done this, uncomment your two null_resource blocks, destroy your configuration, and re-create it. Once your apply has finished, run the AWS CLI command in the output to get the SSH commands for your three instances. Then SSH into one of those instances and run docker node ls followed by docker service ls. You'll see that all of your nodes have successfully initialized/joined your swarm and there are three replicas of your web service.

Congratulations. You've unified the initialize and join logic for your swarm into one script and successfully updated the user_data attribute of your aws_launch_template. Go ahead and delete your initialize.sh and join.sh scripts. You have two steps left in preparing your infrastructure to support autoscaling. First, set up an alarm for the average CPU of your Auto Scaling group and create an autoscaling policy so that your group reacts to this alarm. Second, implement the descaling logic for your Auto Scaling group. In the next section, you'll create the alarms.

Set Up Your CPU Alarm and Autoscaling Policies

So far, you've completed the initial setup of your Auto Scaling group, but it cannot automatically scale itself. To do that, you must add a policy to your group that will react to certain events. You'll create two alarms that watch the average CPU usage of the group and are triggered when the CPU reaches certain thresholds. Then, you'll configure a policy for your Auto Scaling group so that it reacts to these alarms.

To watch metrics from your Auto Scaling group, you'll use CloudWatch.[4] CloudWatch is a service that collects and tracks metrics, collects and monitors log files, sets alarms, and automatically reacts to changes in AWS resources. This is a service that's specific to AWS but is offered across the majority of cloud providers.

In this section, you'll set up one alarm that will be triggered when the average CPU usage of the EC2 instances in your Auto Scaling group is above 45% and another when the CPU usage falls below 35%. We chose 45% and 35% for learning purposes so that you can see the cluster growing and shrinking in a short period of time. In the real world, you would set up alarms that make sense for your application, where triggers would be higher and lower.

The Terraform resource for CloudWatch alarms is aws_cloudwatch_metric_alarm.[5] We've created the two alarms you'll need in the following code snippet, one called high_cpu and the other low_cpu. Copy these into your autoscaling.tf file:

```
# in modules/cloud/aws/compute/swarm/autoscaling.tf
resource "aws_cloudwatch_metric_alarm" "high_cpu" {
  alarm_name          = "high-cpu-usage"
  comparison_operator = "GreaterThanOrEqualToThreshold"
  evaluation_periods  = "1"
  metric_name         = "CPUUtilization"
  namespace           = "AWS/EC2"
  period              = "60"
  statistic           = "Average"
  threshold           = "45"
  alarm_actions       = [aws_autoscaling_policy.scale_up.arn]
  dimensions = {
    AutoScalingGroupName = aws_autoscaling_group.main.name
  }
}
```

---

4. https://docs.aws.amazon.com/AmazonCloudWatch/latest/monitoring/cloudwatch_architecture.html
5. https://registry.terraform.io/providers/hashicorp/aws/latest/docs/resources/cloudwatch_metric_alarm

```
resource "aws_cloudwatch_metric_alarm" "low_cpu" {
  alarm_name          = "low-cpu-usage"
  comparison_operator = "LessThanOrEqualToThreshold"
  evaluation_periods  = "1"
  metric_name         = "CPUUtilization"
  namespace           = "AWS/EC2"
  period              = "60"
  statistic           = "Average"
  threshold           = "35"
  alarm_actions       = [aws_autoscaling_policy.scale_down.arn]
  dimensions = {
    AutoScalingGroupName = aws_autoscaling_group.main.name
  }
}
```

We've set one alarm to be triggered when the Average EC2 CPUUtilization metric is GreaterThanOrEqualToThreshold, where the threshold is 45, and another when the Average EC2 CPUUtilization metric is LessThanOrEqualToThreshold, where the threshold is 35. We've attached these alarms to the Auto Scaling group with an implicit dependency by using the dimensions attribute. The evaluation_periods and period attributes mean that at the end of each minute, a reading will be taken on the average CPU usage over the last 60 seconds. We've set the alarm action values to be aws_autoscaling_policy.scale_up.arn and aws_autoscaling_policy.scale_down.arn. These policies are the actions that your Auto Scaling group will take when your thresholds are met and the alarms are created.

The Terraform resource for autoscaling policies is aws_autoscaling_policy.[6] In the following code snippet, we've created the two scale_up and scale_down resources for you. Look them over and add them to your autoscaling.tf file:

```
# in modules/cloud/aws/compute/swarm/autoscaling.tf

resource "aws_autoscaling_policy" "scale_up" {
  name                   = "scale_up"
  scaling_adjustment     = 2
  adjustment_type        = "ChangeInCapacity"
  cooldown               = 300
  autoscaling_group_name = aws_autoscaling_group.main.name
}
resource "aws_autoscaling_policy" "scale_down" {
  name                   = "scale_down"
  scaling_adjustment     = -2
  adjustment_type        = "ChangeInCapacity"
  cooldown               = 300
  autoscaling_group_name = aws_autoscaling_group.main.name
}
```

---

6. https://registry.terraform.io/providers/hashicorp/aws/latest/docs/resources/autoscaling_policy

You can see that we've linked these two policies to your Auto Scaling group using the autoscaling_group_name attribute. We've set the policies to change the number of EC2 instances by 2 each time their alarms are triggered. This means that any time the average CPU usage of the EC2 instances in your Auto Scaling group goes above 45%, two new EC2 instances will be added to your group. Because of the user_data script, this means that two new nodes and two new kanban_web replicas will also join your swarm. Conversely, when the average CPU usage of your group falls below 35%, two of your EC2 instances will be terminated and removed from the group.

The cooldown attribute has been set to 300. This is the number of seconds after a scaling activity finishes before a new scaling activity can occur. This is useful because when EC2 instances first start up, they often have a high CPU usage due to the initial setup. Adding a cool down period means that any newly created instances will have time to cool down before counting toward the overall average CPU usage of the group for their first five minutes.

Great! Now that you've set up your CloudWatch alarms and autoscaling policies, you need to be sure that your application can descale gracefully. In the next section, you'll see why this is important and how you can add a lifecycle hook to your Auto Scaling group to trigger any maintenance tasks that you need to run before an instance is terminated.

Gracefully Descale Your Application

So far, you've configured the triggers for your autoscaling group and implemented the logic for what your group should do when it scales up (run your launch_node.sh script). But what happens when your autoscaling group scales down?

To answer this, manually descale your autoscaling group to find out how it behaves. Temporarily tweak the min_size of your aws_autoscaling_group resource in your autoscaling.tf file to 2 and add a desired_capacity attribute as we've done here:

```
# in modules/cloud/aws/compute/swarm/autoscaling.tf
resource "aws_autoscaling_group" "main" {
  min_size         = 2
  desired_capacity = 2
}
```

Apply your changes by running terraform apply and wait for the autoscaling group to terminate one of your EC2 instances. You can watch this happen by running the same aws ec2 describe-instances command as in your Terraform output every few seconds using the watch Linux command. Once one of your instances has been terminated, SSH into one of the other instances and run docker node ls. You terminal should look something like this:

```
$ aws ec2 describe-instances \
    --query "Reservations[*].Instances[*].{IP:PublicIpAddress}" \
    --filters "Name=tag:aws:autoscaling:groupName,Values=swarm-asg" \
    "Name=instance-state-name,Values=running" \
    --region eu-west-1 \
    --output text
...
$ ssh -i ./private_key.pem ec2-user@18.133.171.79
...
[ec2-user@ip-172-31-34-208 ~]$ docker node ls
ID         HOSTNAME            STATUS    AVAILABILITY    MANAGER STATUS      ...
rk7...     ip-172-31-3-...     Ready     Active          Reachable           ...
m0f...     ip-172-31-20...     Ready     Active          Leader              ...
p13...     ip-172-31-34...     Down      Active          Unreachable         ...
```

Even though you've terminated one of your EC2 instances and it doesn't exist anymore, your swarm still has three nodes: two ready nodes and one down. Why is this happening?

When a node leaves a swarm, rather than being removed from the node list, Docker changes its status to down and the node becomes unreachable. To actually remove the node from the node list, you need to manually run docker node rm NODE_ID.[7] If the swarm node is a manager, before being able to remove it, you need to demote the node to a worker first.

We mentioned that Docker Swarms are fault-tolerant, which they are, but they do have a caveat. In a Docker Swarm, *if more than half of your manager nodes are down, your swarm will also go down and be totally unreachable.* This is because Docker Swarm relies on a majority consensus (quorum) of the manager nodes to operate correctly. If the quorum is unbalanced and cannot achieve a majority, the swarm cannot make collective decisions, leading to a failure in the swarm's functionality. The following table illustrates how many manager nodes can be down before the swarm becomes inoperable.

No. of Nodes in Swarm	1	2	3	4	5	6	7
Required *Ready* Nodes	1	2	2	3	3	4	4
Acceptable No. of *Down* Nodes	0	0	1	1	2	2	3

In your current swarm, you don't have an issue because, although you have three nodes and one of them is down, you still have two ready nodes. However,

---

7. https://docs.docker.com/reference/cli/docker/swarm/leave/

imagine that an autoscaling event were to happen in your group to scale it up. This would create two new EC2 instances and join two new nodes to your swarm, meaning that you'd have four running EC2 instance and five nodes in your swarm: your two new nodes, your two original ready nodes, and your original down node. Then imagine that a descaling event were to happen. Your two new EC2 instances would be terminated but, again, those nodes would remain in your swarm, meaning you'd still have five nodes in your swarm: two ready and three down. As highlighted in the previous table, this would mean that your swarm would fail and none of the nodes would be reachable.

This is obviously not what you want. Instead, you want your autoscaling group to descale gracefully and remove the EC2 instances that it is terminating as nodes from the swarm. We'll look at how you can achieve this in the next section using the AWS EventBridge service, which listens for an event in the default AWS event bus in your account.

Listen to Autoscaling Events Using the EventBridge Service

Amazon EventBridge[8] is a serverless event bus service that lets you communicate between AWS services and applications using events. Each AWS account comes with a default event bus. When this bus receives an event, it can route that event to specific targets such as other AWS services.

Examples of events that might appear on the event bus include those generated whenever a resource in your AWS account is created, modified, or deleted. For instance, the default event bus in your AWS account will receive an event each time an EC2 instance is launched or terminated, and when an Auto Scaling group scales up or down.

To make your autoscaling group descale gracefully and not leave down nodes in your swarm, you'll do two things. You'll create an EventBridge rule that listens for a certain event —the EC2 instance successfully terminated event. And you'll create an EventBridge target for this rule that runs a script on the non-down instances in your group to remove any dangling down nodes.

The event you'll listen for is EC2 Instance Terminate Successful.[9] This is the event that's triggered as a result of a successful scale-down of an autoscaling group. To listen for this event, create an aws_cloudwatch_event_rule resource.[10] (If you're

---

8. https://docs.aws.amazon.com/eventbridge/latest/userguide/eb-event-bus.html
9. https://docs.aws.amazon.com/autoscaling/ec2/userguide/ec2-auto-scaling-event-reference.html#terminate-successful
10. https://registry.terraform.io/providers/hashicorp/aws/latest/docs/resources/cloudwatch_event_rule

wondering about the resource name, AWS's EventBridge service was formerly known as CloudWatch Events.) We've created the aws_cloudwatch_event_rule resource for you in the following code snippet. Copy it into your autoscaling.tf file, and then we'll go through it:

```
# in modules/cloud/aws/compute/swarm/autoscaling.tf
resource "aws_cloudwatch_event_rule" "autoscaling_terminate_event_rule" {
  name        = "autoscaling-terminate-event-rule"
  description = "Trigger on autoscaling termination events"
  event_pattern = jsonencode({
    source        = ["aws.autoscaling"],
    "detail-type" = ["EC2 Instance Terminate Successful"],
    detail = {
      AutoScalingGroupName = [aws_autoscaling_group.main.name]
    }
  })
}
```

The event rule has the name autoscaling-terminate-event-rule. The event_pattern attribute specifies the event that you want to listen to: EC2 Instance Terminate Successful. It also references your aws_autoscaling_group resource so that this rule is only triggered when an EC2 instance inside your autoscaling group is triggered. Listening to the general events produced when any EC2 instances are terminated would be too broad.

Great! You have an EventBridge rule that pattern-matches the descaling event of your autoscaling group in the default event bus. But how do you actually remove the down node from your swarm? You'll do this using an SSM (AWS Systems Manager) document[11] as an EventBridge target. Recall that you've already used one SSM tool—the Parameter Store—in Chapter 8 to store the join token for your swarm. An SSM document is an action that the Systems Manager can perform on your EC2 instances. The document you'll use is AWS-RunShellScript, which allows you to run shell scripts on Linux EC2 instances. We've created the EventBridge target for you in the following code snippet using the aws_cloudwatch_event_target resource.[12]

Copy it into your autoscaling.tf file and then we'll explain its functionality:

```
# in modules/cloud/aws/compute/swarm/autoscaling.tf
resource "aws_cloudwatch_event_target" "stop_instances" {
  target_id = "SwarmLeave"
  arn       = "arn:aws:ssm:eu-west-1::document/AWS-RunShellScript"
  input = jsonencode({
```

---

11. https://docs.aws.amazon.com/systems-manager/latest/userguide/documents.html
12. https://registry.terraform.io/providers/hashicorp/aws/latest/docs/resources/cloudwatch_event_target

```
    commands = [
      "DOWN_NODE_IDS=$(docker node ls | grep 'Down' | awk '{print $1}')",
      "docker node demote $DOWN_NODE_IDS",
      "docker node rm $DOWN_NODE_IDS",
      "NODES=$(docker node ls | awk 'NR > 1' | wc -l)",
      "docker service update kanban_web --replicas $NODES"
    ],
  })

  rule     = aws_cloudwatch_event_rule.autoscaling_terminate_event_rule.name
  role_arn = aws_iam_role.event_bridge_role.arn

  run_command_targets {
    key    = "tag:Name"
    values = ["docker-swarm-manager"]
  }
}
```

This EventBridge target specifies that any time the aws_cloudwatch_event_rule.autoscaling_terminate_event_rule you created earlier is triggered, the AWS-RunShellScript SSM document should be used in all of the run_command_targets (the EC2 instances in your account that have the docker-swarm-manager tag) to run the commands defined by the input target.

The specified input commands are as follows:

1. Get the ID of the Down node(s) in your swarm.
2. Demote the Down node(s) in your swarm from managers to workers.
3. Remove the Down node(s) from your swarm.
4. Get the total number of nodes in your swarm
5. Update the number of web replicas in your swarm.

Running these commands from the EC2 instances that remain in your autoscaling group means that when an EC2 instance in your autoscaling group is terminated, your Down nodes will be removed from your swarm and the number of web instances in your swarm will be updated accordingly.

You will notice that the role_arn attribute specified a new IAM role called event_bridge_role. This is because you need to give the EventBridge permission to be able to run a shell script on your EC2 instances. You also need to update your EC2 instance permissions so they can receive remote commands. You'll do this now.

Update the IAM Roles

You need to be sure that your EC2 instances can receive the AWS-RunShellScript run command. To do this, attach the ec2messages:* policy to your main role. EC2 messages are API operations made to the Amazon Message Delivery

Service endpoint. Systems Manager uses this endpoint when sending remote commands. You also need to give your EC2 instances the ssm:UpdateInstance-Information permission. This is so that your EC2 instances can keep in touch with the SSM agent.

Add these permissions to your aws_iam_policy.swarm_node_policy resource in your iam.tf file like so:

```
# in modules/cloud/aws/compute/swarm/iam.tf
resource "aws_iam_policy" "ssm_policy" {
  policy = jsonencode({
    Version = "2012-10-17",
    Statement = [
      {
        Sid    = "EventBridge",
        Effect = "Allow",
        Action = [
          "ssm:UpdateInstanceInformation",
          "ec2messages:*"
        ],
        Resource = "*"
      }
    ]
  })
}
```

Lastly, you also need to give the EventBridge permissions to send commands to your EC2 instances. Do this by creating the following new aws_iam_policy, aws_iam_role, and aws_iam_role_policy_attachment resources:

```
# in modules/cloud/aws/compute/swarm/iam.tf
resource "aws_iam_policy" "event_bridge_policy" {
  name        = "EventBridgePolicy"
  description = "Event Bridge"

  policy = jsonencode({
    Version = "2012-10-17",
    Statement = [
      {
        Sid      = "EventBridgeSendSSMCommand",
        Effect   = "Allow",
        Action   = "ssm:SendCommand",
        Resource = "*"
      }
    ]
  })
}
```

```
resource "aws_iam_role" "event_bridge_role" {
  name = "EventBridgeRole"

  assume_role_policy = jsonencode({
    Version = "2012-10-17",
    Statement = [
      {
        Action = "sts:AssumeRole",
        Effect = "Allow",
        Principal = {
          Service = "events.amazonaws.com"
        }
      }
    ]
  })
}

resource "aws_iam_role_policy_attachment" "event_bridge_attachment" {
  policy_arn = aws_iam_policy.event_bridge_policy.arn
  role       = aws_iam_role.event_bridge_role.name
}
```

Fantastic! It's time to witness the fruits of your labor. Reset the min_size of your aws_autoscaling_group resource and comment the desired_capacity attribute. Now destroy your current Terraform configuration and recreate it. Once your configuration has finished creating, wait a minute or so for your EC2 instances to cool down, then change the min_size and desired_capacity attributes back to 2, and reapply. This will manually force one of your EC2 instances to terminate, and therefore your EventBridge rule and target will be triggered. SSH into one of your remaining instances and run watch docker node ls. You'll see that after half a minute or so you only have two nodes in your swarm. You did it! You've set up your Auto Scaling group, alarms, and autoscaling policies.

In the next section, you'll manually stress your application so that you can see your CloudWatch alarms being triggered and your autoscaling group scaling up and down as a result.

Trigger Your Application to Autoscale Using a Prepared Stats Page

In the Kanban application that you saw in the previous chapter, we created a page that lets you visualize your infrastructure. It shows you the different EC2 instances in your autoscaling group, their CPU usage and the containers they are running, the different nodes in your swarm, and the different swarm services. It also has a button in it that will stress each node of your pool by spawning processes in all of the Erlang nodes. The Docker image that will let you see this page is: ghcr.io/beamops/kanban:infrastructure-page. To be able to run this image, you need to do the following:

1. Mount the Docker socket as a volume in your web service (so that you can get the Docker node/service/container information).

2. Replace the replicas sub-attribute of your web service's deploy key with mode: global (to ensure that each of your swarm nodes will have a web service). Generally, specifying the replicas of a service using the replicas sub-attribute is a better way of ensuring that your application is highly available as it allows you to grow your service both horizontally and vertically. But the it doesn't *guarantee* an equal spread, and our image won't work properly if there's a node without a web replica.

3. Enable monitoring in your EC2 instances by editing the launch template.

4. Add five new IAM permissions to your EC2 instances (so that you have the permissions to monitor your EC2 instances and list the scaling activities of your autoscaling group).

The changes you need to make are as follows:

```yaml
# in compose.yaml
services:
  web:
    image: ${WEB_IMAGE:-ghcr.io/beamops/kanban:latest}
    deploy:
      mode: global
    volumes:
      - /var/run/docker.sock:/var/run/docker.sock
```

```
# in modules/cloud/aws/compute/swarm/autoscaling.tf
resource "aws_launch_template" "swarm_node" {
  monitoring {
    enabled = true
  }
}
```

```
# in modules/cloud/aws/compute/swarm/iam.tf
resource "aws_iam_policy" "ssm_policy" {
    {
      Sid    = "KanbanInfrastructurePage",
      Effect = "Allow",
      Action = [
        "cloudwatch:ListMetrics",
        "cloudwatch:GetMetricData",
        "cloudwatch:GetMetricStatistics",
        "cloudwatch:DescribeAlarms",
        "autoscaling:DescribeScalingActivities"
      ],
      Resource = "*"
    }
```

Reset the min_size of your aws_autoscaling_group resource and remove the desired_capacity attribute. Then set the image_to_deploy variable in in your swarm module instantiation in your environments/production/main.tf file to be our ghcr.io/beamops/kanban:infrastructure-page Docker image. When querying the AWS API for information about your EC2 instances, our application uses the same autoscaling group as all of the examples in this chapter: swarm-asg. If you've used a different autoscaling group name, add the AUTO_SCALING_GROUP_NAME environment variable to the web service of your compose.yaml file. Now destroy and reapply your Terraform configuration.

```
$ terraform destroy
...
$ terraform apply
...
```

Now, seed the database of your application using the same method as in Chapter 9 (SSH-ing into one of the instances, running docker ps followed by docker exec -ti bin/seed). After this, log in to the application using one of the default emails (beamops@example.com with the password "password password"), and then navigate to the infrastructure page by clicking on the menu in the top-right corner and selecting Infrastructure. The following image shows you what you should see—a list of your EC2 instances, swarm nodes, and swarm services, as well as a button in the bottom-right corner that brings up a terminal that lets you stress your application and view the autoscaling logs. You'll notice that there's a gold star on one of your swarm nodes and one of the containers inside one of your EC2 instances. These gold stars tell you the node/container that you're being served. Your screen browser looks like the figure shown on page 336.

It may be that the swarm node on the EC2 instance that you're accessing is not the same as the swarm node in the Swarm Nodes list that has a gold star. This is due to Docker's ingress routing mesh. Recall our conversation on this in Chapter 9 on page 304, where Docker's swarm load balancer can route requests from one node to another.

Deploying this image means that you won't have to monitor the EC2 instance dashboard and AutoScaling Group activity page in your AWS dashboard, or run docker node ls and docker service ls inside one of your EC2 instances, to see how your infrastructure behaves when you stress your application. Instead, you'll be able to see everything visually.

Click the "Stress cluster" button inside the logs pop-up and wait for your Auto Scaling group to scale up. You'll see the CPU usage values for each EC2 instance slowly rise. It will take a couple of minutes for the average CPU of

Chapter 10. Autoscaling and Optimizing Your Deployment Strategy • 336

EC2 Instances

Instance	Availability zone	Public IP	Private IP	Containers	Launch time	CPU usage
i-09ba9852c02d92e38	eu-west-1b	54.195.158.250	172.31.32.138	1	6 minutes ago	21.62%
i-0c0a7a2fefa57ce3a	eu-west-1a	52.213.177.202	172.31.25.226	2	6 minutes ago	21.56%
i-0dcfdb8b123cb5ed0	eu-west-1c	34.253.195.1	172.31.15.187	1	6 minutes ago	20.36%

Swarm Nodes

★ wys2uxxot6mnhhgwullnbqoqd ●	hgwullnbqoqdwys2uxxot6mnh ●	ns4tinprx01vr73alsbcpcngs ●
Hostname ip-172-31-25-226.eu-west-1.co...	Hostname ip-172-31-15-187.eu-west-1.co...	Hostname ip-172-31-32-138.eu-west-1.co...
Availability active	Availability active	Availability active
Manager status leader	Manager status reachable	Manager status reachable

Swarm Services

🐘 kanban_db	💧 kanban_web
Image postgres:15.2	Image ghcr.io/beamops/kanban:infrastruct...

your cluster to reach 45% and trigger the cloudwatch alarm that will trigger your scale-up policy. Once your autoscaling group autoscales, you'll see two new logs in the autoscaling logs pop-up, two new instances in your instances list, two new nodes in your swarm nodes list, and the number of replicas of your web service will increase to 5/5, as shown in the figure on page 337.

This means that your CloudWatch alarm has been triggered and your Auto Scaling group has reacted accordingly, thanks to your Auto Scaling group policy. The two new EC2 instances that were created have run your launch_node.sh script and joined your swarm. You'll notice that the CPU of your two new instances is sitting around 80% right after they've been created. This is because they're still booting up. Because of the cooldown attribute that you set in your scaling policy, this high percentage won't cause a new scaling activity because there has to be five minutes in between scaling activities.

Now watch your Auto Scaling group scale back down. Once a scale-up event happens, we've configured our application to kill all of the remaining spawned processes that were causing the CPU spike. Around five minutes after your autoscaling group first scaled up, you should see the average CPU of your Auto Scaling group reduce to below 35% and two of the instances in your group will be terminated. Recall that you added the NewestInstance termination policy to your aws_autoscaling_group resource, so the EC2 instances that are terminated will be the two new ones that were created when your

EC2 Instances							
Instance i-09ba9852c02d92e38	Availability zone eu-west-1b	Public IP 54.195.158.250	Private IP 172.31.32.138	Containers 1	Launch time 17 minutes ago	CPU usage 22.47%	v
Instance i-0c0a7a2fefa57ce3a	Availability zone eu-west-1a	Public IP 52.213.177.202	Private IP 172.31.25.226	Containers 2	Launch time 17 minutes ago	CPU usage 17.32%	v
Instance i-0dcfdb8b123cb5ed0	Availability zone eu-west-1c	Public IP 34.253.195.1	Private IP 172.31.15.187	Containers 1	Launch time 17 minutes ago	CPU usage 19.81%	v
Instance i-0dcfdb8b123cb5ed0	Availability zone eu-west-1b	Public IP 54.194.115.254	Private IP 172.31.35.136	Containers 1	Launch time 8 minutes ago	CPU usage 24.73%	v
Instance i-0dcfdb8b123cb5ed0	Availability zone eu-west-1a	Public IP 34.243.53.174	Private IP 172.31.17.104	Containers 1	Launch time 8 minutes ago	CPU usage 28.29%	v

Swarm Nodes

★ wys2uxxot6mnhhgwullnbqoqd ●	hgwullnbqoqdwys2uxxot6mnh ●	ns4tinprx01vr73alsbcpcngs ●	zhkegdub6ee0z7r3qfc8o9mtwd ✧
Hostname ip-172-31-25-226.eu-west-1.co...	Hostname ip-172-31-15-187.eu-west-1.co...	Hostname ip-172-31-32-138.eu-west-1.co...	Hostname ip-172-31-35-136.eu-west-1.co...

swarm scaled. If you look at the swarm nodes during the descaling event, you'll see that the status of the two nodes being terminated turns to red and their availability is down. Shortly after, they will be removed from the swarm, your EC2 instance list will go back down to 3, and the replicas of your web service will go back to saying 3/3.

Congratulations! You've successfully tested the elasticity of your cluster. You've set up an Auto Scaling group of EC2 instances, which automatically reacts to two CloudWatch alarms that are based on the average CPU usage of your resource pool. Your Phoenix application can officially scale automatically!

In the next section, we'll introduce a load balancer into your Terraform configuration. Load balancers are crucial because they give your Auto Scaling group a fixed DNS and distribute the load between the group's instances.

Add a Load Balancer to Your Auto Scaling Group

You currently have an Auto Scaling group that has a minimum base of three EC2 instances and grows and shrinks the number of instances depending on the group's average CPU usage. This is great. But how do you distribute traffic across your Auto Scaling group?

Real-world applications will most likely have a custom domain name that needs a fixed IP address or DNS. Right now (before your group autoscales), you have three random IP addresses that were assigned when the instances were created. Imagine that your group scales up and you now have five IPs. How could you route the traffic from your domain name to these five resources? You'd have to update the settings of your domain name to include those new IPs. Or, you could use a load balancer!

When you create your load balancer, you can allocate it to your Auto Scaling group. No matter how many instances are created and removed, those IPs will be automatically added and removed from the load balancer's configuration. You can effectively have just one DNS that directs the traffic to all of the instances in your Auto Scaling group.

A load balancer helps to scale your application by dynamically adapting to changes in the number of instances within your Auto Scaling group and effortlessly incorporating new instances into its configuration. Not only that, a load balancer helps to evenly distribute the load of requests among the EC2 instances in your Auto Scaling group. It also helps with high availability and fault tolerance, as it ensures that even if one instance fails, the others can still handle the traffic. But how does a load balancer work?

The Function of a Load Balancer

To implement your load balancer, you need to understand two concepts related to its functionality: a listener and a target group.

A listener checks for connection requests from clients, using the protocol and port that you configure, and forwards requests to one or more target groups based on the rules you define. The listener is the component that checks for incoming traffic and decides how to route that traffic.

A target group routes the requests that it receives from a listener to one or more registered targets, such as EC2 instances, containers, or IP addresses. The target group determines where the traffic will be sent and how the health checks are conducted, ensuring which targets are available to receive traffic. In your case, the target group will distribute the traffic directly to the EC2 instances in your Auto Scaling group.

In the next section, you'll get your hands dirty and create these resources.

Add Load Balancer Components to Your Terraform Configuration

To create your load balancer, you need to create four new resources:

1. A security group, which will allow incoming HTTP requests on port 80 and outbound traffic to any port

2. The load balancer itself, which you'll link to the security group

3. The target group for your load balancer and the necessary health checks it should perform when deciding whether the instances of your Phoenix application are available to receive traffic
4. The listener, which will listen for traffic on port 80 and forward traffic to the target group

You'll then link your load balancer to your Auto Scaling group by setting the target_group_arns attribute of your aws_autoscaling_group resource.

To create these resources, create a new file in your modules/cloud/aws/compute/swarm folder called lb.tf. This is where your load balancer configuration will live.

You'll start with step 1: creating your load balancer's security group. Since you're already familiar with the Terraform resource for security groups, try to create this resource in your modules/cloud/aws/compute/swarm/lb.tf file before looking at our implementation here:

```
# in modules/cloud/aws/compute/swarm/lb.tf
resource "aws_security_group" "http" {
  name        = "allow_http"
  description = "Allow http traffic"

  ingress {
    description = "http"
    from_port   = 80
    to_port     = 80
    protocol    = "tcp"
    cidr_blocks = ["0.0.0.0/0"]
  }
  egress {
    from_port   = 0
    to_port     = 0
    protocol    = "-1"
    cidr_blocks = ["0.0.0.0/0"]
  }
}
```

Now for step 2: dealing with the load balancer itself. The Terraform resource for a load balancer is aws_lb.[13] You'll create an application load balancer that operates at layer 7 of the OSI model and is suited for routing HTTP/HTTPS traffic, so choose application as the load_balancer_type attribute. You'll also link the security group you just created and the subnets used by your Auto Scaling group to this load balancer.

---

13. https://registry.terraform.io/providers/hashicorp/aws/latest/docs/resources/lb

See the following code snippet for the resource configurations that you need to add to your lb.tf file:

```
# in modules/cloud/aws/compute/swarm/lb.tf

resource "aws_lb" "main" {
  ip_address_type     = "ipv4"
  load_balancer_type  = "application"
  name                = "swarm-load-balancer"
  security_groups     = [aws_security_group.http.id]
  subnets             = data.aws_subnets.main_subnets.ids
}
```

Great. Now move on to step 3: creating the target group for your load balancer. The resource you'll need for this is aws_lb_target_group.[14] This target group will be responsible for health checking the EC2 instances in your Auto Scaling group and forwarding the requests it receives to those instances. We've pre-populated the target group for you. Add this resource to your lb.tf file:

```
# in modules/cloud/aws/compute/swarm/lb.tf

resource "aws_lb_target_group" "swarm" {
  ip_address_type                = "ipv4"
  load_balancing_algorithm_type  = "round_robin"
  name                           = "docker-swarm-target-group"
  port                           = 4000
  protocol                       = "HTTP"
  vpc_id                         = data.aws_vpc.main.id

  health_check {
    enabled             = true
    healthy_threshold   = 5
    interval            = 30
    matcher             = "302"
    path                = "/"
    port                = "4000"
    protocol            = "HTTP"
    timeout             = 5
    unhealthy_threshold = 2
  }
}
```

As you can see, this target group will route traffic via HTTP to port 4000 of the resource it is linked to (you'll link it to your Auto Scaling group in a moment) in a round-robin fashion. We've also added a VPC to the target group to control the scope of the load balancing. Given that your Auto Scaling group only has one VPC, this attribute doesn't make a difference to your implementation, but since AWS provides flexibility for different use cases where there

---

14. https://registry.terraform.io/providers/hashicorp/aws/latest/docs/resources/lb_target_group

could be multiple VPCs, adding the VPC is an obligatory attribute when dealing with application load balancers.

This target group also defines a health check to be able to determine whether the instances in your Auto Scaling group are able to receive requests. It does this by accessing the / path on port 4000 and checking that the HTTP response has a 302 status. The status has been set to 302 because our image that you're deploying requires authentication so it automatically redirects to the login page at path /users/log_in when the homepage is visited.

Now for step 4: creating your load balancer's listener. The Terraform resource you'll use to create this is aws_lb_listener.[15] The listener will listen for HTTP requests on port 80, as defined by your security group, and will forward the requests to your target group. To attach this to your load balancer, use the load_balancer_arn attribute and set it to the arn value exposed by your aws_lb resource. The resource you have to add is as follows:

```
# in modules/cloud/aws/compute/swarm/lb.tf

resource "aws_lb_listener" "http" {
  port              = 80
  protocol          = "HTTP"
  load_balancer_arn = aws_lb.main.arn

  default_action {
    target_group_arn = aws_lb_target_group.swarm.arn
    type             = "forward"
  }
}
```

Add Listener and Security Group Rules for HTTPS Traffic

You should also add a listener and security group rules for HTTPS traffic in production environments to provide secure communication between users and your application. To do this, create a certificate in the AWS Certificate Manager and then validate it using DNS validation. We won't cover this in this book but you can read more about it in the official AWS documentation.[16]

You've reached the last step: linking your load balancer to your Auto Scaling group. Do this by setting the target_group_arns attribute of your aws_autoscaling_group resource in your autoscaling.tf file to be the arn attribute exposed by your aws_lb_target_group resource, as shown on the next page:

---

15. https://registry.terraform.io/providers/hashicorp/aws/latest/docs/resources/lb_listener
16. https://docs.aws.amazon.com/acm/latest/userguide/gs-acm-validate-dns.html

```
# in modules/cloud/aws/compute/swarm/autoscaling.tf
resource "aws_autoscaling_group" "main" {
  target_group_arns = [aws_lb_target_group.swarm.arn]
}
```

Your load balancer is now set up! Before applying your configuration, add an output to your modules/cloud/aws/compute/swarm/outputs.tf file of the DNS name for your load balancer. This will allow you to easily recognize the entry point for your load balancer each time you run terraform apply. You can access the DNS name through the dns_name attribute exported by your aws_lb resource. The output you should add looks like this:

```
# in modules/cloud/aws/compute/swarm/outputs.tf
output "load_balancer_dns" {
  description = "The DNS name of the load balancer"
  value       = "open http://${aws_lb.main.dns_name}"
}
```

Remember, you need to carry this output through to your environments/production/main.tf file.

Now apply your configuration by running terraform apply. Your load balancer will be created and the DNS name will appear in the output in your console. You can see an example terminal interaction here:

```
$ terraform apply
...
module.swarm.aws_lb.main: Creation complete after 2m53s
Outputs:

load_balancer_dns = "open http://swarm-load-balancer-16...eu-west-1..."
```

Copy the swarm_lb output, paste it in your terminal, and press Enter. This will open a browser where you'll see the Kanban application running.

Well done! You've added a load balancer to your Auto Scaling group and Docker Swarm architecture. You have a single DNS name that you can access, which will distribute the traffic among your different AWS EC2 instances (Docker Swarm nodes). You have a highly available, robust, fault-tolerant and autoscaling AWS implementation. Your application is reliable, and the load of requests is distributed by both AWS and Docker Swarm. The load balancer you've added in this section adds an extra layer of distribution to your application by allowing new IPs that are added to your Auto Scaling group to receive traffic from one unified DNS name. Not only this, your Docker Swarm also distributes the traffic it receives among its nodes, which will give you further confidence that your application will remain running under periods of high demand.

You've officially automated the scalability of your application and finished adding the main resources of your infrastructure. Congratulations! From here on out, you won't be adding any new resources to your application—only nice extras that will serve as the cherries on top. You can close the "Make Your Application autoscale" issue that you created in Chapter 2. To do this, create a new branch and then commit and push your code from this chapter. Create a PR and merge it. Remember to add closes #ISSUE_ID to your PR description.

Next, we'll look at automatically rolling back your application upon a non-successful deployment. This is crucial in minimizing the impact on users after a failed deployment and avoiding downtime due to a broken application.

Minimize Downtime with Automatic Rollbacks

Now that you've finished creating the main resources for your infrastructure, we want to show you an important tweak you can make when working with orchestrators that run containers. Imagine a scenario in which you make a change to your application that passes all of your current tests but breaks when deployed to your production environment. Perhaps you added a secret to your Compose file but added the wrong secret value. If you were to deploy this change to production, your application would fail to start and you would have a broken deployment. This would mean a complete outage of your production environment, which would certainly impact users.

How can you avoid this? Normally, orchestrators have a feature called health checks that is used to follow the health of your application, similar to the health checks performed by your target group that we saw earlier in the chapter. When a new stack is deployed, your orchestrator will start a new container and run the health check against it. If the health check fails, then the orchestrator will roll back to the previous version of your stack. This will ensure that your application is always running and that you don't have any downtime.

Adding a health check to your application is super easy. There are many ways that you can implement a health check with Docker. In this case, you'll simply install curl in your Docker image and then update your Compose file to curl your application to check that it's working upon deployment.

Let's begin with adding curl to your Docker image.

Add curl to Your Dockerfile

In this section, you'll deploy two new images of our Kanban that we have preprepared: one that works and another that is broken and will fail to start. This will allow you to check that your health check works properly.

To add your health check all you need to do is install curl in the runner stage of your Dockerfile. Throughout the book, we've emphasized that it's a good idea not to manipulate the default Elixir Docker image created by the Phoenix release generator. However, what's important to us is that you understand how to implement a health check in a Docker Compose file, and curl-ing your application with the -f option is a quick and easy health check to implement. Running curl -f means that the curl command will fail if the HTTP response code is 400 or greater.

To install curl in your Docker image, edit your Dockerfile as follows:

```
# in Dockerfile
FROM ${RUNNER_IMAGE}
RUN apt-get update -y && \
  apt-get install -y libstdc++6 openssl libncurses5 locales ca-certificates \
  curl \
  && apt-get clean && rm -f /var/lib/apt/lists/*_*
```

Now that you've installed curl, you need to update your Compose file to include a health check.

Update the deploy Configuration of Your Compose File

The health check you'll add will be a curl to port 4000 of the localhost of the machine running your web service. To run this health check when you deploy your application, add two new sub-attributes to the deploy key of your web service (update_config and rollback_config) as well as a new healthcheck key. Update the web service in your compose.yaml file according to the following code snippet:

```
# in compose.yaml
services:
  web:
    deploy:
      restart_policy:
        max_attempts: ${MAX_ATTEMPTS:-0}
      update_config:
        parallelism: 1
        order: start-first
        delay: 5s
        failure_action: rollback
      rollback_config:
```

```
      parallelism: 0
healthcheck:
  test: ['CMD', 'curl', '-f', 'http://localhost:4000']
  interval: 5s
  timeout: 3s
  retries: 3
```

We've updated the max_attempts value of the restart_policy so that it is dynamic. The default is 0, meaning that the container should always be restarted, but it's possible to set the maximum attempts (for example to 3 as you had before). Making your web service always try to restart will help avoid application outages in production, but being able to set the value means that you can see if your application has a memory leak and fails regularly.

The update_config specifies configuration options for updating your web service. It specifies that when updating a task, the new task should be started first, and the running task briefly overlaps with the new one. It also states that only one container task should be updated at a time, with a delay of five seconds between tasks, and if a task fails, then the deployment should be rolled back. The rollback_config configures the conditions of the rollback. It stipulates that all containers should be simultaneously rolled back at the same time.

Lastly, the healthcheck key defines the health checks that should be run on your application to check if it's healthy. When deploying, this determines whether a rollback is necessary, and when your application is running, this determines whether the swarm should route requests to that task. The health check states that the curl command should be run every 5 seconds, allowing for a 2-second timeout. It defines that if the health check fails three times, then the service should be deemed unhealthy. When the service is deemed unhealthy, your failure_action will take place—your application will roll back. Docker will then run the health check on that rolled-back version. (If that rolled-back version doesn't have the curl installed, then the health check will fail.)

As this health check will run on your application every 5 seconds, we recommend updating the logging level in your config/prod.exs file to :notice as we have done in the upcoming example. This avoids polluting the logs for your application:

```
# in config/prod.exs
config :logger, level: :notice
```

The best way to see this automatic rollback in action is to use the infrastructure page of our Kanban application. Once you have your browser open and ready, deploy our preprepared image called ghcr.io/beamops/kanban:healthy-endpoint that includes curl and has no errors, as we've done here:

```
$ PRIVATE_KEY_PATH=environments/production/private_key.pem \
  SOPS_AGE_KEY_FILE=environments/production/key.txt \
  GITHUB_USER=YOUR_GITHUB_USERNAME \
  ./scripts/deploy.sh ghcr.io/beamops/kanban:healthy-endpoint
```

There won't be any issues with this image because the health check will pass. Scroll down to the Swarm Services section, and you'll see the image of the kanban_web service has been updated successfully. You have to deploy this image before deploying a failing one because now that you've updated your Compose file's deploy configuration, when Docker tries to roll back from the failing image, the image it rolls back to also needs to have the health check and it needs to be healthy.

Now deploy our preprepared image that's broken, called ghcr.io/beamops/kanban:unhealthy-endpoint, as we've done here:

```
$ PRIVATE_KEY_PATH=environments/production/private_key.pem \
  SOPS_AGE_KEY_FILE=environments/production/key.txt \
  GITHUB_USER=YOUR_GITHUB_USERNAME \
  ./scripts/deploy.sh ghcr.io/beamops/kanban:unhealthy-endpoint
```

While this is happening, look at the Replicas of your kanban_web service in the list of swarm services. You will see that the image momentarily updates to ghcr.io/beamops/kanban:unhealthy-endpoint before quickly switching back to ghcr.io/beamops/kanban:healthy-endpoint. This means that your health check has failed and, as a result, your application has been automatically rolled back to its previous version. You'll notice that you never saw any errors in your browser such as the Phoenix socket disconnecting. This is thanks to Docker Swarm's orchestration capabilities that manage the visibility of tasks to end users. Notably, Docker Swarm conducts health checks discreetly, ensuring that health-check containers are never exposed to users. Amazing, right?

Great! You've put the cherry on top of your current deployment strategy. You have a highly available Docker Swarm that autoscales and can perform zero-downtime deployments. You can now close the "Implement automatic rollback upon failed deployments" issue that you created in Chapter 2. As always, commit and push the code you've done in this section and create a PR. Remember to add closes #ISSUE_ID to the description. Merge and then close your PR.

It's time to clean up your Docker architecture when deploying, by removing old images and containers.

Clean Up Dangling Docker Resources

Welcome to the last section of the chapter. You've done a lot of work to get here—well done! But there's one more thing you need to do before wrapping up this chapter: the automation of the cleaning up of your cluster.

There will be always maintenance tasks you'll need to run in your infrastructure. Sometimes, these maintenance tasks aren't obvious until they become an issue, and yet it's impossible to plan for every single scenario. This is why we've been stressing the importance of environment integrity. When your environments are equal and you use them regularly, you'll be able to spot these common maintenance tasks and automate them.

One such example is old/unused Docker resources. When deploying new stacks with Docker, the old images that you've pulled and the containers you've been running don't get deleted. This means that over time, as you deploy more and more stacks in your Docker Swarm, Docker images and Docker containers will accumulate and take up valuable disk space. If you don't clean up your Docker resources in the local registry of your EC2 instances, you'll run out of storage on your EC2 swarm nodes. Unfortunately, there's no way to specify an image retention policy in a Docker Swarm. To solve this issue, you're going to create a global service that will run a task that will remove all the images and containers that aren't being used.

Choosing the global deploy mode means that the service will ensure to at least run one task on every node in the swarm. This is what you want—your clean-up task to be run on every node of your swarm.

The Docker command to clean up your Docker environment by removing all stopped containers, unused networks, dangling images, and build cache is this:

```
docker system prune --all --force
```

The --all option removes unused images, not just dangling ones, and the --force option prevents Docker from asking for confirmation before executing the command.

This docker system prune --all --force command is like the Marie Kondo of Docker – it's a handy way to free up disk space and keep your Docker environment tidy. Running this command also improves the performance of your application, since having unnecessary resources in your local registry means that the Docker daemon takes longer to locate and manage the relevant images and containers.

To run this command on your nodes, you'll create a new Compose file. Using a new file will separate your actual application from your housekeeping tasks. This new file will create a new service that uses the global deploy mode to run the docker system prune --all --force command on each of the nodes of your swarm. Create a new folder called tasks in the root of your project with a file called purge.yaml inside and copy this code snippet into that file:

```yaml
# in tasks/purge.yaml
version: "3.9"
services:
  system-prune:
    image: docker
    volumes:
      - "/var/run/docker.sock:/var/run/docker.sock"
    command: docker system prune --all --force
    deploy:
      mode: global
      restart_policy:
        condition: none
```

The service in this file uses the docker image. You may be thinking: What? Docker inside Docker, isn't that a bit overkill? While it might look a bit much, it's a convenient way to perform Docker-related tasks in containerized environments. This system-prune service mounts the Docker socket of the machine running the container inside the container in the same way that your web service does. Mounting the socket inside this docker container allows you to manage the Docker daemon and run Docker commands within your container.

Once the Docker socket is mounted, this service runs the docker system prune command. And thanks to the mode sub-attribute of the deploy key, this command is run on every node in the swarm. The restart_policy has been set to none so that the task won't restart if it fails.

Now that you've created this new service, it's time to use it in your deployment script. To do this, you need to deploy this system-prune service just after you deploy your kanban service.

Update your deploy script by adding the two following commands just after you deploy your kanban stack. The end of your deploy.sh script should now look like this:

```bash
# in scripts/deploy.sh
# deploy the application
DOCKER_HOST="ssh://ec2-user@$MANAGER_IP" WEB_IMAGE="$IMAGE" \
docker stack deploy -c "$COMPOSE_FILE_PATH" --with-registry-auth "$STACK_NAME"
# remove purge stack if it exists
DOCKER_HOST="ssh://ec2-user@$MANAGER_IP" docker stack rm "system_prune"
# deploy purge stack globally
PURGE_FILE_PATH=${PURGE_FILE_PATH:-"tasks/purge.yaml"}
DOCKER_HOST="ssh://ec2-user@$MANAGER_IP" \
docker stack deploy -c "$PURGE_FILE_PATH" "system_prune"
echo "Deployment completed."
```

You'll notice that your deploy script will now require a new variable to be passed: PURGE_FILE_PATH, which will specify the name of your new purge task. You'll also see that you have to first remove the stack before redeploying it. This is because you've set the restart_policy for your system-prune service to be none so that the command is not run again if it fails. But doing this means that the service won't be automatically restarted when you redeploy the stack. You'll either have to force an update or remove the stack and redeploy it.

The last thing to do is to add the PURGE_FILE_PATH to your swarm_provisioner null_resource. Copy the same logic as your COMPOSE_FILE_PATH variable: create a Terraform variable and pass it to the instantiation of your swarm module. It should have a default value of ../../tasks/purge.yaml. The changes are as follows:

```
# in modules/cloud/aws/compute/swarm/variables.tf
variable "purge_file" {
  type        = string
  description = "Docker purge task file"
  default     = "../../tasks/purge.yaml"
}

# in environments/production/main.tf
module "swarm" {
  purge_file = "../../tasks/purge.yaml"
}

# in modules/cloud/aws/compute/swarm/main.tf
resource "null_resource" "swarm_provisioner" {
  provisioner "local-exec" {
    environment = {
      PURGE_FILE_PATH = var.purge_file
    }
    command = "../../scripts/deploy.sh ${var.image_to_deploy}"
  }
}
```

And that's it! You've added your housekeeping task to your deployment script. SSH into one of your EC2 instances and run the docker images and docker ps -a commands to see all of the images and containers on your instance (both in use and not in use). You'll see a list of images and many exited containers. Then redeploy your application from the root of your project so that your new global system-prune task is run. Once your deployment has finished, rerun the docker images and docker ps -a commands, and you'll see that the images and container lists are much shorter.

You're done! You've successfully created an autoscaling production environment that automatically rolls back deployments if they are unsuccessful and cleans up the resources in your EC2 instances. You're really mastering the "scalability and integrity of environments" BEAMOps principle. And what's more, you did it all using infrastructure-as-code. You now have strategies that you can use in your daily work to better understand how your production environment will behave under periods of high stress. You don't have to worry about rolling back your application if it fails. You've bolstered your confidence in your deployments!

Before we summarize everything this chapter has covered, remember to commit the code you've implemented in this section and destroy your AWS infrastructure after any CI runs have finished executing.

What Have You Learned?

In this chapter, you did many things to optimize your production environment. By adding an AWS Auto Scaling group to your infrastructure, you're enabling your Docker Swarm to grow and shrink horizontally at will and not become overwhelmed during periods of high demand. Integrating an external load balancer with your Docker Swarm bolsters your swarm's orchestration capabilities and enhances the overall performance, availability, and scalability of your application. Adding an automatic rollback policy to your web service improves your deployment strategy. It minimizes the downtime that your application will have upon a non-successful deployment and ensures that your end users don't suffer from any service disruptions. Lastly, your new tasks/purge.yaml file helps clean your Docker environment and improve the performance of your swarm nodes by preventing your EC2 instances from running out of disk space.

This is it for creating new resources for your infrastructure! You officially have a robust, autoscaling, and highly available production environment that has zero downtime and can be created on-demand using Terraform. You've truly mastered infrastructure-as-code, and you've become an expert in the integrity and scalability of environments. You should now feel confident in owning not just the deployment of your application but also its behavior under periods of high demand. Those are invaluable BEAMOps principles that you're now ready to put to use in your daily work.

In the next chapter, we'll move on to the final phase of your BEAMOps journey: instrumenting your application. Collecting data and gathering insights into your application's behavior is crucial for detecting and diagnosing issues, and it can help you identify bottlenecks to see where you could optimize your setup further.

> **The Extra Mile**
>
> If you wish to deepen your knowledge of the themes we've covered in this chapter and refine your BEAMOps developer superpowers, we've created a task for you to do:
>
> 1. Now that you know how to run a global task on all of your swarm nodes, think about how you could do this from your Elixir application.

CHAPTER 11

Instrument Your Application with Logs and Metrics

You're almost at the end of your journey to becoming a developer who practices BEAMOps principles with ease! Let's take a moment to recap what you've accomplished so far. You've packaged your application with mix releases and Docker. You've implemented a Docker Compose file so that you can run and deploy your application in a consistent and efficient manner. You've set up your AWS environment using Terraform and Packer to distribute your application across multiple AZs and ensure that it scales automatically based on the average CPU usage of your EC2 instances. You've also implemented a continuous integration and continuous delivery (CI/CD) pipeline to ensure that you're practicing the Kaizen principle of making small, ongoing changes and reducing the time-to-market of new features.

Well done for getting this far. You're almost there! The last leg of your journey is to understand how to instrument your application.

Throughout this book, we've emphasized the importance of environment integrity and setting up a CI/CD pipeline to make your application reliable. With software, there will always be things that break. Own this truth and fix errors as they arise. A system is only truly reliable if it can recover quickly from any failures. Instrumentation will help you do this.

The goal of instrumentation is to gather information that can be used for analysis, troubleshooting, optimization, and the overall observation of your application. When thinking about instrumentation, you need to ask yourself what you want to observe, how you wish to visualize it, and in what ways you want to be notified when critical errors arise. Because instrumentation is a huge topic, our discussion of instrumentation is split into two separate chapters.

In this chapter, you'll be introduced to Grafana, an open-source set of tools that lets you visualize metrics and logs of applications. You'll use Grafana to scrape and store the logs of your Docker containers. You'll visualize the logs in an interactive site and monitor the performance metrics of your application. By the end of the chapter, you'll be able to close one of the instrumentation issues you created in Chapter 2.

In the next chapter, you'll create your own custom metrics and alerts to measure the average CPU of your EC2 instances.

Let's get to it. We'll start with a brief introduction to instrumentation, and go into more detail on what your instrumentation stack will look like.

Design Your Instrumentation Architecture

Instrumentation is the practice of incorporating code into a software application to gather data, monitor performance, and collect information about its behavior during runtime. Instrumentation is an essential part of software delivery, as it gives you insights into how your application is running and lets you spot potential issues so you can make informed development decisions.

There are three main pillars in instrumentation: logging, monitoring, and tracing. In this book, we'll only focus on logging and monitoring.

A typical instrumentation architecture includes services that collect, store, and visualize data. In this chapter, you'll instrument your application by combining specific Grafana[1] services with other tools such as Prometheus[2] and the PromEx[3] Elixir library.

Grafana is an open-source platform used for monitoring and observability. It has various services within it that, when combined, allow you to visualize time-series data by creating interactive and customizable dashboards.

Prometheus is another open-source tool that collects and stores metrics data from configured targets and provides a query language for analyzing them.

Lastly, PromEx is an Elixir library that collects and exposes metrics to a /metrics endpoint in an application that can later be scraped by services such as Prometheus.

---

1. https://grafana.com
2. https://prometheus.io
3. https://github.com/akoutmos/prom_ex

We chose to use an open-source instrumentation stack in this book rather than the logging and metrics service offered by AWS (CloudWatch) because being able to run your logging and metrics system locally is extremely important for environment integrity. CloudWatch, which you learned about in the previous chapter, is an AWS service that's hosted in AWS and cannot be run locally. Grafana, Prometheus, and PromEx, on the other hand, are open-source tools that can be run locally, meaning that you can replicate the logging and metrics system that you have in production on your local machine. The environment integrity that this instrumentation stack gives you reduces the feedback loop of your application's behavior and speeds up the delivery of metrics, logs, and alerts. This will help you easily develop new observability features and quickly ship them to production with less friction. Another benefit to using an open-source logging/monitoring system is that it decouples your instrumentation implementation to AWS. The fewer cloud-specific parts you use, the easier it is to use a different cloud platform in the future.

Let's take a closer look at the different Grafana services that you'll use in your instrumentation architecture, Prometheus, and PromEx:

1. *Loki*: A horizontally scalable log aggregation store designed by Grafana Labs that's used for saving and searching log data. Loki is multi-tenant, which means that it's able to simultaneously combine logs of different applications in one centralized place without mixing them up. You'll use this service to store the logs of your Docker containers.

2. *Promtail*: An open-source log agent developed by Grafana Labs to collect, enrich, and forward logs to Loki. Promtail scrapes logs from various sources such as files, journal, syslog, and Docker containers. It provides features like log transformations, service discovery, and context switching between metrics and logs. You'll use this service to scrape the logs of your Docker containers and send them to Loki.

3. *Grafana*: A visualization software developed by Grafana Labs that's used to visualize data from different sources. You'll use this service to visualize the logs supplied by Loki and Promtail, as well as the metrics supplied by PromEx and Prometheus.

4. *PromEx*: An Elixir library based on Prometheus that has two main uses. It integrates with the Grafana UI and allows you to save Grafana dashboard templates as JSON files. Its main function, however, is to collect metrics from Elixir applications. Out of the box, it lets you collate the default metrics exposed by the main libraries typically used in Elixir applications, such as Phoenix LiveView, Ecto, and many more. When

PromEx collects metrics, it creates a /metrics endpoint in your Elixir app and exposes these metrics there so that they can be scraped by Prometheus.

5. *Prometheus*: An open-source metric monitoring and alerting toolkit that's used to collect and store time-series data. You'll use it to save the metrics scraped from your application. Prometheus is an external alternative to Grafana Lab's Mimir service, which also handles metric collection. We've chosen to use Prometheus instead of Mimir because of its seamless integration with PromEx.

6. *Alloy*: An open-source OpenTelemetry collector designed by Grafana Labs that has built-in Prometheus pipelines and support for metrics, logs, traces, and profiles. You'll use it to periodically scrape the metrics from your Elixir app and then forward them to your Prometheus data store.

You can see how these services interact with each other in the following diagram:

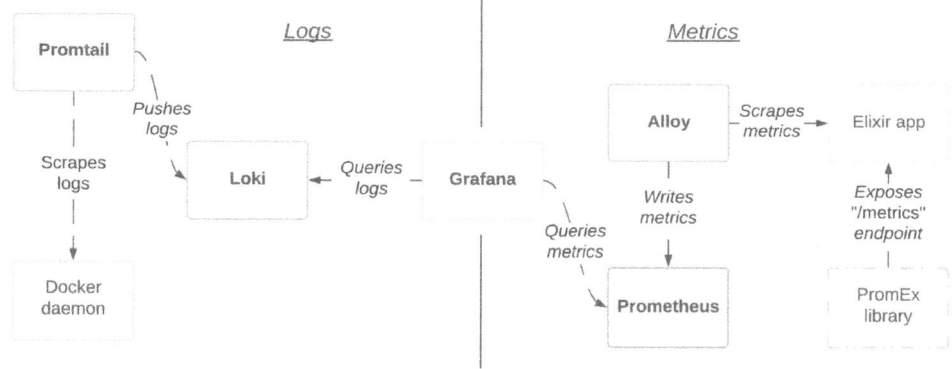

By combining these six components (Loki, Promtail, Grafana, PromEx, Prometheus, and Alloy), you'll have one centralized system for log and metric monitoring that you can run both locally and remotely. This will help you detect and diagnose infrastructure issues, ensuring the reliability of your application.

Now that you have a general overview of instrumentation and what your architecture will include, let's get into the nitty-gritty. You'll start by setting up the logs for your application using Loki, Promtail, and Grafana.

Collect Your Application Logs

When setting up your instrumentation architecture, we recommend that you always start with log collection. This will make it easier for you to add other instrumentation services and see the status of your application. This also means that you'll no longer have to run docker service logs in your local machine or in each of your EC2 instances to find out what's happening if there's an error. Instead, you'll have *one* centralized logging visualization platform that allows you to filter logs by Docker container and Docker service.

The services you'll use to collect and visualize the logs of your application are:

- Loki: to store the logs
- Promtail: to scrape the logs and send them to Loki
- Grafana: to visualize the logs (as well as the metrics that you'll implement later in this chapter, and in the next)

To incorporate these services into your application stack, you'll follow these three steps for each service:

1. Create a configuration file for the solution.
2. Add the solution as a new service in your Compose file.
3. Attach your configuration file created in step 1 to your new Compose service using a new Compose top-level key: configs.

Let's see this in action and start with creating your Loki log store.

Define Your Log Store Service with Loki

To get started, create a Loki configuration file by adding a new folder called instrumentation to the root of your project. Inside that, create a new subfolder called loki, and inside that a file called local.yaml. Then, copy and paste the following snippet into your new file:

```yaml
# in instrumentation/loki/local.yaml
auth_enabled: false
server:
  http_listen_port: 3100

common:
  ring:
    instance_addr: loki
    kvstore:
      store: inmemory
  replication_factor: 1
  path_prefix: /tmp/loki
```

```
schema_config:
  configs:
    - from: 2020-05-15
      store: boltdb-shipper
      object_store: filesystem
      schema: v11
      index:
        prefix: index_
        period: 24h
storage_config:
  filesystem:
    directory: /tmp/loki/chunks
```

This local.yaml snippet sets up your Loki service. It first disables authentication for Loki. This isn't ideal for production scenarios, as Loki should be password-protected, but for simplicity, while you're implementing this service, you can disable the authentication.

The file defines the port that the Loki server will use to listen for HTTP requests of incoming log entries. This is the port that your Promtail service will use when sending POST requests to push the logs entries that it collects. You'll set up this Promtail service in a moment.

The configuration file uses the common key to configure the instance_addr, or listening address, for Loki. This listening address has been set to loki, which is the name you'll use when defining your Loki service in your Compose file. You'll use this hostname, along with the port, later on when you link your Loki log store to your Promtail scraping service. Recall that in a Docker network, Docker uses the name of a service as its DNS name, which is also a service's virtual IP (VIP). Setting the listening address to loki means that your Loki server will only accept requests that use that specific hostname (http://loki:3100). Any requests that don't use that hostname, for example those sent to http://localhost:3100, will be rejected.

After setting the host, the common key sets the kvstore to be inmemory. The kvstore refers to the key-value store used by Loki to store index data, which helps in efficient log querying and retrieval. The common key states that your Loki store will only have one replica, meaning that there's only one copy of each log entry. Should you wish to make your logs more highly available, you could increase this value. But this isn't something we'll look into in this book.

Lastly, the common attribute sets a path_prefix, which is the file path that Loki will use when storing data. Remember, all data in a database is stored in files. In this instance, the file path has been set to the /tmp/loki directory.

The configuration file uses the schema_config key to further define how the log data is stored and indexed. It states that Loki will use the 2020-05-15 schema and the boltdb-shipper store type to save the indexes in an object store. Loki will also refresh the indexes every 24 hours. Creating new indexes each day optimizes your Loki resources by reducing the size of your indexes and, as a result, query time.

This configuration is suitable for a simple Loki setup. It's not optimized for high availability or scalability, as indicated by the in-memory store and the replication factor of 1. For a production environment, you'd typically use a more robust store, such as S3, as well as a higher replication factor.

You've completed the first step of your Loki implementation: creating the configuration file. Now, it's time to add the Loki service to your compose.yaml file. Create a new service called loki (the same as the instance_addr in your configuration file) that uses the grafana/loki image—with the version 2.9.3 pinned to the image, like so:

```
# in compose.yaml
services:
  loki:
    image: grafana/loki:2.9.3
```

That's step two done. Now link your configuration file to this service. To do this, you'll use a new Compose top-level key: configs.[4]

A config in Docker is a file that's mounted into a container when the service is run. A config is typically a configuration file, certificate, or any other configuration data that a service needs. It's similar to a Docker secret in the sense that a config mounts the file that you specify to a specific file path in the container. Like a Docker secret, to update a config, you have to create a new one. However, unlike Docker secrets, the content of a config isn't encrypted. When defining a config for a service, you need to do two things:

1. Add the top-level configs key to create the Docker config and specify where that configuration file can be found on your local machine.
2. Add the configs sub-attribute to a service to add a config to that service.

The top-level configs key is just like the top-level secrets key. It creates a list of configs and, for each config, you have a CONFIG_ID and a file key to tell Docker the name of your config and where it can find the configuration file in your local machine. It's configured like so:

---

4. https://docs.docker.com/compose/compose-file/08-configs/

```
configs:
  CONFIG_ID:
    file: CONFIGURATION_FILE_PATH_IN_YOUR_LOCAL_MACHINE
```

The service sub-attribute `configs` key requires two attributes: a source and a target:

```
services:
  service_name:
    configs:
      - source: CONFIG_ID
        target: PATH_WHERE_THE_FILE_WILL_BE_MOUNTED_INSIDE_THE_CONTAINER
```

The source is the name of the config, and the target is the path in the container to which Docker will mount the configuration file. The source name that you specify in the service must match the name used in the top-level key, that is, the `CONFIG_ID`.

Try to create the configs for your new `loki` service on your own before looking at our implementation:

```
# in compose.yaml
services:
  loki:
    image: grafana/loki:2.9.3
    configs:
      - source: loki
        target: /etc/loki/local-config.yaml
configs:
  loki:
    file: ./instrumentation/loki/local.yaml
```

Default Configuration File Path

We've specified that the target file path in the container is /etc/loki/local-config.yaml because that's the default configuration file path the grafana/loki:2.9.3 image looks for. You can see this if you download the image using `docker pull`, inspect it using the `docker inspect` command, and then look at the CMD value. If you call the file path something other than /etc/loki/local-config.yaml, you'll have to manually override the CMD value of the container using the command service attribute.

Great! You've finished setting up Loki, your log store. The next step is to collect your logs and populate your Loki store using Promtail.

Define Your Log Scraping Service: Promtail

Your Promtail service will collect the logs for your application and send them to Loki. To add this service to your stack, create a Promtail configuration file and a new promtail Compose service. You'll first focus on log collection in a Compose environment. Once you've got your Compose configuration up and running, you'll adapt your configuration for a swarm environment.

To start, add a new folder inside your instrumentation folder called promtail and, inside that, a file called local.yaml. This is where your configurations for Promtail will live. Then copy in the following code:

```yaml
# in instrumentation/promtail/local.yaml
positions:
  filename: /tmp/positions.yaml
clients:
  - url: http://loki:3100/loki/api/v1/push
scrape_configs:
  - job_name: docker_scrape
    docker_sd_configs:
      - host: unix:///var/run/docker.sock
        refresh_interval: 5s
    relabel_configs:
      - source_labels: ["__meta_docker_container_name"]
        regex: "/(.*)"
        target_label: "container"
```

The positions key specifies the location where Promtail should store the current read positions for each log file it's scraping. Promtail keeps track of the current position within each file to ensure it continues reading logs from where it left off in case of restarts or failures. This also ensures that Promtail doesn't duplicate logs. The file where Promtail will store its positions is /tmp/positions.yaml.

The clients key defines where Promtail will send the logs. It's set to be the /loki/api/v1/push path of the loki service you created earlier at port 3100: the listening address and port that you defined for loki.

The scrape_configs key defines the targets that Promtail should scrape. It uses the docker_sd_configs attribute to define one target (the Docker socket) and specifies that it will scrape that target in the environment where it's run every 5 seconds.

The relabel_configs attribute states that each log should be categorized by its container name.

The source_labels specifies the type of data from your target that you wish to capture. _meta_docker_container_name is a metadata attribute saved to Docker's internal logs that links a log entry to a Docker container using its name. Adding this as a source label means that each log will be categorized by the name of its container. regex defines how the container name will be captured and the target_label states the name of the filter that will be displayed in Grafana, in this case "container."

>
> **A Word on Tracing**
>
> We won't discuss tracing in this book (for lack of space), but if you were to implement tracing, it would be a good idea to format your logs into JSON format. By doing so, Tempo[5] (the Grafana tracing tool) can easily connect logs and traces using a trace ID. You can transform your logs from strings to JSON by adding pipeline stages to your Promtail configuration.[6]

The next step is to add a new promtail service to your Compose file. The Docker image you'll use is grafana/promtail, and you should pin the version number 2.9.3. Just like before, to add your configuration file to your service, you must define a new config in the top-level configs key and reference this config in your service using the configs service sub-attribute. You can see the first additions that you have to make here:

```
# in compose.yaml
services:
  promtail:
    image: grafana/promtail:2.9.3
    configs:
      - source: promtail
        target: /etc/promtail/config.yml
configs:
  promtail:
    file: ./instrumentation/promtail/${PROMTAIL_CONFIG-swarm}.yaml
```

You'll notice that we've made the path to the Promtail configuration file dynamic, defaulting to a swarm configuration file that you'll create later on. We've made this config dynamic because the Promtail configuration file you'll use when running your application in a swarm environment will be slightly different than the file you'll use in a Compose environment. In a swarm environment, you'll want to capture different information such as the service

---

5. https://grafana.com/docs/tempo/latest/
6. https://grafana.com/docs/loki/latest/send-data/promtail/pipelines/

logs, which don't exist when running your application using Compose (as you don't have swarm services in a Compose environment).

We've set the target for the config to be /etc/promtail/config.yml. This is the path that the promtail image uses by default to look for its configuration.

Beside defining the config for this service, you'll also need to add one bind mount volume. This is so that you can mount the Docker socket in your promtail containers. Remember that your promtail configuration file has been configured to scrape the Docker socket of the environment that it is run in, and a Docker container doesn't have access to the Docker host's logs by default. So you need to mount the socket in the container, like so:

```
# in compose.yaml
services:
  promtail:
    volumes:
      - /var/run/docker.sock:/var/run/docker.sock:ro
```

Nice. You've set up your Promtail service, and the logs of your Docker containers are now ready to be scraped and pushed to your Loki log store when you run your application in a Compose environment. The next step in setting up the logs is to create the Grafana UI so you can see your logs in one centralized place. You'll do that in the next section.

Define Your Dashboard Visualization Service: Grafana

Grafana is the visualization service that will allow you to see all of the logs for your Docker containers, as well as the metrics that you'll add in the next part of this chapter. It provides charts, graphs, and alerts for the services that you connect to it. To connect a service to Grafana, you use a data source.

A Grafana data source allows you to tell Grafana *where to find your data* and *how to access it*. Each data source in Grafana has a specific plugin that knows how to connect to that type of data source and query it.[7] Once Grafana is connected to a data source, you can use its querying and visualization features to create dashboards that display and analyze the data from that source.

Start by creating your Loki Grafana data source. Create a new folder called grafana in your instrumentation folder with a datasources subfolder nested inside that contains a datasources.yaml file. When creating a data source, you need to configure the name, type, access, and url. We've pre-populated these values for

---

7. https://grafana.com/grafana/plugins/data-source-plugins/

you in the upcoming code snippet. Notice that the URL has the same root as the URL you added to your Promtail configuration file:

```
# in instrumentation/grafana/datasources/datasources.yaml
apiVersion: 1
datasources:
  - name: Loki
    type: loki
    access: proxy
    url: http://loki:3100
    jsonData:
      maxLines: 1000
      manageAlerts: false
```

This tells Grafana that it can find the Loki data source at port 3100 using the loki hostname in the internal Docker network (in the same way that you did with promtail).

Now you need to define your Grafana service. Add a new service to your compose.yaml file called grafana that uses version 9.5.15 of the grafana/grafana image. Then map port 3000 of the container to port 3000 of your host and add the following environment variables, configs, and volumes:

```
# in compose.yaml
  grafana:
    image: grafana/grafana:9.5.15
    environment:
      - GF_PATHS_PROVISIONING=/etc/grafana/provisioning
      - GF_AUTH_ANONYMOUS_ENABLED=true
      - GF_AUTH_ANONYMOUS_ORG_ROLE=Admin
    ports:
      - "3000:3000"
    configs:
      - source: grafana_datasources
        target: /etc/grafana/provisioning/datasources/datasource.yml
    volumes:
      - grafana-storage:/var/lib/grafana
volumes:
  grafana-storage:
configs:
  grafana_datasources:
    file: ./instrumentation/grafana/datasources/datasources.yaml
```

The GF_PATHS_PROVISIONING variable defines the path that Grafana will use to configure itself. Technically, you don't need to set this variable since we're using the default value. But, as you'll see in a moment, it's important that you know the provisioning path that Grafana uses.

Collect Your Application Logs • 365

The GF_AUTH_ANONYMOUS_ENABLED and GF_AUTH_ANONYMOUS_ORG_ROLE environment variables disable the login for the Grafana UI to ease your development process in this chapter.

>
> **Grafana Security in the Real World**
>
> When deploying Grafana to a real production environment, you'd enable the login and create a secure password in your secrets.enc.yaml file inside your secrets folder and then create a new GF_SECURITY_ADMIN_PASSWORD environment variable. Unlike your web and db services, however, this variable cannot be a file path, so you cannot set it to the secret file that would be created with your password once you run your decrypt.sh script. Instead, you'd edit your deploy.sh script to create the environment variable like so: GRAFANA_PASSWORD=$(cat .grafana_password) and then set the compose environment variable like so: GF_SECURITY_ADMIN_PASSWORD=${GRAFANA_PASSWORD}.

The previous snippet also creates a volume: /var/lib/grafana. This is where all of the Grafana settings are saved after reading them from the provisioning folder. This includes data sources, dashboard layouts, as well as any on-the-fly changes you do using the UI. Adding the Grafana data to a volume will allow you to keep the data even if you restart the service.

Lastly, the snippet uses a Docker config to mount your Grafana configuration file inside the grafana service (in the folder that Grafana uses to provision itself).

Great. Now that you've set up your log store (Loki), the service to collect your logs (Promtail), and the UI (Grafana), let's see your log collection in action and run your Compose file in a Compose environment. Run docker compose up, specifying the PROMTAIL_CONFIG to be local so that your promtail service uses the configuration file you created in this section, like so:

```
$ PROMTAIL_CONFIG="local" docker compose up
 ✓ Network kanban_default                      Created        0.0s
 ✓ Volume "kanban_grafana-provisioning"        Created        0.0s
 ✓ Volume "kanban_grafana-storage"             Created        0.0s
 ✓ Volume "kanban_db_data"                     Created        0.0s
 ✓ Container kanban-promtail-1                 Created        0.0s
 ✓ Container kanban-db-1                       Created        0.0s
 ✓ Container kanban-grafana-1                  Created        0.0s
 ✓ Container kanban-loki-1                     Created        0.0s
...
```

Now, visit http://localhost:3000/explore. Select the loki data source in the top left, then the container_name label, and then the name of your web container like so:

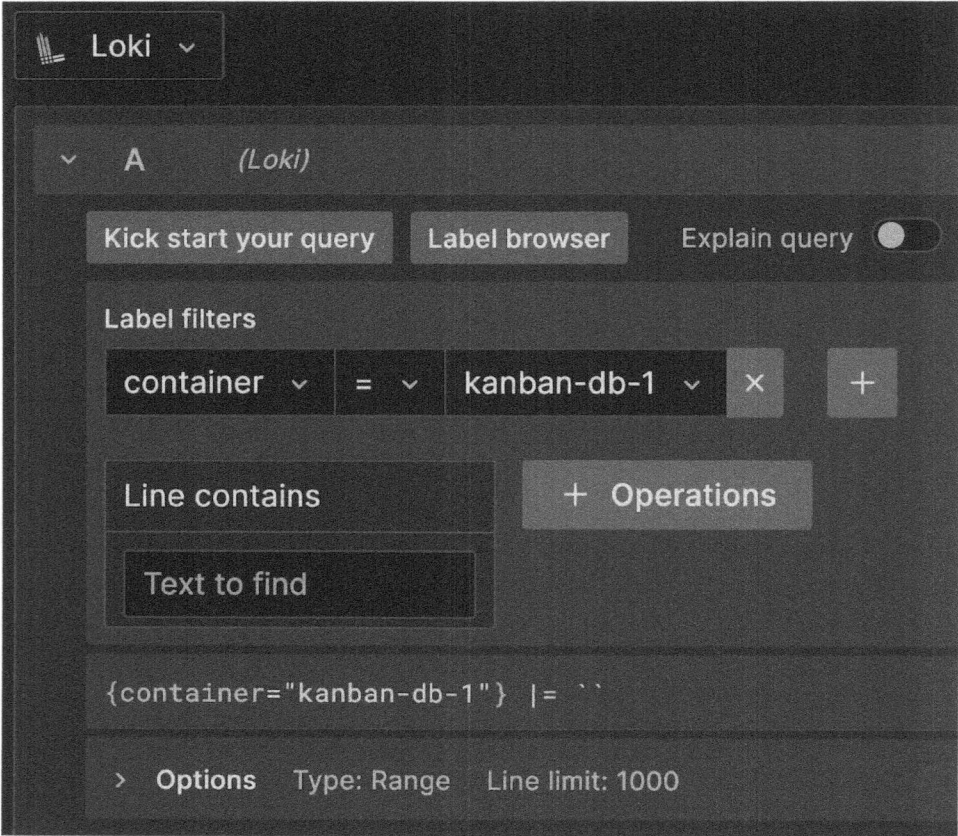

Now press "Run query" in the top right of your screen, and you'll see all of the logs from your db container.

You did it! You have successfully created a logging service and have a centralized place where you can view your logs. Well done. You've made it much easier to debug your application and monitor its behavior. You're one step closer to making your application even more reliable.

As we mentioned earlier, the Promtail configuration will be slightly different in a swarm environment than in a Compose one. This is because you want to capture more logs when running your application in a swarm environment. Being able to log your application in a Compose environment will facilitate your local development environment, and having swarm logging will allow you to log your application in production but also replicate your production environment locally. In the next section, you'll create a new Promtail configuration file to define your swarm scraping configurations.

Add a New Promtail Configuration to Support a Swarm Environment

To adapt your Promtail configuration to efficiently run in a swarm environment, you need to edit your scape_configs key slightly and deploy your promtail service globally. This will enable you to scrape the service logs in your swarm.

To separate your swarm configuration from your Compose configuration, create a new YAML file in your instrumentation/promtail folder called swarm.yaml, and copy over everything in your local.yaml file. But this time, replace your relabel-configs attribute so that your file looks like this:

```yaml
# in instrumentation/promtail/swarm.yaml
positions:
  filename: /tmp/positions.yaml
clients:
  - url: http://loki:3100/loki/api/v1/push
scrape_configs:
  - job_name: "docker_swarm"
    docker_sd_configs:
      - host: unix:///var/run/docker.sock
        refresh_interval: 5s
    relabel_configs:
      - source_labels: [__meta_docker_container_name]
        regex: '^/([^\.]+)\..+'
        target_label: service_name
```

Notice that you haven't needed to change the Loki URL. This is because you're referencing the loki hostname, which is the name of your Loki service (the VIP for that service). Because you're accessing the VIP, Docker Swarm can forward requests to the tasks of a service to accurately capture the logs for all of the service tasks in your swarm.

Now add the deploy attribute to your promtail service in your Compose file and specify that this service should be deployed in global mode, like so:

```yaml
# in compose.yaml
services:
  promtail:
    image: grafana/promtail:2.9.3
    deploy:
      mode: global
```

Deploying your Promtail service in global mode means that each of the nodes in your swarm will have a promtail task. This is important because the docker_sd_configs scrape config can only read the logs of the Docker socket of the node that it deployed in. So, to be able to read the logs of all of the Docker sockets in your swarm, you need to have a promtail task in each swarm node.

> **Promtail Scrape Configs**
>
>
>
> The Promtail documentation states that it uses the same scrape configs as Prometheus.[8] Prometheus has a scrape config that's specific to Docker Swarm environments (dockerswarm_sd_configs), but at the time of writing, this config doesn't work when using Promtail.[9] You'll use that scrape config later on when you set up Prometheus.

OK, you've got your swarm configuration set up. Now test it. Stop your currently running application, start a new swarm, and deploy your stack. Your terminal should look something like this:

```
$ docker compose down -v
...
$ docker swarm init
Swarm initialized: current node (3f6he...) is now a manager.
$ docker stack deploy -c compose.yaml kanban
Creating config kanban_loki
Creating config kanban_grafana_datasources
Creating config kanban_promtail
...
```

In the terminal output you'll see that your configs have been successfully created!

> **Helpful Commands for Docker Configs**
>
>
>
> A couple of useful commands for Docker configs are docker config ls and docker config inspect. These let you list and inspect the configs in a swarm environment. We encourage you to have a look at the documentation and play around with these and other docker config commands.[10]

Now, visit http://localhost:3000 and open the "Label filters" drop-down. Your label filter should now look like this:

---

8. https://grafana.com/docs/loki/latest/send-data/promtail/configuration/#scrape_configs
9. https://prometheus.io/docs/prometheus/latest/configuration/configuration/#dockerswarm_sd_config
10. https://docs.docker.com/engine/reference/commandline/config/

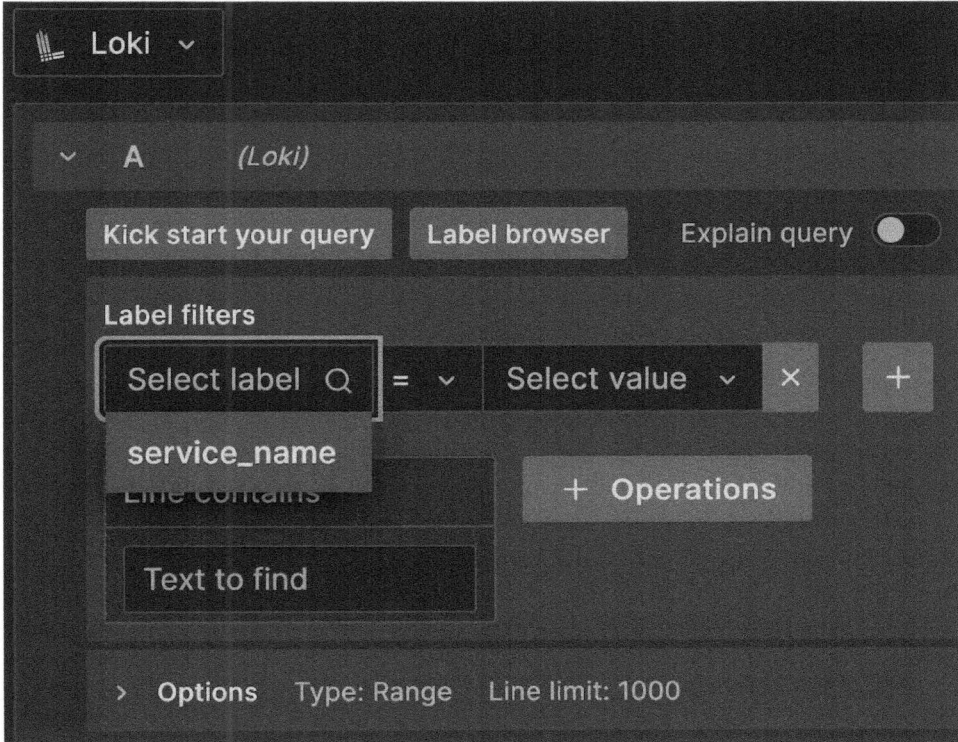

And that's it for the logging. Nice work! You can now see the logs for your application in both Compose and swarm environments. This means that you're able to log your application in both your development and production environments, which will make your life much easier by minimizing debugging time. Figuring out where things went wrong is key to practicing the Kaizen principle and making small, continuous improvements to your application.

In the next section, you'll learn how to monitor the performance of your running application by configuring the default metrics exposed by the main Elixir libraries included in your Phoenix LiveView application.

Configure Default Monitoring Metrics

We mentioned that one of the pillars of instrumentation is monitoring your application. In this section, we'll explore how to monitor an application by implementing metrics. When you implement metrics for your application, you might feel a bit overwhelmed. There are lots of things to measure but which ones are important?

There are generally three different categories of metrics that you can monitor: *application* metrics, *infrastructure* metrics, and *business* metrics. An example of application metrics (in the specific case of an Elixir app) could be the average Ecto query time. Infrastructure metrics can include the host machine's remaining disk space, memory usage, or CPU usage. A business metric is very different depending on the scope of an application, but an example of one for an e-commerce site could be the conversion rate of customers who viewed a product vs. those who bought it. This section will look at application metrics and how you can effectively collect these in an Elixir app.

Elixir has a fantastic library created by Alex Koutmos called prom_ex.[11] PromEx has two main functionalities. First, it collects metrics. Out of the box, it gathers metrics of the BEAM (such as the number of atoms) as well as for the main Elixir libraries like Ecto and Phoenix. You can also use PromEx to create your own custom metrics (which we'll look at in the next chapter). Second, PromEx integrates with Grafana. You can use PromEx to create custom Grafana dashboards and save them as JSON files, which can be sent to the Grafana UI. Defining your Grafana dashboards in PromEx makes them part of your infrastructure-as-code and means that they can be shared easily between environments.

You can think of PromEx in the same way as Promtail—it collects metrics for you but doesn't store them. To store these metrics, you'll need to collect them using Alloy and forward them to Prometheus, a time series database. We'll discuss these two services shortly. PromEx was specifically built for integrating with Prometheus, and they work together seamlessly to collect and store metrics from Elixir libraries.

In this section, you'll use PromEx to collect the metrics that your application's main Elixir libraries produce and expose them at a /metrics endpoint. You'll then configure Prometheus to scrape this endpoint every 5 seconds to retrieve the metrics and store them in its database. After this, you'll link your Prometheus database as a Grafana data source to be able to see the metrics in your centralized UI. Just like with Loki and Promtail, you'll start off doing this in a Compose environment and then will make sure it works in a swarm environment.

Let's start by adding PromEx to your Elixir application and exposing and collecting the metrics for the main Elixir libraries.

---

11. https://github.com/akoutmos/prom_ex

Collect App Metrics with PromEx

The prom_ex library works by using a list of plugins. As we've mentioned, PromEx comes with a set of default plugins that allow you to monitor the main Elixir libraries that are commonly used in an Elixir project. The metrics that PromEx collects are telemetry events published by these libraries. Once these metrics have been gathered, PromEx exposes these metrics at an endpoint (which by default is /metrics) in a format that Prometheus can scrape.

To add prom_ex to your application, add it to your mix.exs file as we've done here:

```elixir
# in mix.exs
  defp deps do
    [
      {:prom_ex, "~> 1.9.0"}
    ]
  end
```

After you've done this, run mix deps.get.

The next steps are to generate the PromEx configuration module, add the default plugins to your application, and include PromEx as a child of your main application supervisor.

To create the configuration module, run the mix prom_ex.gen.config --datasource prometheus command as we've done:

```
$ mix prom_ex.gen.config --datasource prometheus
Successfully wrote out ...kanban/lib/kanban/prom_ex.ex
+--------------------------------------------------------------+
| Be sure to follow the @moduledoc instructions in Kanban.PromEx |
| to complete the PromEx setup process                         |
+--------------------------------------------------------------+
```

Now add the default plugin in your lib/kanban_web/endpoint.ex file like so:

```elixir
# in lib/kanban_web/endpoint.ex
  plug PromEx.Plug, prom_ex_module: Kanban.PromEx
```

Next, add your PromEx module as a child of your application after the Kanban-Web.Endpoint module in your lib/kanban/application.ex file like so:

```elixir
# in lib/kanban/application.ex
    children = [
      # Start the Endpoint (http/https)
      KanbanWeb.Endpoint,
      # Start PromEx
      Kanban.PromEx,
    ]
```

> **Mind the Children**
>
> The order of the children in the supervision tree is important to avoid unnecessary error messages. You need to add first the Endpoint child and then PromEx. For more information, see the PromEx docs.[12]

Great. You've configured PromEx in your application. To test that the metrics are being exposed correctly, start your application locally by running iex -S mix phx.server and go to the /metrics endpoint. You can either do this in your browser, or you can curl the endpoint as we've done here. Remember that you must have a database running to be able to start your application:

```
$ POSTGRES_PORT="5432:5432" docker compose up db -d
...
$ mix ecto.create
...
$ iex -S mix phx.server
...
$ curl -X POST 'http://127.0.0.1:4000/metrics'
# HELP kanban_prom_ex_beam_system_schedulers_online_info
      The number of scheduler threads that are online.
# TYPE kanban_prom_ex_beam_system_schedulers_online_info gauge
kanban_prom_ex_beam_system_schedulers_online_info 8
...
```

Amazing! You can see the metrics exposed by PromEx. You should be able to see the BEAM metric that we've included in our example.

Now that you've checked that the metrics are exposed properly, you're ready to add the Prometheus service to your stack so that you can store these metrics.

Define Your Metrics Database: Prometheus

So far, you've added the prom_ex library to your application. While PromEx collects and collates all of the default metrics for the BEAM and important Elixir libraries, it doesn't save them anywhere. To save them in one centralized place, you need a database. This is where Prometheus comes in.

As we mentioned, Prometheus is a database that saves time-series data. Time-series data is a type of data where the values are recorded at different points in time. Each data point in a time series is associated with a specific timestamp or time period, which means that you can analyze trends, patterns, and behaviors over time.

---

12. https://github.com/akoutmos/prom_ex?tab=readme-ov-file#setting-up-promex

You may be thinking, "isn't log data also time-series data? Why do I need to have two different stores—Loki for logs and Prometheus for metrics?" Technically, yes, log data could also be time-series data if there's a timestamp associated with the log. However, a log is a record of an event or transaction and doesn't inherently have a temporal component. So you can't save all logs inside a time-series database. And time-series data, such as the metric data you're collecting now, cannot be saved to a log store. That's why you need separate data stores—because you're saving two different types of data.

You'll add Prometheus to your application suite using your Docker Compose file, following the same configuration process you used when setting up Loki, Promtail, and Grafana: creating a configuration file and a new Compose service. You'll use the configs Compose key to reference your configuration file and you'll create a volume to persist the saved data.

Start by creating your Prometheus configuration file. This file will set the targets that your prometheus service (that you'll create in a minute) will scrape, as well as the global scrape condition configurations.

To set the scrape conditions, use the global key and set the scrape_interval sub-attribute to be 5s. After this, define the targets that you want to scrape using the scrape_configs key. This key has a list of jobs where each job is a scrape target. Your file should set one target to scrape: the prometheus service itself that will run on port 9090 (the default Prometheus port).

Create a new file called local.yaml inside a new prometheus subfolder within your instrumentation folder. Then add the following code:

```
# in instrumentation/prometheus/local.yaml

# global configurations
global:
  scrape_interval: 5s

# targets to scrape
scrape_configs:
  - job_name: "prometheus"
    static_configs:
      - targets: ["localhost:9090"]
```

We've specified that the target for the prometheus job is localhost:9090 rather than prometheus:9090 to avoid unnecessary network hops, given that this service wants to access itself.

You may be wondering how Prometheus will know which endpoint it needs to access in order to scrape the metrics. The previous snippet never specified the /metrics endpoint anywhere. There's a metrics_path sub-attribute for a scrape_configs job that defines the endpoint that Prometheus should use. The default value for this is /metrics, so you don't need to specify anything. You can see more information and other default settings in the Prometheus documentation.[13]

Next, add Prometheus to your application stack by defining a new prometheus service in your Compose file. The image you'll use for this service is version v2.45.2 of the prom/prometheus image. We've pre-populated the port assignment, volumes, and configs that you need in the following code snippet. Copy these changes into your compose.yaml file, and then we'll go through each part:

```yaml
# in compose.yaml
services:
  prometheus:
    image: prom/prometheus:v2.45.2
    ports:
      - "9090:9090"
    configs:
      - source: prometheus
        target: /etc/prometheus/prometheus.yml
    command:
      - --web.enable-remote-write-receiver
      - --config.file=/etc/prometheus/prometheus.yml
    volumes:
      - prometheus-data:/prometheus
volumes:
  prometheus-data:
configs:
  prometheus:
    file: ./instrumentation/prometheus/local.yaml
```

As you can see, we've exposed port 9090 of the prometheus service. This is so that you can check that your Prometheus targets have been set up properly, using the basic UI that Prometheus offers. We've then created a config that points to your configuration file. This file will be mounted into the prometheus container at the path /etc/prometheus/prometheus.yml, which is the default Prometheus config path. We've also specified the command attribute so that you can enable a remote write receiver. This is so that your alloy service (that you'll create in a moment) can write the metrics that it scrapes from your Elixir app to your Prometheus database. Lastly, we've created a prometheus-data named volume to keep the data that Prometheus saves.

---

13. https://prometheus.io/docs/prometheus/latest/configuration/configuration/#scrape_config

Nice, you've finished setting up your Prometheus database and configuring Prometheus to scrape its own metrics. Now you need to configure your Alloy service that will scrape the metrics that PromEx exposes in your Elixir app and forward them to Prometheus.

Scrape PromEx Metrics and Forward Them to Prometheus

As you saw in the previous section, Prometheus itself does allow you to scrape endpoints and save that data to its database. However, its integration with Docker Swarm doesn't work properly at the time of writing. Luckily, you can use Grafana's Alloy service which emulates Prometheus' scraping behavior and forwards the data it scrapes to remote databases, which in your case will be Prometheus.

You'll set up your Alloy configuration in the same way as Promtail and Prometheus: with a configuration file, a new docker service, and a new Docker config.

Create a new folder called alloy inside your instrumentation folder and then a new file called local.alloy inside the alloy folder. Add the following code into that file:

```
// in instrumentation/alloy/local.alloy
discovery.docker "kanban" {
  host = "unix:///var/run/docker.sock"
  refresh_interval = "15s"

  filter {
    name = "status"
    values = ["running"]
  }
  filter {
    name = "name"
    values = ["web"]
  }
}
discovery.relabel "use_container_name_not_docker_ip" {
  targets = discovery.docker.kanban.targets
  rule {
    source_labels = ["__meta_docker_container_name"]
    regex = "/(.*)"
    target_label = "instance"
  }
}
```

```
// in instrumentation/alloy/local.alloy
discovery.docker "kanban" {
  host = "unix:///var/run/docker.sock"
  refresh_interval = "15s"

  filter {
    name = "status"
    values = ["running"]
  }
  filter {
    name = "name"
    values = ["web"]
  }
}
discovery.relabel "use_container_name_not_docker_ip" {
  targets = discovery.docker.kanban.targets

  rule {
    source_labels = ["__meta_docker_container_name"]
    regex = "/(.*)"
    target_label = "instance"
  }
}
```

As you'll notice, .alloy files use a declarative language syntax that has block names and attributes, similar to the HCL syntax that you're already familiar with. Unlike HCL, which refers to its blocks as resources, these blocks are called *components* in .alloy files. The configuration of an alloy component is as follows:

```
BLOCK_NAME "BLOCK_LABEL" {
  IDENTIFIER = EXPRESSION // an attribute

  NESTED_BLOCK_NAME {
    // nested block body that can contain attributes
  }
}
```

The code in your local.alloy file configures the following four components:

1. discovery.docker: Defines the targets that you want to scrape. It specifies that Alloy should scrape any running containers with the name web from the Docker socket.
2. discovery.relabel: Relabels the data that scraping the target specified by the discovery.docker component so that you can see the container name in the PromEx UI. This is the same behavior as the relabel_configs attribute in your Promtail configuration files.

3. prometheus.remote_write: Configures the URL of your Prometheus database which Alloy should use to send the metrics it scrapes.
4. prometheus.scrape: Borrows the scraping behavior of Prometheus and actually scrapes the metrics from the target specified by the targets attribute every 5 seconds, after which it forwards the metrics to the remote write URL you configured. Notice that the target is the output of the discovery.relabel component, meaning that the metric data that's sent will already be relabeled. Again, you've not had to specify the scrape path (/metrics) as this is a default attribute of the prometheus.scrape component.

Now, add Alloy to your Compose file by adding the following alloy service that uses version v1.1.1 of the grafana/alloy image. This service has the Docker socket mounted to it as a bind volume and a Docker config that points to your configuration file:

```yaml
# in compose.yaml
services:
  alloy:
    image: grafana/alloy:v1.1.1
    configs:
      - source: alloy
        target: /etc/alloy/config.alloy
    volumes:
      - /var/run/docker.sock:/var/run/docker.sock
configs:
  alloy:
    file: ./instrumentation/alloy/${ALLOY_CONFIG-swarm}.alloy
```

You'll notice that the config uses an ALLOY_CONFIG environment variable to allow you to set the configuration file but defaults to a file in the path called instrumentation/alloy/swarm.alloy that you'll create in a minute.

Great! You're all set up to scrape your Elixir app's metrics and save them to Prometheus. Let's see this in action by checking the Prometheus UI.

Rebuild your kanban:latest Docker image so that it includes your PromEx changes, run your application by executing docker compose up with the WEB_IMAGE, PROMTAIL_CONFIG='local', and ALLOY_CONFIG="local" environment variables, and then visit http://localhost:9090/graph and type kanban into the input search. This will show you a list of all of the metrics in the Prometheus database that PromEx has scraped from your kanban application, as you can see on the next page.

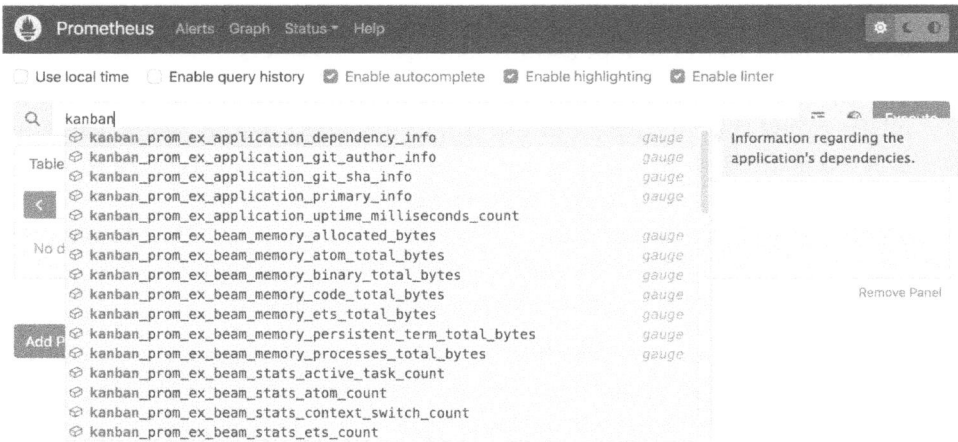

Fantastic! You've successfully added Alloy to your application to scrape the metrics of the main Elixir libraries exposed by PromEx and to save them to a Prometheus database in a Compose environment. Let's integrate this with Grafana and see these metrics displayed visually in a dashboard.

Integrate PromEx and Prometheus with Grafana

Now that you have your prometheus and alloy services up and running and scraping metrics from your application, the next step is to link these metrics to your Grafana UI so you can see visual representations of this data. There are two parts to this. First you must create a new Prometheus Grafana data source, similar to your Loki Grafana data source, in order to share the metric data with Grafana. Then, you must configure PromEx to upload the default Grafana dashboards for the main Elixir libraries.

We mentioned that PromEx has two main functionalities: collecting metrics and uploading Grafana dashboards. Just as PromEx comes out of the box with the configuration to collect the metrics for the main Elixir libraries, it also comes with JSON templates for Grafana dashboards for these libraries. If you wish to see them, they are inside the deps/prom_ex/priv folder.

To integrate PromEx and Prometheus with Grafana, you have to follow these steps:

1. Create a new Prometheus Grafana data source.
2. Disable the authentication type that PromEx uses in your grafana service to remove the need for authentication when uploading new dashboards. (We don't recommend disabling authentication in live production environments, but doing so will ease your learning in this chapter).

3. Upload the default Grafana dashboard templates that PromEx offers to Grafana to be able to visualize the data from Prometheus.

To create your new data source, add the following code under your current Loki data source in your instrumentation/grafana/datasources/datasources.yaml file:

```yaml
# in instrumentation/grafana/datasources/datasources.yaml
apiVersion: 1
datasources:
  - name: prometheus
    type: prometheus
    orgId: 1
    uid: P1809F7CD0C75ACF3
    url: http://prometheus:9090
    basicAuth: false
    version: 1
```

This snippet provides Grafana with the URL it can use to find the data it should import and disables the basic authentication for Prometheus.

Now, disable basic authentication in Grafana so that you can easily upload your PromEx dashboards. You can do this by setting the GF_AUTH_BASIC_ENABLED environment variable in your grafana service to false. The authentication disabling environment variables you added to your grafana service earlier in this chapter were specifically for the UI. This new one is specifically for the PromEx-Grafana integration. You can see the change you have to make here:

```yaml
# in compose.yaml
services:
  grafana:
    image: grafana/grafana:9.5.15
    environment:
      - GF_PATHS_PROVISIONING=/etc/grafana/provisioning
      - GF_AUTH_ANONYMOUS_ENABLED=true
      - GF_AUTH_ANONYMOUS_ORG_ROLE=Admin
      - GF_AUTH_BASIC_ENABLED=false
```

Now, configure your prom_ex library in your Elixir application to upload the default dashboards to Grafana. To do this, uncomment the default metric plugins and their dashboards in your lib/kanban/prom_ex.ex, as shown on the next page:

```elixir
# in lib/kanban/prom_ex.ex
defmodule Kanban.PromEx do
  @impl true
  def plugins do
    [
      Plugins.Application,
      Plugins.Beam,
      {
        Plugins.Phoenix,
        router: KanbanWeb.Router,
        endpoint: KanbanWeb.Endpoint
      },
      Plugins.Ecto,
      Plugins.PhoenixLiveView
    ]
  end

  @impl true
  def dashboards do
    [
      {:prom_ex, "application.json"},
      {:prom_ex, "beam.json"},
      {:prom_ex, "phoenix.json"},
      {:prom_ex, "ecto.json"},
      {:prom_ex, "phoenix_live_view.json"}
    ]
  end
end
```

Lastly, add the following code to your config/config.exs file to tell your application where it should be uploading the dashboards to:

```elixir
# in config/config.exs
config :kanban, Kanban.PromEx,
  grafana: [
    host: "http://grafana:3000",
    upload_dashboards_on_start: true
  ]
```

Great. You're ready to start your application and see the default metric dashboards in Grafana in a Compose environment. Rebuild your Docker image and restart your application using docker compose up. Your terminal should look similar to ours:

```
$ docker build -t "kanban:latest"
...
$ WEB_IMAGE="kanban:latest" \
  PROMTAIL_CONFIG="local" \
  ALLOY_CONFIG="local" \
  docker compose up
```

```
...
[info] Access KanbanWeb.Endpoint at https://example.com
[info] PromEx.DashboardUploader successfully uploaded
       /app/lib/prom_ex-1.9.0/priv/application.json.eex to Grafana.
[info] PromEx.DashboardUploader successfully uploaded
       /app/lib/prom_ex-1.9.0/priv/beam.json.eex to Grafana.
[info] PromEx.DashboardUploader successfully uploaded
       /app/lib/prom_ex-1.9.0/priv/phoenix.json.eex to Grafana.
[info] PromEx.DashboardUploader successfully uploaded
       /app/lib/prom_ex-1.9.0/priv/ecto.json.eex to Grafana.
[info] PromEx.DashboardUploader successfully uploaded
       /app/lib/prom_ex-1.9.0/priv/phoenix_live_view.json.eex to
       Grafana.
[info] PromEx.DashboardUploader successfully uploaded
       /app/lib/kanban-0.1.0/priv/grafana_dashboards/infrastructure.json
       to Grafana
```

You can see from this terminal interaction that PromEx has uploaded the default dashboards that it comes with. Visit http://localhost:3000/dashboards in your browser to see the following list of these different dashboards:

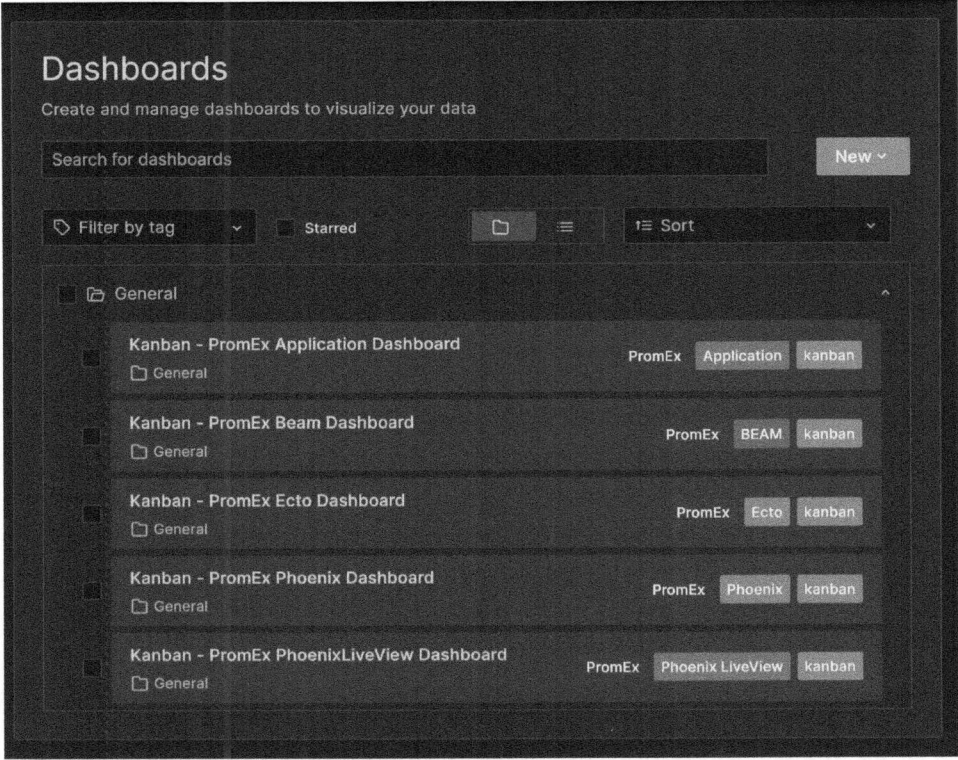

Now select the PromEx Application Dashboard option in your browser. You should see a screen like the one at the top of the next page.

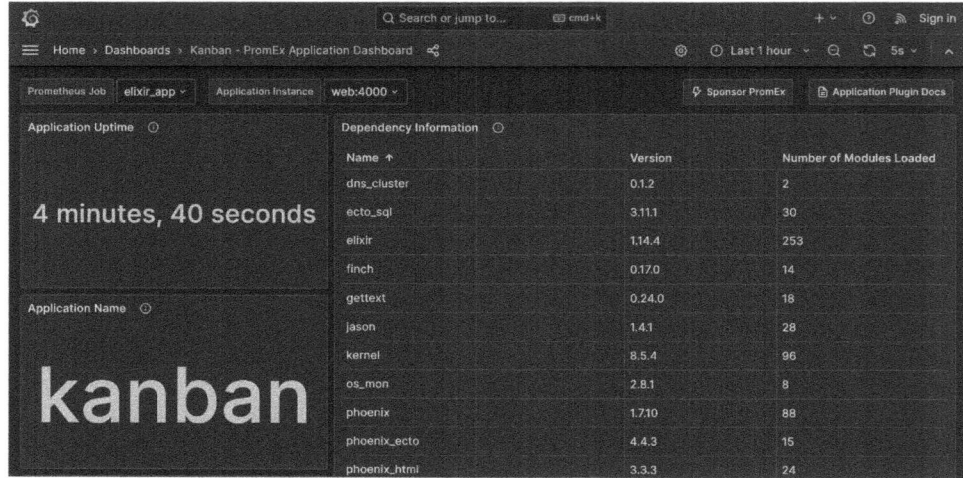

Well done! You've successfully collected the default metrics exposed by Elixir's main libraries, saved them to a Prometheus database, and configured PromEx to send the default dashboards to Grafana. Now that you've done this, you'll be able to see the metrics collected by the main Elixir libraries visually in various dashboards when running your application in a Compose environment. This dashboard is helpful, for example, as it shows the uptime of your application and when it was last deployed, among many other things. We encourage you to go through the different dashboards to see what they do.

Great work so far. What you've implemented is suitable for your local development environment but not for your swarm production environment. Like with Promtail, you must adapt your Alloy configuration slightly so that it works when running your application as part of a Docker Swarm. We'll look at how to do this in the next section.

Add a New Alloy Configuration to Support a Swarm Environment

When running your application in a Compose environment, there's only one instance that runs on port 4000 of your machine (or whatever machine it's being run on). However, as you know, when you run your application in a Docker Swarm, you'll have multiple replicas. This means that there are multiple hosts to consider when collecting your metrics. For this reason, you have to create a new Alloy configuration file that uses a different discovery component.

Create a new file inside your instrumentation/alloy folder called swarm.alloy. Like your local.alloy file, this Alloy configuration should scrape its targets every five seconds. We've created the configuration file for you. Copy it into your new instrumentation/alloy/swarm.alloy file, and we'll go through it:

```
discovery.dockerswarm "kanban" {
  host = "unix:///var/run/docker.sock"
  role = "tasks"
  refresh_interval = "15s"

  filter {
    name = "desired-state"
    values = ["running", "accepted"]
  }
  filter {
    name = "service"
    values = ["kanban_web"]
  }
}
discovery.relabel "use_swarm_node_not_internal_ip" {
  targets = discovery.dockerswarm.kanban.targets

  rule {
    source_labels = ["__meta_dockerswarm_node_id"]
    target_label = "instance"
  }
}
prometheus.remote_write "kanban" {
  endpoint {
    url = "http://prometheus:9090/api/v1/write"
  }
}
prometheus.scrape "kanban" {
  targets    = discovery.relabel.use_swarm_node_not_internal_ip.output
  forward_to = [prometheus.remote_write.kanban.receiver]
  scrape_interval = "5s"
  scrape_timeout = "5s"
}
```

The prometheus.scrape and prometheus.remote_write components are the same as your local.alloy file. Rather than using the discovery.docker component, this file uses the discovery.dockerswarm component to set the scrape target to be all of the tasks of the kanban_web service. The discovery.relabel component specifies that the instance label you see in Grafana should be the swarm node ID.

Let's test this new swarm configuration. Start a new swarm locally and deploy your stack. Your terminal interaction should look something like this:

```
$ docker compose down -v; docker swarm leave --force; docker swarm init
...
$ WEB_IMAGE="kanban:latest" docker stack deploy -c compose.yaml kanban
...
```

Now, visit http://localhost:3000/dashboards and select the PromEx Application Dashboard option again. Notice that the dashboard is the same, but this time it has a different Application Instance label—your swarm node IDs.

Congratulations! You've finished setting up PromEx and Prometheus. You can now collect the metrics exposed by Elixir's main libraries and visualize them in a centralized UI (Grafana) in both a swarm and Compose environment. This means that you can successfully monitor your application's behavior in production. Not only will this let you see errors as and when they happen, but being able to replicate your production metric logging system in your local environment will make it extremely easy to create new metrics or debug current metrics that don't work as expected.

You can now close the "Implement Basic Instrumentation" issue that you created in Chapter 2. To do this, create a new branch, commit the code you've written in this chapter, and create a PR with closes #ISSUE_ID in the description. cd into your environments/production folder and create your infrastructure. Then merge your PR and wait for your CI to finish running. Before moving on to the summary section of this chapter, remember to destroy your production infrastructure.

What Have You Learned?

You now know why instrumentation is an integral part of the software delivery process and how logging and adding metrics to your application will help you not only locate errors or bugs and reduce downtime but also implement the Kaizen principle of making small, ongoing changes. You understand that, when instrumenting an application, you need three different services: a service to collect the logs/metrics, a service to store the logs/metrics, and a service to visualize the logs/metrics. When choosing an instrumentation stack, we hope you'll recall the importance of environment integrity—this will allow you to speed up the metric-collection process and more easily debug your instrumentation setup. You should now feel confident in owning the basic instrumentation stage of an application.

At this point, you only know how to see the default metrics exported by Elixir's main libraries. This is useful, but what happens if you want to create your own metric that's specific to your application? Or what if you want to be alerted when certain metrics are collected, such as when the average CPU of all of your EC2 instances is consistently high? We'll discuss both of these in the next chapter, where you'll create your own PromEx plugin and Grafana alert.

The Extra Mile

If you wish to deepen your knowledge of the themes we've covered in this chapter and refine your BEAMOps developer superpowers, we've created a task for you to do:

1. Throughout this chapter you've disabled the authentication for the Grafana UI. Add in the authentication to make Grafana more secure.

CHAPTER 12

Create a Custom PromEx Metric and Grafana Alert

In the previous chapter, we talked about instrumentation—the last essential component to delivering a reliable software application. You learned how two foundational pillars of instrumentation—logging and monitoring—allow you to quickly spot failures and practice the Kaizen principle of making small, ongoing changes. You implemented logging using Loki and Promtail, and you handled application monitoring using Prometheus and PromEx. You also visualized both the logging and metrics locally inside Grafana.

In this chapter, we'll delve deeper into monitoring your application. You'll first create your own custom PromEx infrastructure metric, which will allow you to measure the average CPU usage of all of your EC2 instances. This is the same metric that your Auto Scaling group monitors to decide if it needs to scale up or down. Next, you'll create a Grafana alert that will send you an email any time the average CPU has been above 40% for over one minute, and another email when the CPU spike is resolved and the average drops consistently below 40%.

You'll first implement these features locally, using your application. Then, you'll deploy our BEAMOps Kanban application to your AWS production environment and see how the email alerts are sent when you stress your Auto Scaling group.

By the end of this chapter, you'll be able to close the last two instrumentation issues that you created in Chapter 2!

Let's jump in and have you create your own CPU metric with PromEx.

Implement Your Own PromEx Metric and Grafana Dashboard

First, let's quickly recap the key points about metrics from the previous chapter. Metrics are defined using PromEx plugins. They are collected and exposed at the /metrics endpoint of your application. Prometheus scrapes the data at this endpoint and saves the metrics to its database. Grafana then links to Prometheus using a data source and PromEx uploads the JSON dashboards (defined in your main PromEx module) to Grafana, which allows you to visualize the metrics.

In this section, you'll create your own metric that measures the average CPU usage of the different host machines that your application runs on (that is, your local machine or your EC2 instances). You'll then create a new Grafana dashboard and add it to your PromEx dashboard list to visualize that data in the Grafana UI. Saving your dashboard to your PromEx configuration means that your dashboard will be available in all environments, demonstrating environment integrity.

To create your custom metric and dashboard you'll do the following:

1. Implement a PromEx plugin to collect the average CPU usage data.
2. Add the custom plugin to your current list of PromEx plugins.
3. Create a custom dashboard layout manually in the Grafana UI.
4. Download this dashboard as a JSON template.
5. Add your custom Grafana JSON dashboard template to your PromEx configuration.

Let's go through these steps one by one.

Create Your CPU Usage PromEx Plugin

Your goal in creating a metric that measures the average CPU usage of the machines running your application is to measure the performance of your application. Of course, there are many other metrics that you could implement, but we chose to demonstrate this one because it's the same metric that your Auto Scaling group monitors. Because of this, you can use the /infrastructure page of our Kanban application (that you saw at the end of Chapter 10), press the Stress Cluster button, and see what happens when you stress your application.

To create your PromEx plugin, you first need to create the function that gets the average CPU data.

Write the Function to Get the Average CPU Usage

As you know, your Auto Scaling group monitors the average CPU usage of EC2 instances in the group using CloudWatch and the AWS logging and metrics service. To collect the average CPU usage of the machines running your application, you'll create two different functions. One function will be used when your application is run in development to fake the monitoring of the CPU usage of your local machine. The other option will be used when your application is run in production to query the AWS CloudWatch API and display the CPU usage of each EC2 instance in your cluster.

Faking production functionalities in development will decouple your data sources and allow you to work on frontend changes without needing to make real API calls. This will speed up your development time and make it easier and smoother for multiple members of your team to work at the same time.

AWS Limits on Free Requests

The AWS API has a rate limiting of the number of free requests you can do per month (one million), so re-creating CloudWatch services in Grafana in production isn't the best solution. However, we've chosen to use the CloudWatch API (rather than manually getting the CPU usage of the host machine) for learning purposes so that you can accurately see the metrics that your Auto Scaling group is reacting to. Just remember to destroy your infrastructure when you're done.

To separate the development and production implementations of getting the CPU usage metric, you'll use a repository. A repository maps to an underlying data store, which is controlled by an adapter. You'll implement one adapter for development and another for production. To create your repository, create a new file called aws_repo.ex inside your lib/kanban folder. Then copy in the following code:

```
# in lib/kanban/aws_repo.ex

defmodule Kanban.AwsRepo do
  @callback get_cpu_average(instance_id :: String.t()) ::
              {:ok, float()} | {:error, term()}
  @callback get_self_instance_id() :: {:ok, String.t()} | {:error, String.t()}

  @spec get_cpu_average(instance_id :: String.t()) ::
          {:ok, [non_neg_integer()]} | {:error, term()}
  def get_cpu_average(instance_id) do
```

```elixir
    adapter().get_cpu_average(instance_id)
  end

  @spec get_self_instance_id() :: {:ok, String.t()} | {:error, String.t()}
  def get_self_instance_id do
    adapter().get_self_instance_id()
  end

  defp adapter,
    do:
      :kanban
      |> Application.fetch_env!(__MODULE__)
      |> Keyword.fetch!(:adapter)
end
```

As you can see, this module has an adapter function, which fetches the adapter that's configured for the environment in which your application is being run. This adapter will be specified in the different config files in your config folder. You may be wondering why we've created this adapter configuration as a function, rather than setting it when the application compiles. This is because we want you to be able to override the adapter at runtime. You'll see why this is useful later on.

In addition to the adapter configuration, this module has a get_cpu_average function that takes an instance ID as an argument and returns the result of calling the get_cpu_average function of the adapter. It also has a get_self_instance_id function that calls the get_self_instance_id of that same adapter.

Let's first focus on the development adapter. To create your development adapter, create a new folder inside lib/kanban called aws_repo. Inside that, create a new file called fixture_adapter.ex. Then copy in the following code:

```elixir
# in lib/kanban/aws_repo/fixture_adapter.ex
defmodule Kanban.AwsRepo.FixtureAdapter do
  @behaviour Kanban.AwsRepo

  alias Kanban.AwsRepo

  @impl AwsRepo
  def get_cpu_average(_instance_id) do
    {:ok, Enum.random(1..99) + 0.123456}
  end

  @impl AwsRepo
  def get_self_instance_id do
    {:ok, "i-09ba9852c02d92e38"}
  end
end
```

This module is called FixtureAdapter because it uses fixed/test data: the get_cpu_average function returns a random float between 1 and 100, and get_self_instance_id returns a hard-coded instance ID.

To use this fixture adapter in your development environment, and to set it as the default adapter for all environments, add the following to your config/config.exs file:

```
# in config/config.exs
config :kanban, Kanban.AwsRepo, adapter: Kanban.AwsRepo.FixtureAdapter
```

Great. At the moment, when you can call the get_cpu_average function, you'll always get a random CPU value.

Now let's implement the function that you'll use in production. To create this function, you'll create a new adapter that will call the AWS API to get real CPU usage percentages for your EC2 instances. To create this adapter, create a new file called aws_adapter.ex in your lib/kanban/aws_repo folder and copy in the following code:

```
# in lib/kanban/aws_repo/aws_adapter.ex
defmodule Kanban.AwsRepo.AwsAdapter do
  @behaviour Kanban.AwsRepo

  import SweetXml

  alias Kanban.AwsRepo

  @base_url "http://169.254.169.254"

  @impl AwsRepo
  def get_cpu_average(instance_id) do
    action = :get_metric_statistics

    action_string =
      action
      |> Atom.to_string()
      |> Macro.camelize()

    start_time =
      DateTime.utc_now()
      |> Timex.shift(minutes: -5)
      |> DateTime.truncate(:second)
      |> DateTime.to_iso8601()

    end_time =
      DateTime.utc_now()
      |> DateTime.truncate(:second)
      |> DateTime.to_iso8601()
```

```elixir
    %ExAws.Operation.Query{
      action: action,
      path: "/",
      params: %{
        "Action" => action_string,
        "Dimensions.member.1.Name" => "InstanceId",
        "Dimensions.member.1.Value" => instance_id,
        "EndTime" => end_time,
        "MetricName" => "CPUUtilization",
        "Namespace" => "AWS/EC2",
        "Period" => 5,
        "StartTime" => start_time,
        "Statistics.member.1" => "Average",
        "Version" => "2010-08-01"
      },
      content_encoding: "identity",
      service: :monitoring,
      parser: &ExAws.Utils.identity/2
    }
    |> ExAws.request()
    |> case do
      {:ok, %{body: xml_body}} ->
        {:ok, parse_cpu_average(xml_body)}

      {:error, reason} ->
        {:error, reason}
    end
  end

  @impl AwsRepo
  def get_self_instance_id do
    url = "#{@base_url}/latest/meta-data/instance-id"

    with {:ok, aws_token} <- get_aws_token(),
         {:ok, %Req.Response{body: body}} <-
           Req.get(url, headers: [{"X-aws-ec2-metadata-token", aws_token}]) do
      {:ok, body}
    else
      {:error, error} ->
        {:error, "Failed to retrieve self instance id, error: #{inspect(error)}"}
    end
  end
```

```
  defp parse_cpu_average(xml_body) do
    xml_body
    |> SweetXml.parse()
    |> SweetXml.xpath(~x"//Datapoints/member"l,
      average: ~x"./Average/text()"f
    )
    |> Enum.reduce({0, 0}, fn %{average: average}, {n, acc} ->
      {n + 1, acc + average}
    end)
    |> then(fn {n, acc} ->
      if {n, acc} == {0, 0} do
        0
      else
        acc / n
      end
    end)
  end

  defp get_aws_token do
    url = "#{@base_url}/latest/api/token"
    headers = [{"X-aws-ec2-metadata-token-ttl-seconds", "21600"}]

    case Req.put(url, headers: headers) do
      {:ok, %Req.Response{body: body}} ->
        {:ok, body}

      {:error, error} ->
        {:error, "Failed to retrieve AWS token, error: #{inspect(error)}"}
    end
  end
end
```

This adapter has the same two functions as your development adapter: get_cpu_average and get_self_instance_id. However, both of these functions call different endpoints of the AWS API.

The get_cpu_average function uses two external libraries—ExAWS[1] and Timex[2] (which you'll add to your mix.exs file in a moment)—to make a GetMetricStatistics call to the AWS CloudWatch API. This get_cpu_average function uses the ExAws module to get the average CPU of a specific EC2 instance over the 5 minutes before the function is called with the help of the Timex module. The AWS API returns its values in XML, so the get_cpu_average function calls a parse_cpu_average function. This function uses the SweetXml[3] library to parse the XML and extract the average CPU data points. It then gets the average of all provided CPU

---

1. https://hexdocs.pm/ex_aws/ExAws.html
2. https://hexdocs.pm/timex/Timex.html
3. https://hexdocs.pm/sweet_xml/SweetXml.html

measurements by taking their sum and dividing it by the number of measurements: acc / n.

The get_self_instance_id function uses the exact same logic as your launch_node.sh script. It calls the internal IP address of the instance in which the application is being run to get an authentication token and then calls the latest/metadata/instance-id endpoint to retrieve the instance ID. It uses the Req[4] library to parse the API request.

For this adapter to work, add the ex_aws, sweet_xml, and req libraries to your project like so:

```
# in mix.exs

  defp deps do
    [
      {:ex_aws, "~> 2.1"},
      {:timex, "~> 3.0"},
      {:sweet_xml, "~> 0.6"},
      {:req, "~> 0.5.7"}
    ]
  end
```

Run mix deps.get. Then, configure the ExAws module in your config/config.exs file like so:

```
# in config/config.exs

config :ex_aws,
  access_key_id: [{:system, "AWS_ACCESS_KEY_ID"}, :instance_role],
  secret_access_key: [{:system, "AWS_SECRET_ACCESS_KEY"}, :instance_role],
  region: "eu-west-1",
  jason_codec: Jason,
  debug_requests: true
```

Excellent. The last thing to do is to update your config/prod.exs file so that your production environment uses this AWS adapter rather than your development (fixture) adapter. To do this, add the following to your config/prod.exs file:

```
# in config/prod.exs

config :kanban, Kanban.AwsRepo, adapter: Kanban.AwsRepo.AwsAdapter
```

You may be wondering why we added the ExAWS configuration to your config/config.exs file and not your config/prod.exs file. This is because we want all environments to have access to your AWS credentials so that you can override the adapter that's being used at runtime. To enable the adapter to be set at runtime, add the following code to your config/runtime.exs file:

---

4. https://hexdocs.pm/req/Req.html

```
# in config/runtime.exs
if System.get_env("USE_AWS_FIXTURE_ADAPTER", "false") == "true" do
  config :kanban, Kanban.AwsRepo,
    adapter: Kanban.AwsRepo.FixtureAdapter

  config :kanban, Kanban.AwsRepo.AwsAdapter, base_url: "http://localhost:1338"
end
```

You'll notice that this if clause uses a USE_AWS_FIXTURE_ADAPTER environment variable, which will allow you to run your application when the MIX_ENV is prod, but using the fixture adapter. You'll see why this is useful at the end of this section, when it comes to running your application.

Fantastic! You've written two adapters: one to mock the CPU usage of your host machine that you can use in development and another for you to use in production that calls the AWS API.

We recommend that you follow this repository/adapter pattern anytime you want to implement data sources that are environment specific. Doing so eases frontend development and helps keep your code clean and DRY. It's one of many great design patterns that our friend and Elixir engineer Ricardo García Vega has taught us.

Now that you've written the functions to get the average CPU usage, the next step is to create the PromEx plugin so that you can expose your CPU metric and add it to a Grafana dashboard.

Write Your PromEx Plugin

With PromEx plugins, there are three different types of metrics that you can collect:

- event metrics: a metric that's collected when a certain event is triggered.
- polling metrics: a metric that should be collected every X milliseconds.
- manual metrics: a general metric function that will be collected on demand.

In this case, you're interested in creating a *polling metric*, as you want to regularly gather the CPU usage of the host machine. If you look at the PromEx docs,[5] you'll see that to create a PromEx plugin that implements a polling metric, you need to create a module that has the following three functions:

1. A public function that collects the CPU usage metric.
2. A private function that expects a poll rate as an argument and creates a Polling struct.

---

5. https://hexdocs.pm/prom_ex/writing-promex-plugins.html#adding-polling-metrics

3. A polling_metrics public function that lists the polling functions that you wish to call.

Let's start by creating the first two functions in this list. Create a prom_ex folder inside your lib/kanban folder, and inside that, create a file called cpu_plug-in.ex. We've defined the module, called Kanban.PromEx.CpuPlugin for you, and we've written the first two functions. Copy the following into your new file:

```elixir
# in lib/kanban/prom_ex/cpu_plugin.ex
defmodule Kanban.PromEx.CpuPlugin do
  use       PromEx.Plugin
  alias     Kanban.AwsRepo
  require   Logger

  @cpu_event [:prom_ex, :plugin, :os, :cpu]

  defp cpu_metrics(poll_rate) do
    Polling.build(
      :os_cpu_polling_events,
      poll_rate,
      {__MODULE__, :execute_cpu_metrics, []},
      [
        last_value(
          [:cpu, :util],
          event_name: @cpu_event,
          description: "The total CPU usage of the host system in seconds",
          measurement: :util,
          unit: :second,
          tags: [:instance_id]
        )
      ]
    )
  end

  @doc false
  def execute_cpu_metrics do
    with {:ok, instance_id} <- AwsRepo.get_self_instance_id(),
         {:ok, cpu_average} <- AwsRepo.get_cpu_average(instance_id) do
      :telemetry.execute(
        @cpu_event,
        %{util: cpu_average},
        %{instance_id: instance_id}
      )
    else
      {:error, error} ->
        Logger.error("Error getting cpu usage: #{inspect(error)}")
        :telemetry.execute(@cpu_event, %{util: 0.0}, %{})
    end
  end
end
```

The execute_cpu_metrics function represents the first of three functions your module must have—a public function that collects the CPU usage metric by calling the get_cpu_average function of the AWSRepo and returning a telemetry metric. Remember that the get_cpu_average function will be different depending on what environment your application is being run in (and therefore which adapter it is using).

The cpu_metrics function represents the second of three functions your module must have—a private function that builds a Polling struct that defines how to get the average CPU usage. Given a poll rate, it calls the execute_cpu_metrics function. Polling.build is a function[6] provided by the prom_ex library. We've configured it to use the last_value telemetry metrics function[7] to always return the most recent value of the CPU usage.

Great. Now add the third and final function your module must have—the polling_metrics/1 public function. Add it to the top of your Kanban.PromEx.CpuPlugin module to define the polling metrics that you want to collect—the cpu_metrics function you just created. You can see how to do this here:

```
# in lib/kanban/prom_ex/cpu_plugin.ex
defmodule Kanban.PromEx.CpuPlugin do
  @impl true
  def polling_metrics(opts) do
    poll_rate = Keyword.get(opts, :poll_rate, 1_000)

    [
      cpu_metrics(poll_rate)
    ]
  end
end
```

As you can see, this calls your cpu_metrics function with a default poll rate of 1 second.

Fantastic, you've defined your plugin! The next thing to do is add your plugin to your PromEx plugin list and see it in action.

Add Your Custom CPU Usage Plugin to Your PromEx Plugin List

Adding your custom metric plugin is fairly simple. You just need to add it to the list of plugins that you have in your lib/kanban/prom_ex.ex file, as shown on the next page:

---

6. https://hexdocs.pm/prom_ex/PromEx.MetricTypes.Polling.html#build/4
7. https://hexdocs.pm/telemetry_metrics/Telemetry.Metrics.html#last_value/2

```
# in lib/kanban/prom_ex.ex
defmodule Kanban.PromEx do
  @impl true
  def plugins do
    [
      Kanban.PromEx.CpuPlugin
    ]
  end
```

Now, let's test it locally by starting your application. Remember that you must have a database running for your application to start, so run POSTGRES_PORT="5432:5432" docker compose up db -d and set up the database first. Then curl your application and pipe the grep function to your curl request to filter the response by cpu_util. Your terminal should look something like this:

```
$ POSTGRES_PORT="5432:5432" docker compose up db -d
...
$ mix ecto.setup
...
$ iex -S mix phx.server
...
$ curl -v X POST 'http://localhost:4000/metrics' | grep cpu_util
...
# HELP cpu_util The total CPU usage of the host system in seconds
# TYPE cpu_util gauge
cpu_util{instance_id="i-09ba9852c02d92e38"} 2.0050125313283207
```

Great! Now, let's test the production functionality. To do this, run terraform apply, and then create a branch and PR with the code you've written in this chapter. *Do not merge it, however.* You'll merge this PR later. Once your CI has finished running, run your deploy.sh script to deploy the image that your CI created for your PR. Once your image has been deployed, repeat the same curl request as before, but this time, changing localhost to one of your EC2 IPs.

> **Wrap the /metrics Endpoint**
>
>  You'll have noticed that the /metrics endpoint of your EC2 instances are being exposed and accessible to anyone. We recommend that you use another package from Alex Koutmos: Unplug,[8] which will allow you to put a wrapper around the /metrics endpoint and hide it.

Amazing. You can see your fancy new average CPU usage metric is being collected by PromEx and exposed at the /metrics endpoint of your application in both development and production. Alloy will now scrape the most recent

---

8. https://hexdocs.pm/unplug/Unplug.html

value of this metric every five seconds and add it to its database. Because you've already hooked Prometheus up to Grafana, the Grafana UI will now also have access to this data. The next step is to create a new Grafana dashboard so that you can display this CPU metric visually.

Create a Dashboard for Your CPU Metric Using the Grafana UI

Now that you've exposed your custom metric in the /metrics endpoint, you can add it to your dashboard. You could add it to one of your existing default dashboards, but we would discourage doing that for two reasons. First, it is good to separate your dashboards by domain (such as application metrics and infrastructure metrics). Second, you shouldn't add functionality to the default dashboards provided by PromEx. If you were to do that, you'd have to constantly maintain that change if PromEx were to update its default dashboards. This is the same reason why you shouldn't edit or alter the default Dockerfile that's generated by the Phoenix release generator (apart from the environment variable needed to make the Dockerfile support multiple architectures), as we discussed back in Chapter 3.

In the previous chapter, we mentioned that the default Grafana dashboards that PromEx provides are saved in deps/prom_ex/priv as JSON files. Having these dashboards as part of your infrastructure-as-code gives you environment integrity and ensures that all of your dashboards appear in all of your environments. For this reason, any custom dashboards that you create must also be saved as JSON files and added to your PromEx configuration. You could create your new JSON template manually. However, the Grafana UI lets you create new custom dashboards and then download them as JSON files that you can add to your PromEx configuration. Creating your dashboard manually and then downloading it is a much easier and more visual way of dashboard creation than trying to manipulate a JSON template manually.

To create your dashboard, rebuild your Docker image so that it includes your PromEx changes and run your application using docker compose up. Remember to add the PROMTAIL_CONFIG and ALLOY_CONFIG environment variables. You'll also have to add the USE_AWS_FIXTURE_ADAPTER environment variable. This is because your Docker image sets the MIX_ENV of your application to be prod. When this is the case, your application uses your AWSAdapter module, which expects the application to be running on an EC2 instance that has the internal metadata API. Adding the USE_AWS_FIXTURE_ADAPTER environment variable will allow you to continue running your application locally in a Compose/swarm environment. Now do you see why being able to override the adapter at runtime is useful?

To be able to set this environment variable, add the following to the web service in your compose.yaml file:

```
# in compose.yaml
services:
  web:
    environment:
      USE_AWS_FIXTURE_ADAPTER: ${USE_AWS_FIXTURE_ADAPTER:-false}
```

Now build your Docker image and run your application. Your terminal should look like ours:

```
$ docker compose down -v
...
 ✓ Volume db_data           Removed                         0.1s
 ✓ Volume grafana-data      Removed                         0.0s
$ docker build -t "kanban:latest"
...
$ WEB_IMAGE=kanban:latest PROMTAIL_CONFIG='local' ALLOY_CONFIG='local' \
  USE_AWS_FIXTURE_ADAPTER=true docker compose up
...
```

Visit http://localhost:3000/dashboards, click New, and then click New Dashboard like so:

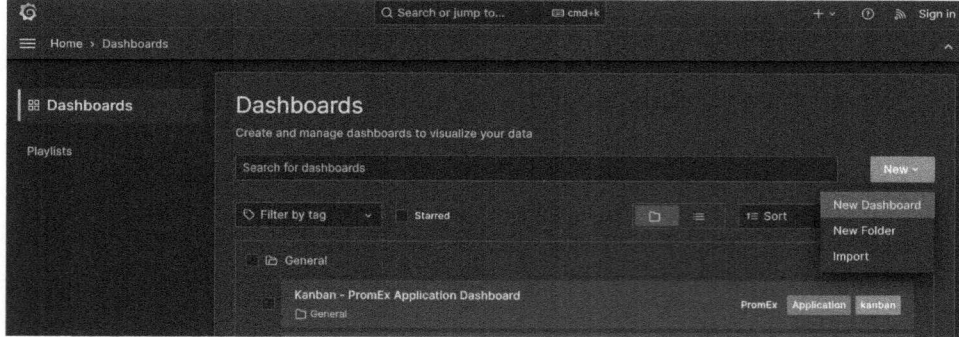

After you've done this, click the "+ Add visualization" button. The first step is to tell Grafana which type of graph you wish to create: a gauge graph. Gauge graphs have colored ranges, or bands, that represent different levels of a metric such as normal, warning, and critical. Using this graph type to display the average CPU level of the hosts running your application will allow you to quickly and intuitively identify when the CPU usage exceeds acceptable limits. Go to the right navigation bar and follow these instructions:

1. Change the graph from a "Time series" chart to a Gauge graph by clicking on the top right drop-down.

2. Set the title as "Average Host CPU Utilization".

3. Set the description to "The average CPU usage percentage of the host machine(s)".

4. Click the Calculation drop-down and select the "Last *" option.

5. Enable the "Show threshold labels" and "Show threshold markers" options in the Gauge section.

6. In the "Standard options" section, click the Unit drop-down and select "Misc -> Percent(0-100)".

7. Set min to 0 and max to 100.

8. Scroll down to the Threshold section and add the following thresholds with the following colors:
   - 30% = yellow
   - 45% = red

9. Set the "Thresholds mode" to Percentage.

The different parts of the configuration form should look like this:

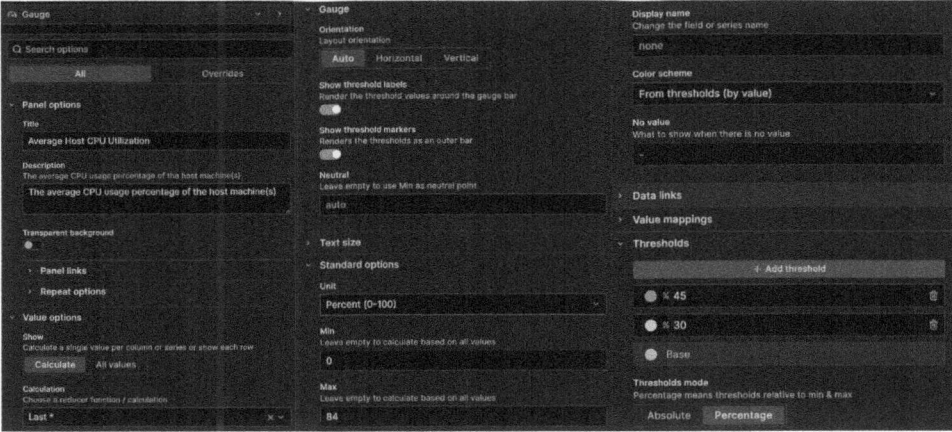

You've just defined what your dashboard's graph will look like. Now it's time to build the query so that Grafana can pull the CPU usage metric from your Prometheus database. To do this, go to the query builder (Query) beneath your gauge graph and follow these instructions:

1. Select "prometheus" as the "Data source".

2. On the right-hand side, make sure Code is selected rather than Builder.

3. In the Metrics Browser input, type "avg (cpu_util)".

4. Open the Options section and select the following options:
   - Legend = Verbose
   - Format = Table
   - Type = Instant

Your query configuration should look like this:

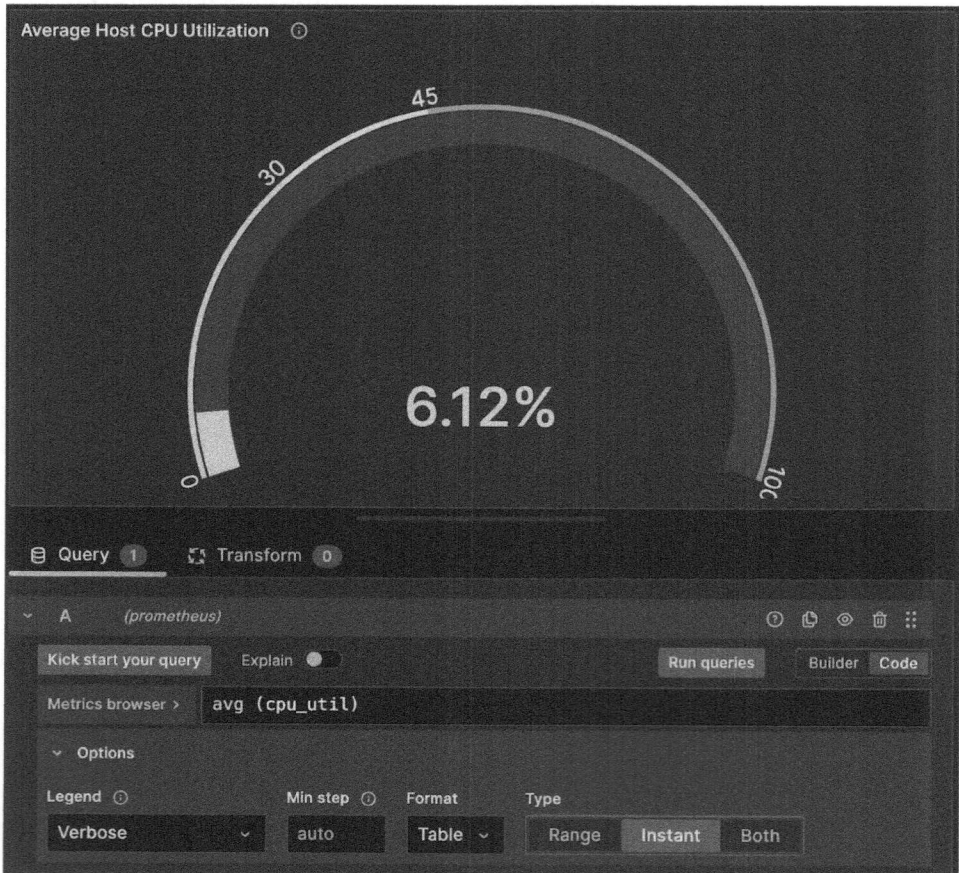

Now click Apply and you'll see your new chart. You've created your first custom dashboard! Keep this tab open for the moment. The next step is to download your new dashboard as a JSON file so that you can import it in your PromEx configuration.

Download Your New UI Dashboard as a JSON File

To download your dashboard as a file, create a subfolder inside your priv folder called grafana_dashboards, and inside that create a JSON file called infrastructure.json. Then navigate back to the browser and click on the settings icon at the top right of your new dashboard. Select the JSON model tab, copy the JSON code, and paste this into the file you just created.

Open your priv/grafana_dashboards/infrastructure.json file, and you'll see something that looks like this:

```
{
  "panels": [
    {
      "datasource": {
        "type": "prometheus",
        "uid": "P1809F7CD0C75ACF3"
      }
    }
  ],
  "title": "New dashboard"
}
```

Update the title of the dashboard to be Infrastructure Metrics.

Set UID and ID to null

It's important that you find the uid and the ID of the dashboard in the JSON file and set them to null. This is because PromEx uses a PUT when uploading the dashboard to Grafana, and Grafana won't allow you to update a dashboard if the uid and ID are set.

The last step in implementing your custom PromEx metric and dashboard is to add your new JSON file to your PromEx configuration.

Add Your Custom JSON Dashboard File to Your PromEx Configuration

To add your dashboard to your PromEx configuration, you need to add it to your list of dashboards in your main PromEx module in your lib/kanban/prom_ex.ex file like so:

```
# in lib/kanban/prom_ex.ex
defmodule Kanban.PromEx do
  @impl true
  def dashboards do
    [
      {:kanban, "grafana_dashboards/infrastructure.json"}
    ]
  end
end
```

You may notice that this snippet tells PromEx to look for the dashboard in your application's codebase rather than the prom_ex library. It also doesn't include priv in the file path. This is because PromEx automatically looks in the priv folder of your application for custom dashboard configurations. If you were to add priv to the path, PromEx would try to look for priv/priv/grafana_dashboards/infrastructure.json.

And that's it! Now, you just need to test that it works in both a local compose and swarm environment. To do so, rebuild your Docker image so that it includes your PromEx changes and run your application using docker compose up.

Your terminal should look like ours:

```
$ docker compose down -v
...
 ✓ Volume db_data           Removed                         0.1s
 ✓ Volume grafana-data      Removed                         0.0s
$ docker build -t "kanban:latest"
...
$ WEB_IMAGE=kanban:latest PROMTAIL_CONFIG='local' ALLOY_CONFIG='local' \
  USE_AWS_FIXTURE_ADAPTER=true docker compose up
...
```

Visit http://localhost:3000/dashboards and you should see your new Infrastructure Metrics. It worked, you created an idempotent dashboard!

Now start your application in a swarm environment to be sure that it works:

```
$ docker compose down -v && docker swarm leave --force; docker swarm init
...
$ WEB_IMAGE=kanban:latest USE_AWS_FIXTURE_ADAPTER=true \
docker stack deploy -c compose.yaml kanban

Creating config kanban_prometheus
Creating config kanban_loki
Creating config kanban_grafana_datasources
Creating config kanban_promtail
...
Creating service kanban_loki
Creating service kanban_promtail
Creating service kanban_grafana
Creating service kanban_prometheus
```

Visit the /dashboards page of your Grafana UI again and select your custom dashboard. You'll see that your CPU usage gauge chart is there monitoring the average CPU usage of your swarm as expected.

Your new dashboard is working in both a Compose and a swarm environment! You can officially collect the average CPU usage of your swarm in your local environment. This will help you better understand the behavior of your application and how you could potentially optimize your infrastructure.

Now that you've added the dashboard to your PromEx configuration, which automates the process of uploading it to Grafana, you're ready to set up an alert for your CPU metric.

Before we move on, leave your local Docker Swarm.

Add Alerts to Your Metrics Configuration

Visualizing your metrics is great, but you don't want to be like the monkey in *Toy Story 3* whose eyes are red from staring continuously at the security cameras of the day care center to see if anything is happening. Rather than having to monitor your application yourself, you want monitoring to be automated, and you want to be notified automatically when something goes wrong. This is where alerts come in.

Alerts are a way to notify you when a certain metric crosses a certain threshold. In this section, you'll learn how to create an alert in Grafana and then automate its creation using a configuration file. Once you've done this, you'll set up your alert so that you get an email notification whenever the metric threshold has been triggered. There are several contact points (as Grafana calls them), such as Slack and PagerDuty, that you can use to communicate the alert. However, we've chosen to do an email alert because, well, nearly everyone has an email account.

Let's start by creating the alert manually in Grafana.

Manually Create an Alert in Grafana

As we've emphasized throughout your BEAMOps journey, when implementing a new feature, it's good practice to first approach the issue manually to try and understand what is happening. This is exactly what we'll do with alerts.

Open your local Grafana UI and click the Alerting button on the navigation bar. Then click the Alert Rules tab and then the "Create alert rule" button.

When you create a rule, you must always define three things:

1. The query to get the information you want to monitor (section A).
2. A function that reduces the values gathered by the query into one value (section B).
3. The threshold that will determine when the alert should be sent (section C).

To implement all of this, fill in the alert rule form as follows:

1. Set your alert rule name as High CPU Usage.
2. Select the "Grafana managed alert" option.
3. In section A (which defines how you'll get the information that you want to monitor):
   a. Select "prometheus" as the data source.
   b. Select "now-1m to now" as the time range.
   c. Select the Code option and write the following query: "avg (cpu_util)". Note that this is the same query as in the dashboard you implemented earlier.
   d. In the Options section, select the following:
      i. Legend = Verbose
      ii. Format = Table
      iii. Type = Instant
   e. Choose Stat as the visualization type and click the "Run queries" button to see the results of your query.
4. In section B (which defines how to reduce the results of your query into one value):
   a. Select Last as the function option.
   b. Select Drop Non-numeric Values as the mode.
5. In section C (which defines the threshold for when to send the alert):
   a. Select B as the input.
   b. Select IS ABOVE and 40 for the threshold.
6. In the alert evaluation behavior section:
   a. Create a new folder called "alerts" (you have to press Enter after typing in the name of the folder to create it).
   b. Create a new evaluation group called "main."
   c. Set the "Evaluation interval" to 1m and write 1m in the "for" section. This means that the CPU will be measured every minute, and the alert will be triggered if the threshold is being met (that is, the CPU is above 40%) consistently for one minute.

You're done! Click Save to create the alert. Once you've done this, go back to the "Alert rules" page. You'll see that you now have one alert set up.

Now that you've created the alert, add it to your Grafana provisioning folder. This automates the creation of the alert and makes sure it will be created in each environment your application is run, giving you environment integrity. To make this alert part of your configuration, click the Export button, which will trigger a download of a YAML file. Create a new subfolder in your instrumentation/grafana folder called alerting and move this YAML file into that folder. Rename the file alert_rules.yaml. Now add this configuration file to your grafana service in your Compose file by creating the following Docker config:

```
# in compose.yaml
services:
  grafana:
    configs:
      - source: grafana_alert_rules
        target: /etc/grafana/provisioning/alerting/alert_rules.yaml
configs:
  grafana_alert_rules:
    file: ./instrumentation/grafana/alerting/alert_rules.yaml
```

To test that the automatic provisioning of this alert works, run docker compose up to start your Docker suite, remembering to specify the WEB_IMAGE, USE_AWS_FIXTURE_ADAPTER, PROMTAIL_CONFIG, and ALLOY_CONFIG environment variables. You'll see the alert is there.

Great! You've created the alert. But you haven't defined what should happen when that alert is triggered. You'll do this next by setting up a contact point.

Enable Email Notifications

To complete this section, you need to have a Gmail account, have enabled 2FA, and create an app password. If you don't already have an app password, you can find more information in Google's docs.[9]

The methods of receiving alert notifications are what Grafana refers to as *contact points*. To set up your email contact point, first give Grafana access to your email. To do this, define the following environment variables in your Compose file's grafana service (we've added a description to each one so that you know what each environment variable is):

- GF_SMTP_ENABLED = enables or disables SMTP (Simple Mail Transfer Protocol), the protocol used for sending emails
- GF_SMTP_HOST = specifies the hostname or IP address of the SMTP server that Grafana will use to send emails—Gmail

---

9. https://support.google.com/accounts/answer/185833?hl=en

- GF_SMTP_USER = the username or email address that Grafana will use when authenticating with the SMTP server to send emails
- GF_SMTP_PASSWORD = sets the password Grafana should use to authenticate with the SMTP server—your app password
- GF_SMTP_FROM_NAME = sets the "From" name for the emails sent by Grafana
- GF_SMTP_FROM_ADDRESS = sets the "From" email address that Grafana should use when sending emails

Add these environment variables to the grafana service like so:

```
# in compose.yaml
grafana:
  image: grafana/grafana:9.5.15
  environment:
    - GF_SMTP_ENABLED=true
    - GF_SMTP_HOST=smtp.gmail.com:587
    - GF_SMTP_USER=YOUR_EMAIL_ADDRESS
    - GF_SMTP_PASSWORD=YOUR_GMAIL_APP_PASSWORD
    - GF_SMTP_FROM_NAME=Grafana
    - GF_SMTP_FROM_ADDRESS=YOUR_EMAIL_ADDRESS
```

Ensure App Password Is a Secret

 You'll notice that we've hardcoded the app password as the GF_SMTP_PASSWORD. Ideally, this would be a secret in your secrets.enc.yaml file. You would then cat the secret file in your deploy script and set it as a GMAIL_PASSWORD environment variable and update the GF_SMTP_PASSWORD to be GF_SMTP_PASSWORD=${EMAIL_PASSWORD}. We're hard coding it for now for learning purposes.

Now that you've created these environment variables, it's time to set up a contact point in Grafana. A contact point defines how and where to send notifications for a specific alert. To configure your contact point, restart your Docker suite, visit http://localhost:3000/alerting, and click the "Contact points" tab. Click the Edit button of the grafana-default-email and type in your email address. To test that it has been properly configured, click the Test button and send a predefined test notification. You should see a success message in the UI:

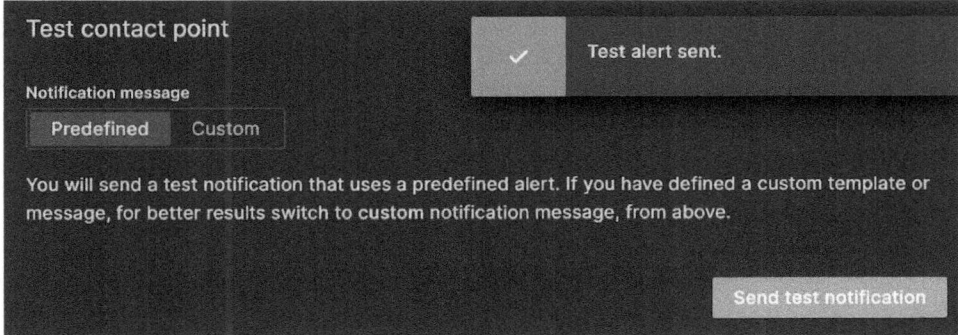

And you should receive an email in your inbox like so:

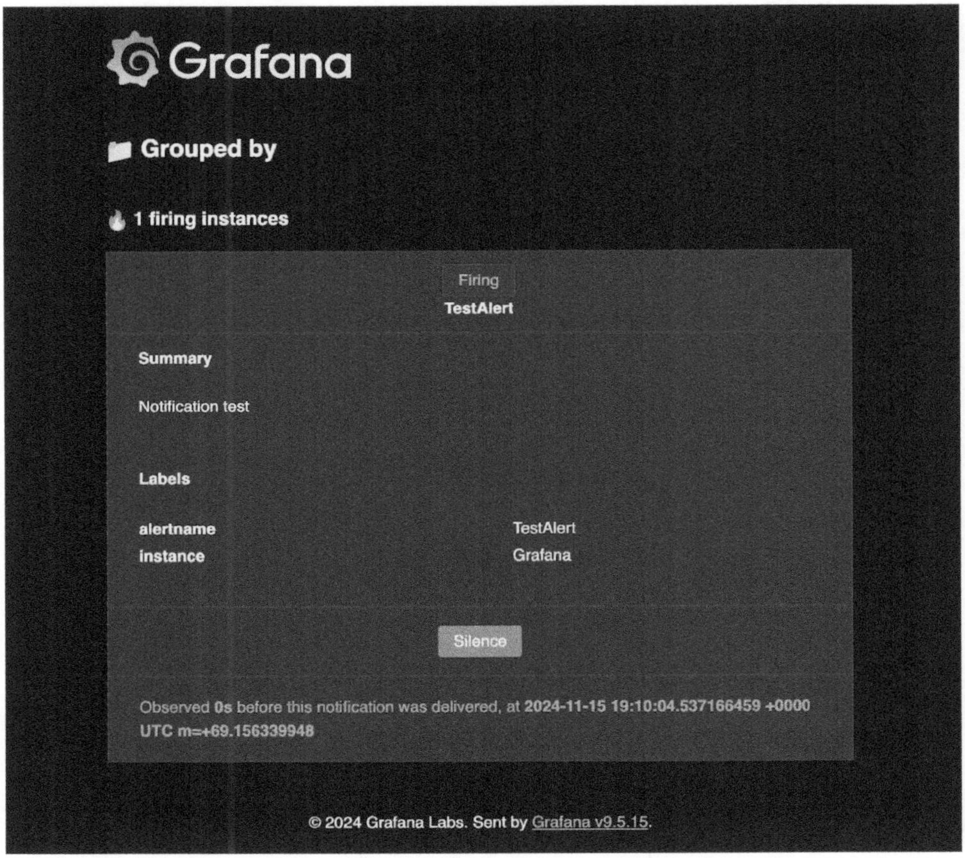

Wonderful. Now let's automate the setup of your contact point so that it's available in all of your environments.

Automate the Contact Point Setup

For this section, we'll provide you with the YAML files that you need to automate the provisioning of your contact point. We're doing this because the version of Grafana we're using here doesn't have an option in the UI to export this resource.

To add the contact point setup to your Grafana configuration, you'll repeat the same process as the alerting rules. You'll create a YAML configuration file in an instrumentation/alerting subfolder and then add a new config to your grafana service to include this file. So, create the alerting subfolder inside your instrumentation folder. Inside, create a new file called alert_resources.yaml and paste in the following code:

```yaml
# in instrumentation/grafana/alerting/alert_resources.yaml
apiVersion: 1
policies:
    - orgId: 1
      receiver: My Contact Email Point
      group_by:
        - grafana_folder
        - alertname
      routes:
        - receiver: My Contact Email Point
contactPoints:
    - orgId: 1
      name: My Contact Email Point
      receivers:
        - uid: my_contact_email_point_uid
          type: email
          settings:
            addresses: YOUR_EMAIL_ADDRESS
            singleEmail: false
          disableResolveMessage: false
```

This file sets up two separate things: a contact point and a policy. The contact point tells Grafana that when the My Contact Email Point is used, it should send out alert notifications to your email address. The policy states that all of the alerts on your Grafana configuration should use the My Contact Email Point. It's possible to use the object_matchers policy configuration to only route certain alerts to certain contact points. But, as you only have one alert in your configuration, you don't need this attribute.

Now that you have this configuration file, add a new config to your grafana service that references this new file, like so:

```
# in compose.yaml
services:
  grafana:
    configs:
      - source: grafana_alert_resources
        target: /etc/grafana/provisioning/alerting/alert_resources.yaml
configs:
  grafana_alert_resources:
    file: ./instrumentation/grafana/alerting/alert_resources.yaml
```

You're done! It's pretty easy to automate the provisioning of resources, right?

Let's test that your contact point has been successfully added. Stop your Docker suite (without removing the volumes) and start it up again. You'll see that your new contact point has been created. Now stop your Docker suite again, this time removing the volumes, and start it again. You'll see that everything is provisioned as expected: your alert, your contact point, and your notification policy (as well as your data sources and dashboards).

Go ahead and run your application in a local Docker Swarm and then visit your Grafana dashboard. You'll see that everything is still being provisioned as it should.

So far in this chapter, you've only been logging and collecting metrics for your application locally. The last step is to confirm that this all works in your AWS production environment. In the next section, you'll deploy an image we created, which includes the PromEx dashboards you made both in this chapter and the last. It also includes the same /infrastructure page you saw in Chapter 10 that lets you stress your application.

Deploy the BEAMOps Kanban Image to AWS in Production

Rather than deploying your own image to production, you'll deploy one of our images. This is so that you can use our infrastructure page (which you saw in Chapter 10), stress the application, and monitor how our CPU usage gauge dashboard (which is the exact same as the one you've implemented in this chapter) increases/decreases and triggers an alert notification to be sent.

The first step is to make sure that you can access port 3000 (the Grafana UI) of your swarm nodes. To do this, add the following ingress rule to your aws_security_group resource in your modules/cloud/aws/compute/swarm/sg.tf file, as shown on the next page:

```
# in modules/cloud/aws/compute/swarm/sg.tf
resource "aws_security_group" "swarm_sg" {
  ingress {
    description = "Grafana"
    from_port   = 3000
    to_port     = 3000
    protocol    = "tcp"
    cidr_blocks = ["0.0.0.0/0"]
  }
}
```

Apply this change by running terraform apply. To deploy our BEAMOps Kanban image, run your deploy script as you've been doing throughout this book—with the PRIVATE_KEY_PATH, SOPS_AGE_KEY_FILE, GITHUB_USER, and WEB_REPLICAS environment variables—using the following image tag: ghcr.io/beamops/kanban:instrumented. Following is the command you have to run:

```
$ PRIVATE_KEY_PATH=environments/production/private_key.pem \
  SOPS_AGE_KEY_FILE=environments/production/key.txt \
  GITHUB_USER=YOUR_GITHUB_USERNAME \
  ./scripts/deploy.sh ghcr.io/beamops/kanban:instrumented
```

Once the deploy has finished, run terraform output to display your ssh_commands output. This will tell you the IPs of your different EC2 instances. Open two separate windows in your browser. In one window, visit the /infrastructure page of port 4000 on one of your EC2 instances. Either create a new account to log in to the application or seed your database using the docker exec command.

Now visit the /dashboards endpoint of port 3000 of that same instance to bring up the custom CPU dashboard. It should look like this:

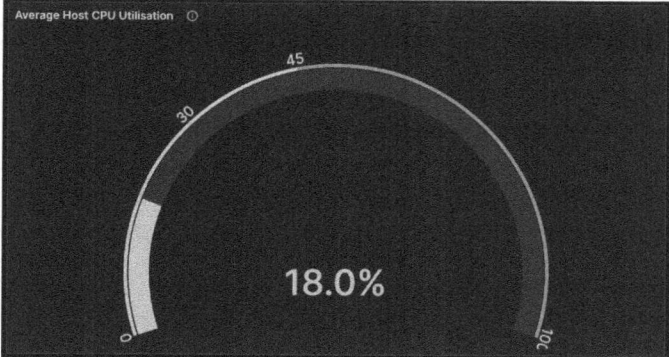

Now press the Stress Cluster button on the infrastructure page. You'll see that, as the load in your swarm spikes, the CPU usage metric in your Grafana dashboard increases. Once the CPU usage of your EC2 instances has been over 40% for over one minute, your Grafana alert will fire and you'll receive an email. Then, when your Auto Scaling group autoscales and the average CPU usage of your Auto Scaling group drops, you'll see the CPU usage metric in your Grafana dashboard go back to green, and you'll receive a second Grafana email that says that the high CPU spike has been resolved. The scale-down event could take a while to take effect (longer than when you tested in Chapter 10) because AWS has to drain the terminating EC2 instances from your load balancer.

Congratulations! You've done it—you're finished. You've successfully deployed an application to production and can monitor the average CPU usage of the machines hosting your application. This will give you confidence in monitoring the state of your application in production and resolving any potential issues that arise.

You can now close the final two issues that you created in Chapter 2: the "Create Your Own Custom PromEx Metric" and "Create A CPU Alert For Your Application" issues. Commit the rest of the changes you've made in this chapter to your open PR. Add closes #ID for each of the issues to the description and merge it. Once your CI finishes running, destroy your production infrastructure.

What Have You Learned?

You now have a deeper understanding of the monitoring pillar of instrumentation. You've implemented your own custom PromEx metric to measure the CPU usage of your EC2 instances. You've implemented a repository and adapter that allows you to mock the metric locally while using the AWS CloudWatch metric in production. You've created a custom PromEx plugin and Grafana dashboard to collect and display the average CPU usage of the hosts running your Elixir applications. And you've set up an email alert so that you can be automatically notified any time the average CPU usage of the machines hosting your application has been above 40% for over one minute, as well as when the CPU spike has finished.

With what you've learned in this chapter, you should feel confident in creating reliable applications and owning the instrumentation stage of software development. You now understand why instrumentation is important—it provides system behavior and performance analysis, and it enables efficient troubleshooting and debugging when errors occur. You also understand how implementing customized metrics and alerts allows you to practice the Kaizen principle of making small, continuous improvements to your application.

> **The Extra Mile**
>
> If you wish to deepen your knowledge of the themes we've covered in this chapter and refine your BEAMOps developer superpowers, we've created a task for you to do:
>
> 1. Let's close with a big one, shall we? You're currently using version 9.5.15 of Grafana. Newer versions of Grafana allow you to export provisioned resources into Terraform code. Upgrade the version of Grafana that you use to 10.3.1 and refactor your Grafana configuration away from YAML provision files to Terraform provisioning.

Wrapping Up the Journey

Congratulations! You've made it to the end of your BEAMOps journey. It's been a long, winding road, but you've made it to the top. You're now a BEAMOps developer!

In Chapter 1, we introduced the seven BEAMOps principles:

- Project Management
- Ownership
- Infrastructure-as-Code (IaC)
- Environment Integrity
- Scalability
- Kaizen Principle
- Continuous Deployment

Throughout each chapter in this book, you've tackled each one and should now feel confident practicing all of them in your daily work.

Project management "typically" doesn't fall within the scope of software development. In reading this book, though, you've planned and executed the delivery of a software application from start to finish. In Chapter 2, you created a list of issues and you've closed all of these issues as you've worked through the chapters. You've done project management!

We hope that you feel a sense of ownership in all of the areas that we've covered in this book: the packaging of an application, CI/CD pipelines, remote infrastructure provisioning and automation, creating distributed Erlang clusters, autoscaling, and instrumentation. Remember that you've just deployed a distributed application to a fully provisioned AWS environment that scales up/down based on the average CPU usage of the machines hosting your application. You can also stress your cluster and receive automated alerts that tell you when there is a CPU spike. While we couldn't delve into every single detail about every single thing—we've had to make compromises here and there (such as security)—we're confident that you now have a fantastic foundational knowledge of each stage of software delivery. Rather than throwing any of the more "operational" tasks over the fence into someone else's territory, you can now jump over that fence and show you're a pragmatic and empathetic engineer who's ready to take on anything.

Throughout the book, we've emphasized that defining your infrastructure in code isn't optional. It's always a *must*. Aim to automate any process, wherever you can. Not only will it save you time in the long run by getting rid of manual (human) intervention, it will also help you ensure consistent results across environments. Related to infrastructure-as-code is the critical principle of environment integrity, which is especially important when working on a team. We hope that you never again hear the phrase, "But it works on my machine."

When delivering a software product, you should always consider implementing autoscaling. As you've seen in this book, autoscaling will help you better understand your infrastructure, its orchestration capabilities, and how your application behaves when the group of host machines grows and shrinks. Autoscaling will only make your application more reliable!

One of the phrases that we hope you remember from this book is: "Make it work, then make it beautiful." These words, by Joe Armstrong, really convey what it means to be a BEAMOps developer. Being a BEAMOps developer is about striving for the best, but not letting perfectionism get in the way of even starting. Use the Kaizen principle and CI/CD pipelines to help you submit small features often. As John C. Maxwell famously said, "fail early, fail often, but always fail forward." Failing, or code-breaking, isn't a bad thing. As long as you can be alerted of the error and can fix it, the world won't end.

Above all, we hope you've enjoyed the process of reading this book and navigating the different stages of software delivery. We believe the most important thing is to love what you do. That's the exact reason we wrote this book—to share our love of programming. After all, knowledge shouldn't be exclusive.

And, with that, we'll sign off.

Ellie and Josep

Index

SYMBOLS

&&, cloud-init, 199
* (asterisk), GitHub Action workflow logs, 84
. (period)
 context for Docker images, 62
 context for Packer, 194
: (colon), pinning image versions, 139
=
 Dockerfile ARG statements, 64
 multistage Dockerfiles, 68

DIGITS

1password, 224

A

-a option (docker ps), 73
account_id variable, IAM policies, 260
Action attribute, IAM policies, 260
action.yaml file, 242
actions, *see* GitHub Actions
adapters, custom plugins, 389–395, 404
add (Date), 29
age command (SOPS), 223
age key
 enabling continuous deployment with GitHub Actions, 236, 239
 SOPS, 223
age-keygen (SOPS), 223
alarm action, 326
alarms, autoscaling, 312, 325–327, 336
alerts, custom Grafana, 387, 405–411
algorithm attribute, key pairs for EC2 instances, 183
aliases
 continuous integration exercise, 117
 multistage Dockerfiles, 67
Alloy
 about, 356, 370
 collecting metrics in swarm environment, 382–384
 components, 376
 configuring, 375–378
 scraping and forwarding metrics, 375–378
AMD architecture
 building images, 111–115, 121
 continuous development exercise, 250
ami argument
 importing EC2 instances, 201
 importing EC2 instances with Terraform, 171
AMIs (Amazon Machine Images)
 EC2 instances, connecting, 165
 EC2 instances, creating manually, 159
 ID, finding, 172
 names, 193, 200
 with Packer, 190–207
 provisioning with cloud-init, 198
 using latest version, 196, 198
 viewing in EC2 dashboard, 195
any restart policy option (Docker Compose), 132
application metrics, implementing, 369–384
apply (Terraform)
 importing resources, 166
 vs. plan (Terraform), 24
 refactoring with, 26
 state and, 15
 Terraform provisioning cycle, 21–23
ARG (Dockerfile), 64
arguments
 ARG statements, 64
 Terraform registry, 20
 Terraform/HCL syntax, 16
ARM architecture
 building images, 111–115, 121
 continuous development exercise, 250
Armstrong, Joe, 4, 157, 251, 415
AS (Dockerfile), 67
asdf, 7–10

assets
  multistage releases, 70–72
  releases with mix, 53
asterisk (*), GitHub Action workflow logs, 84
authentication
  GitHub provider, 24
  Grafana, 7, 378, 385
  Loki, 358
authentication tokens, 264
Auto Scaling groups
  alarms, creating, 312, 325–327
  alarms, with stats page, 336
  automatic rollbacks, 343–346
  creating, 312–324
  deploying images with custom plugins, 412
  descaling gracefully, 327–333
  housekeeping, 347–350
  load balancers, 337–343
  policies, 314, 325–327
  setup, 313–318
.auto.pkrvars.hcl file, 197
autoscaling
  about, 308, 311, 415
  alarms, creating, 312, 325–327
  Auto Scaling groups, creating, 312–324
  deploying images with custom plugins, 412
  descaling gracefully, 327–333
  enabling, 312–337
  with EventBridge service, 329–333
  housekeeping, 347–350
  with load balancers, 335, 337–343
  policies, 314, 325–327
  rollbacks, 308, 343–346
  script for, 318–324
  setup, 313–318
  SSM documents, 312, 330–333
  triggers, 312, 325–327
  triggers with stats page, 333–337
autoscaling_group_name attribute, 327
availability zones
  autoscaling, 313, 316
  creating multiple EC2 instances for Docker Swarm, 252–278
  defined, 252
  distributing EC2 instances for Docker Swarm, 253–254
  manager nodes, 252, 255
  in production environment diagram, 1
AWS, see also Auto Scaling groups; EC2 instances; SSM Agent
  about, 6
  access keys, creating, 168
  account owner ID, 201
  account setup, 11
  CodePipelines, 6
  costs, 11
  credentials and machine images with Packer, 195
  destroying resources, 11
  ECS service, 6
  EventBridge, 329–333
  limits on free requests, 389
  machine images with Packer, 190–207
  production environment, automated setup, 166–190
  production environment, manual setup, 158–166
  region and machine images with Packer, 196
  in tech stack for this book, 5
AWS Certificate Manager, 341
AWS CLI
  installing, 9
  obtaining IP addresses of EC2 instances, 229
  querying instances for autoscaling, 317
AWS ECR, 59
AWS ECS, 149
AWS Systems Manager Agent, see SSM Agent

B

bash shell
  checking if command was successful, 80
  creating multiple EC2 instances for Docker Swarm, 252–278
  manually connecting distributed Erlang clusters with Docker Compose, 296
  running Docker containers, 65
BEAM
  about, 285
  advantages, 2
  embedded vs. interactive mode, 50
  QEMU-Erlang bug, 114
  release scripts, 215
  releases, understanding OTP, 50
BEAMOps paradigm
  development of, xv
  principles of, xv, 2–5, 414
beauty, Kaizen and, 4, 157, 251, 415
bind mounts, 131, 363
blocks
  labels, 16
  nested, 18
  Terraform/HCL syntax, 16
Bob the builder, 62, 67
booting
  Docker containers and, 58
  virtual machines and, 57
bourne shell, 216, 219
branch protection, 246–249
bridge network driver, 124
build (Docker), 58, 62, 76
build (Packer), 193
build (PromEx plugins), 397
build block (Packer), 192
--build-arg option, 64
builders, Packer, 191, 195
buildx builders, 109
business metrics, 370

C

-c option (docker stack deploy), 152
cache-from key (Docker), 109
cache-to key (Docker), 109
caching
  conditional, 91–93
  dependencies in continuous integration pipeline, 86–93

distributed Erlang advantages, 287
Docker builds, 109
Docker Compose, 134
Dockerfile and layer caching, 60, 68–69
enabling in continuous integration pipeline, 88
exercise, 117
Persistent Lookup Tables (PLTs), 100
restoring caches, 89, 92
cgroups, 57
--check-formatted flag, 96
--chmod option, 68
--chown option, 68, 76
clean (mix), 101–103
clients, Docker architecture, 58
clients key, Promtail setup, 361
cloud, *see also* autoscaling
cloud providers, 17
cloud-init setup assistant, 198
cloud-init, 198
CloudWatch
about, 325
autoscaling alarms, 325
CPU usage custom metric with PromEx, building, 388–405
limits on free requests, 389
vs. open-source instrumentation, 355
clusters, *see* distributed Erlang clusters
CMD (Dockerfile)
about, 61
Docker Compose service configuration, 130
multistage Dockerfiles, 76
overriding, 147
Phoenix release tasks, 126
using, 65–66
--cmd option, 66
code, *see also* infrastructure-as-code
analysis and continuous integration pipeline, 97–101
compilation and continuous integration pipeline, 80–86

compiling locally, 80
formatting and continuous integration pipeline, 96
preloading of in OTP releases, 50
source code for this book, xix
testing and continuous integration pipeline, 93–96
CodePipelines, 6
colon (:), pinning image versions, 139
command Docker Compose service configuration, 130
command attribute, Prometheus, 374
common attribute, Loki setup, 358
common key, Loki setup, 358
compile (mix), 70, 80
compiling
code locally, 80
in continuous integration pipeline, 80–86
dependencies in multistage Dockerfile releases, 70
errors, 81, 94, 105
JIT compiling and QEMU-Erlang bug, 114
components, Alloy, 376
Compose, *see* Docker Compose
--compose-file option, 152
compose.yaml file, 129–132, 134, 137, 150
config (Docker Compose), 138
CONFIG_ID, 359
configs (Docker)
creating, 359
inspecting, 368
listing, 368
configs key, Docker Compose top-level configuration, 359
configs sub-attribute, Docker Compose service configuration, 359
configuring, *see also* Terraform
AWS access keys, 168
checking services in Docker Compose Files, 138

cloud-init setup assistant, 198
with Docker Compose, 128
EC2 instances, 159–160
mix, 51
multistage Dockerfile releases, 70
OTP releases, advantages, 50
Phoenix, 51
Phoenix projects, 53
reusing Terraform configuration files, 13, 23
console (Terraform), 27
contact points, Grafana alerts, 405, 407–411
containers, *see also* Docker Swarms
canceling, 124
checking status of, 73
defined, 4, 60
Docker architecture diagram, 58
environment integrity and, 4
inspecting, 65
listing, 73
logs, 154
mounting sockets inside containers, 348
names, 125
networks, 124–126
OTP releases, advantages, 50
parsing, 65
publishing ports, 124
removing, 124, 128, 134
replicating with Docker Swarm, 152
running, 60, 63–66, 73–77
running and multistage releases, 71
running interactively, 65, 71
security, 60, 124
service containers, 148
stopping, 133
vs. virtual machines, 58
volumes, sharing, 131
content attribute, key pairs, 184
context
building Docker images, 62
exercise, 207

GitHub, 107, 109
Packer, 194
continuous deployment
  BEAMOps paradigm principles, 2, 4, 250, 414
  branch protection, 246–249
  Docker secrets, 227–236
  Docker Swarm, 277–283
  enabling with GitHub Actions, 236–249
  encrypting Docker secrets, 222–226
  exercises, 250
  kaizen and, 209, 226
  packaging and, 77
  with Postgres database, 147
  project milestones, 28
  pushing images to GitHub registry in continuous integration pipeline, 103–115
continuous improvement, see kaizen
continuous integration
  advantages, 79
  caching builds, 109
  caching dependencies, 86–93
  cleaning dependencies, 101–103
  code analysis, 97–101
  code compilation, 80–86
  code formatting, checking, 96
  exercises, 117
  kaizen and, 79, 117
  main branch and, 84, 115
  multi-architecture images, 111–115, 121
  packaging and, 77
  pipeline steps, 80–103
  with Postgres database, 147
  project milestones, 28
  pushing images to GitHub registry, 103–115
  testing and, 80
  testing code, 93–96
  .tool-versions file, 9
  triggers, amending, 115–117
  warnings and, 81, 94
  workflow, 80

cookies (distributed Erlang clusters), 286, 290, 295
cooldown attribute, autoscaling, 327
COPY (Dockerfile), 61, 67, 76
costs, EC2 instances, 159
count (Terraform), 44
CPU usage
  autoscaling alarms, 312, 325–327, 336
  custom metric with PromEx, alerts, 405–411
  custom metric with PromEx, building, 388–405
  custom metric with PromEx, dashboard for, 399–405
  function for, 389–395
create (Docker), swarm services, 152
create (Ecto), 140, 143
CREATE–DESTROY–IMPROVE–REPEAT motto, 40–43, 47, 187
credentials, IAM roles, 258
curl
  adding to Dockerfile, 344
  health checks with, 343–346

D

-d option (docker network create), 124
data block (Terraform), 16
data centers, see availability zones
data replication and distributed Erlang, 287
data sources, for VPCs and security groups, 181
data sources, Grafana
  creating, 363
  setup, 363–366
databases
  adding to app, 119–122
  autoscaling, testing, 335
  conditionally exposing ports, 136–139
  connection errors, 146
  creating Phoenix projects without, 51

deploying services with Docker Swarm, 149–155, 278
  with Docker secrets, 211–222
  encrypting Docker secrets, 223–226
  health checks, 135
  manually running multi-service applications, 122–128
  migrations, 121, 125–128, 140, 143, 145
  releases and, 53
  running Postgres containers, 123
  running releases as Erlang nodes, 291
  seeding, 143, 303
  starting in detached mode, 140
DeBenedetto, Sophie, 308
--decrypt option for sops, 224, 230
decryption, automatic deployment script, 234
dependencies
  automatically installing with --install flag, 120
  caching in continuous integration pipeline, 86–93
  cleaning in continuous integration pipeline, 101–103
  compiling code for continuous integration, 83
  Docker Compose service configuration, 132–133, 146
  minimizing production, 98
  modules and cross-dependencies, 87
  multistage releases, 67–70, 74
  Phoenix projects creation, 52
  searching for, 102
depends_on Docker Compose service configuration, 132–133, 146
depends_on meta-argument (Terraform), 43
deploy (Docker)
  about, 149
  Compose files, 153

Index • 421

deploying manually with secrets, 231
swarm services, creating, 152
using, 206
deploy Docker Compose service configuration, 132
deploy attribute, Promtail setup, 367
deploying
　Docker Compose service configuration, 132
　with Docker secrets, automating, 232–236
　with Docker secrets, manual, 227–232
　with Docker Swarm, automated, 277–283
　housekeeping, 347–350
　specifying deploy mode, 347
　with stack deploy, 149, 152–153, 206
　summary of steps, 231
deployment, *see* continuous deployment
description AWS security group attribute (Terraform), 178
description property, Terraform variables, 31
destroy (Terraform), 41, 189
destroying
　CREATE–DESTROY–IMPROVE–REPEAT motto, 40–43, 47, 187
　destroying resources and AWS costs, 11
　destroying resources and Terraform state, 15
　destroying resources vs. updating, 35
　EC2 instances, 189
　errors while, 41
　exercise, 284
DevOps paradigm, xv, 2, 415, *see also* BEAMOps paradigm
Dialyxir, 97–101, 120
Dialyzer, 98
dialyzer (mix), 98
dimensions attribute, autoscaling alarms, 326
directives, Docker Compose, 129–132

directories
　viewing file structure, 19
　working directory for multistage Dockerfiles, 67
discovery Alloy component, 376, 382
distributed Erlang clusters
　about, 284
　advantages, 286
　connecting nodes, 289
　cookies, 286, 290, 295
　Docker Swarm, automated creation, 300–308
　Docker Swarm, IP addresses, 298
　exercises, 309
　listing nodes, 289, 296
　manually connecting with Docker Compose, 295–298
　manually implementing, 288–299
　message passing, 302–308
　node names, 288, 293
　running Phoenix applications as Erlang nodes, 291–295
　scaling with, 285–287, 295
　understanding, 285–287
distributed environment, *see* Docker Swarm
distributed environments, network drivers, 125
DNS
　load balancers setup, 342
　names lookup, 297
　polling, 300, 306
DNSCluster library, 300, 306
Docker, *see also* containers; Docker Compose; Docker Desktop; Dockerfile; images; secrets, Docker
　about, 56
　advantages of, 6
　architecture, 58
　architecture diagram, 58
　assigning ports, 138
　caching builds, 109
　CLI commands, 58
　development cycle diagram, 65

　EC2 instances installation with Packer machine images, 196, 198–200
　EC2 instances installation with user-data attribute, 189, 203
　exercises, 78
　hosts, 58
　licenses, 10
　manually running multi-service applications, 122–128
　mounting sockets inside containers, 348
　network drivers, 124
　networks, 124–126
　objects, 59
　orchestration and, 6
　registries, 59, 61, 104, 206
　running commands, 11
　specifying hosts, 204
　tech stack for this book, 5–7
docker commands, specifying Docker hosts, 205
Docker Compose
　about, 117, 128
　CLI commands, 133–144
　Compose file, understanding, 128–132
　conditionally exposing ports, 136–139
　configs, 359, 368
　creating Docker Compose files, 134–149
　deploying with Docker Swarm, 149–155, 206
　directives, 129–132
　distributed Erlang clusters, 295–298
　with Docker secrets, 211, 217–222
　exercises, 155
　installing, 10
　Phoenix application, adding to Compose file, 144–147
　Postgres service, creating, 134–140
　specifying files, 152
　in tech stack for this book, 5
　understanding, 128–134
Docker daemon (dockerd)
　authentication with GitHub registry, 206

commands, 58
in Docker architecture, 58
enabling Amazon Linux AMI, 165
installing, 10
Docker Desktop, installing, 10
--docker flag (mix phx.gen.release), 56, 121
Docker Hub, 59, 61
Docker Swarm, *see also* nodes
about, 58
advantages, 251, 255
architecture, 149
automatic deployment script, 235
automatic rollbacks, 343–346
autoscaling script, 318–324
autoscaling setup, 313–318
basics, 149–155
CLI commands, 150
collecting metrics, 382–384
creating multiple EC2 instances for, 252–254
creating swarms, 255–258
deploying, automated, 277–283
deploying, to production, 203–207
diagram, 150
distributed Erlang clusters, IP addresses, and, 298
distributed Erlang clusters, automating, 300–308
Docker Compose service configurations, 132
EC2 instances and production, 158
exercises, 351
housekeeping, 347–350
initialization script, 267–272
initializing, 150, 153
join script, 272–275
joining nodes, 256
joining swarms, automated, 266–275
joining swarms, autoscaling, 322

with load balancer, 338–343
machine images with Packer, 200–203
manager nodes, creating, 151
manually deploying with secrets to, 227–232
network driver for, 125
in production environment diagram, 1
Promtail setup, 362, 367–369
pruning, 347
quorums, 328
removing, 155
replicating containers, 152
restart policies, 132
rolling updates, 152
routing mesh, 304, 335
starting, 204
starting multiple versions of a service, 298
in tech stack for this book, 5
testing, 263–266
using separate initialization and join scripts, 266–275
docker-compose.yaml file, 129
DOCKER_HOST environment variable, 204, 235
docker_sd_configs attribute, Promtail setup, 361
Dockerfile
automatically creating in Phoenix, 56
curl, adding, 344
defined, 56, 59
images, building, 58–59, 62
layer caching, 60, 68–69
releases with, 56
specifying, 62
statement order, 61
syntax, 60
Dockerfiles
ARG statements, 64
creating with Phoenix release generator, 120
multistage, 67–77
releases with, 67–77
documentation
importance of, 37
project milestones, 28
down (Docker Compose), 133

--driver option, 124
drivers, networks, 124

E

-E option, cloud-init, 199
-e option
bash scripts, 234
docker run command, 72
EC2 instances
adding to Terraform configuration, 174–176
AWS EC2 dashboard, 159, 195, 200
configuring manually, 159–160
configuring permissions for swarms, 258–277
connecting to, 160–166
costs, 159
creating manually, 158–160
creating multiple for Docker Swarm, 252–254
defined, 158
Docker installations with Packer machine images, 196, 198–200
Docker installations with user-data attribute, 189, 203
Docker Swarm nodes, 158
IAM instance profiles, attaching, 262
ID, obtaining, 264
instance connect, 183
key pairs, 159, 182–189, 191, 195
machine images with Packer, 190–207
production environment, automated setup, 166–190
production environment, manual setup, 158–166
security groups, 160, 176–180
in tech stack for this book, 5
terminating, 189
testing Docker Swarm, 263–266
EC2 messages, 331
ECS service, 6
Ecto, creating Phoenix app with, 119–122

Index • 423

EEF (Erlang Ecosystem Foundation), 62
Effect attribute, IAM policies, 260
egress AWS security group attribute (Terraform), 178
egress security group attribute, 271
Elixir
    base images, 62
    compilation and releases, 50
    ecosystem evolution, xi
    files and .gitignore file, 52
    installing, 9, 83
    parsing in continuous integration pipeline, 108
    releases with mix, 51–56
    setting in continuous integration pipeline, 83
    in tech stack for this book, 5
    version and running Docker containers, 63
email notifications (Grafana), custom alerts, 405, 407–411
encryption
    automatic deployment script, 234
    Docker secrets, 210, 222–226
ENTRYPOINT (Dockerfile), 61, 65–66
--entrypoint option (docker run), 66
env (GitHub workflow file key), 82
ENV (Dockerfile), 61, 67, 76
.env files, 210
env option (docker run), adding environment variables, 72
environment
    exercise, 78
    setup for, 7–11
    setup with cloud-init, 199
environment Docker Compose service configuration, 130
environment integrity
    BEAMOps paradigm principles, xv, 2–3, 49, 414
    containers, 60
    continuous integration pipeline, 81, 83, 108
    dashboards, custom, 399
    Docker advantages, 58

Docker Compose and, 128
Docker secrets, 211
housekeeping, 347
importance of, 415
instrumentation, 353, 355, 384, 388
machine images with Packer, 191
multi-architecture builds and, 112
package management and, 7
pinning image versions, 139
resources, 167
swarm services, creating, 152
environment variables
    Docker Compose service configuration, 130
    encrypting Docker secrets, 223–226
    _FILE suffix for, 212
    GitHub workflow files, 82–83
    handling with Docker secrets, 210–222
    multistage Dockerfiles, 68
    QEMU-Erlang bug and, 114
    releases, 54, 70
Erlang, see also distributed Erlang clusters
    base images, 62
    ERTS, 51
    installing, 9
    parsing in continuous integration pipeline, 108
    QEMU-Erlang bug, 113
    releases, understanding OTP, 50
    version and running Docker containers, 63
Erlang Ecosystem Foundation (EEF), 62
Erlang runtime system (ERTS), 51
Erlang Virtual Machine, see BEAM
errors
    automatic deployment script, 234
    compiling, 81, 94, 105
    database connections, 146

destroying resources, 41
type errors and code analysis in continuous integration pipeline, 97–101
ERTS (Erlang runtime system), 51
escape characters, Terraform, 321
event metrics (PromEx), 395
EventBridge, 329–333
ExAWS library, 393
expressions, Terraform, 16

F

-f option
    curl, 344
    docker compose, 133
fault tolerance
    distributed Erlang advantages, 286
    Docker Swarm advantages, 251, 255
--file option
    docker build, 62
    docker run, 133
file_permission attribute, key pairs (Terraform), 184
filename attribute, key pairs (Terraform), 184
files
    copying and multistage Dockerfiles, 68, 76
    Docker image context, 62
    specifying Docker Compose files, 133
    viewing file structure, 19
filter (Terraform data block), 181, 200
filtering
    AMIs, 198, 200
    data sources, 181
    EC2 instances, 229
--filters option (AWS CLI), 229
for_each
    autoloading variables, 32–42
    GitHub secrets, 238
    labels, 39
--force option (docker swarm leave), 151, 155
format (mix), 96
--format github option for mix dialyzer, 100

formatting, checking code in continuous integration pipeline, 96
FROM (Dockerfile), 61, 64, 67
functions, running in Terraform, 28

G

García Vega, Ricardo, xii, 285, 302, 395
gauge graphs, 400
-generate-config-out option, terraform plan, 170
generated_resources.tf file, 170
GenServers, 351
GH_PAT
    building and pushing images in continuous integration pipeline, 107
    continuous deployment with secrets, 240
GitHub
    about, 13
    branch protection, 246–249
    committing to, 47
    container registry, 59, 206
    encrypting Docker secrets, 222–226
    issues, closing, 77
    issues, setup, 44–47
    marketplace, 83
    milestones labels, 37–42, 44–47
    milestones setup, 28–30
    project management with, 13–47
    provider for Terraform setup, 17–26
    registry, pushing images to in continuous integration pipeline, 103–115
    repositories, creating and adding to configuration file, 20
    secrets, 107
    token, 24, 105, 107, 239
GitHub Actions
    about, 6
    continuous deployment, composite action, 242–249
    continuous deployment, enabling, 236–249
    continuous integration pipeline, amending triggers, 115–117
    continuous integration pipeline, building and pushing images, 106–109
    continuous integration pipeline, caching dependencies, 86–93
    continuous integration pipeline, code compilation, 80–86
    continuous integration pipeline, enabling caching, 88
    continuous integration pipeline, with Postgres database, 147
    costs, 115
    predefined, 83
    in tech stack for this book, 5
    triggering workflows manually, 90, 110
    UI, 100
    verbose output, 92
    workflow file, creating, 81
    workflow file, keys, 81
    workflow file, main branch and, 84, 115
    workflow file, manually triggering, 82
    YAML file for, 81
GitHub CLI
    installing, 9
    setup, 11
    using, 84
    viewing workflows, 83
GitHub UI
    opening, 85
    viewing workflows, 83
github_owner, specifying in Terraform configuration file, 26
.gitignore file
    creating resources, 21
    Packer files, 203
    Phoenix projects, 52
    secrets, 222
global deploy mode (Docker Swarm), 347, 367
Grafana
    alerts, custom, 387, 405–411
    authentication, 7, 378, 385
    dashboards, custom, 388, 399–405
    dashboards, defining in PromEx, 370
    dashboards, uid and ID, 403
    dashboards, uploading, 378–384
    default configuration file path, 360
    instrumentation architecture, 354–356
    PromEx and Prometheus integration, 378–384
    running queries, 365
    security, 7, 365
    services, list of, 355
    setup, 363–366
    in tech stack for this book, 5
    Terraform provisioning exercise, 414
    tracing, 362
    visualizations, 355, 378–384, 399–405

H

Hashicorp Configuration Language, *see* HCL
HCL
    basics, 16
    infrastructure-as-code and, 14
    Packer and, 16, 191–194
    Terraform and, 14, 16
    variables, using, 31–42
health checks, 135, 343–346
healthcheck key (Docker Compose service configuration), 344
heredoc syntax, 34, 188
hex, 51, 67
host network driver, 124
hostname, Loki setup, 358
hosts, Docker, 58, 204
housekeeping, automating, 347–350
HTTP
    EC2 instances configuration, 160
    server options and releases, 55
HTTPS
    load balancers and security group rules, 341
    server options and releases, 55
hypervisors, 57

I

IaC, *see* infrastructure-as-code
IAM instance profiles
    attaching to EC2 instances, 262
    creating, 262
    defined, 258
    swarms, 258–277
    testing, 263–266
IAM policies
    attaching to IAM roles, 261
    creating, 259–261
    defined, 258
    swarms, 258–277
    testing, 263–266
IAM roles
    attaching IAM policies, 261
    autoscaling with EventBridge, 331–334
    AWS access keys, 168
    creating, 261
    defined, 258
    swarms, 258–277
    testing, 263–266
id key in caching in continuous integration pipeline, 88
identifiers, Terraform, 16
iex, manually implementing distributed Erlang clusters, 288–290
ignore_changes lifecycle meta-argument (Terraform), 276
image, Docker Compose service configuration, 130
images
    automatic deployment script, 234
    base images, 62, 67
    for this book, xix
    building, 58, 61–63, 104–106
    building automatically in continuous integration pipeline, 106–109
    building dynamically, 63
    building multi-architecture, 111–115, 121
    caching builds, 109
    continuous deployment with composite actions, 244
    custom metrics, deploying to production, 411–413
    defined, 59
    deploying with composite GitHub Actions, 242
    deploying with secrets, manually, 231
    derived, 59
    Docker architecture diagram, 58
    Docker Compose service configuration, 130
    Docker registries, 59, 61
    exercises, 78
    housekeeping, 347–350
    lean images, 62, 74
    pinning versions, 139
    Postgres, 123
    pushing to GitHub registry in continuous integration pipeline, 103–115
    removing local, 106
    size of, 74
    specifying in Docker Compose file, 145
    tagging, 108, 244
    testing, manually, 104–106
immutability, machine images with Packer, 191
import (Terraform), 166
import blocks (Terraform)
    configuring, 169
    idempotency, 176
    removing, 188
    using, 166, 170–176
importing
    key pairs for EC2 instances, 186
    resources, Terraform, 166–190
    resources, diagram, 175
    security group, 176–180
index attribute
    assigning subnets to availability zones, 254
    for count (Terraform), 44
indexes
    Loki setup, 359
    refreshing, 359
:inet_res.lookup/3 function, 297
infrastructure metrics, 370
infrastructure-as-code
    advantages of, 14
    BEAMOps paradigm principles, xv, 2, 414
    environment integrity and, 3
    HCL and, 14
    importance of, 415
    importing resources, 159
    project milestones, 28
ingress AWS security group attribute (Terraform), 178, 269
init (Docker Swarm), 150, 153, 256
init (Packer), 193
init (Terraform), 168
init (mix), 215
inline attribute (Packer), 193
inspect (Docker)
    docker inspect, 65
    docker service inspect, 154, 228
inspect (Packer), 193
--install flag for dependencies, 120
instance connect, 183
instance profiles, *see* IAM instance profiles
instance_type argument, importing EC2 instances with Terraform, 171
instrumentation
    architecture, designing, 354–356
    custom alerts, 387, 405–411
    custom metrics, 387–405
    custom metrics, deploying to production, 411–413
    dashboards, custom, 399–405
    definition, 354
    diagram, 356
    goal of, 353
    kaizen and, 369
    logging, 354
    metrics, implementing, 369–384
    monitoring, 354
    project milestones, 28
    running queries, 365
    setup, 357–369
    tracing, 354, 362
    visualization with Grafana, 355, 378–384, 399–405
--interactive option, running containers, 65
interval option, DNS polling, 300

IP addresses
   Docker Swarm and distributed Erlang clusters, 298
   EC2 instances, deploying with secrets, 229
   EC2 instances, joining swarms and, 256
   EC2 instances, output for SSH key pairs, 187
   joining swarms automatically, 266
   manager nodes in swarms, 151
   primary nodes, 260
   running releases as Erlang nodes, 293, 297
   specifying Docker hosts, 205

J
jobs, GitHub workflow file key, 82
join (Docker swarm), 151
jq, 9, 65, 89, 110
JSON, custom Grafana dashboards, 399, 402

K
kaizen
   BEAMOps paradigm principles, 2, 4, 414
   beauty and, 4, 157, 251, 415
   continuous deployment and, 209, 226
   continuous integration and, 79, 117
   instrumentation and, 369
key, caching in continuous integration pipeline, 89
keys
   AWS access keys configuration, 168
   caching in continuous integration pipeline, 88
   Docker secrets, 211
   EC2 instances key pairs, 159, 182–189, 191, 195
   encryption with SOPS, 222
   GitHub workflow file, 81
   specifying Docker hosts, 205
Koutmos, Alex, 370, 398
Kubernetes, 6, 10, 149

L
labels
   GitHub milestones, 37–42, 44–47
   relabeling data with Alloy, 376
   Terraform blocks, 16
last_value telemetry metrics, 397
:latest tag, Docker images, 108
launch_template argument, importing EC2 instances with Terraform, 171
layer caching, Dockerfile, 60, 68–69
leave (Docker swarm), 151
length (Terraform), 44
licenses, Docker Desktop, 10
lifecycle attribute (Terraform), 271
list, resources, 26
listeners, load balancers, 338, 341
listening addresses, Loki setup, 358
lists
   GitHub issues setup, 44–47
   obtaining length of, 44
load balancers
   about, 158
   autoscaling and, 335, 337–343
load distribution, distributed Erlang, 286, 304
local provider (Terraform), 184
local-exec provisioner (Terraform), 278, 280
locals block (Terraform)
   about, 16
   declaring local variables, 25
   vs. variables, 31
locks
   cleaning dependencies in continuous integration pipeline, 101–103
   lockfiles and caching, 89, 91
   .terraform.lock.hcl, 19
--log-failed option (gh run view), 85
logs
   autoscaling, 335
   containers, 154
   Docker Compose, 133
   Docker Swarm services, 154
   GitHub Action workflows, 84
   health check and automatic rollbacks, 345
   instrumentation with CloudWatch, 355
   instrumentation with Grafana, setup, 357–369
   loading secrets with scripts, 217
   time-series data and, 372
   viewing failed, 85
Loki
   about, 355
   authentication, 358
   linking to Promtail, 358
   setup, 357–360

M
machine images
   building local versions, 200
   defined, 190
   Packer, 190–207, 266
main.tf file, creating, 18–26
MANAGER_IP variable, 234
manager_tag variable, 274, 314
manual metrics, 395
--max-failures option (mix test), 94
Maxwell, John C., 209, 415
memory, Docker containers vs. virtual machines, 58
message passing
   distributed Erlang advantages, 287
   with distributed Erlang clusters, 302–308
   Erlang advantages, 285, 295
   with Pub/Sub, 285, 295, 306
meta-arguments (Terraform), using, 17
_meta_docker_container_name, Promtail setup, 362
metadata
   EC2 instances IDs, 264
   Terraform state and, 15
   Terraform state and EC2 instances, 174

metrics
  collecting and exposing with PromEx, 354, 356, 370–372
  collecting and storing with Prometheus, 354, 356, 370, 372–375
  collecting in swarm environment, 382–384
  custom PromEx, 387–405
  custom PromEx, deploying to production, 411–413
  dashboards, custom, 399–405
  dashboards, separating, 399
  event, 395
  implementing, 369–384
  instrumentation with CloudWatch, 355
  integrating Grafana, PromEx and Prometheus, 378–384
  last_value telemetry metrics, 397
  manual, 395
  polling, 395–397
  scraping and forwarding with Alloy, 356, 375–378, 382–384
  types of, 370
/metrics endpoint, 354, 373, 398
metrics_path sub-attribute, Prometheus, 373
migrations
  adding Phoenix application to Docker Compose file, 145
  running, 121, 125–128
  schema_migrations table, 140, 143
milestones (GitHub)
  due dates, 29
  issues, closing, 77
  issues, setup, 44–47
  labels, 37–42
  project management, 28–30, 37–42, 44–47
Mimir, 356
mix
  caching dependencies in continuous integration pipeline, 86–93
  cleaning dependencies in continuous integration pipeline, 101–103
  code analysis in continuous integration pipeline, 97–101
  creating projects, 51
  formatting code and continuous integration pipeline, 96
  releases with, 51–56
  searching for dependencies, 102
  testing code in continuous integration pipeline, 93–96
module block (Terraform), 16
modules
  configuring resources automatically, 170
  cross-dependencies, 87
  defined, 167
  file for, 19
  importing EC2 Instances, 167
  machine images with Packer, 200–203
  outputs and child modules, 188
  path, 185
  providers setup, 19
most_recent attribute, AMIs, 198, 201
Mozilla, 222
multistage Dockerfiles, 67–77

N

name key, GitHub workflow file key, 82
--name option, Docker containers, 125
--name parameter, Erlang nodes, 289
names
  AMIs, 193, 200
  Docker containers, 125
  Erlang nodes, 288, 293
  labels, 37
  providers, 17
  resources, 20, 29
  secret files, 212
  secrets, 211
  security groups, 188
  stacks, 152
  stages in multistage Dockerfiles, 67
  volumes, 141
namespaces, virtualization and, 57
needs key, GitHub Action job, 107
--network flag, Docker containers, 125
networks
  adding Phoenix application to Docker Compose file, 144–147
  automatic creation with Docker Compose, 136
  containers, 124–126
  deployment with Docker Swarm, 149
  drivers, 124
  EC2 instances configuration, 160
  health checks, 135
  removing, 134
networks directive (Docker Compose), 144
newlines, heredoc syntax, 34
--no-ecto option (mix phx.new), 51
nobody user, 76
node() function (Elixir), 289
nodes, *see also* distributed Erlang clusters
  automated deployment, 277–283
  autoscaling and distinguishing between primary and secondary, 319
  Docker Swarm architecture, 149
  EC2 instances as, 158
  joining swarms, 151, 256
  joining swarms, automated, 266–275
  listing, 151, 153
  manager nodes, availability zones and, 252, 255
  manager nodes, creating, 151
  manager nodes, defined, 255
  manager nodes, joining to swarm, 153
  manager nodes, tokens, 256–258
  pruning, 347
  quorums, 328
  removing, 328, 330–333
  roles of, 257
  unreachable, 328

worker nodes, defined, 255
worker nodes, joining to swarm, 153
none restart policy option (Docker Compose), 132

O

-o flag, encryption with SOPS, 223
objects, Dockers, 59
on, GitHub workflow file key, 82, 115
on premise providers, 17
on-failure restart policy option, 135, 145
on-failure restart policy option (Docker Compose), 132
onetimesecret, 224
orchestration, *see also* Docker Swarm
    automatic rollbacks, 343–346
    AWS ECS and, 149
    Docker and, 6
    Kubernetes and, 6, 149
order
    Dockerfile statements, 61
    PromEx children, 372
OTP releases
    advantages, 50
    building, 50–56
    with Dockerfile, 56
    with mix, 51–56
-out flag (terraform plan), 23
output block (Terraform), 16
OVA files, 190
overlay network driver (Docker), 125
overlays folder, 53
ownership
    BEAMOps paradigm principle, 2, 250, 414
    continuous deployment and, 4, 250
    packaging and releasing, 77
    project management and, 3, 28, 47

P

-p option (docker ps), 73
packages
    hex package manager, 51
    setup for book, 7–10

Packer
    advantages, 190
    basics, 191–194
    commands, 193
    formatting exercises, 207
    HCL and, 16
    installing, 9
    machine images, 190–207, 266
    in tech stack for this book, 5
    Terraform integration, 200–203
packer block, 192
Parallels, 200
Parameter Store
    adding secret to Terraform, 275–277
    autoscaling, 314, 318
    IAM policies, 259
    joining swarms, automated, 266
    storing tokens, 257, 264
parsing, containers, 65
--password-stdin flag (docker login), 105
passwords
    GitHub Docker registry, 105
    Grafana, 365
    password managers, 224
    Postgres containers, 123
path, key in caching in continuous integration pipeline, 89
${path.module} function, 185
path_prefix, Loki setup, 358
.pem file, 160, 164
permissions
    autoscaling with EventBridge, 331–334
    AWS access keys, 168
    EC2 instances configuration, 160, 164, 258–277
    multistage Dockerfiles, 68, 76
    SSH key pairs, 184
    testing, 263–266
Persistent Lookup Tables (PLTs), 99–101, 103
Phoenix, *see also* Presence; Pub/Sub message passing
    adding application to Docker Compose file, 144–147

    canceling containers, 124
    creating projects, 51
    creating projects with databases, 119–122
    Dockerfile creation, automatic, 56
    installing, 51
    manually running multi-service applications, 122–128
    release generators, 120
    release tasks, 126–128
    releases with Docker secrets, 215–222
    running applications as Erlang nodes, 291–295
    version, 51
Phoenix.Digester, 54
plaintext_value attribute, GitHub secrets, 238
plan (Terraform)
    vs. apply (Terraform), 24
    -generate-config-out option, 170
    importing resources, 166, 170–176
    Terraform provisioning cycle, 21–23
platform as service providers, 17
platforms key, GitHub Action job, 113
PLTs (Persistent Lookup Tables), 99–101, 103
plugins
    adding custom plugins to PromEx plugin list, 397
    environment integrity and, 8
    Grafana data sources, 363
    machine images with Packer, 192–193
    PromEx, about, 371
    PromEx, creating, 388–397
    providers setup, 19
    setup for book, 8–10
    types of metrics, 395
policy_arn attribute, IAM policies, 261
polling metrics, 395–397
ports
    assigning, 138
    autoscaling, 319

conditionally exposing database ports, 136–139
custom metrics, deploying image to production, 411
Docker Compose service configuration, 130
Docker Swarm configuration, 152
Docker Swarm routing mesh, 304
Grafana setup, 364
joining swarms, 256, 264
joining swarms automatically, 266
load balancers, 340
Loki setup, 358
manager nodes in swarms, 151
manually connecting distributed Erlang clusters with Docker Compose, 296
mapping, 138
Prometheus configuration, 373
Promtail setup, 358
publishing, 73, 124
running releases as Erlang nodes, 292
security groups, 179
ports Docker Compose service configuration, 130
positions key, Promtail setup, 361
post-processors, 191, 200
Postgres
　Docker image, 123
　with Docker secrets, 211–222
　installing, 9
　pinning image version, 139
　running Postgres containers, 123
　running releases as Erlang nodes, 291
　service with Docker Compose, creating, 134–140
　volume persistence, 140–144
Presence, 287, 306
private_key_pem attribute (Terraform), 184, 186
processes, global registry and distributed Erlang, 287

production
　Docker Swarm, initializing, 203–207
　machine images with Packer, 190–207
　production environment, automated setup, 166–190
　production environment, diagram, 1, 158
　production environment, manual setup, 158–166
Programming Phoenix LiveView, 308
project management
　BEAMOps paradigm principles, 2, 414
　GitHub issues, closing, 77
　GitHub issues, setup, 44–47
　GitHub milestones labels, 37–42, 44–47
　GitHub milestones setup, 28–30
　milestones, 44–47
　ownership and, 3, 28, 47
　responsibility for, 2
　with Terraform and GitHub, 13–47
Prometheus
　about, 356
　collecting and storing metrics, 372–375
　configuring, 372–375
　Grafana integration, 378–384
　instrumentation architecture, 354–356
　scrape config, 368
PromEx
　about, 355, 370
　collecting metrics, 370–372
　configuring, 371–372
　custom metrics, 387–405
　custom metrics, deploying to production, 411–413
　Grafana integration, 378–384
　instrumentation architecture, 354–356
Promtail
　about, 355
　linking to Loki, 358
　setup, 358, 361–363, 367–369

promtail task (Docker Swarm), 367
providers
　initializing, 18, 21
　names, 17
　Terraform registry, 17
　types of, 17
provisioner block, cloud-init, 199
provisioners, Packer, 191, 195, 199
prune (Docker), 347
ps (Docker), 73
psql, 136
Pub/Sub message communication, 285, 287, 295, 306
public_key_openssh attribute (Terraform), 184, 186
--publish option (docker run), 73
pull (Docker), 58
Pulumi, 14
PURGE_FILE_PATH variable, 349
push (Docker), 58, 105
${PWD}/ for bind mounts, 131

Q
QEMU, 112
QEMU-Erlang bug, 113
query option, DNS polling, 300

R
race conditions, 274
RAFT logs, 210
rebar, 52, 67
region variable, IAM policies, 260, 274
registries
　Docker, 59, 61, 104, 206
　GitHub, 103–115
relabel Alloy component, 376
relabel_configs attribute, Promtail setup, 361, 367
release (mix), 52, 70, 215
RELEASE_COOKIE variable, 295
RELEASE_DISTRIBUTION variable, 293
RELEASE_NAME variable, 294
RELEASE_NODE variable, 293
RELEASE_NODE_NAME variable, 294
releases
　compiling assets in multi-stage releases, 70–72
　contents of, 50

defined, 50
with Docker secrets, 215–222
with Dockerfiles, 56, 67–77
environment variables, 54, 70
with mix, 51–56, 215
OTP, building, 50–56
ownership of, 77
Phoenix release generators, 120
Phoenix release tasks, 126–128
running Phoenix applications as Erlang nodes, 291–295
security, 76
starting, 54
workflow for, 56
remote_write Alloy component, 377
replace (Terraform), newlines, 34
replicas attribute, deploying with Docker Swarm, 277
repositories, custom plugins, 389–395
repository attribute, GitHub secrets, 238
Req library, 394
required_providers block, 18
reset (Ecto), 143
resource address (Terraform), 26
Resource attribute, IAM policies, 260
resource block (HCL), 16
resources
  addresses, 26
  configuring automatically, 170
  CREATE–DESTROY–IMPROVE–REPEAT motto, 40–43, 47, 187
  creating with GitHub provider, 17–26
  dependencies between and Terraform management, 42–43, 45
  destroying and AWS costs, 11
  destroying and Terraform state, 15
  destroying exercise, 284
  distributed Erlang advantages, 287

Docker Swarm advantages, 251, 255
environment integrity and, 3
exercises, 48
HCL blocks, 16
housekeeping, 347–350
IAM policies, 260
implicit dependencies vs. explicit dependencies, 43
implicit resources exercise, 48
implicit vs. explicit dependencies, 45
importing, 166–190
importing, and infrastructure-as-code, 159
listing, 26
listing attributes, 27
metadata, 15
names, 20, 29
parametrizing with variables, 31–36
Terraform mapping, 15
Terraform registry, 20, 29
responsibility, continuous deployment and, 4, 250
restart policies
  adding Phoenix application to Docker Compose file, 145
  automatic rollbacks, 345
  Docker Compose service configuration, 132, 135, 145
restart_policy Docker Compose service configuration, 132, 135, 145
restore-keys, caching in continuous integration pipeline, 89, 92
rm (Docker), 124, 128, 154, 328
rmi (Docker), 106
role attribute, IAM policies, 261
roles, see IAM roles
rollback_config (Docker Compose), 344
rollbacks, automatic, 308, 343–346
rolling updates, Docker Swarm, 152
routing mesh, 304, 335

rsa_bits attribute, key pairs for EC2 instances, 183
run (Docker)
  about, 58
  interactive containers, 65–66, 71
  manually running multi-service applications, 122–128
  using, 63
RUN (Dockerfile), 61, 67, 76
runners
  building multi-architecture images, 112
  GitHub workflow file, 82

S

-S flag, Elixir shell, 291
scale (Docker), 323
--scale option, Erlang nodes, 296
scaling, see also autoscaling
  about, 308
  BEAMOps paradigm principles, xv, 2, 4, 414
  distributed Erlang clusters and, 285–287, 295
  Docker Swarm advantages, 152
  manual, 311
schema_config key, Loki setup, 359
schema_migrations table, 140, 143
scrape Alloy component, 377
scrape_configs attribute, Prometheus configuration, 373
scrape_configs key, Promtail setup, 361, 367
scrape_interval attribute, Prometheus, 373
scripts, exiting, 234
secret (mix), 55, 105
secret keys
  creating, 55
  releases and, 54–56, 72
secret_name attribute, GitHub secrets, 238
secrets (Docker), 211
Secrets Operations, see SOPS
secrets, Docker
  encrypting, 210, 222–226
  vs. GitHub secrets, 237
  IDs, 211

manually deploying with, 227–232
names, 211
regenerating script for, 230
secrets file for, 211–213
using, 210–222
secrets, GitHub
continuous deployment, 237–244
creating, 237–241
vs. Docker secrets, 237
security
conditionally exposing ports, 136–139
containers, 60, 124
cookies and distributed Erlang clusters, 295
disclaimer, 7
Docker containers, 58
Docker secrets, encrypting, 222–226
Docker secrets, using, 210–222
EC2 instances configuration, 160, 164
EC2 instances connections, 160–166
Grafana and, 7, 365
HTTPS, 341
IAM roles, 258
nobody user, 76
publishing ports, 124
releases, 76
virtual machines, 57
VPCs, 180
security groups
EC2 instances, 160, 176–180
ID, linking, 179
ID, obtaining, 177
joining swarms, automated, 269
load balancers, 338, 341
machine images with Packer, 191, 195
names, 188
VPCs, 179, 181
:server option, releases, 55
servers
Docker architecture, 58
hypervisors, 57
releases, 55, 75
service containers
creating, 148
secrets, 212

services
adding Phoenix application to Docker Compose file, 144–147
checking configuration in Docker Compose Files, 138
cloud-init setup assistant, 198
creating swarm services, 152
creating with Docker Compose, 134–140
database health checks, 135
Docker Swarm architecture, 149
inspecting, 154, 228
isolating in Docker Compose files, 133
listing Docker Swarm, 153
logs, 154
manually running multi-service applications, 122–128
starting in detached mode, 140
starting multiple versions of a service, 298
swarm commands, 151
updating multiple, 323
services Docker Compose directive, 129–132
services key, GitHub Actions, 148
setup (Ecto), 143
setup.sh file, 199
:sha-xxx tag, 245
shell provisioner (Packer), 193
shells, *see also* bash shell
bourne shell, 216, 219
iex, 291, 293
short names, Erlang nodes, 288, 293
Sid attribute, IAM policies, 260
--sname parameter, Erlang nodes, 288
software as service providers, 17
SOPS
continuous development exercise, 250
editor, 224

encrypting Docker secrets, 222–226
in tech stack for this book, 5
sops command, 223
.sops.yaml file, 223–226
source block (Packer), 192
source_labels attribute, Promtail setup, 362
SSH
EC2 instances configuration, 160
EC2 instances connections, 160–166
EC2 instances key pairs, 182–189
machine images with Packer, 191, 195
multiple EC2 instances for Docker Swarm, 253
username, 193
ssh-agent, specifying Docker hosts, 205
SSM Agent, Parameter Store, 257
SSM documents, autoscaling, 312, 330–333
stack, tech stack for this book, 5–7
stack deploy (Docker)
about, 149
Compose files, 153
deploying manually with secrets, 231
swarm services, creating, 152
using, 206
stacks
names, 152
removing, 154
stages, multistage Dockerfiles, 67–77
start, releases, 54
start (Docker Compose), 133
state
Terraform, examining, 26
Terraform, provisioning cycle, 21–23
Terraform, understanding, 15
state show (Terraform)
EC2 instances, adding, 174
listing resource attributes, 27

stop (Docker Compose), 133
subnet_id attribute (Terraform), 180
subnets
    assigning to availability zones, 254
    autoscaling, 315
    EC2 instances, 160, 180–182
    multiple EC2 instances for Docker Swarm, 252–254
swarm (Docker swarm), 150
SwarmReady tag
    assigning, 264
    autoscaling, 323
    deployment with Docker Swarm, 279–280
    joining swarms automatically, 266
    node responsibilities, 257
swarms, *see* Docker Swarms
SweetXml, 393

T

--tag option (docker build), 62
tagging
    images, 62
    images in continuous integration pipeline, 108
target groups, load balancers, 338–341
tasks
    Docker Swarm architecture, 149
    listing, 154
Tate, Bruce A., 308
TCP, distributed Erlang clusters, 286
tech stack for this book, 5–7
templatefile function (Terraform), 274
templates
    Packer, 191–193, 196, 207
    releases, 215
Tempo, 362
termination_policies attribute, autoscaling, 314
Terraform, *see also* modules
    about, 13
    advantages, 13
    AWS access keys, 168

configuration files, adding EC2 instances, 174–176
configuration files, creating, 18–26
configuration files, reusing, 13, 23
configuration files, splitting, 259, 263
console, 27
CREATE–DESTROY–IMPROVE–REPEAT motto, 40–43, 47, 187
data sources, 181
escape characters, 321
GitHub issues, setup, 44–47
GitHub provider setup, 17–26
GitHub secrets, creating, 237–241
HCL basics, 14, 16
importing resources, 166–190
installing, 9
meta-arguments, 17
Packer integration, 200–203
Parameter Store integration, 275–277
production environment, automated setup, 166–190
project management with, 13–47
providers, types of, 17
provisioning cycle, 21–23
provisioning exercise, 414
registry, 17, 20
running apply for refactorings, 26
running init after changes, 168
state, examining, 26
state, provisioning cycle, 21–23
state, understanding, 15
in tech stack for this book, 5
variables, using, 31–42
workflow, 14
terraform block, 16, 18
Terraform Core
    declaring resources, 17–26
    understanding, 15
    variables and, 31
.terraform folder, 19

.terraform.lock.hcl, 19
terraform.tfstate file, 15
Terragrunt, 239
testing
    async and sync tests, 94
    code in continuous integration pipeline, 93–96
    continuous integration and, 80
    IAM roles, policies, and instance profiles, 263–266
    images, manually, 104–106
    resources on, 93
    running tests locally, 93
    test coverage exercise, 117
Testing Elixir, 93
.tf files, 16, 167, 259
.tfvars file, 32
-ti option
    docker exec, 296
    docker run, 65, 71
time-series data, 372
Timex library, 393
tls provider, 183
--token option docker swarm join, 151
tokens, *see also* cookies
    API token and autoscaling, 320
    authentication, 264
    GitHub, 24, 105, 107, 239
    Parameter Store integration with Terraform, 275–277
    swarm nodes, 151
    swarm tokens, autoscaling and, 320
    swarm tokens, joining swarms, 256–258
    swarm tokens, joining swarms automatically, 266
    swarm tokens, storing with Parameter Store, 257, 264
.tool-versions file
    continuous integration pipeline, 9, 83, 108
    setup, 7
--trace flag for tests, 94
tracing, 354, 362

triggers
    autoscaling, 312, 325–327
    autoscaling, with stats page, 333–337
--tty option (docker run), 65
type=sha tag, 108
typing, code analysis in continuous integration pipeline, 97–101

U

-u flag, GitHub Docker registry, 105
uncategorized project milestones, 28
--unlock option, cleaning dependencies, 101
--unused option, cleaning dependencies, 101
up (Docker Compose), 133
update (Docker Swarm), 152
update-in-place (Terraform), 173
update_config (Docker Compose), 344
USER (Dockerfile), 76
user notifications, with Pub/Sub and distributed Erlang clusters, 287, 306
user-data attribute, 189, 203
UTF-8 encoding, 74

V

-v flag for deleting volumes, 134
Vagrant box, 200
validate (Packer), 193, 197
values, declaring local, 25
variable block (Terraform)
    about, 16
    using, 31
variables
    autoloading, 32–42
    building Docker images dynamically, 63
    vs. local blocks, 31
    Packer, 196
    separating from main.tf file, 185
    SSH key pairs in, 184
    using, 31–42
vault, 223
--verbose option (gh run view), 92
version Docker Compose directive, 129
version control, Docker secrets, 222–226
versioning, machine images with Packer, 191
versions
    parsing in continuous integration pipeline, 108
    providers, 17
    setting in continuous integration pipeline, 83
    tools, checking, 9
view
    GitHub Action logs, 84
    GitHub Action workflows, 84
Virtual IP (VIP), swarms and, 278, 299
virtual machines, see also EC2 instances
    about, 57
    vs. Docker Containers, 58
    OVA files, 190
VirtualBox, 200
virtualization, see also Docker
    about, 57
    building machine images, 200
VMWare ESXI, 57
--volumes flag (docker compose down), 134
volumes
    creating, 130
    deleting, 134
    deployment with Docker Swarm, 149
    Docker Compose directive, 129, 131
    Docker Compose service configuration, 131
    Docker Swarm configuration, 152
    explicit, 140–144
    names, 131, 141
    persistence, 134, 140–144
    sharing, 131
    syntax, 131
volumes Docker Compose directive, 129, 131
volumes Docker Compose service configuration, 131
vpc_id attribute (Terraform), 181
vpc_zone_identifier attribute (Terraform), 313, 315
VPCs
    EC2 instances, 160, 179–182
    load balancers, 340
    security, 180
    security groups, 179, 181

W

--wait option, cloud-init, 199
warnings, compiling, 81, 94, 105
--warnings-as-errors flag (mix test), 81, 94
--web flag, GitHub CLI, 85
--with-registry-auth flag (docker stack deploy), 206
WORKDIR (Dockerfile), 61, 67, 76
workflow file, GitHub, 81
workflow_dispatch GitHub Action trigger, 82, 84

X

-x option for scripts, 234
XML, parsing, 393

Z

-z option for scanning nodes, 264
zero-downtime updates, see rolling updates

Thank you!

We hope you enjoyed this book and that you're already thinking about what you want to learn next. To help make that decision easier, we're offering you this gift.

Head on over to https://pragprog.com right now, and use the coupon code BUYANOTHER2024 to save 30% on your next ebook. Offer is void where prohibited or restricted. This offer does not apply to any edition of *The Pragmatic Programmer* ebook.

And if you'd like to share your own expertise with the world, why not propose a writing idea to us? After all, many of our best authors started off as our readers, just like you. With up to a 50% royalty, world-class editorial services, and a name you trust, there's nothing to lose. Visit https://pragprog.com/become-an-author/ today to learn more and to get started.

Thank you for your continued support. We hope to hear from you again soon!

The Pragmatic Bookshelf

Designing Elixir Systems with OTP

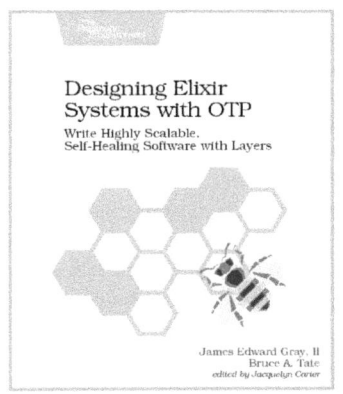

You know how to code in Elixir; now learn to think in it. Learn to design libraries with intelligent layers that shape the right data structures, flow from one function into the next, and present the right APIs. Embrace the same OTP that's kept our telephone systems reliable and fast for over 30 years. Move beyond understanding the OTP functions to knowing what's happening under the hood, and why that matters. Using that knowledge, instinctively know how to design systems that deliver fast and resilient services to your users, all with an Elixir focus.

James Edward Gray, II and Bruce A. Tate
(246 pages) ISBN: 9781680506617. $41.95
https://pragprog.com/book/jgotp

Small, Sharp Software Tools

The command-line interface is making a comeback. That's because developers know that all the best features of your operating system are hidden behind a user interface designed to help average people use the computer. But you're not the average user, and the CLI is the most efficient way to get work done fast. Turn tedious chores into quick tasks: read and write files, manage complex directory hierarchies, perform network diagnostics, download files, work with APIs, and combine individual programs to create your own workflows. Put down that mouse, open the CLI, and take control of your software development environment.

Brian P. Hogan
(326 pages) ISBN: 9781680502961. $38.95
https://pragprog.com/book/bhcldev

Adopting Elixir

Adoption is more than programming. Elixir is an exciting new language, but to successfully get your application from start to finish, you're going to need to know more than just the language. You need the case studies and strategies in this book. Learn the best practices for the whole life of your application, from design and team-building, to managing stakeholders, to deployment and monitoring. Go beyond the syntax and the tools to learn the techniques you need to develop your Elixir application from concept to production.

Ben Marx, José Valim, Bruce Tate
(242 pages) ISBN: 9781680502527. $42.95
https://pragprog.com/book/tvmelixir

Machine Learning in Elixir

Stable Diffusion, ChatGPT, Whisper—these are just a few examples of incredible applications powered by developments in machine learning. Despite the ubiquity of machine learning applications running in production, there are only a few viable language choices for data science and machine learning tasks. Elixir's Nx project seeks to change that. With Nx, you can leverage the power of machine learning in your applications, using the battle-tested Erlang VM in a pragmatic language like Elixir. In this book, you'll learn how to leverage Elixir and the Nx ecosystem to solve real-world problems in computer vision, natural language processing, and more.

Sean Moriarity
(372 pages) ISBN: 9798888650349. $61.95
https://pragprog.com/book/smelixir

From Ruby to Elixir

Elixir will change the way you think about programming. Use your Ruby experience to quickly get up to speed so you can see what all of the buzz is about. Go from zero to production applications that are reliable, fast, and scalable. Learn Elixir syntax and pattern matching to conquer the basics. Then move onto Elixir's unique process model that offers a world-class way to go parallel without fear. Finally, use the most common libraries like Ecto, Phoenix, and Oban to build a real-world SMS application. Now's the time. Dive in and learn Elixir.

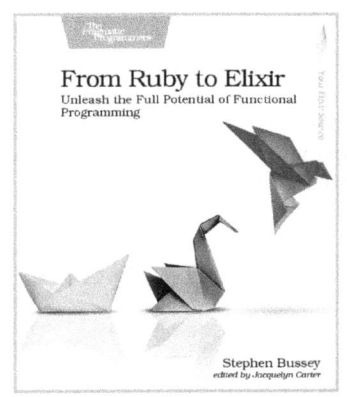

Stephen Bussey
(222 pages) ISBN: 9798888650318. $48.95
https://pragprog.com/book/sbelixir

Functional Web Development with Elixir, OTP, and Phoenix

Elixir and Phoenix are generating tremendous excitement as an unbeatable platform for building modern web applications. For decades OTP has helped developers create incredibly robust, scalable applications with unparalleled uptime. Make the most of them as you build a stateful web app with Elixir, OTP, and Phoenix. Model domain entities without an ORM or a database. Manage server state and keep your code clean with OTP Behaviours. Layer on a Phoenix web interface without coupling it to the business logic. Open doors to powerful new techniques that will get you thinking about web development in fundamentally new ways.

Lance Halvorsen
(218 pages) ISBN: 9781680502435. $45.95
https://pragprog.com/book/lhelph

The Pragmatic Bookshelf

The Pragmatic Bookshelf features books written by professional developers for professional developers. The titles continue the well-known Pragmatic Programmer style and continue to garner awards and rave reviews. As development gets more and more difficult, the Pragmatic Programmers will be there with more titles and products to help you stay on top of your game.

Visit Us Online

This Book's Home Page
https://pragprog.com/book/beamops
Source code from this book, errata, and other resources. Come give us feedback, too!

Keep Up-to-Date
https://pragprog.com
Join our announcement mailing list (low volume) or follow us on Twitter @pragprog for new titles, sales, coupons, hot tips, and more.

New and Noteworthy
https://pragprog.com/news
Check out the latest Pragmatic developments, new titles, and other offerings.

Save on the ebook

Save on the ebook versions of this title. Owning the paper version of this book entitles you to purchase the electronic versions at a terrific discount.

PDFs are great for carrying around on your laptop—they are hyperlinked, have color, and are fully searchable. Most titles are also available for the iPhone and iPod touch, Amazon Kindle, and other popular e-book readers.

Send a copy of your receipt to support@pragprog.com and we'll provide you with a discount coupon.

Contact Us

Online Orders:	*https://pragprog.com/catalog*
Customer Service:	*support@pragprog.com*
International Rights:	*translations@pragprog.com*
Academic Use:	*academic@pragprog.com*
Write for Us:	*http://write-for-us.pragprog.com*

www.ingramcontent.com/pod-product-compliance
Ingram Content Group UK Ltd.
Pitfield, Milton Keynes, MK11 3LW, UK
UKHW050454150426
5217IPUK00025B/1680